ΣBEST
シグマベスト

最高水準
問題集

中学英語長文

佐藤誠司　著

文英堂

本書のねらい

▶みなさんは，“定期テストでよい成績をとりたい”とか，“希望する高校に合格したい”と考えて毎日勉強していることでしょう。そのためには，**どんな問題でも解ける最高レベルの実力**を身につける必要があります。では，どうしたらそのような実力がつくのでしょうか。それには，よい問題に数多くあたって，自分の力で解くことが大切です。

▶この問題集は，最高レベルの実力をつけたいという中学生のみなさんの願いに応えられるように，次の3つのことをねらいにしてつくりました。

1 出題形式・内容ごとに自分の弱点が確かめられるようにする。

2 おさえておかなければならない内容をきめ細かく分析し，問題を1問1問練りあげる。

3 最高レベルの良問を数多く収録し，より広い見方や深い考え方の訓練ができるようにする。

▶この問題集を大いに活用して，どんな問題にぶつかっても対応できる最高レベルの実力を身につけてください。

本書の特色と使用法

1 すべての章を「標準問題」→「最高水準問題」で構成し，段階的に無理なく問題を解いていくことができる。

▶本書は，「標準」と「最高水準」の2段階の問題を解いていくことで，各章の学習内容を確実に理解し，無理なく最高レベルの実力を身につけることができるようにしてあります。
▶本書全体での「標準問題」と「最高水準問題」それぞれの問題数は次のとおりです。

標準問題……21題　最高水準問題……17題

豊富な問題を解いて，最高レベルの実力を身につけましょう。
▶さらに，学習内容の理解度をはかるために，章ごとに「**実力テスト**」を設けてあります。ここで学習の成果と自分の実力を診断しましょう。

2 「標準問題」で，各章の学習内容を確実におさえているかが確認できる。

▶「標準問題」は，各章の学習内容のポイントを１つ１つおさえられるようにしてある問題です。１問１問確実に解いていきましょう。

▶どんな難問を解く力も，基礎学力を着実に積み重ねていくことによって身についてくるものです。まず，「標準問題」を順を追って解いていき，基礎を固めましょう。

▶その章の学習内容に直接かかわる問題に 重要 のマークをつけています。じっくり取り組んで，解答の導き方を確実に理解しましょう。

3 「最高水準問題」は各章の最高レベルの問題で，最高レベルの実力が身につく。

▶「最高水準問題」は，各章の最高レベルの問題です。総合的で，幅広い見方や，より深い考え方が身につくように，難問・奇問ではなく，各章で勉強する基礎的な事項を応用・発展させた質の高い問題を集めました。

▶特に難しい問題には， 難 マークをつけて，解答でくわしく解説しました。

4 「標準問題」にある〈ガイド〉や，「最高水準問題」にある〈解答の方針〉で，基礎知識をおさえたり適切な解き方を確認したりすることができる。

▶「標準問題」には， ガイド をつけ，学習内容の要点や理解のしかたを示しました。

▶「最高水準問題」の下の段には， 解答の方針 をつけて，問題を解く糸口を示しました。ここで，解法の正しい道筋を確認してください。

5 くわしい〈解説〉つきの別冊解答。どんな難しい問題でも解き方が必ずわかる。

▶別冊の「解答と解説」には，各問題のくわしい解説があります。答えだけでなく， 解説 もじっくり読みましょう。

▶ 解説 には 得点アップ を設け，知っているとためになる知識や高校入試で問われるような情報などを満載しました。また， 精読 では，難関校ならではの難しい長文問題への取り組み方を解説しています（くわしくは次ページ）。

6 難関校の英語長文問題の“読み方”がわかる。

▶難関高の英語長文問題には，中学英語のレベルを超えた，難しい文法事項や構文がたくさん含まれています。また，特に物語文などでは，そうした文法や構文の難しさに加え，国語力まで駆使して解かねばならない問題も登場します。本書では，別冊の「解答と解説」に 精読 というコーナーを設けて，中学生のみなさんが課題となっている長文をしっかり理解して正しく意味をつかみ，どんな難問にも立ち向かえるよう，くわしくていねいな解説を心がけました。

▶ 精読 で取り上げている文法事項や構文は，難しいけれど，覚えておけば実際の入試で確実に役立つものばかりです。問題を解いて答え合わせをしたらそれで終わりではなく，もし間違った問題や読んでも意味がよくわからない部分などがあれば，解説 や 精読 をじっくり読んでから，もう一度問題に取り組んでください。この機会に知識を自分のものにして，実際の入試でも活用できるようにしておきましょう。

7 スマートフォンやタブレットで「英語音声」を聞くことができる。

▶英語長文は，ただ目で追って黙読するだけでなく，実際のネイティブの発音を聞いて，自分でも声を出しながら読むと，「英語のリズム」が身につき，英文を適切なところで区切りながら読む「自然な読み方」ができるようになってきます。

▶本書では，各大問の英語長文の右上に，英語音声を聞くためのQRコードを掲載しています。ぜひ，問題を解くだけでなく，英語音声を活用した音読学習にも取り組んでみてください。

【音声の利用方法】

以下の方法で，簡単に再生することができます。

1．紙面のQRコードを，スマートフォンやタブレットで読みとります。
2．表示されるURLにアクセスすると，プレーヤーの画面が表示されます。
3．タップして再生を開始してください。

●音声は無料でご利用いただけますが，通信料金はお客様のご負担となります。●すべての機器での動作を保証するものではありません。●やむを得ずサービス内容に予告なく変更が生じる場合があります。●QRコードは㈱デンソーウェーブの登録商標です。

もくじ

1 会話・メール

標準問題

解答 別冊 p.2

001 彩(Aya)と帰国を控えた留学生のボブ(Bob)が昼休みに教室で話しています。二人の会話を読んで，問いに答えなさい。 (愛知県)

001

Aya: Hi, Bob. When will you go back to your hometown?

Bob: Hi, Aya. I'll go back to San Francisco next month.

Aya: [A]

Bob: Wonderful! I have learned about Japan in our school since last year, so I often talk about it with my host family.

Aya: Please tell me more.

Bob: Well, I learned about *QR codes in the class last week. So I talked about them with my host grandfather. I told him that the codes were made in Japan. (1)Then he told me that he (　　) for a Japanese company which first invented the QR code in 1994.

Aya: Did he?

Bob: [B] When I went to a restaurant with my family, my mother sometimes *scanned the code with her smartphone to pay the money after the meal. It was very convenient. The Japanese technology has supported our daily lives in America.

Aya: [C] Did you talk about anything else?

Bob: Yes, we talked about evacuation drills. I think it's another strong point of Japan. Japanese drills are different from American drills.

Aya: Is that so?

Bob: [D] Then fire alarms in the school make *loud (2) suddenly, and let us know the drill has started.

Aya: Some schools in Japan have that kind of drill.

Bob: Great! During my stay here, I've known that many Japanese prepare for disasters, such as fires, earthquakes and heavy rain.

Aya: [E] My family has made an emergency kit and we keep it in the house.

Bob: Oh, have you? (3)My host family knows how much food and water they should store, and they also know (　　) the local shelter is during a disaster. It's amazing!

Aya: Our family, too. It's important for everyone to prepare for an emergency.

Bob: I agree with you. After going back to America, I'll tell my family to store food and water in case of a disaster.

(注) QR code 二次元コードの一つ　scan ～を読み取る　loud 大きい

① 次の各文を[A]～[E]に入れて対話を完成するとき，[B]と[D]に入るものを答えなさい。ただし各文は1回しか使えません。　[B]（　　）　[D]（　　）

ア Yes. The codes are also popular in San Francisco.

イ I see. Japan has a variety of disasters every year.

ウ Your stay in this school has passed quickly. How's Japanese school life?

エ Yes. On a fire drill day, students in my school don't know about it at all.

オ Sounds good. Technology is a strong point of Japan.

② 下線部(1)，(3)が適切な文となるよう，それぞれの空所に入る語を答えなさい。

(1)（　　　　）　(3)（　　　　）

③ （ 2 ）に入る最も適切な語を，次の中から選びなさい。　（　　）

ア voices　イ laughter　ウ sounds　エ songs

④ 次の英文は，対話があった日の夜，彩が英語の授業で発表するために書き始めたスピーチ原稿の一部です。この原稿が対話文の内容に合うように，英文中の[X]，[Y]に入る適切な語を答えなさい。　[X]（　　　　）　[Y]（　　　　）

Strong points of Japan

Japan is so wonderful. One day, I learned a new fact when I talked with Bob, a student from America. He knew about QR codes in America and he learned, in the class, that they were created in Japan. A Japanese technology is spreading to another country, giving the people a convenient life and [X] their daily lives!

In addition, many Japanese are ready [Y] a disaster. Bob was surprised to know that many Japanese have stored some food and water in case of a disaster ....

ガイド　公立高校入試でよく出題される形式の会話問題の例。①～③は空所に入る文や語句を答える問い，④は英語の文章を完成する問い。感想文やプレゼンテーションの台本を完成する④のような問いは，多くの都道府県の公立高校入試で出題されている。④は本文の該当箇所を探すのがポイント。

重要 002 高校２年生のかおるさんと留学生のトムさんが，かおるさんの家族とドライブの途中で立ち寄った施設で話をしています。二人の会話を読んで，問いに答えなさい。

002

（兵庫県）

Kaoru: Let's have a break here.

Tom: OK. What's this place?

Kaoru: This is a *roadside station. It's a station for cars. We can use the toilets and take a rest.

Tom: Look! A lot of vegetables and fruits are sold here. They are very fresh and not so expensive.

Kaoru: Yes, farmers bring them from their fields near here. They can decide the prices of their products.

Tom: Nice! (1), what's printed on the box of tomatoes?

Kaoru: It's the name of a farmer, Mr. Tanaka. It also tells us that he grew his tomatoes without using *agricultural chemicals.

Tom: I see. I feel safe if I know (2) and how they were grown.

Kaoru: I think so, too.

Tom: Well, do farmers sell anything else?

Kaoru: Yes, they also sell their handmade products. For example, my grandmother sells her jam in all seasons. She makes it from *blueberries she grows in her field. It's popular and is sold quickly.

Tom: That's nice.

Kaoru: Roadside stations are good for local farmers because the farmers can (3).

Tom: I agree. We can buy original products sold only in this roadside station.

Kaoru: Also, we can enjoy original events planned to attract a lot of people at roadside stations.

Tom: Really? What kind of events do they have?

Kaoru: For example, this roadside station has a *knife sharpening event every month. Some companies in this town have made excellent knives since the *Edo* period. There is a museum about their products next to this building.

Tom: Oh, we can learn about the history, too.

Kaoru: In addition, people can get a lot of convenient information for their travels. Roadside stations spread information about their towns. Many people from other cities visit them, and they're always crowded on weekends. Local people become more cheerful.

Tom: That's true. Roadside stations attract many visitors. I think those visitors (4). I want to visit many different roadside stations, too.

Kaoru: How about visiting another roadside station next week?

Tom: That sounds wonderful.

(注) roadside station 道の駅 agricultural chemicals 農薬 blueberry ブルーベリー knife sharpening 刃物研ぎ

① (1)に入る最も適切なものを，次の中から選びなさい。 ( )

ア By the way イ In total ウ For example エ Of course

② (2)に入る最も適切なものを，次の中から選びなさい。 ( )

ア who made them イ why he grew them

ウ when they were sold エ what made the price low

③ (3)に入る最も適切なものを，次の中から選びなさい。 ( )

ア have a break and learn about the history of the town

イ grow their products and see the name of visitors

ウ decide the price by themselves and sell their products

エ visit other local museums and show more products

④ (4)に入る最も適切なものを，次の中から選びなさい。 ( )

ア have the chance to sell local products

イ help local farmers buy other products

ウ tell local people to go to other cities

エ make the local community more active

⑤ トムさんは，この日の出来事をメールに書きました。会話の内容に合うよう，(A)～(C)に入る適切な1語を本文中から抜き出して答えなさい。

(A)( ) (B)( ) (C)( )

Dear Mom,
Today, I visited a wonderful place. It is called a roadside station.
Local farmers can sell fresh vegetables and fruits there. They also sell their handmade products such as (A) in all seasons. I hear many interesting (B) are planned to attract many people. Also, visitors can collect useful (C) for sightseeing.
I am looking forward to visiting another roadside station next week!
Take care,
Tom

ガイド 会話文とメールを組み合わせた問い。この問題も 001 と同様に，最後の⑤で英語の文章を完成する問いが出題されている。道の駅での会話なので，ドライブなどで道の駅に行った経験があれば会話の状況と内容をつかみやすい。

003 次の2通のメールを読んで，問いに答えなさい。 （大阪・早稲田摂陵高）

003

From: Mayumi SATO
To: Gardening Club Members
Date: January 3, 2022 09:15

e-mail #1

Happy New Year,
Are you enjoying the holidays? I had a plan to stay with my grandparents in Nagano, but had to give up the idea *because of COVID-19. So I am staying home and enjoying (1) TV with my father and mother.
I am thinking of the club meeting on January 12. I think we would like to talk about this year's gardening plan on the day. We *dug the ground to make the bed for roses near the entrance of the school building last year. February is one of the best months to put roses in the garden.
(2)Roses are sleeping now with the leaves off and waiting for the coming spring. I would like to know your ideas for the garden.
Regards,
Mayumi SATO
Manager, WS Gardening Club

From: Kent SAITO
To: Mayumi SATO
Date: January 3, 2022 11:40

e-mail #2

Happy New Year,
I am (3) to read your e-mail about our new garden. I want to tell you my idea to make the garden popular among the students. I think the place is the key. It is beside the entrance and it would be a good time to pass by the roses when we enter and get out of the school building. I would like to *recommend two roses for the garden. One of them is *Ophelia* and the other is *Tiny Grace*. Ophelia is from France and one of the world famous roses. It was named after a *character in William Shakespeare's *drama *Hamlet*. Tiny Grace is, on the other hand, from Japan. The rose has the other name, *Fragrant Hill*. The name says that it has wonderful (4)fragrance. The roses are loved by a lot of people in the world because they have excellent scent.
Best Regards,
Kent SAITO
WS Gardening Club

（注） because of COVID-19 新型コロナウイルス感染症が原因で　dug ＜ dig 〜を掘り起こす
recommend 〜を推薦する　character 登場人物　drama 劇

① （ 1 ）に入る最も適切な語句を，次の中から選びなさい。（　　）

ア watch　　イ to watch　　ウ watching　　エ watched

② 下線部(2)が表すバラの状態として最も適切なものを，次の中から選びなさい。（　　）

ア　　イ　　ウ　　エ

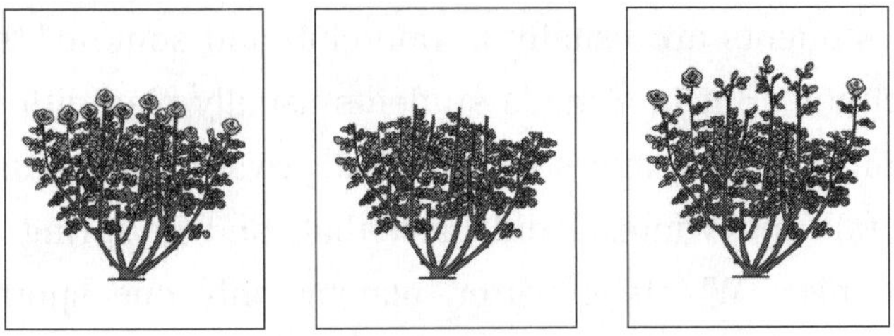

③ （ 3 ）に入る最も適切な語句を，次の中から選びなさい。（　　）

ア excite　　イ to excite　　ウ exciting　　エ excited

④ 下線部(4)とほぼ同じ意味を表す語を，e-mail #2 の本文から抜き出して答えなさい。

（　　　）

⑤ マユミのEメールの内容に一致するものはア，一致しないものはイで答えなさい。

[1] Mayumi is spending time with her grandparents in Nagano.（　　）

[2] The club meeting will be held in January.（　　）

[3] The club members made the bed last year to put it in the school building.（　　）

[4] It is not good to put roses in the garden in winter.（　　）

[5] Mayumi wants to know club members' ideas about the rose garden.（　　）

⑥ ケントのEメールの内容に一致するものはア，一致しないものはイで答えなさい。

[1] Kent has a good idea to make the garden nice for the students.（　　）

[2] Kent wants to put Ophelia and William Shakespeare in the garden.（　　）

[3] People sometimes call Tiny Grace Fragrant Hill.（　　）

[4] Both Ophelia and Tiny Grace are from France.（　　）

[5] Many people love the roses because they like William Shakespeare's dramas.（　　）

⑦ バラの花壇の位置(★)として正しいものを，次の中から選びなさい。ただし，[■　■]は校門を，[●　●]は校舎入口を表すものとします。（　　）

ア　　イ　　ウ　　エ

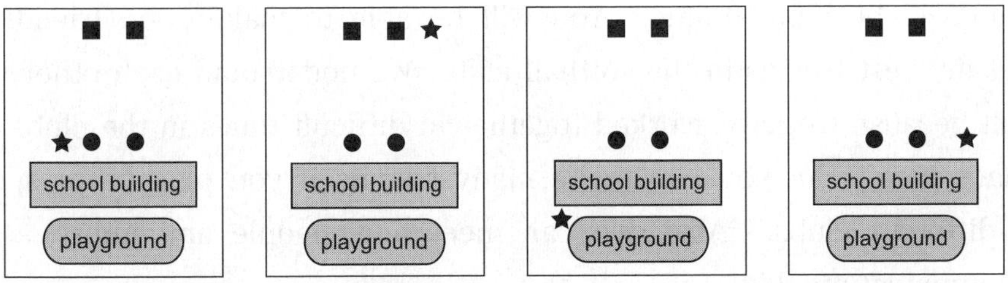

004 昼休みの英語サークルで，英語ネイティブ講師の Mr. Jones が高校生のアヤノ，エマ，ミカの３人と話をしています。この会話を読んで，問いに答えなさい。

004

（東京・日本大豊山高）

Mr. Jones: Hi, everyone. Today, we're going to talk about sports and club activities. In Japan students are usually in one club and some of them play one sport at school. But in Canada students usually play different sports in each season at school and sometimes at private clubs outside school. [A], in fall and winter I did basketball and in spring and summer I played tennis. Which is better, playing only one sport or playing different sports?

Ayano: I think that playing more than one sport is better. I'm in the basketball club, but I'm also interested in other sports. It's great to be able to enjoy different sports.

Emma: [B]I don't agree with you. I'm in the volleyball club at school. If you want to be a good player, you have to practice only volleyball.

Mika: I think so too. I've played softball [C]. I think I have improved a lot because I have focused on it.

Ayano: But you can find the sport [D] you really like if you play many different sports.

Mika: I don't think I have to do that because I like softball the best.

Mr. Jones: You really like softball, Mika. Do you have any other ideas, Ayano?

Ayano: You can learn things from other sports. [A] if you play different sports, you will learn different ways of moving your body. They will be useful for playing softball, Mika.

Mika: [E]I see. I've heard that even some professional athletes play different sports.

Mr. Jones: That's right. Some of them do that. It could be a great chance to learn many things from different sport activities.

Emma: I'm beginning to think that it's a good idea to try different sports.

Mika: Well, listen. If you continue to play one sport for a long time, your team will be more united. You will be able to make good friends. I met my best friends in the softball club. We understand each other very well because we have worked together in difficult times in the club.

Ayano: That's nice. But you can make many friends if you play other sports in different clubs. Also, we can meet new people and improve our communication skills too.

Emma: [F]I understand that. But I also met my best friends because I continued to play volleyball. I don't know which is better. Both ways of thinking about sports have good points.

① Which one is correct? Choose the best answer from below. (　　)

ア Canadian students usually like to do sports in only one season.

イ Canadian students think it is better to play sports at private clubs.

ウ Canadian students can join some clubs not only at school but outside school.

エ Canadian students do not want to try many sports.

② Choose the best answer for [A]. (　　)

ア According to　　イ By the way　　ウ First of all　　エ For example

③ What does [B] mean? Choose the best answer from below. (　　)

ア I don't want to belong to the basketball club.

イ It's not a good idea to play other sports.

ウ Playing volleyball is better than basketball.

エ It's great to enjoy many sports.

④ In [C], choose the best sentence from below. (　　)

ア since I was six years old　　イ when I was in the elementary school

ウ after I was eight　　エ for I am sixteen years old

⑤ In [D], choose the best word from below. (　　)

ア so　　イ and　　ウ that　　エ when

⑥ What does [E] mean? Choose the best answer from below. (　　)

ア Mika saw that people were moving their bodies a lot.

イ Playing softball is important and could be useful for life.

ウ If you want to be good at one sport, you don't need to think about other sports.

エ It is good for people to do other sports.

⑦ What does [F] mean? Choose the best answer from below. (　　)

ア Mika and her friends have worked together in difficult times and they made a good friendship.

イ It is important to try many sports to make new friends.

ウ For our better communication skills, focusing on one sport is the best way to do.

エ You can make new friends and improve communication skills by joining different clubs.

⑧ 会話の中で述べられていないものを選びなさい。 (　　)

ア We should focus on one sport for years to be a better player.

イ Playing more sports can be helpful to improve our communication skills.

ウ There are no easy ways when you want to become a professional athlete.

エ When you spend lots of time together with friends, your friendship may be stronger.

⑨ 次の文は，4人での会話を終えた後にエマが残した感想である。会話の流れに合うように[1]～[3]の文を空所に入れるとき，適切な順番を下から選びなさい。 (　　)

Which is better, playing one sport or playing different sports?
Today we talked about it. (　　) (　　) I also heard that we can meet our best friends by playing only one sport. (　　)

[1] I think both ideas I heard today are true, so it is difficult to decide which is better.

[2] But my idea started to change when I heard that we can learn new things from other sports.

[3] I believed that I should play only one sport to be a better player.

ア [1]→[2]→[3]　　イ [2]→[3]→[1]　　ウ [3]→[1]→[2]　　エ [3]→[2]→[1]

005 次の会話と予定表について，問いに答えなさい。 (神奈川県)

Kana and Mary are high school students. They are looking at their schedules for this summer.

Kana: Hi, Mary. Kamome Museum is going to *hold a music festival from July 22 to August 11. Do you want to come with me?

Mary: That sounds great!

Kana: Every morning at the music festival, they will hold a guitar *concert, a piano concert, and more. I'm especially interested in the popular *musical, *Singing Girls in New York*. The musical is going to *show every Tuesday, Thursday, and Saturday during the music festival at 2:00 p.m.

Mary: I'd like to see it! When should we visit the museum?

Kana: Let me see. July 23 or August 10 is good for me.

Mary: I'm sorry, but I have plans on *both of those days. How about on August 1 or August 3?

Kana: I have a tennis lesson every Thursday afternoon. On August 3 and 4, I will go to Kamome *Lake.

Mary: We're really busy. We can't find a day that is good for our schedules.

Kana: Well, I will move one of my tennis lessons to the next day, so we can go to the music festival on that day.

Mary: Thank you. I'm also interested in the piano concert in the morning. How about meeting at 10:00 a.m. at the museum on that day?

Kana: OK. I can't wait!

〈Kana's schedule〉

<table>
<tr><th>Monday</th><th>Tuesday</th><th>Wednesday</th><th>Thursday</th><th>Friday</th><th>Saturday</th><th>Sunday</th></tr>
<tr><td>7/22</td><td>23</td><td>24</td><td>25
Tennis Lesson</td><td>26</td><td>27</td><td>28</td></tr>
<tr><td></td><td></td><td></td><td></td><td></td><td colspan="2">Visit Grandmother's House</td></tr>
<tr><td>29</td><td>30</td><td>31</td><td>8/1
Tennis Lesson</td><td>2</td><td>3</td><td>4</td></tr>
<tr><td colspan="2">Visit Grandmother's House</td><td></td><td></td><td></td><td colspan="2">Go to Kamome Lake</td></tr>
<tr><td>5</td><td>6</td><td>7</td><td>8
Tennis Lesson</td><td>9</td><td>10</td><td>11
Watch a Movie</td></tr>
<tr><td colspan="3">Summer Class (English)</td><td></td><td></td><td></td><td></td></tr>
</table>

〈Mary's schedule〉

<table>
<tr><th>Monday</th><th>Tuesday</th><th>Wednesday</th><th>Thursday</th><th>Friday</th><th>Saturday</th><th>Sunday</th></tr>
<tr><td>7/22</td><td>23
Guitar Lesson</td><td>24</td><td>25</td><td>26</td><td>27</td><td>28
Piano Lesson</td></tr>
<tr><td></td><td></td><td></td><td colspan="3">Go to Kyoto</td><td></td></tr>
<tr><td>29</td><td>30</td><td>31</td><td>8/1</td><td>2</td><td>3</td><td>4
Piano Lesson</td></tr>
<tr><td></td><td colspan="2">Summer Class (Math)</td><td></td><td></td><td></td><td></td></tr>
<tr><td>5</td><td>6
Guitar Lesson</td><td>7</td><td>8</td><td>9</td><td>10</td><td>11
Piano Lesson</td></tr>
<tr><td></td><td></td><td></td><td colspan="3">Go to Kamome Mountain</td><td></td></tr>
</table>

（注） hold ～を開催する　concert コンサート　musical ミュージカル
show 上演される　both 両方　Lake 湖

問 When will Kana and Mary go to the music festival? (　　)

ア July 31.　イ August 1.　ウ August 2.

エ August 8.　オ August 10.

重要 006 放課後，高校生の太郎(Taro)が，アメリカ合衆国からの留学生マイク(Mike)と話をしています。二人の会話を読んで，問いに答えなさい。 (福島県)

006

Mike: Hey, Taro. Can I ask you a question?

Taro: Sure, Mike. What do you want to know?

Mike: *Before I came to Japan, some people around me said people in Japan worked long hours. I've been here for a year, but I'm not *sure of this. What do you think about this?

Taro: I'm not sure, either. But my parents often come home *late.

Mike: [A]

Taro: Well, I'll ask them about it tonight, and tell you about it tomorrow.

Mike: Great! Thanks, Taro.

[The next day]

Taro: Hi, Mike. Do you have some time?

Mike: Sure, Taro. Did you talk with your parents last night?

Taro: I only talked with my father. But I found some interesting articles, too.

Mike: Oh, thanks! What did he say?

Taro: Well, my father doesn't think he works long hours. But he thinks it takes a long time from our house to his office.

Mike: Oh, is his office far from your house?

Taro: Yes, it is. It takes an hour. My father said he wants more time with us.

Mike: I see. You want more time with your father, too, right?

Taro: Yes, of course, and all my family members wish the same. My mother says she needs more time with my father, especially because she takes care of my eight-year-old brother.

Mike: I see.

Taro: According to an article I found, young Japanese people these days think their family is more important than their jobs. Look at this graph. It shows the survey results of three thousand people in 2011 and ten thousand people in 2017. These people were 16 to 29 years old.
Which is more important, your family or job?

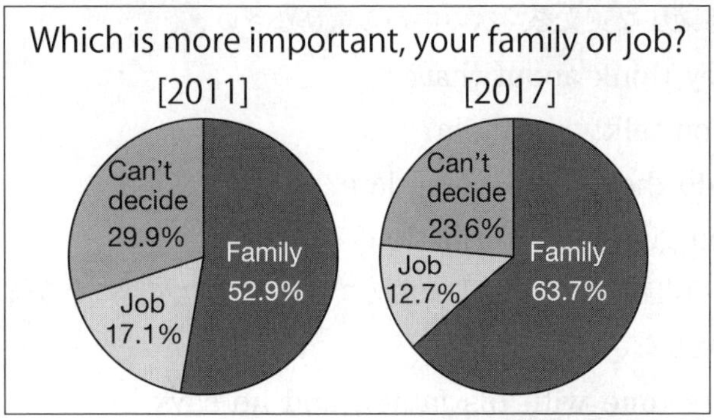

（内閣府資料により作成）

Mike: Oh, more than 63 percent of them thought their family was more important in 2017.

Taro: Right. The number rose *by about 11 percent from 2011.

Mike: I see. So, we can say more and more young people think their family is more important, right?

Taro: Right. I think a lot of people need to think about how they work. Oh, here's an idea. If my father can choose to work *either at his office or at home, he can spend more time with me. Technology has made that possible, right? I think every *worker will be happy about that.

Mike: You think so? I think [B]

Taro: Oh, really? Why?

Mike: Well, for example, think about the workers who build roads, bridges, or buildings. Doing such things at home is not possible, right?

Taro: Oh, you're right. People in different jobs work in different ways. Actually, my mother is a *nurse and I think it's not possible for her to work at home. She goes to work at the hospital to help her patients, and she says she is proud of her job.

Mike: That's great! I hope I can be proud of my job like your mother! I also hope I can get a job which gives me time to spend with my family and *on my hobby.

Taro: Me, too. If we have a better *private life, we can enjoy our work more!

（注） before　～する前に　　sure of ～　～を確信している　　late　遅くに
by about 11 percent　約11パーセント分だけ　　either ～ or ...　～か…かのどちらか
worker　働く人　　nurse　看護師　　on my hobby　自分の趣味に　　private　個人の

① [A]に入る最も適切な英文を，次の中から選びなさい。 ( )

ア What do they think about that?

イ Where do you talk with them?

ウ How often do they come home late?

エ Why can you give me information?

② 次の英文は，本文の内容の一部を示したものです。本文の内容に合うように，下線部に4語を補って，英文を完成しなさい。

Taro wants more time with his father, and he says ________________ wish the same.

③ 本文やグラフの内容に合うように，それぞれの英文の空所に入る最も適切な数字を選びなさい。

[1]( ) [2]( )

[1] In 2011, ( ) percent of young Japanese people thought their family was more important.

ア 17.1 イ 29.9 ウ 52.9 エ 63.7

[2] In 2017, ( ) percent of people thought their family was less important than their job.

ア 12.7 イ 23.6 ウ 29.9 エ 63.7

④ [B]に入る最も適切なものを，次の中から選びなさい。 ( )

ア things are so simple.

イ things are not so simple.

ウ they will be happy about working at their office.

エ they will not be happy about working at their office.

⑤ 本文の内容に合うものを，次の中から1つ選びなさい。 ( )

ア Mike knows that people in Japan work long hours because he came to Japan one year ago.

イ Mike thinks that Taro's mother needs to get more help from Taro and his brother.

ウ Taro says that a lot of people need to think about the workers who build roads, bridges, or buildings.

エ Taro and Mike want to get a job that gives them time to spend with their family and on their hobbies.

ガイド 会話問題を解きながら，会話特有の表現に慣れておこう。特に応答の表現をたくさん知っておくと，スピーキングにも利用できる。この問題には，Sure., I'm not sure(, either)., I see., Yes, of course., You think so?, (That's) Great!, Me, too. など，実際の会話で使えるさまざまな表現が含まれている。

最高水準問題

解答 別冊 p.10

007 次の会話を読んで，問いに答えなさい。 （京都・同志社高）

Dorothy: Chocolate and cookies! Wow, are you eating all of them?

Hannah: Well, today, I've just finished an important presentation. As soon as I relaxed after a hard task, I felt hungry for these. I understand (1)食べ過ぎるのは健康によくない, but I can't stop.

Dorothy: So, these are your comfort foods.

Hannah: [A]

Dorothy: Something that will make you happy when you eat it.

Hannah: [B] Chocolate and cookies calm me down. So I sometimes want to eat them though I am not hungry.

Dorothy: Yeah. I heard that it is partly because of your brain. One of the reasons is "*dopamine." When you eat a comfort food that tastes good to you, you get a lot of dopamine. To your brain, dopamine sends good feelings that are connected with your comfort food. Your brain remembers those good feelings. (2)That's why you will want to continue to eat comfort food. Chocolate and cookies are all good examples of comfort food.

Hannah: I see.

Susie: Hi, Dorothy! Hi, Hannah! [C]

Hannah: Hi, Susie. [D]

Susie: Oh, you are enjoying eating sweets!

Dorothy: Hi, Susie. Well, we are talking about comfort food. Hannah's comfort food is chocolate and cookies.

Susie: Comfort food! My comfort food is different. I remember chicken soup that my mom made when I was a child and sometimes want to eat it. You know I am living alone.

Hannah: Oh. That reminds me of the words of a famous chef, "Food is like a hug." Food often helps us feel less lonely especially when we are left alone.

Dorothy: Comfort food also gives us a feeling of (3)"connection."

Hannah: I see. [E] What is your comfort food, Dorothy?

Dorothy: Umm, a meat pie. It is a food that I often had in my childhood. On special days, like Christmas and my birthday, my grandmother cooked a meat pie for me and we had a good time together.

Susie: Comfort food is connected with past experiences from your childhood. We can remember our family and people who took care of us. Comfort food brings back happy memories from our past.

Hannah: Connections between food and memories are very strong. It is like our brain eats food. Comfort food is different from person to person.

Dorothy: Talking about food makes me hungry! Well, (4)明日私の家に来ない？ I'll invite you to dinner! I'm going to make a pie whose recipe I found online. I'll prepare chocolate cake for dessert, Hannah, and for you, Susie, I'll cook chicken soup!

Susie: Sounds wonderful! I know you are good at cooking, but is it ok? It may take a lot of time to cook these kinds of dishes.

Dorothy: Oh, I really enjoy cooking. I can forget bad things when I cook. I also read in a book that making comfort food gives us control over our feelings.

Hannah: Ah, Dorothy, just thinking about delicious dishes makes me happy. That is also our brain's work, isn't it? (5)明日のディナーを楽しみにしています！

（注） dopamine ドーパミン（神経伝達物質の一つ）

① 下線部(1), (4), (5)の日本語を英語に直しなさい。

(1) ____________________

(4) ____________________

(5) ____________________

② ［ A ］～［ E ］に入る最も適切な文を，下から１つずつ選びなさい。

［A］（　　）　［B］（　　）　［C］（　　）　［D］（　　）　［E］（　　）

ア How about you?　　イ What do you mean?　　ウ What's up?

エ Would you like some?　　オ You said it.

③ 下線部(2)に「comfort food を食べ続けたくなる」とあるが，なぜそのようになるのか。次の文の空所に適切な言葉を入れなさい。

comfort food を食べるとドーパミンが出て____________________から。

④ 下線部(3)の “connection” とは，どういうことを述べているのか。次の文の空所に適切な語を入れなさい。

You won't feel (　　　) when you eat comfort food, and you can feel that you are (　　　) to people.

⑤ Dorothy と comfort food の関係について述べた次の文の空所に適切な語を入れなさい。

Dorothy (　　　) the time she spent with her grandparents. Comfort food brings back (　　　) about good times. (　　　) comfort food also helps her control her feelings.

解答の方針

②のア～オのような会話特有の慣用表現は意味や使い方を知らないと問題が解けない。覚えることが大事。

難 008 次の会話を読んで，問いに答えなさい。 （東京・都立日比谷高）

*Rina, Hana, Yuta, and Oliver are in the classroom after school. Oliver is a student from *Norway. Hana is sitting in her seat by herself and she looks like she has something on her mind.*

Rina: What's wrong, Hana?

Hana: I was thinking about my group science project. Things aren't going well.

Yuta: You're the leader of the project, right?

Hana: Yeah, we have to make a presentation in two weeks but we aren't ready at all.

Oliver: I often see you getting together after school, so I thought it was going well.

Hana: We often get together, but only a few members express their opinions. Yesterday, some didn't even come to the meeting because they said they had other things to do! I don't think that everyone is serious about the project.

Rina: Being the leader is hard, right?

Hana: I sometimes think to myself, I want our group to be like a *flock of *pigeons.

Yuta: What?

Hana: (1)<u>A flock of pigeons.</u> You've seen pigeons flying in the sky, right? I'm always surprised when I see a big group of pigeons suddenly turn in the same *direction at the same time.

Oliver: Why do you want to be like them?

Hana: I want everyone in my group to be able to do things together as one team. I want to know how the leader of the flock can make the other pigeons follow along.

Rina: Is there actually a leader? I thought they were just doing the same thing that the pigeon next to them is doing.

Hana: People thought so before. But according to scientists, pigeons change direction by following the leader, and not any member of the flock.

Oliver: I've heard about that from my grandpa. He loves bird watching.

Yuta: How did they find that out?

Hana: By putting tiny GPSs on pigeons and checking where they are every 0.2 *seconds.

Yuta: How do pigeons decide who the leader is?

Oliver: I heard that the fastest pigeon is usually the leader. However, my grandpa told me an interesting fact. Sometimes slower pigeons also lead the flock, so in that case, the leader is not the same even during one flight.

Rina: Really? That's surprising. I thought that in the animal world, usually the strongest *male becomes the leader.

Yuta: I thought so, too. But sometimes that is not true. For example, elephants. I saw a TV program last week and it said that the leader is the oldest *female. By the way, have you heard of the expression, "to have a memory like an elephant"?

Hana: Never. What does it mean?

Yuta: It means that if you have a memory like an elephant, (2). In the program, they talked about an elephant leader that saved her group from a *drought because she had a good memory. In her group, many of the elephants survived, but in a different group, almost half of them lost their lives.

Rina: What was the difference between them?

Yuta: Both groups had a leader that had a lot of experience. However, the second group had a younger leader that did not experience the *previous drought 35 years ago. According to researchers, the first group was able to survive because of the leader's memory about the previous drought.

Oliver: (3)That sounds similar to *killer whale leaders. I often went to see killer whales in Norway.

Rina: You can see them in Norway?

Oliver: Yeah, especially in the winter season. Hey, did you know that for killer whales, living with their (4a) is the key to a long life? According to research, when young killer whales lost a (4b), their lives were *more likely to be in danger.

Yuta: Why not (4c)?

Oliver: You see, male killer whales usually live until they are 35 years old, but females often live until they are 60.

Rina: I can't believe that there is such a big difference!

Oliver: They live longer, so they have more experience and know where they can find food.

Hana: So for some animals, it is important to follow the one that has the *knowledge to help them live longer.

Oliver: That's right.

Yuta: And there are *chimpanzees. Even the smallest one can become the leader.

Hana: Really? How?

Yuta: Some use their *strength, but others use their brain to climb to the top.

Hana: And how do they do that?

Yuta: When chimpanzees want to become leaders, they think about others instead of themselves and then take action. For example, they share their food easily. And after they become leaders, when other chimpanzees are having a fight, they support the one that doesn't have a chance of winning.

Rina: Why do they do that?

Yuta: They do that to get supporters. When other chimpanzees see such *behavior, they feel safe and show respect to the leader.

Oliver: Chimpanzees are so smart!

Hana: Now I know why things weren't going well with the science project.

Oliver: You do?

Hana: The reason is me. I'm not a good leader.

Rina: Oh, don't say that. You're always working so hard.

Hana: Talking about the behavior of animal leaders has given me some hints about how to become a good leader.

Yuta: Like what?

Hana: From chimpanzees, I learned that if I want to become a good leader, I should think about my group members more and do things to get their support. By doing so, we can build good *relationships and learn to trust each other.

Yuta: Was there anything else you learned?

Hana: Leaders with a lot of knowledge can make good decisions for the group.

Oliver: Like elephants and killer whales?

Hana: Yes. As you know, I don't have the experience that those leaders have, but it's OK because I can *make up for that.

Yuta: How?

Hana: With the help of my group members. We humans are able to communicate with language, so we can share our knowledge that we got through experience.

Yuta: That's true! Was there anything you learned from pigeons?

Hana: I learned that sometimes a different member of the group can lead the group. The important thing is to reach the goal as a team.

Oliver: Everyone is an important part of the group and we should all share the *responsibility.

Hana: You're right! Thank you. I think our science presentation is going to go well.

Rina: I'm so happy to hear that!

Hana: There are a lot of things that I can do to become a good leader, but (5)I think the first thing to do is to get to know my group members better.

Oliver: That sounds like a good place to start!

Yuta: Good luck with your science project!

（注） Norway ノルウェー　flock 群れ　pigeon ハト　direction 方向　second 秒
male 雄　female 雌　drought 干ばつ　previous 以前の
killer whale シャチ　more likely to *do* より～しそうな　knowledge 知識
chimpanzee チンパンジー　strength 力　behavior 行動　relationship 関係
make up for ～ ～を補う　responsibility 責任

① 下線部(1)について，ハナが会話を通して理解したことを次の中から選びなさい。　(　　)

ア Only the fastest pigeon can become the leader of the flock.

イ The leader of the flock checks where they are every 0.2 seconds.

ウ The leader of the flock may change during one flight.

エ Pigeons fly together in flocks by watching the pigeon next to them.

② (　2　)に入る最も適切なものを，次の中から選びなさい。　(　　)

ア elephants give you a lot of good memories

イ elephants remind you of good times

ウ you like things from the past like elephants

エ you are good at remembering things like elephants

③ 下線部(3)に関する次の質問に対する答えとして最も適切なものを，下から選びなさい。

質問：According to the passage, how are elephants and killer whales similar?

(　　)

ア It is hard to find them in nature during the winter.

イ The leader of the group has a lot of experience.

ウ Males can hunt so they live longer than females.

エ The leader of the group is the strongest female.

④ (　4a　)～(　4c　)に入る語の最も適切な組み合わせを，次の中から選びなさい。　(　　)

ア (a) grandmothers　(b) grandfather　(c) grandmothers

イ (a) grandmothers　(b) grandmother　(c) grandfathers

ウ (a) grandfathers　(b) grandfather　(c) grandmothers

エ (a) grandfathers　(b) grandmother　(c) grandfathers

⑤ 下線部(5)のためにハナがとる行動として最も適切なものを次の中から選びなさい。 (　　)

ア She will spend the day together with her group members outside of school and develop a good relationship.

イ She will read books about animals in the library and learn more about how to become a good leader.

ウ She will stop depending on her group members too much and show them that she is the leader.

エ She will put information about her science project on the Internet and tell her group members about it.

⑥ 本文の内容に一致するものを，次の中から2つ選びなさい。 (　　)(　　)

ア Hana feels that things are not going well in the science project though everyone comes to all the meetings.

イ Many elephants did not survive in one of the groups because they experienced the previous drought.

ウ Hana is like killer whale leaders because she has the knowledge to make good decisions for the group.

エ Chimpanzees that want to become leaders think about themselves instead of others and share food.

オ The behavior of chimpanzee leaders affects their group members, so it is important for them to support their members.

カ Hana learned from pigeons that leaders need to show their power by leading the flock all the time.

キ After talking with her friends, Hana realized everyone should share the responsibility, so she will make someone else the leader.

ク Hana learned many things from animals and thought she could be a better leader than before.

第 1 回 実力テスト

▶解答→別冊 p.16

時間 30 分　目標 70 点

得点　／100

次の会話を読んで，問いに答えなさい。　（愛媛・愛光高）（①各 10 点，②③各 20 点，④各 10 点，計 100 点）

201

Tomoya: Hello, Susan. How was your summer holiday?

Susan: Hi, Tomoya. It was fantastic! I traveled in Edinburgh and had a very good time there.

Tomoya: Edinburgh? Where is it?

Susan: Edinburgh is the *capital of Scotland and I stayed there for a week.

Tomoya: Oh, Scotland. What did you do there?

Susan: Well, I went to some famous tourist spots [A] Edinburgh Castle and Calton Hill. I also enjoyed Royal Edinburgh Military Tattoo very much.

Tomoya: Royal Edinburgh Military Tattoo? What's that?

Susan: It's a music festival. *Army bands from various countries play music in the event. (1)[so / was / got / their / wonderful / that / performance / goosebumps / I].

Tomoya: That sounds so nice. I want to go to see it someday, too.

Susan: You should. (2)[the / I / ever / was / been / music festival / to / it / best / have]. However, I had a terrible experience [B] the trip.

Tomoya: A terrible experience?

Susan: Yeah. When I arrived at Edinburgh Airport, my *baggage didn't *come out.

Tomoya: What? Why did that happen?

Susan: This time, I flew from Haneda Airport to Heathrow Airport in London. Then, I caught another flight in London and flew to Edinburgh Airport. And as I said, when I arrived there, I realized that my baggage was *missing. So I asked a member of the *ground staff and she told me that it was still in London.

Tomoya: That's too bad. I've heard that sometimes happens when you travel abroad.

Susan: That actually happened to me this time. After all, I had to wait two days [C] my baggage until it arrived in Edinburgh. So I couldn't change clothes or use other things.

Tomoya: You had such a bad experience ....

Susan: Yes, but *apart from that, the trip was perfect and it was a special holiday.

（注）capital 首都　army 軍隊　baggage 荷物　come out 出てくる
missing 見当たらない　ground staff 地上勤務員　apart from ～ ～を除けば

① ［ A ］〜［ C ］に入る最も適切な語を，下から1つずつ選びなさい。ただし，同じ語をくり返し使わないこと。　［A］（　　）　［B］（　　）　［C］（　　）

ア across　イ into　ウ like　エ for　オ over　カ during

② 下線部(1)が次の日本文の意味になるように，［　　］内の語を正しく並べ替えなさい。ただし，文頭にくる語も小文字で記してあります。

「彼らの演奏は鳥肌が立つほど素晴らしいものだった。」

____

③ 下線部(2)が次の日本文の意味になるように，［　　］内の語を正しく並べ替えなさい。ただし，文頭にくる語句も小文字で記してあります。

「それは私がこれまで行った中で一番の音楽祭だった。」

____

④ それぞれの文が本文の内容と一致すればア，一致しなければイ，本文の内容からだけでは判断できなければウで答えなさい。

［1］ Susan had some terrible experiences while she was traveling in Edinburgh.　（　　）

［2］ In Edinburgh, Susan went to see Holyrood Palace.　（　　）

［3］ Susan couldn't receive her baggage when she arrived at Edinburgh Airport.　（　　）

2 論説文－文化・社会

標準問題

（解答）別冊 p.17

009 次の文章を読んで，問いに答えなさい。（山梨・駿台甲府高）

009

[1] Do you read comic books? If you do, are they paper comic books or *digital comic books? A few years ago, paper comic books were more popular. But since the *pandemic, this situation has changed. People stayed home and started to read more digital comic books on the Internet. In 2020, more than half of comic book *sales in Japan were digital. Digital comic books are becoming more popular.

[2] Digital comic books have some good points. People can buy digital comic books everywhere. You don't need to go to a bookstore. You can find the comic book you want and buy it with your smartphone while you are lying on the sofa at home. After you buy it, you can start to read it *at once.

[3] Another good point is that you can buy all kinds of comic books from all over the world. For example, Japanese manga-style comic books are popular. Their stories and characters are loved by people around the world. Graphic novels are an American type of comic books. The stories are long and serious, so they are big, and they are usually read by adults. Bandes Dessinées are another type of comic books, from France. Most of them are full color and the stories are usually very *poetic, so some people think that they are kind of art. Reading foreign comic books is a great way to learn language and culture.

[4] The third point is you don't need a lot of space. After you read a comic book, you may want to read another. If you buy a lot of paper comic books, you will need a big *bookshelf. If you read digital comic books, you only need a smartphone. You don't have to worry about where to put them, and you can keep your room *neat.

[5] The fourth point is that you can carry them easily. Carrying a lot of paper books is hard work because they are very heavy. On the other hand, if you read digital comic books, you don't have to carry the books. Of course, some people say that it's difficult to read small *print on a smartphone. For those people, a *tablet is better. It is as big as paper comic books, so you can read it easily.

[6] More people are choosing digital comic books than before. They are more convenient than paper comic books. You can buy them everywhere, and try all kinds of comic books from around the world. You can buy a lot of books and you don't need a bookshelf. You can easily carry them in a smartphone. More people

will probably choose digital comic books in the future.

（注） digital デジタルの　pandemic 感染症の広範囲の流行　sale(s) 売上
at once すぐに　poetic 詩的な　bookshelf 本棚　neat 片付いている
print 文字　tablet タブレット端末

① According to paragraph [2], which statement is true? （　　）
ア There are a lot of problems with digital comic books in Japan.
イ Bookstores must not sell digital comic books.
ウ Smartphones are not useful for finding comic books.
エ You can buy digital comic books with your smartphone.

② According to paragraph [3], which statement is true? （　　）
ア The stories of Japanese manga are too long for people around the world.
イ One of the American types of comic books is graphic novels.
ウ The stores of Bandes Dessinées are usually very serious.
エ A good way to learn culture is to visit France.

③ According to paragraph [4], which statement is NOT true? （　　）
ア You may want more paper comic books after reading one of them.
イ You should share paper comic books with others after reading them.
ウ You can read digital comic books on your smartphone.
エ You don't need a lot of space to keep digital comic books.

④ According to paragraph [5], which statement is true? （　　）
ア It is hard to carry paper comic books because they are heavy.
イ People think that small smartphones are better than big ones.
ウ It is difficult to carry digital comic books.
エ Everybody likes to read comic books on a smartphone.

⑤ What is the best title for this passage? （　　）
ア The most popular digital comic book
イ A famous comic book writer
ウ A new way of reading comic books
エ The history of digital comic books

ガイド 一般に説明文は，「導入－本論－結び」という構成が多い。この文章も，[1]が導入，[2]～[5]が本論，[6]が結びである。[2]～[5]は非常にわかりやすい構成で，[2]の第1文で「デジタルコミックにはいくつかの長所がある」と述べ，それに続いて第1の長所が示される。[3]～[5]がそれぞれ第2・3・4の長所の説明であることは，各段落の最初の文からわかる。このように段落(パラグラフ)ごとの論理的な関係を考えながら読む方法を，パラグラフリーディングという。

重要 010 次の文章を読んで，問いに答えなさい。 （岡山朝日高）

010

When you buy a nice bag you have wanted, you feel happy. When you eat a good dinner at a famous restaurant, you feel happy. However, there are better ways to spend money to make you happier.

A *study showed that people who *spent money on others felt happier than people who bought themselves something they wanted. In the study, people received a paper bag which had $5 or $20. When the *researchers gave the people the paper bag, they asked them the *level of their happiness and told them to spend the money that day. Half of them were told to use it for something they wanted, and the other half were told to spend it on someone else. That evening, the researchers called each of them and asked their happiness levels and how they spent their money. People from (1)the first group bought drinks, cake, or clothes. The second group bought picture books for younger brothers, bought toys for poor children, or gave the money to *charity groups. Can you imagine how they felt after the *experiment? You may be surprised, but people from the second group were happier than people from the first group. The *amount of money they got did not *affect how they felt.

You may worry that spending money on yourself isn't good. Don't worry. (2) But spend it on experiences. Spending it (3)[makes / on things / on experiences / than / you / happier / it / spending]. When you buy things, you feel happy, but the happiness the things give you will *disappear after you use them many times. However, the *pleasure and memories that experiences give you can stay longer in your heart. Here is some advice when you spend money on experiences. First, join some events with your friends, your family, or even *strangers, and you can share memories with them. You can also develop a good *relationship, and it will make you happier. Climbing a high mountain with your friends is a good example. Even when you feel bad about the experience at that time, if you talk with your friends later, you will feel better. Second, don't spend a lot of money on special experiences but spend a small amount of money on smaller experiences more often. [A] makes you happier than [B]. If you want to make your experiences better, buy something which helps to make experiences more *meaningful. A good example is buying a good camera or [C].

You now know that there is a *relation between how you spend money and your (4). How will you spend your money tomorrow? Find your own answer.

（注） study 研究　spend ～ on ... ～を…に費やす　researcher 研究者　level レベル
charity group 慈善団体　experiment 実験　amount 量　affect ～に影響する
disappear 消える　pleasure 楽しみ　stranger 見知らぬ人　relationship 関係

meaningful 意味のある　relation つながり

① 下線部(1)はどのような集団ですか。30字以内の日本語で説明しなさい。

② (2)に入る最も適切な文を，次の中から選びなさい。 (　　)

ア It isn’t.　イ It is.　ウ You do.　エ You don’t.

③ 下線部(3)の[　　]内の語句を，適切な意味になるように並べ替えなさい。

____

④ [A]～[C]に入る最も適切な表現を１つずつ選びなさい。ただし，同じものをくり返し使わないこと。文頭にくるべきものも小文字で示しています。

[A] (　　)　[B] (　　)　[C] (　　)

ア going abroad every year

イ talking with your friends at a coffee shop every weekend

ウ getting a new bicycle

⑤ (4)に入る１語を文中から抜き出して答えなさい。 (　　)

⑥ 筆者がすすめていることを，次の中からすべて選びなさい。 (　　)

ア To buy something nice for other people

イ To get everything you want

ウ To use money only for others

エ To share experiences with others

オ To spend a lot of time to choose what to buy

ガイド 「結論(読者の興味を引きそうな意外な事実や発見)＋根拠(結論を裏付けるための研究や調査)」は，説明文の典型的な構成の１つである。この文章はその例。第１段落で本文のテーマを導入し，第２段落(A study showed ...)以下が具体的な事実と根拠の説明になっている。

なお，条件つきの問いでは，その条件を満たさなければ不正解になる。たとえば④で同じ記号をくり返し使っていれば，全部が０点となる。また⑤は「文中から抜き出して」という指示だから，本文中に出てきた語を同じ形で答える必要がある。たとえば「本文中の語はboys[makes] だが正解はboy[make]」というようなことはありえない。

011 次の文章を読んで，問いに答えなさい。 （千葉・日本大習志野高）

The ‘peace sign,’ the two-fingered gesture that many Japanese children make when they are being photographed, (1) to have been invented by the British Prime Minister, Winston Churchill. Churchill used it to mean ‘V for Victory’ during World War II. After the time of the Vietnam War, President Nixon also used the gesture to mean victory. But people *protesting against the Vietnam War started to use the gesture to mean ‘peace.’ [A]

During a visit to Australia in the 1990s, the first President Bush tried to give the peace sign to the crowd of Australians welcoming him at the airport. (2), he held his hand the wrong way round. In the United States that doesn’t matter very much. But in England and Australia, if the back of your hand faces the audience, the gesture becomes very (3)offensive and is used to insult people. [B] The Australians were very shocked!

Photographs of President Bush’s mistake were widely *distributed, but few people know that Churchill also used the gesture the wrong way round in the early days of World War II. However, people quickly (4) out his mistake, so Churchill reversed it, inventing the gesture that came to be known as the peace sign.

Another common gesture in the West, the ‘thumbs-up’ sign, can also be misunderstood. In England and the United States, it means that ‘everything is O.K.’ or ‘job well done.’ But you should avoid ‘giving the thumbs-up’ in Latin America, West Africa, Greece, Russia, and southern Italy, where it is a very offensive gesture. [C] In particular, you shouldn’t use it at all in Arab countries (5) you may be challenged to a fight!

One other gesture can cause trouble. To call someone over to you in Japan and the Philippines you extend your hand with the palm facing downwards and wave your hand up and down. [D] The Japanese aren’t upset by this gesture. But in the Philippines, calling someone over with one finger held up is very offensive. It is a gesture that is only used for dogs. In the old days, (6)children using it to call adults sometimes had their fingers broken as a punishment.

（注） protest 反対する　distribute ～を配信する

① （ 1 ）に入る最も適切なものを，次の中から選びなさい。 （　　）

ア says　イ said　ウ saying　エ is said

② （ 2 ）に入る最も適切なものを，次の中から選びなさい。 （　　）

ア Probably　イ Unfortunately　ウ Successfully　エ Finally

③ 下線部(3)の意味として最も適切なものを，次の中から選びなさい。 （　　）

ア 侮辱的な　イ 本能的な　ウ 悲観的な　エ 宗教的な

④ （ 4 ）に入る最も適切なものを，次の中から選びなさい。 （　　）

ア kept　イ got　ウ paid　エ pointed

⑤ （ 5 ）に入る最も適切なものを，次の中から選びなさい。 （　　）

ア so　イ but　ウ because　エ although

⑥ 下線部(6)の意味として最も適切なものを，次の中から選びなさい。 （　　）

ア 子どもたちを呼ぶのにそれを使った大人たちは，罰としてときどき指を折られた。

イ 子どもたちにそれを使って呼ばれた大人たちは，不幸にもときどき指を骨折した。

ウ 指を骨折したことがある子どもたちは，大人を呼ぶのにときどきそれを使った。

エ 大人を呼ぶためにそれを使っていた子どもたちは，ときどき罰として指を折られた。

⑦ 次の質問の答えとして最も適切なものを，次の中から選びなさい。

［1］（　　）　［2］（　　）

［1］ Who started to use the two-fingered gesture as the ‘peace’ sign?

ア President Nixon

イ Winston Churchill

ウ The crowd of Australians

エ People who were against the Vietnam War

［2］ What is true in England below?

ア People use the thumbs-up sign to show ‘Good job.’

イ Using the thumbs-up sign can cause trouble.

ウ It is polite for people to hold up their first finger when they call someone.

エ It is a good habit that the back of the hand faces the audience when people make the peace sign.

⑧ 本文の内容と一致するものを，次の中から２つ選びなさい。 （　　）（　　）

ア The peace sign originally means ‘peace.’

イ Many Japanese children make the peace sign to mean victory.

ウ The thumbs-up sign can be trouble in Arab countries.

エ It is said that the first President Bush invented the peace sign.

オ In the Philippines, the thumbs-up sign is sometimes used to call someone.

カ The same gesture has different meanings from country to country.

⑨ 本文中で述べられていない gesture を，次の中から1つ選びなさい。　(　　)

ア

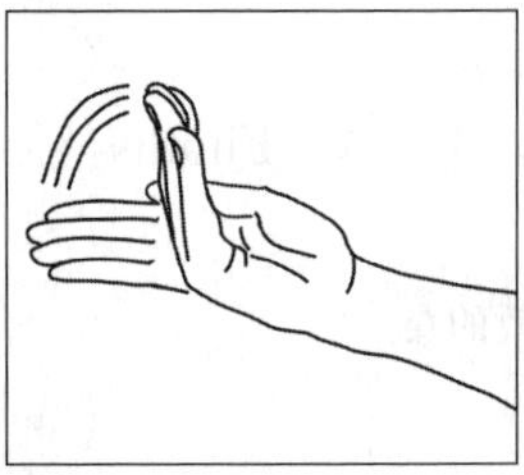

イ

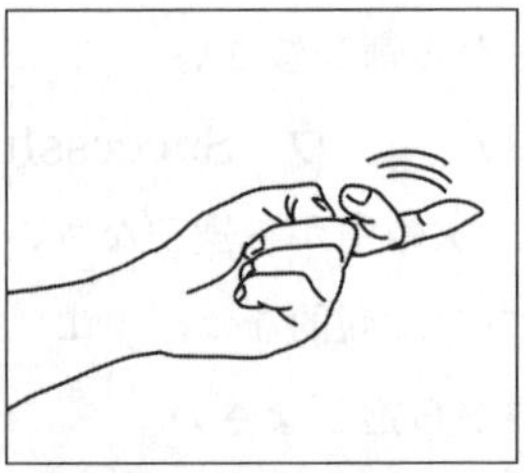

ウ

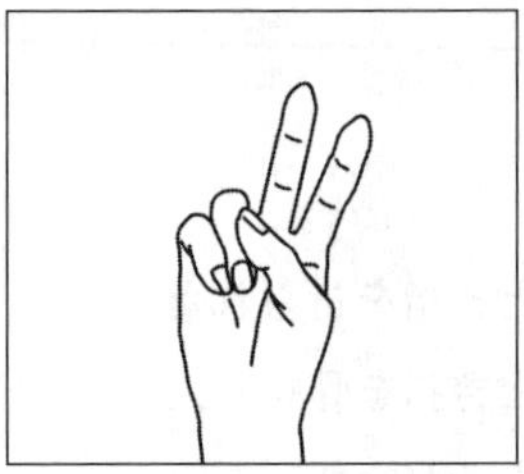

エ

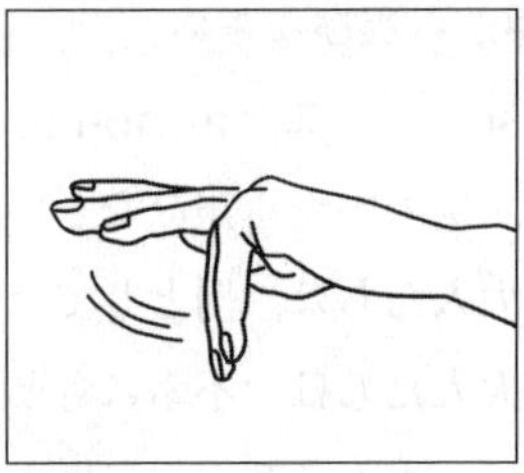

⑩ 本文には次の文が欠けている。この文を入れる適切な位置を，[A]～[D]から選びなさい。

(　　)

In England and the U.S. people use only the first finger with the hand facing upwards.

ガイド **本文の主題や結論は，しばしば文章の最初に書かれている。**この文章の場合，最初の文に出てくる「ピースサイン」が1つの中心的な話題になっている。ただし第4段落に Another common gesture ...(もう1つのよく使われるジェスチャーは…)，第5段落に One other gesture ...(もう1つのジェスチャーは…)とあり，それぞれ別のジェスチャーの話になる。文章全体は個々のジェスチャーの単なる説明ではなく，それらが持つ文化的な意味である。ジャンル分けするなら，本文は**比較文化論**(異なる文化間の違いや共通点の研究)に関する文章といえる。

本文中の空所に入る適切な語句を選ぶ問いの正解には，**(1)内容的に正しいもの，(2)文法的に正しい形，(3)熟語やコロケーションを完成させるもの**，の3つのパターンがある。この問題の場合，①は(2)，②⑤は(1)，④は(3)のパターンである。それぞれの問いがどのパターンに当たるかを考えながら解くとよい。

最高水準問題

解答 別冊 p.23

012 次の文章を読んで，問いに答えなさい。（東京農業大第一高）

In 1974, serious flooding in *Bangladesh caused a terrible shortage of food. Throughout Bangladesh, about one million people *starved to death over the next few years.

During that period, a worried young professor at *Chittagong University, *Muhammad Yunus, was disappointed that all he could do to help society was to teach economics. He wanted to do more to help his fellow countrymen and women. He wanted to put away the economics theories and textbooks, and find out about the real lives of the poor of Bangladesh. With this in mind, he took his students on a field trip to the local village of *Jobra.

In Jobra, the professor and his students met a woman named *Sophia who made small bamboo seats for a living. They were shocked to discover that she only made 2 cents a day from her work. Most of her money went into paying back high-interest loans that she used to buy the *raw materials she needed. Their research in Jobra showed many more poor people living just like Sophia.

[A] So, villagers such as Sophia had to borrow money from local dealers, who *charged terribly high interest rates. None of the villagers could make enough money to escape their poverty because they were all having to pay back high-interest loans.

[B] So, he lent 42 poor women the 27 dollars he had with him to buy raw materials to make their bamboo seats, etc. It was important that he trusted these poor women to pay him back — if they didn't, there would be nothing he could do.

Yunus's lower *repayment rate allowed the women to make enough to live on and to make a *profit. He continued his banking system for the poor based purely on trust, and it soon became successful in several villages. So in 1983, Yunus decided to start his own bank, *Grameen Bank, with the single purpose of loaning money to the "poorest of the poor." The word "gram" means village in *Bengali, reflecting the bank's origins.

[C] To get a loan, all you need to show is that you are poor and you have the will to work hard. Then, five of you make a group, and each of you receives a small, individual loan. People who borrow from the bank repay the trust they are given by repaying their loans. As a result, they paid in record numbers.

[D] This social pressure encourages the members to pay their loans back on time. However, the rest of the group do not have to repay an unpaid loan — Grameen Bank accepts it as a loss. By trusting these people with their tiny loans,

Yunus allowed them to help themselves.

[E] Yunus believes that women living in poverty use the money more directly for their families than men. Not only do they repay their loans, but they also clothe, educate and feed their children with their profits.

Over the last few years, the *greed and mistakes of traditional banks have caused great problems in the world economy. At the same time, Grameen Bank has continued to make life a little better for the poor of the world. The contrast between these banks and Grameen Bank is clear: they work to make money; Grameen works to help the poor.

Grameen Bank has so far loaned about 6.4 billion dollars to 7.4 million families, and now many *financial institutions around the world have copied Muhammad Yunus's simple model. It is worth remembering that the poor are not poor because they are lazy. They are no (X) from the rich. They just happen to have been born into (X) families. In 2006, the great work done by Yunus and the bank itself was recognized, and they were *awarded the Nobel Peace Prize.

（注） Bangladesh バングラデシュ　starve 飢える　Chittagong University チッタゴン大学
Muhammad Yunus ムハマド・ユヌス（グラミン銀行の創始者）
Jobra ジョブラ（バングラデシュの小さな村）　Sophia ソフィア（ジョブラの貧しい女性）
raw material 原材料　charge ～を請求する　repayment rate 返済利率
profit 利益　Grameen Bank グラミン銀行　Bengali ベンガル語　greed 強欲
financial institution 金融機関　award （賞）を与える

① [A]～[E]に入る適切な英文を，次の中から1つずつ選びなさい。

[A]（　　）　[B]（　　）　[C]（　　）　[D]（　　）　[E]（　　）

ア It is an interesting fact that about 97 percent of Grameen borrowers are women.

イ Traditional banks would not lend money to these poor people because they did not trust the poor to pay them back.

ウ If one of the group cannot repay their loan, the rest of the group will feel the pressure.

エ Grameen Bank has a unique system.

オ Yunus saw that if these people could borrow money at a more reasonable rate, it would help them greatly.

② 次の各問いに対する最も適切な答えを，下から1つずつ選びなさい。

[1] Why did Yunus take his students to the local village of Jobra?（　　）

ア He wanted to throw away his teaching materials.

イ He wanted to teach them economics with products made in Jobra.

ウ He wanted to show them real lives in Bangladesh.

エ He wanted to get along with Sophia through the field trip.

［2］ What was Sophia's life like? （　　）

ア She couldn't get out of poverty because of a high-interest loan.

イ She earned enough money to support her family.

ウ She could earn only 2 cents and spent all the money for her family.

エ She became independent by making hand-made products.

［3］ What did Yunus do for the women in Jobra? （　　）

ア He gave them raw materials to produce their hand-made products.

イ He lent a small amount of money with high interest rates.

ウ He introduced local dealers in order to lend them a small amount of money with low interest rates.

エ He used his own money for poor women to help them buy raw materials to make their bamboo seats, etc.

［4］ According to Yunus, how were women living in poverty different from men? （　　）

ア They directly used money they got for their families.

イ They bought their own clothes with their profits.

ウ They educated their children because their husbands didn't.

エ They spent much more money on education and amusement than men.

［5］ What was special about Grameen Bank? （　　）

ア Grameen Bank made a lot of money by lending money to the poor.

イ Grameen Bank had a big impact on the world economy.

ウ Grameen Bank continued to improve the standard of living of the poor.

エ Grameen Bank loaned more than 6 billion dollars, which made it famous.

［6］ What happened because of Yunus's effort? （　　）

ア Women around the world were fully saved by Yunus's low-interest loans.

イ Many banks around the world introduced Yunus's bank model.

ウ Most people noticed poor people were not poor because they were lazy.

エ Yunus and the bank itself were awarded the Nobel Peace Prize because they gave people a lot of money without any profit.

③ グラミン銀行の特徴について述べた次の英文のそれぞれの空所に入る1語を答えなさい。

(1) (　　　　) (2) (　　　　) (3) (　　　　) (4) (　　　　)
(5) (　　　　)

"Gram" means village in Bengali, which reflects the bank's origins. Grameen Bank lends a small individual loan to people who show their will to work hard although they are (1). Five people make a (2) and cooperate with each other to pay the loan back. As a result, people who borrowed from Grameen Bank repaid their loans with a surprisingly (3) percentage. This is because social pressure to repay their loans allows the members to pay it back (4) time. However, the fellow members don't have to repay any unpaid money even if someone can't pay it back. The bank thinks of the unpaid money as a (5). The policy helped poor people become independent.

④ 本文中の空所(X)に共通して入る1語を答えなさい。　(　　　　)

⑤ 次の英文は，本文の内容をふまえたN君の感想である。空所に入る1語を答えなさい。

(1) (　　　　) (2) (　　　　)

This story was impressive. Muhammad Yunus and his Grameen Bank were a shining example to everyone. They showed us that making money was not the only goal, even for a bank. In the Edo period, Japan also had a similar five-family neighborhood system (Gonin-Gumi). However, the villagers at that time had to take responsibility for not paying a tax. In other words, it worked as a system to (1) the other villagers. There was little room for believing in other people. On the other hand, Muhammad Yunus and his Grameen Bank tried to save the poor by expecting their good will. They showed the power of (2). In that sense, it was worth being awarded the Nobel Peace Prize.

013 次の文章を読んで，問いに答えなさい。 (東京・桐朋高)

The names of companies and products have many different origins. Older companies often got their names from (1). Car companies are a good example. Many car companies, such as Ford, Toyota, and Tata, all have the names of the men who started them. Other car companies, such as SAAB, FIAT, and BMW have names that are (2). For example, BMW stands for Bavarian Motor Works. Today, most new companies do not choose names like these. They want more interesting names, because they know that company and product names are very important.

A new company must choose its name carefully. It must also think carefully when it names its products. A name (3)[people / can / about / what / think / influence] a company or a product. People will remember a good name. They may choose that company or product because of its name. This means that a company or a product with a good name may not need many advertisements. This can save the company a lot of money.

Companies *consider many things when they choose a name. They want a name that customers will connect with the company or product. If a company makes shoes for running, it should consider names that are *related to feet or shoes. *Green Moon* or *Crazy Cow* would not be good names for shoes. A good name should also be easy to remember. However, the name should not be too ordinary. It is probably not a good idea to choose a name like *Best Shoes* or *The Shoe Company*. These names are (4) and do not show how the company is unique.

(5)Perhaps the most important factor that a company must consider is the emotion that people will feel when they hear the name of the company. What will they think about when they hear the name? When the online company Amazon began, it sold only books. The *founder of the company chose the name because the Amazon River is vast and powerful. It is the largest river in the world. He wanted his company to be the biggest bookseller in the world.

A good name tells a story. If a shoe company chooses a name like *Fast Feet*, this explains the business to the customers. There is a clear connection between shoes and their purpose, but the name is a little ordinary. Two companies that make running shoes chose names that are more interesting: Nike — the Greek *goddess of victory — and Reebok — a large animal from Africa that runs very (6-a). These names tell good stories. The companies hope their customers will think about (6-b) and speed when they buy their shoes.

The names of some electronic and technology products also give good examples of responses to products. The names for these products should make people think about modern science and technology. [A] Sometimes this choice relates to sounds. [B] In English, words that begin or end with *x*, such as x-ray, often sound very scientific or technical. [C] A good example of a product name is Xerox. [D] It sounds very technical, but it is also easy to remember. Another good example is the company name Google. This name comes from the word *googol*, which means a very large number: 10^{100}. The company's original name was Back Rub, but as it grew, the directors decided it needed a better name. They chose the new name because it makes the company sound scientific and powerful. Today, Google is a very successful company.

Finally, sometimes businesses want to find a new name. Kentucky Fried Chicken sells lots of fried chicken. Today, many customers worry that they eat too much fat. Kentucky Fried Chicken didn't want its customers to just think about its fried food. (7)The company decided to change its name to KFC. KFC wanted customers to think about its other products, which are not fried. A company may also change its name when something bad happens. For example, there was an airplane crash in Florida in 1997. Many people died in the crash. The company that owned the airplane, ValuJet, wanted its customers to (8) the crash, so it changed its name to AirTran.

Choosing and changing names is an important part of any business. Names can have a powerful influence on customers. With a good response from customers, a company can make a lot of money. With a bad response, a company may lose a lot of money.

（注） consider ～を熟考する　related to ～ ～に関連した　founder 創立者
goddess 女神

① (1)に入る最も適切な語を，次の中から選びなさい。 (　　)
ア animals　イ computers　ウ people　エ products

② (2)に入る最も適切な語を，次の中から選びなさい。 (　　)
ア capitals　イ images　ウ initials　エ symbols

③ 下線部(3)の[　]内の語を並べ替えて，意味の通る英文を完成しなさい。

④ (4)に入る最も適切な語を，次の中から選びなさい。 (　　)
ア boring　イ short　ウ difficult　エ interesting

⑤ 下線部(5)を日本語に直しなさい。

⑥ （ 6-a ）と（ 6-b ）に入る最も適切な語を，それぞれ1語の英語で答えなさい。

(a)（　　　　　） (b)（　　　　　）

⑦ 本文には次の文が欠けています。この文が入る位置を［ A ］～［ D ］から選びなさい。

（　　　）

For example, words that begin with *e*- or *i*-, like e-mail and iPhone, make people think about technology.

⑧ 下線部(7)の理由を日本語で説明しなさい。

---

⑨ （ 8 ）に入る最も適切な語を，次の中から選びなさい。（　　　）

ア avoid　イ forget　ウ survive　エ remember

014 次の文章を読んで，問いに答えなさい。 （神奈川・桐蔭学園高）

A Japanese college student who stayed in America for a few months was surprised to discover that Americans weren't interested in how good or bad his English was, if he could make his meaning clear.

People were interested mainly in his personal ideas and opinions, and his reasons for holding them. They didn't judge him by form, by how well he speaks in English. They judged him by content, by things that he had to say.

(1)<u>This</u> made a real problem for him, because it was usual for Japanese people to accept the opinions of others, either by agreeing with everything they said, or by continuing to be silent, and he mostly did so in Japan. Japanese people's idea is that "you and I are members of a group, and therefore you and I think and feel in the same way."

But he quickly discovered that if he acted this way in America, people thought that he was stupid, not clever. American people's idea is that "you and I are different persons, and therefore you and I are original." It is important for you not only to have a personal opinion about every subject that comes up, but to be ready at all times to express it.

It doesn't matter whether your opinion is right or wrong, if you show that you are thinking about the matter. You don't have to know all the answers, or reach a final decision. But if someone asks you, "What do you think about X?" and you really know nothing at all about it, it's not a good idea just to answer, "I don't know" or "[A]" That sounds *rude, because they may think you are saying that you are not interested in the conversation.

In such a case, you can always ask a question in return, like "I don't know what to think about X; what do you think?" (2)<u>This</u> shows that you are at least ready to think about the matter. And the other person, if he is an American, will be happy to tell you.

But after he has told you his idea, (3)<u>you should not just agree</u>. If you just say, "Oh, I see" or "Yes, that's true," he will think that you are too stupid to have an opinion of your own.

In America, if you don't express an opinion, it means you don't have one. You must show that your *brain is working and that you have been paying active attention. You do this by offering reasons of your own for agreeing with him, or by asking questions or finding problems about his opinion.

Questioning each other's opinions is so natural to Americans that most of the time they don't even think that they are doing it. Americans don't think it is rude to question someone's ideas even if he is in a higher social position. Ideas are seen as something separate from the person who expresses them, so disagreeing with an idea does not show *disrespect for the person.

Teachers like students who don't easily believe but ask questions about things that teachers say in class, because it shows that (4). Students don't have to accept everything the teacher says. So, if you want to make a good impression on an American teacher, ask a lot of questions.

Of course, it can sound rude if you *contradict someone by saying something like "No, that's not right" or "[B]" But it is always perfectly good to ask, "Why do you think so?", or to show that you are not satisfied with his opinion by saying, "[C]"

American teachers in Japan feel frustrated in their English conversation classes. They enjoy challenges from students, as a way of creating original opinions and ideas.

But for Japanese, the idea of questioning someone's opinion seems very rude. Japanese teachers do not often ask for a student's opinion in class. And even when they do, they don't usually ask questions about it; they simply respond by saying something like "[D]"

But American teachers are always asking their students for their opinions. And when a student gives his opinion, the teacher always asks him, "Why do you think so?" This question is so surprising that the Japanese student feels he has given a "wrong" answer.

(Adapted from *Polite Fictions in Collision*)

（注） rude 失礼な　brain 脳　disrespect 無礼　contradict ～を否定する

① 下線部(1)が指す内容として最も適切なものを，次の中から選びなさい。 (　　)

ア 英語をうまく話せないので，言うべきことが伝わらないこと

イ 英語の上手さではなく，発言の内容で判断されること

ウ いつも黙っているのではなく，何を言ったらよいかわからないこと

エ 人の意見を聞き流してしまうことがよくあること

② [A]～[D]に入る最も適切な文を，次の中から1つずつ選びなさい。ただし，同じものをくり返し使わないこと。

[A] (　　) [B] (　　) [C] (　　) [D] (　　)

ア Yes, but what about X?　イ You are wrong.　ウ Never mind.

エ I have no opinion.　オ That's very interesting.

③ 下線部(2)が指す内容として最も適切なものを，次の中から選びなさい。 (　　)

ア 知らないことを自分で調べること

イ 話し手に対して質問をすること

ウ 話し手に対して同意をしておくこと

エ 話題に関する失礼な表現を避けること

④ 下線部(3)の理由として最も適切なものを，次の中から選びなさい。 (　　)

ア すぐに人にだまされてしまうから　　イ 相手との会話がはずまなくなるから

ウ まずは反論をするべきだから　　エ 自分で物事を考えられないと思われるから

⑤ (4)に入る最も適切なものを，次の中から選びなさい。 (　　)

ア they disagree with the teachers

イ they don't understand the teacher's ideas

ウ they can speak English very well

エ they are thinking actively

⑥ 本文の内容に合うようにそれぞれの英文を完成させるとき，空所に入る最も適切なものを選びなさい。

[1] Japanese people usually (　　). (　　)

ア judge others by the content of their opinions

イ continue to be silent only when they are not interested in the opinions of others

ウ accept the opinions of others without any question

エ ask a lot of questions to show that they have been paying active attention

[2] American people's idea is that (　　). (　　)

ア people who have different opinions from other members should leave the group

イ every person is a member of a group, and thinks and feels in the same way

ウ every person is unique, and should have his or her own opinion

エ people shouldn't start talking before they find the right answer

[3] Americans think (　　). (　　)

ア it is bad manners to express a different opinion against people in higher social positions

イ disagreeing with someone's idea doesn't mean that you don't respect the person

ウ questioning someone's opinion will break the friendship

エ students have to accept everything their teacher says

⑦ 本文中に述べられているアメリカ人の考え方に基づいているものはア，日本人の考え方に基づいているものはイ，どちらにも基づいていないものはウで答えなさい。

[1] Students must be ready to express their personal opinions about every subject. (　　)

[2] Students should make small groups to think and feel in the same way. (　　)

[3] Teachers must change the subject if the students don't have any opinions about it. (　　)

[4] Teachers usually accept a student's opinion without asking questions. (　　)

難 015 次の文章を読んで，問いに答えなさい。 （東京・中央大杉並高）

KINTSUGI

You probably have not heard the word '*kintsugi*' before. That is not very surprising. *Kintsugi* is a Japanese word. It is made up of two Japanese words: the first part, *kin*, means 'golden,' and the second part, *tsugi*, means 'fixing.' When you put the two words together, it means repairing a broken thing in a beautiful way. Normally, if something is broken, you feel it is not useful anymore. You may want to throw it away and get a new one. But that is not the *kintsugi* way.

Kintsugi started a long time ago in Japan. The ancient Japanese people loved pots and cups, and they had a tradition of making beautiful ones. However, because those pots and cups were so delicate, they got broken easily. Most owners threw away the broken ones right away and bought new ones. But, in the middle of the 16th century, some people felt that they should not throw away the beautiful pots, cups and bowls as waste. They thought they should try to fix them. This idea gradually became popular among the Japanese at that time. People began to fix their broken *ceramics. At first, they put the broken pieces back together with *glue only, but later they started to mix the glue with gold *powder. This meant you could see very clearly which part was repaired. By doing this, they were not *pretending that the cup or pot was not broken before; they were clearly showing that it was fixed. They were showing that they did not *mind accepting those facts, and they were also showing that they could create even more beautiful things by fixing them. This is the *kintsugi* way.

<u>*Kintsugi* is a big idea.</u> It started from a very small thing — fixing a broken cup — but the same idea can be used for thinking about more important things as well. For example, people can be broken easily because they are so delicate. It is not just the physical breaking of bones or hurting the body. Breaking can also happen if you get truly angry and say something bad, or if you do something unkind. When this happens, you feel as if something good in yourself is damaged. Maybe you feel like other people will not want you anymore.

However, you can cure yourself in the *kintsugi* way. For example, you feel sorry when you do something terrible, and you say sorry to the person. It is a kind of repairing. You are repairing your feelings and the relationship with that person. You do not forget that a terrible thing has happened, and you are not pretending that you never said or did that bad thing. At the same time, you are trying to improve the situation and fix the problem. In this way, you are doing your best with 'gold powder' just like *kintsugi*.

When you *make up with someone, your relationship can become better than it was before. After you have made up, you can be sure that an *argument will not mean the end of a friendship and sometimes the friendship becomes stronger through it. For example, sometimes you can be angry with your parents. But if you explain what the problem is, talk, and listen, you can understand each other more. Then, your relationship with your parents becomes better than before. It is helpful to know that our feelings can be repaired. Sometimes you hurt other people's feelings, and sometimes they hurt yours. That is never nice. But remember that you can repair things in a good way, if you keep the idea of *kintsugi* in your mind.

（注） ceramics 陶磁器，焼き物　glue 接着剤　powder 粉
pretend (that) ～ ～であると装《よそお》う，偽《いつわ》る　mind ～ing ～することを気にする
make up 仲直りする　argument 口論，口げんか

① Which of the following is NOT true about *kintsugi*? (　　)
- ア People made the word *kintsugi* by putting words together.
- イ *Kintsugi* is a Japanese tradition of making beautiful and delicate ceramics.
- ウ *Kintsugi* is a technique to fix things in a beautiful way.
- エ People show the broken part of the ceramics in *kintsugi*.

② Which was true about Japanese pots and cups before the middle of the 16th century? (　　)
- ア They were so delicate that they got broken easily, and Japanese people did not mind throwing away the broken ceramics as waste.
- イ They were treated very carefully because it was a Japanese tradition to take care of them.
- ウ Japanese people never thought of fixing the broken ceramics because it was too expensive to do so.
- エ Japanese people loved their beautiful pots and cups so much that they kept even the broken pieces for a long time.

③ In the *kintsugi* way, why do people put gold powder into the glue to fix the broken ceramics? (　　)
- ア With the gold powder, the broken part of ceramics can be hidden.
- イ With the gold powder, the broken ceramics become stronger and easier to use.
- ウ In that way, they try to show that it is very difficult to fix the delicate ceramics.
- エ In that way, they can show the broken part and make the broken ceramics more beautiful.

④ What does the underlined part "*Kintsugi* is a big idea." mean? (　　)

ア The idea of *kintsugi* can be used in repairing the human mind.

イ The idea of *kintsugi* can repair any broken cups and pots.

ウ The idea of *kintsugi* can be used in fixing humans' broken bones.

エ The idea of *kintsugi* can change other people's mind when you don't like them.

⑤ How can the *kintsugi* way help you when you hurt someone? (　　)

ア It can help you to feel sorry and say "sorry" in your mind.

イ It can help you to try to think that nothing terrible has happened.

ウ It can help you to repair your feelings and improve the situation.

エ It can help you to use 'gold powder' to forget that terrible thing.

⑥ According to the article, choose two correct sentences from the following. (　　)(　　)

ア Before the birth of *kintsugi*, Japanese people used all pieces of the broken ceramics to create new pots and cups.

イ Repairing broken ceramics with only glue was more difficult than repairing them with gold powder.

ウ The human mind is as delicate as ceramics, so people shouldn't hurt others' feelings.

エ The *kintsugi* way can make your friendships stronger than before.

オ Our feelings toward our parents can be repaired more easily than our feelings toward our friends.

カ Even if you hurt other people's feelings, you can repair the relationship with them by using the *kintsugi* way.

解答の方針

「金継ぎ」という日本の伝統技術に関する文章。第1・2段落は金継ぎの技法の具体的な説明だが，第3段落の冒頭の *Kintsugi* is a big idea. で話の内容が変わる。ここからは「金継ぎという技術の根底にある考え方を，別の面に応用する」という説明になっている。簡単に言えば，前半は具体的な話，後半は抽象的な話である。人の心を修復するプロセスの中で，金継ぎの物理的な工程が比ゆとして使われている。その関係を正確にとらえることが大切である。

なお，この問題では設問文がすべて英文になっている。近年の入試ではこのような出題が増えているので，英文の設問形式にも慣れておこう。たとえば⑥の According to the article は「本文によれば」の意味。article（記事）の代わりに passage（文章），text（本文）なども使われる。

難 016 次の文章を読んで，問いに答えなさい。 （東京・開成高）

Megan entered my *therapy office looking for help because she was feeling stressed out and *overwhelmed. She said there weren't enough hours in the day to accomplish everything she needed to do.

At age thirty-five, she was married and had two young children. She worked a part-time job, taught Sunday school, and was the Girl Scout troop leader. She *strived to be a good wife and (1), but she felt like she just wasn't doing a good enough job. She was often *irritable and *grumpy toward her family and she wasn't sure why.

The more Megan talked, the clearer it became that she was a woman who couldn't say [A]. Church members frequently called her on Saturday nights, asking her to bake muffins for Sunday morning's church service. Parents of her Girl Scout troop sometimes relied on her to drive their children home if they were stuck at work.

Megan also frequently babysat for her sister's kids, so her sister wouldn't have to spend money on a sitter. She also had a cousin who sought favors and always seemed to have some sort of last-minute problem, ranging from being short on cash to needing help with a home improvement project. Lately, Megan had stopped answering her cousin's phone calls because (2a)she knew that every time (2b)she called (2c)she needed something.

Megan said to me that her number one rule was to never say [B] to family. So each time her cousin asked for a favor or her sister asked her to babysit, she automatically said [C]. When I asked her what impact that had on her husband and children, she told me that sometimes it meant (3)[dinner / for / home / in / she / time / wasn't] or to put the kids to bed. Just admitting that out loud helped Megan begin to realize why saying [D] to *extended family meant she was saying [E] to her *immediate family. Although she valued her extended family, her husband and her children were her top priorities, and she decided she needed to start treating them accordingly.

We also reviewed her desire to be liked by everyone. Her biggest fear was that other people would think she was selfish. However, after a few therapy sessions she began to recognize that her need to always be liked was actually much more selfish than saying [F] to someone. (4)Helping others really wasn't about improving their lives; she was mostly *giving of herself because she wanted to be held in higher *regard. Once she changed the way she thought about people pleasing, she was able to begin changing her behavior.

It took some practice for Megan to begin saying [G] to people. In fact, she wasn't even sure how to say [H]. She thought she needed an excuse but she didn't want to lie. But I encouraged her to simply say something like "No, I'm not able to do that," without providing a lengthy reason why. She began practicing saying [I] and she found that the more she did it, the easier it became. Although she had imagined people would become angry with her, she quickly noticed that (5). The more time she spent with her family, the less irritable she felt. Her stress level also decreased and after saying [J] a few times, she felt less pressured to (6) others.

(注) therapy 療法　overwhelm ～を精神的に参らせる　strive : try hard
irritable 怒りっぽい　grumpy 不機嫌な
extended family : family that includes grandparents, aunts, uncles, etc.
immediate family : family such as your parents, children, husband, or wife
give of oneself 人のために尽力する　regard 尊敬

① (1)に入る適切な1語を答えなさい。　(　　　)

② 下線部(2a)～(2c)が指すものを，次の中から1つずつ選びなさい。同じものをくり返し使ってもよい。　(a) (　　)　(b) (　　)　(c) (　　)

ア Megan　イ Megan's sister　ウ Megan's cousin

③ 下線部(3)の[　　　]内の語を，文脈に合うよう並べ替えなさい。

④ 下線部(4)を日本語に直しなさい。

⑤ (5)に入る最も適切なものを，次の中から選びなさい。　(　　)

ア they didn't really seem to mind
イ they were going to ask her for another favor
ウ they didn't actually have good feelings about her
エ they were very grateful for what she had done so far
オ they had the attitude that they would never ask her for a favor again

⑥ (6)に，直前の段落中の1語を適切な形にして入れなさい。　(　　　)

⑦ [A]～[J]のうち，2つにはyesが入り，それ以外にはnoが入る。yesが入る2つの空所を記号で答えなさい。　(　　)(　　)

解答の方針

文章の内容はそれほど難解ではない。冒頭のMegan entered my therapy office ... から，この文章はミーガンという女性を診察したtherapist(セラピスト[療法士])が書いたものだとわかる。ちなみにtherapy(療法)とは一般には薬を使わずに患者の症状を改善する方法のことで，たとえば音楽を通じて精神の安定を図るmusic therapy(音楽療法)などがある。

ただし，文章中で使われている表現や構文，および設問のレベルは高い。解説の「精読」をよく読んで，文法・構文の知識を確認しておこう。

第2回 実力テスト ▶解答→別冊 p.36

時間 30 分　目標 70 点　得点　／100

次の文章を読んで，問いに答えなさい。　（東京・城北高）　（①～④⑥各 10 点，⑤各 10 点，⑦各 6 点，計 100 点）

202

Partners and children appear later in our lives. Parents usually leave us too early. But brothers and sisters are often with us for almost all our lives for better or for worse ....

Bringing up two or more kids under the same roof often means trouble. [A] *Siblings take each other's things and fight for their parents' (1). In fact, a recent study in England showed that 31 percent of children were unhappy because a sibling fought with them a lot.

But these fights can be good for us, too. They are a chance to face problems in an *emotionally safe environment. A fight at breakfast is forgotten by lunch. As British poet Dylan Thomas once said, "I made a *snowman and my brother knocked it down and I knocked my brother down and then we had tea."

It seems especially helpful for us to have sisters. [B] A study at the University of Ulster in the U.K. found that when we have girls for siblings, honest communication in the family increases. This is (a) for our *emotional health.

Now let's think about another family matter! What do Barack Obama, Ben Affleck, and JK Rowling have in common? They're all rich, successful, and first-born children. In fact, more than half of US Presidents and Nobel Prize winners were first-born. A study by the newspaper USA TODAY found that 43 percent of the *bosses of large companies were also first-born. Why can this be?

Well, parents usually give more attention to first-born children, and they *expect great things from them. As a result, these children are often (b) and confident. They do well at school, and some studies (2)[are / than / suggest / they / their / siblings / smarter / younger]. But the first-born can have weak points, too. They sometimes expect too much of themselves and try too hard to be perfect. This can make them worry and feel (c) of making mistakes.

Last-born children — the "babies of the family" — usually get a lot of attention, too. They are often loving, sociable, and *charming. They are freer than their older siblings and more *likely to do unusual or (d) things. They often break the rules, like the Polish scientist Copernicus. (3)He was the youngest of all the children in his family. In 1543, he shocked the world when he wrote a book saying that the Earth moves around the Sun. [C] At that time, everybody was sure that the Sun moved around the Earth, and some people were very angry when Copernicus said they were wrong.

What about the poor kids in the middle? (4)(　　　)(　　　)(　　　)(　　　)

Is it sad to be brought up as an only child, with no brothers and sisters to play with? [D] But lots of recent studies show that only children are often happy and successful. The actress Natalie Portman once said that her parents allowed her to become an actress because she was an only child. Her parents didn't have to worry about her being seen as "special" or (e) from any siblings. She didn't steal attention away from anyone. She could be happy doing everything she wanted.

Lastly, we have the question of *multiple births. How does it feel to be a *twin? (5)Twins can have extremely close relationships, and this can help them get through life. But sometimes it's difficult for twins to show their own characters. They have to remind people: "Please, it's not us. It's me!"

（注） sibling （男女の別なく）きょうだい　emotionally 感情面において　snowman 雪だるま
emotional 感情面の　boss 社長　expect ～を期待する　charming 魅力的な
be likely to *do* ～する可能性が高い　multiple 複合的な，多数の　twin 双子

① （ 1 ）に入る適切な1語を本文中から探して答えなさい。　　　　（　　　　）

② 下線部(2)の［　　］内の語を，正しく並べ替えなさい。

____

③ 下線部(3)を以下のように言い換えるとき，空所に適切な語を入れなさい。

He was (　　　) than (　　　) (　　　) (　　　) in his family.

④ 下線部(4)に入る次の4つの文を，適切な順に並べ替えなさい。

（　　→　　→　　→　　）

ア Bill Gates, John F. Kennedy, and Madonna are all middle children.
イ But don't worry if you're a middle child.
ウ There are some great members in your club.
エ Studies say they get less attention and are not usually favorites.

⑤ 下線部(5)について，双子であることの利点と懸念点を次のように説明するとき，［1］［2］に適切な言葉を入れなさい。［1］は5字以内，［2］は15字以内とし，句読点も字数に含めます。

［1］

［2］

双子は，非常に［ 1 ］関係であることが彼らの人生において支えになるが，一方で時に［ 2 ］ことが難しい，という側面もある。

⑥ 本文中には次の1文が欠けている。この文が入る正しい位置を，［ A ］～［ D ］から選びなさい。

In the past, people thought so.　　　　（　　　）

⑦ （ a ）～（ e ）に入る最も適切な形容詞を，次の中から1つずつ選びなさい。同じ語はくり返し使うことはできません。

(a)（　　） (b)（　　） (c)（　　） (d)（　　） (e)（　　）

ア different　イ good　ウ dangerous　エ afraid　オ responsible

3 論説文－科学・技術

標準問題

解答 別冊 p.39

重要 017 次の文章を読んで，問いに答えなさい。[1]～[5]は段落の番号です。（奈良県）

017

[1] Have you ever seen the 2D codes which have a special *mark on the corners? For example, you can find the 2D codes in your textbooks. When you *scan them with a *tablet computer, you can see pictures or watch videos. Today, a lot of people around the world use them in many different ways. This *type of 2D code was invented by *engineers at a car *parts *maker in Japan.

[2] When cars are produced, many kinds of parts are needed. Car parts makers have to *manage all of the car parts. About 30 years ago, car companies needed to produce more kinds of cars, and car parts makers had to manage many different kinds of car parts for each car. At that time, they used barcodes to manage the car parts, but they could not *put a lot of information in one barcode. So, they used many barcodes. *Workers had to scan many barcodes. A worker at a car parts maker had to scan barcodes about 1,000 times a day. It took a lot of time to scan them. The workers needed some help to improve their *situation.

[3] The engineers at a car parts maker in Japan knew the situation of the workers. They started to learn about 2D codes because 2D codes can *contain more information than barcodes. There were already some types of 2D codes in the U.S. One type could contain a lot of information, but it took a lot of time to scan that type. Another type was scanned very *quickly, but it contained less information than other types. The engineers at the car parts maker did not use these types. They decided to create a new type of 2D code which had both of those good points. The engineers needed a long time to create this new type which could be scanned quickly. Finally they *thought of an idea. They thought, “If a 2D code has a special mark on the three corners, it can be scanned very quickly from every *angle.” In this way the new type of 2D code with special marks was invented by the engineers at a car parts maker in Japan.

2D code
（2次元コード）

[4] How did people around the world start to use the new type of 2D code? After car parts makers started to use it, other *businesses also started to *pay attention to it. For example, a *mobile phone company started to use it to help people visit websites *directly by using their mobile phone cameras. By scanning a 2D code with their

9784578233589
barcode
（バーコード）

mobile phones, *users can get a lot of information quickly and easily. With this technology, people learned that the new type of 2D code was very useful.

[5] Today, the 2D code invented by the engineers at a car parts maker in Japan has become popular in people's lives around the world. It was invented by engineers to help workers, but now, it helps people around the world a lot.

（注） mark 目印　scan ～を読み込む　tablet computer タブレットコンピューター
type 種類　engineer エンジニア　part 部品　maker 製造業者
manage ～を管理する　put (情報など)を入れる　worker 労働者　situation 状況
contain ～を含む　quickly 素早く　think of ～ ～を思いつく　angle 角度
business 事業　pay attention to ～ ～に注目する　mobile phone 携帯電話
directly 直接　user 利用者

① 英文の段落ごとの見出しを下の表のようにつけるとき，（ A ）～（ C ）に入る適切なものを下から1つずつ選びなさい。　(A)（　　）　(B)（　　）　(C)（　　）

段落	見出し
[1]	The 2D codes in our daily lives
[2]	（ A ）
[3]	（ B ）
[4]	（ C ）
[5]	The 2D code for people around the world

ア A new type of 2D code invented by engineers in Japan
イ The barcode which can improve the situation of workers
ウ Another way of using the new type of 2D code
エ The way of using some 2D codes from the U.S.
オ The company which started to use mobile phone cameras
カ The problems of using barcodes

② 英文の内容について，次の問いにそれぞれ3語以上の英語で答えなさい。コンマやピリオドなどは語数に含みません。

(1) Did the engineers at the car parts maker in Japan use the 2D codes from the U.S.?

____

(2) Where did the engineers put a special mark when they invented the new type of 2D code?

____

③ 英文の内容に一致するものを，次の中から２つ選びなさい。 (　　) (　　)

ア A car parts maker in Japan invented barcodes.

イ Car parts makers used barcodes to sell more cars.

ウ Barcodes can contain more information than 2D codes.

エ The 2D code with special marks can be scanned quickly.

オ A mobile phone company used the new type of 2D code to help users visit websites easily.

カ The engineers from Japan and the U.S. worked together to invent the new type of 2D code.

ガイド 論理展開が明快な標準レベルの論説文。５つの段落は「[1]導入＋[2][3][4]本論＋[5]結び」の構成であり，本論の部分を正確に読む必要がある。

重要 018 Read the passage and choose the answer which best completes each sentence ①〜⑤. (大阪府)

Our *daily lives are supported by a lot of *satellites in space. Now, there are about 4,300 satellites around the earth. By 2030, about 46,000 satellites will be there. These satellites help our activities and communication. For example, weather information, the Internet, and cellphones can be used with this satellite technology.

However, *space debris makes the situation of satellites (1). Space debris is trash in space. For example, old satellites which are not working, and, some parts which were *separated from a *rocket are all space debris. There are various sizes and shapes of space debris. The space debris flies around the earth very fast. What will happen if the fast space debris hits a satellite? It may destroy the satellite. Now, the number of pieces of space debris has been getting bigger. This means there may be more accidents in the near future. If we do nothing, the accidents will have an influence on our daily lives.

Now, scientists and many teams around the world are trying three things to solve this problem. First: finding and watching space debris. Second: reducing the number of new pieces of space debris. This means improving technology to reduce the number of the separated parts from rockets. Making satellites which can work longer is also helpful. Third: removing space debris which is already in space.

Many people have thought the third point was too difficult, but a Japanese team is now trying to do it. How can the team remove space debris? The team invented a machine which used the power of *magnets. After the machine finds space debris which is not *tumbling, it follows and catches the space debris. Some kinds of space debris are tumbling, so it is too difficult for the machine to catch those kinds of space debris. To catch the tumbling space debris, the team will keep improving the machine.

"Let's reduce trash." This has been an important topic when we think about our daily lives and the global environment. (2)Both should be protected, but today, we have to protect the environment of space, too. We are responsible for a good environment both on the earth and in space.

（注） daily 日々の　satellite 人工衛星　space debris スペースデブリ（宇宙ゴミ）
separate ～を切り離す　rocket ロケット　magnet 磁石　tumble 回転する

① The word which should be put in (1) is ( )
ア better. イ convenient. ウ dangerous. エ wrong.

② One of the problems in space is ( )
ア various pieces of trash which may destroy satellites.
イ many kinds of satellites which are working for our daily lives.
ウ the satellites which move fast and cause serious accidents.
エ the number of space debris which helps our activities.

③ The plan which is not tried for solving the problem of space debris is ( )
ア finding and watching space debris.
イ making satellites work longer.
ウ reducing the number of rockets and satellites.
エ taking space debris out from space.

④ The word (2)Both refers to ( )
ア our daily lives and the global environment.
イ our activities and communication.
ウ scientists and many teams around the world.
エ space debris and satellites.

⑤ According to the passage, ( )
ア old satellites are not space debris because they are not working.
イ scientists and many teams in the world are trying to separate space debris from rockets and satellites.
ウ the machine made by a Japanese team can catch space debris which is tumbling.
エ space debris may hit satellites more often in the near future because the number of pieces of space debris is getting bigger.

ガイド キーワードは第2段落の最初の文にあるspace debris(スペースデブリ[宇宙ゴミ])。この言葉を聞いたことがなくても，第2段落を読めばspace debrisが何であるかがわかる。第3段落にはFirst ... Second ... Third ... という3つの情報が箇条書き的に述べられている。それを受けて次の段落の最初の文にthe third point was ...(第3点は…)とある。文章中のこのような指示関係に注意しながら読むようにしよう。

019 次の文章を読んで，問いに答えなさい。 （京都・立命館高）

The amount of beef that people eat is increasing year by year. Foods like hamburgers and steak are more popular than ever. This is not a big surprise. Beef not only tastes good but also has some things that are good for our bodies. However, we may not be able to continue eating beef as much as we do now.

Beef is one of the most difficult kinds of food to produce. Of course, we need cows to produce beef, but to *raise them, a lot of land, food and water are needed. Also, cows produce a lot of *greenhouse gases which cause global warming. It has become one of the most serious problems in the world to solve. Because of (1)these facts, producing beef is sometimes seen as a bad thing. Beef is an important food for many people, so we can't stop producing it so soon. But the world population is growing and it may become about 9.7 billion in 2050. This means more beef will be needed in the near future and the situation will get worse.

From such facts, some people worry that they will have to live without beef in the near future. Then, some companies and scientists have started working on new projects. For example, some companies make foods that look and taste similar to beef but are not made from cows. One of them is made from tofu. Tofu hamburgers and tofu meatballs are popular in many countries. In the near future, more and more companies and scientists will (2)try to do such projects.

Actually, there is a new way to produce beef, too. The meat is not from a farm but from a *lab. This kind of meat is called lab-grown meat. A new technology is used to produce this meat. This technology is the same as the one which is used in medical care. To produce lab-grown beef, scientists use *cells from cows. They put the cells in a special *liquid, and then the number of cells starts to increase. When the number of the cells is enough, the cells begin to connect. In this way, scientists can produce beef little by little.

In the last ten years, researchers and companies around the world have been using these technologies to produce lab-grown meat products. In 2013, a hamburger made with lab-grown meat was shown to the world. Later, an American company made lab-grown chicken meat. In February 2021, a company in Israel announced they made the first thick steak from lab-grown meat by using a special 3D printer. It can make lab-grown meat that is just like steak.

The technology to produce lab-grown meat is wonderful. However, some people say (3)it is difficult to make the meat popular. The technology is new, so there has not been a way yet to produce lab-grown meat at a low cost. To make the first hamburger made from lab-grown meat in 2013, it cost about 325,000 dollars! So scientists and companies are trying to reduce the cost. Also, some people worry about its safety. Some governments say lab-grown meat is safe and will allow companies to sell it in the near future, but that is not enough to change people's ideas. Scientists need to do more research.

Now more companies have started to pay attention to lab-grown meat. There are still some problems to solve, so it will take time before lab-grown meat is accepted by everyone as food. But we can say that (　　).

(注) raise ～を育てる　greenhouse gas 温室効果ガス　lab 実験室　cell 細胞
liquid 液体

① 下線部(1)が具体的に表す内容として最も適切なものを，下から選びなさい。 (　　)

ア cows need a lot of greenhouse gases

イ it is easy for us to produce beef

ウ producing beef is not good for the earth in many ways

エ we will not be able to see beef in our future lives

② 下線部(2)が具体的に表す内容として最も適切なものを，下から選びなさい。 (　　)

ア try to use tofu to raise animals for meat

イ try to raise animals without producing greenhouse gases

ウ try to produce things which can be enjoyed just like meat

エ try to find an easier way to produce tofu to make foods like beef

③ 下線部(3)の理由を２つ，日本語で簡潔に答えなさい。

④ 本文の最後の空所に入る最も適切な語句を，次の中から選びなさい。 (　　)

ア it may be one of the great inventions that change how we produce food

イ not meat but other kinds of food can be produced in labs

ウ we should work hard to stop producing lab-grown meat

エ everyone will notice that meat from farms isn't as good as lab-grown meat

⑤ 本文の内容に合うものを次の中から２つ選びなさい。 (　　)(　　)

ア Beef is difficult to produce and the amount of beef produced in the world is getting smaller.

イ The technology for producing meat in labs comes from the same one used to help patients.

ウ The lab-grown meat is a kind of meat which is made from tofu in labs.

エ Some people are worried about eating lab-grown meat.

オ There are some companies which have already started to sell lab-grown meat.

⑥ 以下の英文は本文の内容をまとめたものです。それぞれの空所に入る1語を答えなさい。

Beef is a kind of food which is very important for many people now. However, in the future we may have to live with [A] beef than now. This is because the [B] is increasing in the world and there may not be [C] beef for everyone. Also, raising cows can be [D] for the environment. Some companies have already made meat using tofu. Also, by [E] cells, people can produce meat in a lab. Before selling it all over the world, some problems must be solved.

［A］(　　　　)　［B］(　　　　)　［C］(　　　　)　［D］(　　　　)
［E］(　　　　)

重要 020 次の文章を読んで，問いに答えなさい。 （東京・中央大高）

We know a lot about what sleep is, but we don't know what causes sleep. Sleep is a *state of rest. When we sleep, our body *recovers from *fatigue caused by the day's activities. After a good sleep, we become active again and ready for our daily activities.

Scientists have found that sleep is also important in the process of learning. When we sleep, the brain takes the new information we received during the day, and carries it to a holding area. Then, the information is moved to more *permanent storage, kept deep in your memory.

(1)When we wake up in the morning, it is not always possible for us to remember what happened in our mind when we were asleep. We may remember a dream, but the rest of our sleep was a kind of darkness and nothing seems to have taken place.

Several things happen to our body as we go deeper into sleep. Our muscles relax. Our heartbeats become slower. Our temperatures and *blood pressure go down. The brain also slows down so that we can't think or act *consciously. But we can dream. When we first wake up, our temperatures and blood pressure rise to (2). Our heartbeats and breathing also become (2) and we become more *fully awake. Then, we often forget most of the dreams that we had while sleeping.

What is a dream? It is an activity of the mind that takes place when we are asleep. Dreams seem to be important for several reasons. One is that (3)a dream can help us to sleep through noise. For example, the alarm clock rings, but our mind causes us to dream that the telephone or doorbell is ringing and that we are awake and answering it. Dreams also *reveal a lot about one's problems and can provide a solution to them.

Some dreams are *realistic while others are not. (4)This means that [ ] could happen when we are awake. Others could not. But we must remember (5)one thing. Dreams cannot be used as a way to tell the future. They simply can never tell the future.

（注） state 状態　recover 回復する　fatigue 疲労
permanent storage 永久記憶装置　blood pressure 血圧　consciously 意識的に
fully 十分に　reveal ～を明らかにする　realistic 現実になる

① 下線部(1)を日本語に直しなさい。

② (2)に共通して入る語を，次の中から選びなさい。 (　　)

ア normal　　イ common　　ウ fast　　エ active

③ 下線部(3)が表す内容を，本文の記述に従って45字程度の日本語で具体的に説明しなさい。

														45

④ 下線部(4)が「つまり，夢の中で起きることの一部は，目が覚めているときにも起こりうる」という意味になるようア～キの語句を並べ替えるとき，[A][B]に入るものを記号で答えなさい。 [A] (　　)　[B] (　　)

This means that [　　] [A] [　　] [　　] [B] [　　] [　　] could happen when we are awake.

ア dreams　　イ the things　　ウ happen　　エ some

オ that　　カ in　　キ of

⑤ 下線部(5)が指す内容として最も適切なものを，次の中から選びなさい。 (　　)

ア Some dreams are realistic.

イ Other dreams are not realistic.

ウ Dreams are used to tell the future.

エ Dreams can never tell the future.

⑥ 本文の内容に合うものを，次の中から１つ選びなさい。 (　　)

ア 日中の疲労を回復させるには，良質な睡眠と翌日の活発な運動が必要である。

イ 睡眠中，脳は日中に得た新しい情報を取り込み，最終的に記憶の中に保存する。

ウ 夢を見ている時は暗闇のような状態にあり，何も起きなかったように感じる。

エ 夢は未来を予測することはできず，人々の問題を解決する手段にもならない。

ガイド 睡眠をテーマにした文章。①のような下線部和訳問題では，複雑な構造の英文が出題されることが多い。この問いも，不定詞，間接疑問(あるいは関係代名詞)，否定など，さまざまな文法知識を使って考える必要がある。そのためには，文法・構文の豊富な知識が求められる。中学の教科書には出てこない知識が問われることもあるので，解説中の「精読」の内容を重点的に学習しておこう。なお，③の「45字程度」という指示に対しては，40～50字程度で答えるのが望ましい。

最高水準問題

解答 別冊 p.45

021 2021年に書かれた次の記事を読んで，問いに答えなさい。 (神奈川・法政大第二高)

Young People Win Climate Case in Germany

021

Germany's top *court has reached a decision that parts of the country's 2019 *climate action law must be changed because they don't do a good job of protecting young people. The result was a big victory for the nine young people who started the *lawsuit.

The court case gives great attention to an important part of the *climate crisis: (A). That's because the impacts of global warming will become more serious in the near future. Since the adults have paid no attention to these problems, young people will be left to handle them as they become adults.

In 2019, Germany passed a new law and the government promised, in the law, that the country would be *carbon neutral by 2050. The law made a plan of action until 2030. But the law didn't have any clear rules or plans for climate actions that would be taken between 2031 and 2050.

A group of nine young people aged 15 to 24 took the government to court about the law. They said that the government didn't make a careful plan and it was putting their future lives in danger. Under the government's plan, they felt they would be left to face the most difficult *emissions challenges when they were adults.

On April 29, 2021, the *judges of Germany's highest court agreed with the young people and said that parts of the German law didn't follow Germany's *Constitution. The judges said that if the government does not take climate action, it might take away the basic right of young people to a better future.

The young people *challenged the government's law in four areas. The judges didn't agree with all of the challenges. They agreed with only a part of their challenges. But even a part of their case is seen as a big victory.

Luisa Neubauer is one of the young people who took the government to court. She works with the climate action group Fridays For Future. Ms. Neubauer said, "(1)Climate protection is our basic right and that's official now. This is a huge win for the climate movement. It changes a lot."

The court has given the German government a year, until the end of 2022, to fix the law. The climate law will now need to have a much more careful plan for the actions that will be taken after 2030 to cut Germany's pollution and lead the country to be carbon neutral by 2050.

Germany's government has said that (2)it will quickly begin working to make the needed changes. One important part of high court decisions like this is that they act as guides or examples for future decisions. This means that in the future, Germany's lawmakers will more probably think about the climate future of young people when they create their (B).

Other groups of young people around the world are also bringing lawsuits against governments. Last year a group of six young people from Portugal began a lawsuit against 33 European countries in *the European Court of Human Rights. Recently young people in Australia, Brazil, and the United Kingdom have also taken their governments to court about climate action.

（注） court　裁判所　　climate action law　気候保護法　　lawsuit　訴訟
climate crisis　気候危機
carbon neutral　カーボンニュートラル(環境用語)。二酸化炭素の排出を「全体としてゼロにする」こと。つまり排出量と植物などが吸収する量を差し引きゼロにすること。
emissions challenges　排出量の課題　　judge　裁判官　　constitution　憲法
challenge　～に関する妥当性を問う
the European Court of Human Rights　欧州人権裁判所

① (A)に入る最も適切なものを，次の中から選びなさい。 (　　)

ア the climate crisis will influence young people much more than adults
イ the climate crisis will destroy the natural environment all over the world
ウ the climate crisis will cause the country to lose a lot of money
エ the climate crisis will result in record-breaking high temperatures

② Ms. Neubauer が下線部(1)のように言った根拠として最も適切なものを，次の中から選びなさい。 (　　)

ア In 2019, the German government created a new law about becoming carbon neutral.
イ Germany's highest court said that the climate crisis was a difficult problem to solve.
ウ Germany's top court agreed that a basic right of young people should be protected by taking climate action.
エ The new climate action law didn't follow the German constitution.

③ 下線部(2)の it が具体的に指すものを，本文の中から抜き出して答えなさい。 (　　　　　　　　　　)

④ (B)に入る最も適切なものを，次の中から選びなさい。 (　　)

ア government　　イ groups　　ウ problems　　エ laws

⑤ 次の英文のそれぞれの空所に入る年を，算用数字(西暦)で答えなさい。 (X) (　　　　) (Y) (　　　　)

Germany's top court ordered that the government should change the climate action law by the end of (X) and the new law should have more careful plans for climate action by (Y).

⑥ 本文の内容と一致するものを，次の中から1つ選びなさい。 (　　)

ア The judges of Germany's highest court agreed that the 2019 climate action law protected young people's future enough.

イ The young people challenged the climate action law in four areas, but the judges didn't agree with any of them.

ウ The top court's decisions will influence the government's action for the climate future of the country's young people.

エ The climate action group Fridays For Future talked with young people around the world and they started a lawsuit against the government.

難 022 次の文章を読んで，問いに答えなさい。解答に固有名詞を含む場合は英語表記でよい。

（鹿児島・ラ・サール高）

A company called Neuralink has shared a video which appears to show a monkey playing a video game. That's fairly unusual, but what makes the video even stranger is that the monkey is playing the video game with just its (1).

Neuralink is a company owned by Elon Musk, who also owns the car company Tesla and the rocket company SpaceX. Neuralink is working to develop *devices that could allow people to control things using just their brains. It sounds like something from (2) movie, but Neuralink is already showing progress in doing similar work with other animals, like pigs.

The monkey in the video is called Pager, and he has two of Neuralink's special "Link" devices inside his brain. The devices were planted in Pager's brain by a surgeon. These devices are connected to 2,048 wires (3)[movements / of Pager's brain / that control / to the parts / which lead] of the arms and hands. Scientists taught Pager to play a video game. They used a banana smoothie as a special treat to reward him when he played the game correctly. Soon Pager was eager to play well in order to get more smoothie.

At first, Pager controlled the video game using a joystick, which is a normal gaming controller. But as Pager played, his "Link" devices wirelessly sent out information about the signals his brain was using to control his arms and hands. Neuralink's scientists recorded all of (4)these signals.

Then they used computers to match up the signals from Pager's brain to the movements that his hands were actually making. (5)This was challenging work and the scientists had to use artificial intelligence (AI) to help them decode Pager's brain signals.

The final step was to have a computer make moves in the video game as if Pager had actually moved the joystick. If Pager thought about moving the joystick up, the computer would send an "up" signal to the video game. (6)At first, the researchers let Pager keep moving the joystick with his hand, even though it was connected to the computer. But soon Pager was able to play the video game using just his brain.

Even though Neuralink's work right now focuses on animals and video games, there's a very serious purpose behind it. (7)Neuralink wants to make it possible for humans who have lost the ability to control their bodies to communicate and connect with the world around them.

Mr. Musk says that in the near future Neuralink hopes to allow a paralyzed person to control a smartphone just by thinking. He believes they'll be able to do it faster than someone who is using their hands. The next step would be to allow them to control a computer.

When people are paralyzed, it's often because the brain has lost the ability to send signals to different parts of the body. Neuralink hopes that one day in the future, its system will allow (8).

（注） device 装置

① 文章全体の内容をふまえて，（ 1 ）に入る最も適切な語を次の中から1つ選びなさい。

ア eyes　イ hands　ウ joystick　エ mind　（　　）

② （ 2 ）に入る最も適切な語句を次の中から1つ選びなさい。　（　　）

ア an action　イ an adventure　ウ a science fiction　エ a suspense

③ 下線部(3)の語句を正しい順に並べ替えなさい。

④ 下線部(4)の内容を日本語で説明しなさい。

⑤ 下線部(5)の内容を日本語で説明しなさい。

⑥ 下線部(6)のどこかにnotを入れると意味が通る。notを入れる適切な位置の直前と直後の1語ずつを答えなさい。　（　　）（　　）

⑦ 下線部(7)を和訳しなさい。

⑧ （ 8 ）に入る最も適切な語句を次の中から1つ選びなさい。　（　　）

ア paralyzed people to use their arms or legs again
イ any animal to communicate using a smartphone
ウ better video games to be developed
エ Elon Musk to create a robot using AI

解答の方針

AI(人工知能)，脳科学，情報工学などに関する文章は，入試でもしばしば出題される。この文章ではサルを使った実験が説明されている。実験，研究，調査などを説明する文章では，**「目的→具体的な手順→結果→今後の展望」**のように話が展開することが多い。研究者たちはサルを使って何を調べようとしたのか？ また，実験の結果は今後どのような形で生かされるのか？ という視点で読み進めるとよい。

④⑤のような指示語の内容を説明する問いでは，その直前の部分に着目するのがポイント。たとえば④では，直前の文にthe signals ... とあるので，these signalsはこの部分を指しているとわかる。⑥⑦の下線部は文法・構文のポイントを多く含むので，解説の説明を読んで確認しておこう。

難 023 次の文章を読んで，問いに答えなさい。 （東京・都立西高）

Some people say that we now live in "the Anthropocene." The Anthropocene is the name of an *epoch which some scientists started to use at the beginning of the twenty-first century. *Anthropo* means "man" in English, and *cene* means "new." They call the newest period in the Earth's history the Anthropocene epoch because human activity has a great influence on the Earth's environment. Animals are, of course, an example of this.

Every *species of animal has *evolved for billions of years to survive in their environment. For example, the process of each species' *evolution has decided how each animal looks. [ア] Because of this, each species can better protect itself from its *predators and survive in the environment around it. [イ] Since the Anthropocene epoch started, however, some species have changed how they look over a very short period of time. [ウ] In this epoch, human activity is *causing quick changes. [エ] One example of these changes is a species of *moth called the peppered moth. [オ]

Peppered moths live in Europe. Their bodies are white, with some *marbled patterns on the wings. Most of the moths that live in England once had that same light color. In the late nineteenth century, however, peppered moths began to become dark especially in factory areas.

(1)Why did this change happen? In the early nineteenth century, more and more factories were built. The air pollution caused by the black smoke from these factories killed a lot of *lichens on the *bark of trees that lived near the factories, and the color of the bark became dark. Peppered moths rest on these trees during the day. When lichens live on the bark and the trees look light, it is easy for white moths to hide themselves from their predators, birds. When lichens do not cover the bark and the trees look dark, however, it is hard for birds to find dark peppered moths. Dark moths have a higher chance of surviving in this changed environment. In fact, the same species of the peppered moths that live in the *countryside, away from factories, have stayed light.

An English researcher did experiments in 1953 and 1955 to show that it was easier for dark peppered moths to hide themselves from birds. His group *released many peppered moths in the woods both near factory areas and in the countryside. Then, after some time, they caught the moths that survived. The results are shown in the table on the next page. In the table, the numbers show how many light and dark moths were released and caught again. We can see that more of the dark peppered moths in factory areas were able to survive. Where the peppered moth lives and how it looks is very important for the species to survive.

area (year)	released / caught again	light moths	dark moths
[(a)] (1953)	released	137	447
	caught again	18	123
[(b)] (1955)	released	64	154
	caught again	16	82
[(c)] (1955)	released	496	473
	caught again	62	30

However, some scientists have said that other *factors may be influencing the increase of dark peppered moths. In fact, scientists are now doing some research on the *genes of these moths, so we will know more about it someday. Though we are still researching this, it is clear that the changes in their environment are connected in some ways to the changes in the color of the moths. This is one example to show how during the Anthropocene epoch human activity is influencing on animal life more than before.

In fact, human activity has not only influenced animals but also plants in the Anthropocene epoch. Just like the peppered moth, a species of plant has changed [2] in a very short time. In the peppered moth's case, humans changed their environment, and then some of the moths became dark to hide themselves from their predators. But in this plant's case, the predators are humans. This means that human activity influences this plant more *directly. The name of this plant is Fritillaria delavayi.

Fritillaria delavayi grows in China. In the past, its flowers were only bright yellow, and its leaves were only bright green. It has a *herbal component in its *bulbs, so people have picked it to make medicine for at least 2,000 years. In the late twentieth century, however, the need for the medicine started to increase not only in China but also in other countries. Since then, people in China have picked the plants more often. Something strange has started to happen to the plants because of this.

What has happened to Fritillaria delavayi? The answer is this: the colors of its flowers and leaves have become dark. Some of the plants are now grey, and others brown. Why? They grow in mountain areas near rocks and stones, so dark colors like grey or brown are less *noticeable.

[3]

Why has this happened?

According to research done over six years in China, the plants growing in places that humans cannot reach easily, like very high places near the tops of the mountains, stay bright, while the plants growing in places that humans can reach easily are becoming dark. If nobody comes to pick the plants, the next *generations will stay bright because they will not have to make themselves less noticeable. However, the next generations of the plants living near humans will become dark to make themselves less noticeable. Again, where Fritillaria delavayi grows and how it looks is very important for the species to survive.

There may be other factors that have caused these changes in color. Though no researchers have started studying the genes of this plant yet, more and more scientists want to research Fritillaria delavayi because it is one of the very few examples of plants that have experienced quick changes in color.

Many factors have influenced how life on the Earth has evolved for billions of years, but today, the influence that [4] is having on it is greater than before. Though some people call this epoch "the Anthropocene", the Earth is not just for humans, but for everything living on it. We should all make every effort to move from the Anthropocene epoch into a new better epoch in the future. We do not know when we will be able to realize this, but we can say *for sure that it is better to realize it sooner than later.

（注） epoch 時代　species 種《しゅ》　evolve 進化する　evolution 進化
predator 捕食者　cause ～を引き起こす　moth 蛾《が》
marbled pattern 霜降り模様　lichen 岩石や樹木に生育するコケなどの生物群
bark 樹皮　countryside 田園地帯　release ～を放つ　factor 要因
gene 遺伝子　directly 直接的に　herbal component 薬草成分　bulb 球根
noticeable 目立つ　generation 世代　for sure 確実に

① 次の英文を入れるのに最も適切な場所を，［ ア ］～［ オ ］から選びなさい。（　　）

In the Earth's history, such evolutions have usually taken a long time.

② 下線部(1)の問いの答えとして最も適切なものを，次の中から選びなさい。（　　）

ア Because many lichens on the bark of the trees in the woods near factory areas died and the bark lost the original dark color.

イ Because more lichens started to cover the bark of the trees in the woods near factory areas after many were built there.

ウ Because the color of the bark of the trees in the woods near factory areas became dark after a lot of lichens growing on their bark died.

エ Because the smoke from the factories began to cover the bark of the trees in the woods near them and the color of the trees became light.

③ 表中の(a)～(c)に入るものの組み合わせとして最も適切なものを，次の中から選びなさい。
( )

	(a)	(b)	(c)
ア	factory area	factory area	countryside
イ	countryside	countryside	factory area
ウ	countryside	factory area	countryside
エ	countryside	countryside	factory area

④ 本文の流れに合うように，[2]に入る本文中の英語3語を答えなさい。
( )

⑤ [3]には次のうち3つの文が入る。それらの文の正しい配列を，下から選びなさい。( )

A Some of the plants, however, have stayed as bright as before.

B Which will be easier for their predators, humans, to find in such places, bright plants or dark plants?

C Of course, dark plants will be easier for them to find.

D It is easy to answer this question.

ア A→B→C　イ A→B→D　ウ B→C→A　エ B→D→A
オ C→B→D　カ C→D→A　キ D→A→C　ク D→B→C

⑥ 本文の流れに合うように，[4]に入る本文中の英語2語を答えなさい。
( )

⑦ 本文の内容に合う英文の組み合わせとして最も適切なものを，下から選びなさい。( )

[1] Some scientists started to use the name “the Anthropocene epoch” just after the twentieth century began, because they thought it was an epoch of a new kind of humans.

[2] We can say by looking at the example of peppered moths that humans started to quickly reduce the speed of the changes in color of some species of animals in the Anthropocene epoch.

[3] The color of the peppered moths living in the countryside did not change even after more factories were built in other areas because the color of the bark of the trees there stayed the same as before.

[4] Some scientists are studying the genes of peppered moths, so we will know in the future why many peppered moths in the factory areas in England have changed their environment.

[5] We can say that humans are influencing peppered moths more directly than Fritillaria delavayi because the predators of peppered moths are not birds but humans.

〔6〕 People in China have thought that Fritillaria delavayi is an important plant for their health for a long time because it has a herbal component in its flowers and leaves.

〔7〕 How easy it is for people to visit places will decide the colors of the next generations of Fritillaria delavayi which grow in these places.

〔8〕 The number of scientists who do research on Fritillaria delavayi will increase in the near future because there are very few other plants which have moved to different places.

ア 〔1〕〔4〕　イ 〔2〕〔6〕　ウ 〔3〕〔4〕　エ 〔3〕〔7〕　オ 〔4〕〔8〕
カ 〔1〕〔2〕〔5〕　キ 〔2〕〔3〕〔7〕　ク 〔2〕〔7〕〔8〕　ケ 〔3〕〔4〕〔7〕　コ 〔5〕〔6〕〔8〕

解答の方針

英文の分量が多く聞き慣れない言葉もたくさん入っているので，難しく感じるかもしれない。ただ，段落ごとに意味を整理してとらえれば，話の展開は比較的わかりやすい。peppered moth と Fritillaria delavayi という２つの生物種が取り上げられているので，文章を前半と後半に分けて考えるとよい。

第3回 実力テスト

▶解答→別冊 p.54

時間20分　得点　　／100
目標80点

次の文章を読んで，問いに答えなさい。　　（東京・明治大付中野高）（各20点，計100点）

The term “robot” was first used in the 1920s, and today there are millions of robots in use throughout the world, according to the International Federation of Robotics. In the health industry, robots are being used more each day.

Increasingly, *surgeons use robots for remote surgery, also called *telesurgery*. In other words, they *operate on patients without having to be in the same physical location: in fact, they may be far away. Although it might seem scary to have a robot performing an operation on you, robotic surgery has many *benefits. Robots do not get *distracted or become bored by *repetitive tasks. In addition, they are much more *precise. As a result, a patient may feel less pain during an operation and recover more quickly.

Medical students also use robots to learn about the human body. They practice on *human simulators*, *mannequins with the latest technology. These pieces of equipment not only look like real people, but they also act like them. They can cry, sweat, produce *saliva, and open and close their eyes. They can make breathing and heartbeat sounds, and they can *bleed and respond to drugs. There are many varieties of these mannequins: male and female versions, teenage versions, and even pregnant and baby versions. Because they are so lifelike, these robotic patients can prepare future doctors for the real-life scenarios they might face in their careers. They can “suffer” from almost any emergency situation possible, like a heart attack or *epileptic seizure. This experience of realistic “emergencies” may help prevent medical errors, which unfortunately are all too common.

Robots can help nurses, too. A common problem in hospitals is that nurses constantly have to move people from one bed to another, pick them up, or put them into a wheelchair. Robots are strong, so they can help with tiring tasks like these. Because they do not get tired, they can help prevent injury, and in addition, they never get angry, bored, or frustrated.

Finally, robots can also improve life for people who have lost mobility. Robotic pants allow *paralyzed patients to move around independently instead of being *confined to a wheelchair. The pants have advantages that are not only physical. One patient commented: “I never dreamed I would walk again. I forgot what it’s like.” He continued: “I have a 3-year-old daughter. The first time she saw me walking, she was silent for the first few minutes and then she said: ‘Daddy, you are tall.' It made me feel so good, like I was flying."

（注） surgeon 外科医　operate 手術をする　benefit 利点　distracted 気が散った
repetitive くり返しの　precise 正確な　mannequin マネキン人形　saliva 唾液
bleed 血を流す　epileptic seizure てんかん性発作　paralyzed 麻痺した
confine ～を閉じ込める

① Which is NOT written about robotic surgery in the passage?　(　　)

ア Robotic surgery does not cost much.
イ Robots do not lose focus or get tired.
ウ Robotic surgery causes less damage to the patients.
エ Doctors do not have to be in the operating room.

② Which is true about what medical students can do with *human simulators*?

ア They can directly see how to do remote surgery.　(　　)
イ They can practice moving people from one bed to another.
ウ They can learn how to use robots in a real situation.
エ They can get ready for emergency situations they may face.

③ What can robots do instead of nurses?　(　　)

ア Reducing the pain of patients after surgery.
イ Doing physical work without getting tired.
ウ Recording the condition of patients every day.
エ Moving beds for people who are going to stay in hospital.

④ Which is true about robotic pants?　(　　)

ア They help patients recover from paralysis.
イ They assist patients in getting in and out of a wheelchair.
ウ They support patients both physically and emotionally.
エ They allow paralyzed patients to jump high.

⑤ Which is the best title for this passage?　(　　)

ア Great Improvement in Remote Surgery
イ Various Robots That Improve Health Care
ウ Doctors with Excellent Medical Tools
エ Robots, Mannequins, and Special Pants for Patients

4 物語・随筆

標準問題

（解答）別冊 p.56

024 〉次の文章を読んで，問いに答えなさい。 （東京・実践学園高）

Mary was a junior high school student. One day her teacher said, "Next Friday we are going to learn about jobs. Think about which location you would like to visit. Make groups of four people and talk about it." Mary and her friends talked together and (1)(decide) to go to a *textile mill near their school. Her teacher said, "Decide what you will do [A] a member of your group. One student will ask questions. (あ) Two students will write a report and one student will take pictures." "I don't want to write a report. Who will write the report?" Mary asked. No one answered. Mary's friend said, "I want to take pictures." Another friend said, "Me too." "It's hard to make questions," said her friend. (い) No one wanted to make questions, so they stopped (2)(talk) about it.

A few days later Mary and her friends visited the textile mill, but they could not decide what they should do. A man was waiting [B] them in the textile mill. (3) He said, "Good morning." "Good morning," they said, (4)but they were not happy. He told them many things about cloth. He said, "A long time ago, cloth was *valuable for many people and making cloth was hard. They had to help each other." (5) "Do you have any questions?" he asked. They looked [C] and did not answer him.

Mr. Green said, "Well, let's learn how to make a piece of cloth. Now we must make strong *threads. A single thread is short and weak, but by *twisting several threads together, we can make strong threads." The girls tried to do it, but it was hard. Mary could not do it alone, but her friends helped her. (6) Mr. Green said, "Next, let's use these threads to make a piece of cloth." They tried together. At (7)[ア single / イ a / ウ didn't / エ first / オ say / カ word / キ they], but soon one of her friends said, "Mary, could you pull this thread?" "All right," Mary said. Another friend said, "Making cloth is difficult, but it is fun." Mary and her friends smiled. They worked for one hour but they only made a very small piece of cloth. (う) Mr. Green said to Mary and her friends, "A single thread is short and weak. (8) You are [D] this cloth. Working together is important. When you do something in the future, please remember this." Then Mary said to her friends, "I'm sorry. I will write the report." "No, Mary. Let's write it together," they said.

The next day Mary and her friends talked about their report. (え) They said, "We learned many things about making cloth and we learned something important to us too."

（注） textile mill 織物工場　valuable 価値がある　thread 糸
twisting より合わせること

① 下線部(1)(2)の語をそれぞれ適切な形にするとき，正しい組み合わせを次の中から選びなさい。 (　　)

ア (1) decided　(2) to talk　　イ (1) decide　(2) to talk
ウ (1) decided　(2) talking　　エ (1) decide　(2) talking

② [A]～[D]に入る最も適切な語を，次の中から1つずつ選びなさい。ただし，同じ語をくり返し使わないこと。 [A] (　　) [B] (　　) [C] (　　) [D] (　　)

ア for　イ like　ウ down　エ as

③ 次の文が入る最も適切な箇所を，(あ)～(え)の中から選び答えなさい。 (　　)

However, they were happy.

④ (3)，(5)，(6)に次の文を入れるとき，最も適切な組み合わせを下から選びなさい。 (　　)

a. They made many strong threads together.
b. His name was Mr. Green.
c. He also showed them how to make cloth and how many kinds he made at the textile mill.

ア (3) a　(5) b　(6) c　　イ (3) a　(5) c　(6) b
ウ (3) b　(5) a　(6) c　　エ (3) b　(5) c　(6) a
オ (3) c　(5) a　(6) b　　カ (3) c　(5) b　(6) a

⑤ 下線部(4)の理由を日本語で答えなさい。

⑥ 下線部(7)の[　　]内の語を適切に並べ替えたとき，[　　]内で2番目と4番目と6番目にくる語の記号を順に答えなさい。 (　　) (　　) (　　)

⑦ (8)に入る最も適切なものを，次の中から選びなさい。 (　　)

ア So it is impossible to combine many threads.
イ But if you combine many threads, you can make a strong piece of cloth.
ウ But you can make a strong piece of cloth without combining many threads.
エ So you should buy many clothes to combine many threads.

⑧ 先生が，グループの中で決めるように伝えた役割は何か，具体的に3つ日本語で答えなさい。

⑨ 本文の内容に一致するものを，次の中から２つ選びなさい。 (　　)(　　)

ア Mary's teacher told Mary and her friends to go to the textile mill.

イ Mary wanted to write a report on the textile mill before visiting it.

ウ Mary asked several questions when Mr. Green said, "Do you have any questions?"

エ Mary and her teacher were glad after they made a small piece of cloth together.

オ Mr. Green said it was important to help each other.

カ Mary and her friends learned many things about jobs.

重要 025 次の文章を読んで，問いに答えなさい。 （東京・お茶の水女子大附高）

025

It was getting late on a cold December evening. The wind was strong and it started to rain. A man was driving a car. He was very tired and worried.

He lost his job when the factory *closed down two weeks ago, so he had to find a new job.

This morning he drove to the town for a *job interview, but he was too late. All the *positions were already taken, so they *turned him away. He walked around the town all day to find some kind of work, but couldn't find any. If he didn't get a job soon, he didn't know what he would do.

It got dark and very late. *Up ahead, the man saw a car on the side of the road. He slowed down to *have a look as he *drove by. The car looked new and expensive. An older woman was standing by the car and waving her arms. The man *pulled over and got out of his car. "What's your trouble?" the man asked.

The woman didn't say anything. She was scared and didn't know *if she could trust this man. The woman knew she looked rich. She was wearing an expensive coat and standing next to a nice car. But she was also cold and wet. She had to trust this man.

"I *have a flat tire. I tried calling for a *tow truck, but there's no *cell phone reception here," she said.

"Hah, yeah. But don't worry. I'll change the tire for you," said the man with a smile.

"My name is Paul, by the way," he said.

"I'm Edna," the woman said. "Thank you so much for helping me. I was worried no one was going to come."

"No problem. (1)<u>You are lucky.</u> There is nothing around here," Paul said. He got the *spare tire and the tools out of Edna's car. "Why don't you wait in my car and *warm yourself up?" he suggested.

Edna *nodded and got inside. It was warm. Soon Paul finished changing the tire. Edna got out of his car and thanked him. "I can't thank you enough." She opened her *purse to give Paul some money. Paul thought about it for a moment. (2)<u>He really needed the money</u>, but he shook his head. "I said don't worry about it," he said with a smile. Edna thanked him again and they got back into their cars. They *drove off into the night.

About an hour later, Edna saw a town. She was getting tired and *stopped in a small restaurant for a cup of coffee and some food.

A *waitress came to *take her order. She looked very tired. Edna could *tell that the waitress was about eight months *pregnant by the size of her stomach.

But she still had a cheerful smile on her face. She was very friendly when she was taking Edna's order.

Edna ate her meal and drank her coffee. She watched the waitress as she served the other customers. She made friendly *small talk with everyone as she took their orders. She didn't stop for a second to rest. When Edna finished eating, she gave the waitress a hundred-dollar *bill to pay for the meal. As the waitress went to the *cash register to get the *change, Edna stood up and quietly walked out the door. When the waitress came back, she saw that Edna was *gone. She hurried out the door to catch her, but Edna already left. When she came back inside to clean Edna's table, she saw (3)another hundred-dollar bill on the table. The *tip was left for the waitress. She picked it up. She couldn't believe it. How did that woman know she needed that money right now?

The waitress finished work. She got in her car and drove home. She had a big smile on her face, but it was a different smile from the one she usually had. When she got home, her husband was sitting on the sofa and watching TV. She ran to him and gave him a big *hug. He was surprised and looked at her.

"Oh Paul, you'll never guess what happened at work today!" she said.

[Adapted from Blake, S. *Price of Love Heartwarming Stories*.]

（注） close down 閉鎖する　job interview 仕事の面接　position 職
turn ～ away ～を追い払う　up ahead 行く手に　have a look ちらりと見る
drive by 車で通りかかる　pull over 車を道の片側に寄せる　if ... …かどうか
have a flat tire タイヤがパンクしている　tow truck レッカー車
cell phone reception 携帯電話の電波　spare 予備の　warm ～ up ～を暖める
nod うなずく　purse 財布　drive off 車で立ち去る　stop in ～ ～に立ち寄る
waitress ウエイトレス，接客係　take her order 注文を取る　tell わかる
pregnant 妊娠している　small talk 世間話　bill 紙幣　cash register レジ
change おつり　gone いなくなって，行ってしまって
tip チップ（サービスに対する慰労や感謝の気持ちとして，客が接客係などに渡すお金）
hug ハグ，抱きしめること

① 下線部(1)について，Paul がそう考えた理由を具体的に説明しなさい。

② 下線部(2)について，その理由を具体的に説明しなさい。

③ Ednaがそのウエイトレスのために下線部(3)を置いていった理由を，レストランに着く前に起きたことをふまえて説明しなさい。

ガイド　この文章は，a heartwarming story(心温まる物語)の一種である。このような物語には「落ち」(人生訓など)があり，全体としてどんなことが言いたいのかを理解する必要がある。また，この文章には，ポール，エドナ，ウエイトレスの３人が出てくる。３人の人物像や置かれた境遇についての説明を本文中から探し出し，どんな関係で結びついているかを考えながら読み進めよう。「行間を読む(read between the lines)」ことも大切であり，直接的に書かれてはいない登場人物の心情も推測しながら読む必要がある。

026 次の文章を読んで，問いに答えなさい。 （東京・都立国立高）

Hello, my name is Lisa Smith. My friends call me Lisa. I'm fifteen years old. I live with my parents and my brother in a small town in Canada. The other day, something important happened and I have realized that pet animals have special powers. Why do I think pet animals have special powers? I'll tell you why.

I'm a junior high school student. I walk to and from school every day. I enjoy walking to school and it takes about half an hour. One warm spring day, when I was on my way home from school, a small friend was following me. This friend was different from any other friend. She was very small. "What a cute *kitten!" She had no *identifying marks of any kind. "Is she a *stray cat?" I thought. She followed me all the way. When I arrived home, she was just behind me.

When my parents came back home from work that evening, they were surprised to see the kitten. I told them that my friend gave her to me, but it was a *lie. My parents knew that I was telling a lie. My parents love cats but told me that we should find the owner and give her back. They said I should think of the owner. "What should I do?" I thought. I thought about a *notice in the town newspaper. However, that was the last thing I wanted to do. "If I put a notice in the town newspaper, her owner may appear," I thought. The kitten was so cute. I started to think, "(1)" I did not want to lose her.

My brother said that the kitten was maybe about six months old. The cat liked us right away. After dinner she climbed on to my legs and watched TV with us. By now I was asking my parents to keep her.

By the end of the week, the new cat was part of our family. She was very smart and good with me. My parents started to change their minds about the cat. My father said to me, "Lisa, I think no one is looking for this cat. Now, it's time for you to take *responsibility for another life. This will be a good chance for you to learn something important. You'll learn something you'll need when you become a parent in the future."

The next week, something told me to check the town newspaper. One very small notice jumped out at me. When I saw it, I was surprised. A woman near my house was looking for her lost cat. My hands were shaking. I knew I should call the woman, but I couldn't pick up the phone. Instead, I tried to believe that I didn't see the notice. I quickly threw the newspaper away in the closet in my room and continued to do my homework. I (2) said a word about it to my parents.

We gave a name to the kitten. She was all white like snow, so we decided to call her Snow. When I was studying at my desk, she was quiet. However, when I went into the garden, she followed me and asked me to play with her. When I was doing the dishes, she was there to lend a hand (or should I say *paw?).

There was only one problem with this perfect picture. I could not forget the notice in the town newspaper. One day, I started to think what I really should do. I knew in my heart that I should call the woman. I knew she really wanted to see her cat again. I thought, "Is our Snow the cat the woman wants to see?" I didn't sleep well that night.

The next morning, I talked about the notice to my parents, and, at last, I started to push the numbers on my phone. In my heart, I was hoping no one would answer, but someone did. "Hello." It was the voice of a young woman. I explained to her about the cat and she asked me a lot of questions. She said she really wanted to come. After the phone call, I was very nervous. I asked my parents to stay with me.

I was with my parents at the kitchen table. I hoped a *miracle would happen. Snow was sitting at my feet the whole time and sometimes looked up at me with those pretty eyes. (3)Snow noticed something was wrong.

Within minutes the woman was at the front door. I saw her through the window. She was standing there with a map in her hand. She *knocked on the front door. "Excuse me, is this the home of Mr. and Mrs. Smith?" she asked. When she knocked on the door again, a thousand *thoughts crossed my mind. I could say to her, "(4)" But it was too late; my mother opened the door. I also went there to face my fear.

The woman looked at Snow and the woman's face changed. I saw a big smile on her face. "Here, Lucy," she called. "Come to me, girl." Now I realized the cat was called Lucy by the woman. The cat looked very happy at the woman's voice. It was clear that she belonged to the woman.

I was in tears. I couldn't do anything. I wanted to run away with Snow. Instead, I smiled a little and my parents asked the young woman to come in.

The young woman was already holding Snow up into her arms. She opened her *purse and tried to give my parents some money.

"For your trouble," she said.

My parents shook their heads. My mother said, "Oh, we can't. She has been a joy. We should pay you some money." With that, the woman smiled and *hugged Snow again.

Snow was really happy to see the woman again. I knew it was time for them to go home. I opened the front door. When the woman was leaving, I noticed a little girl with her father. The girl was sitting in the front seat of the car. When the girl saw the kitten, I saw a big smile on her face. The girl said, “Come here, Lucy!”

Before I said something, the woman started to explain. “My family moved to this town last month. The girl in the car is my daughter. She did not know anyone in this town and she felt very lonely every day. Lucy was given to her because my husband and I know that she loves cats.”

The woman continued, “When Lucy *disappeared, my daughter was very shocked. She was crying all day. She was in her room all the time. Every day she said she wanted to see Lucy again. Lucy is her only friend at this new place. She has a special *bond with the kitten.”

Suddenly I realized that I was thinking only about myself. My heart went out to that little girl. When I saw the car going away, the smile on my face was real. I knew I did the right thing. I knew that the kitten was exactly at the right place. I learned something important from the cat.

（注） kitten : A kitten is a very young cat.　identifying mark 身元を示すしるし
stray cat のら猫　lie うそ　notice 告知　responsibility 責任感
paw : The paws of an animal such as a cat or dog are its feet.　miracle 奇跡
knock ノックする　thought 考え　purse 財布　hug ～を抱きしめる
disappear いなくなる　bond きずな

① （ 1 ）に入る最も適切な文を，次の中から選びなさい。（　　）

ア I have to find her owner and give her back as soon as I can.
イ I must go and check the newspaper at the school library now.
ウ I really want to know why my friend gave me such a pretty cat.
エ I cannot understand why her owner did not watch her enough.

② （ 2 ）に入る適切な1語を答えなさい。（　　）

③ 下線部(3)とほぼ同じ意味を持つ文を，次の中から選びなさい。（　　）

ア Snow felt something was going to happen.
イ Snow thought she made a terrible mistake.
ウ Snow thought she should feel sorry for me.
エ Snow felt we should think more carefully.

④ （ 4 ）に入る最も適切な文を，次の中から選びなさい。（　　）

ア Hello, welcome. Open the door, please.
イ I'm afraid you have the wrong address.
ウ Sorry, I don't know anything about Lucy.
エ Who is it? My mother is coming soon.

⑤ 本文の内容に一致するものを，次の中から2つ選びなさい。 (　　) (　　)

ア Lisa walks to junior high school with her small friend every day. She spends about thirty minutes going to school.

イ At first, Lisa's parents told Lisa to return the cat to the owner because they thought Lisa was still a child and should not keep a cat.

ウ Finally, Lisa agreed to meet a woman who was looking for her cat, so her mother made a phone call to the woman.

エ The woman who came was the owner of the cat. She said "thank you" and gave some money to Lisa's parents.

オ The kitten was called Snow by Lisa because it was all white, and the same cat was called Lucy by the girl in the car.

カ For the girl in the car, the cat was her only friend in the town. She had no other friend there because she was new there.

最高水準問題

解答 別冊 p.62

難 027 次の文章を読んで，問いに答えなさい。 （兵庫・灘高）

My son's first season of playing basketball was when he was ten years old. Often, when I picked him up from his father's house, he was *shooting hoops. On one such day, he came running over to my car and said, "Mom, can I pleeease get another basketball?"

"Why do you need two basketballs, Tyler?" I asked.

"Because then I could have a basketball at my mom's house and at my dad's house," he replied.

I thought that was a fine idea, especially since all Tyler could talk about was basketball. (1)Sometimes he'd ask me to take him to the gym an hour before practice began. He enjoyed meeting his new teammates and thought the basketball drills were fun. I often had to convince him to leave the gym after practice was over. He usually wanted to hang around and shoot baskets.

Tyler and I have always had our most special talks when I go into his room to say good night. One night, he expressed some concern over his basketball shoes. He told me that maybe he needed better ones. (2)I closed my eyes tightly, wishing that his last sentence would just go away. Being a single mom, the topic of new shoes was always difficult for me. I looked [A] at his *"broken-in" shoes sitting next to his perfectly folded uniform. They looked just fine to me. I quickly changed the subject.

Finally, the first game of the season arrived. The gym was surprisingly crowded. Tyler's team, the Hornets, was playing the Magic. I saw the happy look in my son's eyes when he saw his dad sitting in the stands a few yards down [B] me.

There was a look of determination on Tyler's face as he joined his teammates. As I watched the other kids running up and down the court, I saw my son sitting on the bench. By the fourth quarter, Tyler hadn't even touched the ball, and his team had won the game.

The games that followed were pretty much the same. The team kept winning, but Tyler barely touched the ball. He ran so hard when he was on the court, but when he got the ball, he would quickly throw it to a teammate. I would sit there with my heart *pounding out of my chest.

On the way home from one of his games, I asked, "Tyler, do you still enjoy basketball?"

He replied, "I like basketball a lot. But I know that some of the kids play better than me, so when I get the ball, I just throw it to them."

The next day, I ran into an old friend of mine who used to play basketball when we were younger. I shared [C] him how I thought that Tyler played somewhat cautiously.

"Does he have good shoes?" he asked. I remembered how earlier in the season, Tyler had mentioned that he thought he needed better shoes. My friend must have noticed the look on my face as I thought about Tyler's worn-out shoes. Before I knew it, we were shoe shopping. (3)He insisted on buying Tyler a pair of beautiful, high-quality basketball shoes. It was the kind of gesture that inspires deep gratitude for any single mom, especially the mother of a son.

As I put Tyler to bed, he told me that he had wanted new basketball shoes for a long time. He loved them. They were awesome. He hoped that his new shoes would help him with his game.

Weeks of Tyler's unending enthusiasm and devotion to basketball flew by. Once more, Tyler told me that he knew he wasn't the best player on his team but that it was okay because he liked basketball so much. He played hard and kept practicing. I watched him improve. He never became discouraged. He said that he felt more comfortable [D] his new shoes and once more thanked me for them. He gave me detailed descriptions of new plays he had thought of. He told me how he was proud to be on such a good team. So far, they were undefeated.

The team made it to the play-offs. In front of a standing-room-only crowd, Tyler scored eight points at the end of a very close and exciting game.

The season came to a close, and the time for the awards ceremony was coming up. Tyler was guessing which kids would be getting awards for Most Valuable Player, Best Defense, Most Improved and Best All-Around Player. Tyler's team had come in second place, and each player received a trophy. Toward the end of the ceremony, the director got up and thanked everybody. Then he said, "We aren't finished yet. We have one last, special award for a very special player. He shows up for every game with a positive attitude. He has never argued with a referee or another player, never been late and never missed a practice or a game. He knows his place while playing, and his teammates speak highly of him. He plays because he obviously loves the game, and he always runs hard and tries his best. (あ) goes to Tyler Marsden!"

Suddenly, all the attention was [E] Tyler. His teammates and friends were giving him high-fives and slaps on the back. I felt tears welling up in my eyes. I looked a few yards down into the stands and saw his father with the same tears in his eyes. We actually smiled at one another.

The other kids were still congratulating him when Tyler walked over and picked up his second trophy. I overheard other parents saying, "He got the most impressive award of the evening."

Tyler proudly said, "Now I have a (い) for my mom's house and a (い) for my dad's house!"

(注) shoot hoops バスケットボールをする　broken-in 履き古した　pound どきどきする

① 下線部(1)を日本語に直しなさい。

② 下線部(2)のように筆者が考えた理由を，次の中から１つ選びなさい。 (　　)

ア もう就寝時間を過ぎていて早く寝させたかったから

イ バスケットボール以外のことを話したかったから

ウ シングルマザーであることに触れられたくなかったから

エ 息子の願いをかなえるには経済的に苦しかったから

③ [A]～[E]に入れるのに最も適切な語を，次の中から１つずつ選びなさい。ただし，同じ語をくり返し使わないこと。

[A] (　　)　[B] (　　)　[C] (　　)　[D] (　　)　[E] (　　)

ア from　イ in　ウ on　エ over　オ with

④ 次の文が下線部(3)とほぼ同じ意味になるように，空所に適切な語を入れなさい。

He firmly said that he (　　) buy a pair of beautiful, high-quality basketball shoes (　　) Tyler.

⑤ (あ)に入れるのに最も適切な語句を，次の中から１つ選びなさい。 (　　)

ア Coach of the Year　イ Rookie of the Year

ウ The Best Shooter Award　エ The Sportsmanship Award

⑥ (い)に共通して入る語を，本文から抜き出して答えなさい。 (　　)

⑦ 本文のタイトルとして最も適切なものを，次の中から１つ選びなさい。 (　　)

ア Coming Down　イ Running Down

ウ Showing Up　エ Throwing Up

解答の方針

この文章には，比較的レベルの高い語句が多く含まれている。文中に意味を知らない語が出てきた場合は，とりあえずその語を無視して読んでみよう。たとえばHe lived in a X house. という文のXが未知の語であっても，「彼は～な家に住んでいた」という意味であることは推測できる。未知の語があるために文の構造がつかめない場合は，文脈を考慮して「ここではたぶんこういうことが言いたいのではないか」と推測する必要がある。ただし，その推測が間違っている可能性もあるので，読み進めながら必要に応じて最初の解釈を軌道修正する柔軟性は持っておこう。

また，タイラーの発言中の「パパの家とママの家」という言葉に着目する必要がある。彼の父親と母親はどんな関係なのか？ ―この点を正確にとらえることが，このストーリーを理解するカギとなる。

028 次の文章を読んで，問いに答えなさい。 (東京学芸大附高)

Antonio Canova was a little boy who lived in Italy. His parents were dead, and he lived with his poor grandparents. His grandmother took care of her husband and the boy, and his grandfather cut stone to make statues to sell to rich people.

Antonio was not very strong. He didn't like to play with other boys of the town, but he often went out with his grandfather to look for big pieces of stone which were strong and beautiful enough for statues. Antonio enjoyed working with his grandfather so much that he soon learned how to make a statue like his grandfather. "The boy will be a great stone artist some day," said his grandfather.

Every evening after work, Antonio's grandmother sang to him, and told him stories that filled his mind with pictures of wonderful and beautiful things. And the next day, when he went back to look for stones, Antonio tried to make some of those pictures in stone.

There was a rich man in the same town, and he was called the *Count. He often had dinner parties, and his rich friends from other cities came to visit him. At these times Antonio's grandfather often helped in the kitchen because he was also a great cook.

One day Antonio went with his grandfather to the Count's great house because there was going to be another big party. The boy could not cook, and he was not old enough to serve food to the guests, but he could wash the pots and frying pans, and as he was smart and quick, he could help in many other ways.

Just before the dinner started, there was a big sound in the dining room, and a man rushed into the kitchen. He looked [A].

"What should I do? What should I do?" he cried. "I have broken a statue that should stand at the center of the table. The table will not be pretty without the statue. What will the Count say?"

And now all the other people around Antonio were troubled. Was the dinner going to be a failure? The table had to look very nice. The Count would be very angry without the nice [B]. "Oh, no! What are we going to do?" they all said to each other.

Then little Antonio Canova went up to the man who broke the statue.

"I can make a statue. May I make one for you?"

"Little boy," said the man, "The new statue must be exactly the same size as the one that I broke."

"All right. That is no problem," said Antonio. "Perhaps I can make one that will be as beautiful as the broken one."

(1)The man laughed. "Who are you, young boy? Why can you say you can make a statue in one hour?"

"I am Antonio Canova," said the boy.

All the other people knew that the boy was good at making statues, so they all said, "[C]"

On the kitchen table, there was a huge square piece of yellow butter. It weighed almost 100 kilograms. With a kitchen knife, Antonio began to cut and carve this butter. In a few minutes, he made it into the shape of a sitting lion.

"How beautiful!" they cried. "It is much prettier than the statue that was broken."

When it was finished, the man carried it to (2)its place.

When the Count and his friends came in to dinner, the first thing they saw was the yellow lion.

"What a beautiful work of art!" they cried. "Only a very great artist can carve such a figure, but isn't it interesting to make it of butter!" And then they asked the Count to tell them the name of the artist.

"Well, to tell the truth, [D]. Who made this wonderful statue? Does anyone know?"

One of the kitchen boys said, "It was carved only an hour ago by a little boy in the kitchen."

This was much more of a surprise to the guests, and the Count called the boy into the room.

"My dear boy, you have created such a wonderful piece of art," said the Count. "What is your name, and who is your teacher?"

"My name is Antonio Canova," said the boy, "and (3)I have no teacher but I [ア my grandfather / イ carve / ウ from / エ to / オ sculptures / カ how / キ learned / ク of / ケ out] stone."

All the guests were delighted, and were also proud because they could meet a future fine artist at this party. They wanted the boy to have dinner with them, and Antonio was very happy to sit down at the table.

The next day, the Count asked Antonio's grandfather to send Antonio to his house, and his grandfather was very pleased because Antonio was asked to live with the Count. The best artists in the country started to live with the Count to teach Antonio the skill of carving art. He carved stone, not [E], and in a few years, Antonio Canova became one of the greatest stone carving artists in the world.

（注） Count 伯爵

① [A]に入る最も適切な語を，次の中から選びなさい。 (　　)

ア pale　イ pleased　ウ smart　エ angry

② [B]に入る最も適切な語を，次の中から選びなさい。 (　　)

ア stone　イ table　ウ dinner　エ statue

③ 下線部(1)に関して，次の質問に対する答えとして最も適切なものを選びなさい。 (　　)

Why did the man laugh?

ア Because the man thought it was a great idea for the boy to make a statue.

イ Because the man couldn't believe that the boy would make a statue in one hour.

ウ Because the man thought the boy was as beautiful as the statue.

エ Because the man was just amazed to know that the boy was so brave.

④ [C]に入る最も適切なものを，次の中から選びなさい。 (　　)

ア He can do it! He can do it!　イ Yes, we will! Yes, we will!

ウ He did it! He did it!　エ Attention, please! Attention, please!

⑤ 下線部(2)が表す具体的な場所を，本文中から５語で抜き出しなさい。

____

⑥ [D]に入る最も適切なものを，次の中から選びなさい。 (　　)

ア the broken statue has made me sad

イ I am as surprised as you all

ウ I know why there is butter here

エ I am shocked to see the new statue

⑦ 下線部(3)が意味の通る英文になるように[　　]内の語句を並べ替え，[1]～[3]に入るものの記号を答えなさい。 [1] (　　)　[2] (　　)　[3] (　　)

I have no teacher but I [　　] [1] [　　] [2] [　　] [　　] [　　] [3] [　　] stone.

ア my grandfather　イ carve　ウ from　エ to

オ sculptures　カ how　キ learned　ク of　ケ out

⑧ [E]に入る適切な１語を答えなさい。 (　　　)

⑨ 本文の内容と一致するものを，次のア～キの中から２つ選びなさい。 (　　)(　　)

ア Antonio enjoyed playing outdoors with other boys, but he was not a very strong boy.

イ Antonio's grandmother told stories every night, and Antonio drew their pictures on the stones.

ウ Antonio and his grandparents often went to the Count's house to help in the kitchen.

エ When the statue was broken in the kitchen, the staff workers thought that the Count would be angry.

オ The man who broke the statue went up to Antonio and asked him to make a butter statue.

カ It took Antonio only a few minutes to carve a large piece of butter into the shape of a lion.

キ The guests at the Count's party wanted to know who made the wonderful statue of a lion.

解答の方針

本文は比較的平易で読みやすく，語いのレベルもあまり高くない。ただし思考力を要する問いが多く，話の流れや人物の心情を正確にとらえる力が求められている。また問いを解くには一定の語い力・文法力も必要になる。たとえば①②の選択肢には合計８つの単語があるが，これらの意味を全部知っていただろうか。この中にもし未知の単語があったなら，語い力を強化する必要がある。

⑨の各選択肢は本文のどこかの箇所に対応しているので，該当箇所をていねいに探す必要がある。１つ１つの選択肢をていねいに読み，「誰が何をしたか」などが本文の内容と正確に一致しているものを選ぶ。「本文に似た内容が書かれているが，本文が言っていることとは少し違う」という選択肢を選ばないようにしよう。

難 029 司書(librarian)として図書館で働く「私」と，その図書館に住んでいた猫の「デューイ(Dewey)」に関する次の英文を読んで，問いに答えなさい。 (東京・巣鴨高)

Have you ever been in a library after closing? Of course not! (Or at least I hope not.) Well, let me tell you: a library after closing is a lonely place. It is very quiet, and the *rows of shelves create a lot of dark corners that make you nervous. (1)Most of the librarians I know won't stay alone in a library after dark. But I worked at the Spencer Public Library almost every night after everyone else had gone home, and I was never scared. I was strong. I was *stubborn. And above all, I was never alone. I had Dewey.

While I worked, Dewey sat on top of my computer screen, slowly moving his tail. When I stopped working, he always jumped down onto the keyboard. *No more*, he *would say. *Let's play*. Dewey had (2) of timing.

"All right, Dewey," I told him. "You go first."

Dewey's game was *hide-and-seek, so as soon as I gave the word he would take off around the corner. I often found the back half of a *long-haired orange cat right away. To Dewey, hiding meant pushing your head into a bookshelf, he seemed to forget he had a (3).

"I wonder where Dewey is," I said out loud as I *sneaked up on him. "Boo!" I shouted when I got within a few feet, sending Dewey running.

Other times he was better hidden. I would walk around a few shelves with no luck, then turn the corner to see him *prancing toward me with that big Dewey smile.

You couldn't find me! You couldn't find me!

"(4)That's not fair, Dewey. You only gave me twenty seconds."

Sometimes he stayed in a very small spot quietly. I'd look for five minutes, then start calling his name. "Dewey! Dewey!" That dark library could get a little frightening, but I always imagined Dewey hiding just a few feet away, laughing at me.

"All right, Dewey, that's enough. [A]"

Nothing. Where could that cat be? Just when I was giving up, I'd turn around and there he was. He was standing in the middle of the *aisle, looking at me.

"Oh, Dewey, you clever boy. [B]"

I'd run and hide behind a bookshelf, and one of two things always happened. I'd get to my hiding place, turn around, and Dewey would be standing right there. He had followed me.

Found you. That was easy.

His other favorite thing to do was to run around the other side of the shelf and get to my hiding spot before I did.

Oh, is this where you're thinking about hiding? Because, well, I knew it.

I'd laugh and *pet him behind the ears. "Fine, Dewey. Let's just run for a while."

We'd run between the shelves, meeting at the end of the aisles. After fifteen minutes I would completely forget my troubles. Anything that had been troubling me was gone. (5)The weight, as they say, was lifted.

"Okay, Dewey. [C]"

Dewey never complained. I'd climb back into my chair, and he'd climb back on top of the computer and start moving his tail in front of the screen. The next time I needed him, he'd be there.

Those games of hide-and-seek with Dewey got me through a lot of hard nights. Maybe I should tell you Dewey put his head on my *lap and *whimpered while I cried, or that he *licked the tears from my face. You could understand that, right? And it is almost true, because sometimes when (6)the ceiling started falling in on me and I found myself looking down at my lap, tears in my eyes, Dewey was there, right where I needed him to be.

Dewey was a loving cat. But he was still a cat, so he liked his personal space. However, he always knew when I needed a warm body, and he knew when the best thing for me was a silly, mindless game of hide-and-seek.

He'd give me anything I needed, without thought, without wanting something in return, and without me asking. It wasn't just love. It was more than that. It was respect. It was *empathy. And it went both ways. That connection Dewey and I had felt when we met? Those nights alone together in the library turned it into an unbreakable bond.

（注） rows of shelves 何列もの書棚　stubborn 頑固な　would ～したものだ
hide-and-seek かくれんぼ　long-haired 長い毛の　sneak up on ～ ～に忍び寄る
prance 意気揚々と歩く　aisle 通路　pet ～を優しくなでる　lap ひざ
whimper かぼそい声で鳴く　lick ～をなめる　empathy 共感

① 下線部(1)を日本語に直しなさい。

② (2)に入る最も適切なものを，次の中から選びなさい。 (　　)

ア an amazing sense　イ a terrible sense

ウ an ordinary sense　エ a narrow sense

③ (3)に入る適切な1語を，それより前の本文中から抜き出して答えなさい。 (　　　　)

④　下線部(4)について，このような発言をした理由を，具体的な場面に触れながら25～35字の日本語で説明しなさい。

									25					
				35										

⑤　[A]～[C]に入る最も適切なものを，次の中から１つずつ選びなさい。ただし，同じものをくり返し使わないこと。　[A]（　　）　[B]（　　）　[C]（　　）

ア　Now it's my turn.

イ　Let's get back to work.

ウ　You win!

⑥　下線部(5)が表している心情に最も近いものを，次の中から１つ選びなさい。　（　　）

ア　excited　　イ　interested　　ウ　relaxed　　エ　impressed

⑦　下線部(6)の意味していることとして最も適切なものを，次の中から１つ選びなさい。　（　　）

ア　デューイがどこかに行ってしまったと思い，気持ちが沈んでいる。

イ　突然目の前に建物が崩れてきて，身の危険を感じている。

ウ　かくれんぼのせいで仕事が終わらず，焦り始めている。

エ　不安がのしかかってきて，心が押し潰されそうになっている。

⑧　本文の内容に合うものを，次の中から２つ選びなさい。　（　　）（　　）

ア　デューイは狭い場所は平気だが，「私」と同じく暗い図書館を少し怖がっていた。

イ　デューイが隠れる時に，「私」はその後をこっそりついていくことがあった。

ウ　デューイは「私」の隠れようとする場所に先回りをすることがあった。

エ　デューイは一匹でいる時間が必要で，「私」が望んでもそばにいないことがあった。

オ　デューイは「私」が必要なものをくれたが，それはすべて愛情からだった。

カ　デューイと「私」は夜を何度も一緒に過ごし，互いのきずなを深めていった。

解答の方針

この文章は語いのレベルが高く文体も文学的で，読みやすいとは言えない。主人公の心情が比ゆ的に表現されている部分もあるので，筆者がどのような気持ちでデューイと触れ合っていたのかを推し量ることが大切。また，その場の状況をイメージする力や，言葉を凝縮した表現を解釈する力も求められている。いわば「英文を使った国語の試験」とも言える。このような文章を面白いと思う人は，易しい英語で書かれた物語を自分で探して読むとよいだろう。また，時間があれば英文を１つ１つ日本語に直した上で全文訳と見比べることで，英語・国語の両方の勉強になる。

030 次の文章を読んで，問いに答えなさい。 （埼玉・立教新座高）

030

There's an Alien on the Internet

Andy's best friend is Joey, but they've never actually met. He met him on the Internet. He learned all the things about the solar system from Joey, so it made his *Star Wars* games fun. Joey doesn't go to school. He chooses to get his education at home. *I wish that Joey would come to our school here in Portland,* thought Andy.

Last week Andy's teacher, Mrs. Becker, put a big circle on the blackboard and said it was a pizza.

"Andy," she said, "if we divide the pizza, would you like one-third or one-tenth?" Ten is the bigger number, so that's what he picked.

Kevin started waving his hand in the air and shouted that he chose one-third. Mrs. Becker drew lines on the circle and then, Kevin showed that his piece of the pizza was bigger than Andy's. "(1)<u>Andy's gonna get hungry,</u>" Kevin joked.

Then the whole class was laughing. (2)<u>*I wish that the recess bell would ring,*</u> thought Andy.

Mrs. Becker's loud and strong voice made the room quiet. "Andy, do you see how the more you divide the whole pizza, the smaller the pieces become?"

"Yes, Mrs. Becker," Andy lied. The recess bell didn't ring for another half hour, and by then Mrs. Becker gave twenty problems in the class math book. Each problem had two *fractions with an empty circle between the fractions. The students were supposed to put a sign, > (*greater than*), or < (*less than*), in each circle. Looking at all those fractions and circles made Andy dizzy. He decided he had a fifty-fifty chance of guessing which one is right, but he often guessed wrong.

After school, when Andy got online with Joey, he typed: "I failed my math quiz today. I don't understand fractions and how to tell which is bigger."

Joey typed back: "Here's a good trick." Then he went to his drawing board and showed Andy how.

The next week, when Mrs. Becker gave a fractions test, Andy was the only kid who got 100 percent. The class didn't think Andy was so stupid anymore, thanks to Joey.

One day Andy said they should trade pictures in the mail. Andy sent his picture; he was in his baseball uniform with his bat over his shoulder like he was going to hit a home run. Then, when Andy asked Joey if he received his picture yet, Joey answered, "Your picture came, and it's impressive. Thanks!"

"Great!" Andy replied. "Then I should be getting yours soon." But Joey's picture never came.

It was strange. No photo and no comment from Joey. He just changed the subject. Then one day when they were talking about stars and aliens, Andy asked him, “Do you think there are aliens *in disguise on earth?” (3)It seemed like a long time before the screen lit up with his reply.

“Can you keep a secret?”

“I guess,” Andy answered.

“Promise? It’s really important!”

“Sure. I promise.”

“I’m an alien from another planet. That’s why I can’t send you a photograph. My image can’t be caught on film.”

Andy sat there, while he was staring at the computer, in shock. He thought, “*Was this one of Joey’s jokes? Then why didn’t he send a picture? Is this why he knows so much more than other kids about spaceships and outer space? Why is he not so open about himself?*”

At dinner, Dad announced, “Good news! My *transfer request was accepted. We’ll move to the head office in Denver at the end of this month. The company has found us a home. It’s close to a good school for Andy and large enough for Grandma to live with us.” Andy’s mom was happy because her mother lived in Denver and recently broke her leg so she wanted Grandma to live with them. But Andy just felt confused.

That night in bed, Andy thought about being a new kid in a new school. *I remember how I felt when we moved here. It was hard to make new friends. The other kids treated me differently for a while until they got to know me.*

The next morning, as Andy was sitting at the kitchen table and eating breakfast, his mom was watching a show on TV. A newscaster was interviewing a lady in Florida. “Tell me about the role the Internet plays in Joey’s life,” the newscaster asked.

“Well, it has allowed him a freedom he’s never known before. He is not only able to have access to information from his wheelchair, but most importantly, he has made new friends.”

The newscaster then asked, “Tell us about your Internet friends, Joey.”

The camera shifted to the kid in a wheelchair, who was sitting in front of his computer. He was a little thin with disabled legs. His head hung to one side, and when he answered, his words were hard to understand. He had to make a big effort to say them. “When other kids see me, they just see that I’m different. It’s hard for me to talk and be understood. But when I’m on the Internet, they think I’m just another kid because they can’t see me. I’ve been making friends with lots of different people,” Joey explained.

All day at school, Andy’s mind was full of mixed thoughts. He wondered: *His*

Internet friend, Joey; Joey the alien; Joey the kid on TV; making new friends in Denver; Grandma. As soon as he got home, he ran to his computer and switched it on.

He decided: *It doesn't matter where Joey came from — another planet or Florida. It doesn't matter what Joey looks like. I know who Joey is. Joey is my friend.*

Andy typed into the computer: "Joey, guess what? We're moving to Denver. (4)Boy, I am so glad to have a friend who goes with me everywhere I go."

出典：*Joanne Peterson "There's an Alien on the Internet"*

Chicken Soup for the Kid's Soul (Revised)

（注） fractions 分数　in disguise 変装した　transfer 異動，転勤

① それぞれの問いの答えとして最も適切なものを，下から１つずつ選びなさい。

［1］ Why did Kevin say, (1)Andy's gonna get hungry?　(　　)

ア Because he wanted to make fun of Andy's mistake.

イ Because Andy started moving his hand and shouting.

ウ Because he thought Andy couldn't get his piece of pizza.

エ Because Andy already ate the pizza he chose.

［2］ Why did Andy answer "one-tenth" to the teacher's question?　(　　)

ア Because he wanted to divide the pizza among his ten classmates.

イ Because Kevin answered one-third first, Andy chose the other.

ウ Because he thought one-third is smaller than one-tenth.

エ Because there were more than three classmates in his class.

［3］ Why did Andy think (2)*I wish that the recess bell would ring*?　(　　)

ア Because he easily finished solving all the problems.

イ Because he felt embarrassed when his classmates laughed at him.

ウ Because he wanted to play with other kids.

エ Because he wanted to have lunch soon.

［4］ How are the problems done in the math book?　(　　)

ア Draw 20 circles between fractions.

イ Line up 20 fractions in order.

ウ Do a guessing game that makes them dizzy.

エ Tell which fraction is bigger in each problem.

［5］ What does Andy look like in his picture? (　　)

ア Andy has his team's uniform on and his name plate.

イ Andy has his bat which he hit a home run with.

ウ Andy looks like he can hit a home run.

エ Andy is in his school uniform with his classmates.

② 下線部(3)<u>It seemed like a long time before the screen lit up with his reply.</u> について，次の質問の答えとして最も適切なものを選びなさい。 (　　)

Why did it take so long for Joey to answer Andy's alien question?

ア Joey couldn't find a good answer to Andy's question right away.

イ Joey's computer broke down.

ウ Joey was taking a picture of himself.

エ It took time for Joey to get messages from earth.

③ 次の質問に対して<u>当てはまらないもの</u>をすべて選びなさい。 (　　　)

What were the roles the Internet played in Joey's life?

ア A tool to get a lot of information.

イ A tool to connect with friends.

ウ A tool to make his condition better.

エ A tool to make him different from others.

④ 下線部(4)<u>Boy, I am so glad to have a friend who goes with me everywhere I go.</u> から，Andy のどのような気持ちが読み取れるか。次の書き出しに続く最も適切なものを選びなさい。 (　　)

Andy felt happy because he would be able to ...

ア always be with his best friend.

イ make new friends at a new school.

ウ start his new life in a city he would first visit.

エ live with his grandmother again.

⑤ 本文の内容と異なるものを3つ選びなさい。 (　　)(　　)(　　)

ア Andy has not met Joey directly.

イ Joey studies at his house instead of going to his local school.

ウ Andy chose the smaller piece of pizza for the math quiz by Mrs. Becker.

エ Joey's picture came at last but his image was not clear and difficult for Andy to see.

オ Joey knows much more about outer space than other kids.

カ Andy's family planned to live with his grandmother.

キ When Dad announced his move to Denver, every member of Andy's family was happy.

ク Andy was worried if he could get along with new friends when he heard about them moving to Denver.

ケ Andy knew Joey came from another planet from the beginning.

コ Andy decided he didn't mind what Joey looked like after he watched him on TV.

解答の方針

まず「インターネットにエイリアン(宇宙人)がいる」というタイトルに着目しよう。これはどういう意味だろうか？ と考えながら読むと，途中でその答えがわかる。主要な登場人物であるAndyとJoeyがそれぞれどんな性格であり，彼らに何が起きたかを考えながら読み進めよう。いくつかの文がイタリック(斜字)体で書かれているのは，その文が人物の気持ちを表しているから。たとえば第1段落は「Andyの親友はJoeyだ」で始まっているが，その段落の最後の *I wish* ... のIとはAndyのことである。

第4回 実力テスト

▶解答→別冊 p.75

時間 30 分　得点
目標 70 点　／100

次の文章を読んで，問いに答えなさい。（兵庫・関西学院高等部）（①～④⑥各 10 点，⑤ 20 点，⑦⑧各 15 点，計 100 点）

204

As a young puppy, Lucky was different from her brothers and sisters. During play time, they usually ran around in the garden while she was lying calmly on the grass. She was interested in the world around her, and liked to follow the movements of the *insects as they flew from flower to flower. When it was time for dinner, instead of jumping and *barking like the others, she sat patiently and waited for her turn.

Her owners (1)were concerned about Lucky's behavior. They thought that she didn't know how to play with other people, and that she was too quiet and shy. However, that changed after one event. One day, their friends were visiting the house with their 1-year-old child, Kento. [A] Kento learned to take his first steps recently, and so he could not walk for a long time before falling down. [B] Step by step, she moved along with him in order to help him keep his balance. [C] At that moment, Lucky's owners realized that Lucky could be more than just a pet; she could be a guide dog and help those who could not see. [D]

It was a tough decision for Lucky's owners to say goodbye to her, but they knew that it was the right thing to do. They took her to the Japan National Guide Dog Training Center. For 6 months, Lucky worked with professional trainers. The trainers taught her how to listen to *commands and walk along the streets. She was always very focused on the (2)surroundings, and could sense dangers from far away. Being a guide dog was a tough job, but Lucky seemed to enjoy it. When her trainer put the *collar on her, her tail always started *wagging to show that she was happy because it was time for work.

After the 6 months of training, Lucky was ready to meet with her first blind owner. She was sent to the Ishida family to help their 15-year-old daughter, Rumi. Rumi had a rare eye disease as a child, and her *vision slowly began to get worse after she entered junior high school. In the beginning of her third year, she could no longer see at all. Because of that, she was scared to move around, and stayed alone in her room. (3)It was difficult for her to go to school. When Lucky first met Rumi, Lucky naturally walked over to Rumi's side, and stood by her just like she did for Kento.

From that moment on, the *bond between them grew stronger and stronger. Rumi became more (4)confident, and started going on short walks outside the house with Lucky next to her. Soon, she became able to do things like other teenagers, such as going to the shopping mall, and visiting amusement parks, all with Lucky by her side. In fact, Rumi and Lucky could move around so well that Rumi's friends forget that Rumi sometimes needs help.

It is just the beginning of a wonderful journey for the pair. While they may face many problems along the way, Lucky will be by her owner's side, and guide the way through the road that lies *ahead.

（注）insect 虫　bark 吠える　command 命令　collar 首輪　wag ～を振る
vision 視力　bond きずな　ahead 前に

① Luckyを表す最も適切な文を，次の中から選びなさい。　(　　)

ア She was a quiet dog that was born in the Japan National Guide Dog Training Center.

イ She liked the smell of flowers and running in the garden.

ウ She was a noisy dog that became excited when it was time for dinner.

エ She was a patient dog that understood what was happening around her.

② 下線部(1)の意味に最も近い語句を，次の中から選びなさい。　(　　)

ア enjoyed　イ were worried about　ウ changed　エ were proud of

③ 次の英文が入る適切な位置を，第2段落中の[A]～[D]から選びなさい。　(　　)

When Kento tried to stand, Lucky moved by his side to act as a support for the child.

④ 下線部(2)の意味に最も近い語を，次の中から選びなさい。　(　　)

ア feelings　イ environment　ウ strangers　エ sounds

⑤ 下線部(3)の理由を日本語で詳しく述べなさい。

⑥ 下線部(4)の意味に最も近い語を，次の中から選びなさい。　(　　)

ア precious　イ creative　ウ positive　エ curious

⑦ 次の質問に対する最も適切な解答を，下から選びなさい。　(　　)

What do Rumi's friends think about Rumi?

ア They believe that Lucky's support is not enough, and that they also need to help her actively.

イ They were hoping that Rumi would get more attention for her courage, and that she and Lucky would become famous.

ウ They began to feel that Rumi didn't want any support because she enjoyed her time with Lucky.

エ They did not notice that Rumi had any disabilities because she could do so many things with Lucky's help.

⑧ 次の質問に対する最も適切な解答を，下から選びなさい。　(　　)

What is the story about?

It is about ...

ア how a guide dog's abilities can improve a person's life.

イ how a guide dog was trained to help people who have difficulties in hearing.

ウ a girl who had bad vision and how she was able to live by herself.

エ how dogs are the best pet that people can own.

5 ビジュアル読解

標準問題

解答 別冊 p.76

031 以下は観光ツアーの案内です。これを読んで，内容に合う英文を下から２つ選びなさい。

（東京・実践学園高）

031

Hakone Tour

*Book Online & Get 10% OFF

This is a hiking tour to enjoy the natural beauty of Hakone. There are many fun activities which you can try.

☆ Tour Route

Shinjuku Station (8:00 start) → bus → Northern Hotel in Shibuya (8:30 [guests only]) → bus →

Gotemba Station (1-hour free time) → bus → Otomeguchi Bus Station → bus →

Mt. Kintoki & Mt. Nagao (3-hour guided hike) → bus → Otomeguchi Bus Station → bus →

Northern Hotel in Shibuya (15:30) → bus → Shinjuku Station (16:00 finish)

Your tour guide will be waiting for you at the information counter in Gotemba Station.

☆ Tour Schedule and Times

Month	Price per person
January to March	4,000 yen
April to June	6,000 yen
July to September	6,500 yen
October to November	5,000 yen

(Bus fare, lunch, guide fee included)
Children of five and under: FREE

（注） book 予約する

ア You should meet the tour guide at Otomeguchi Bus Station.

イ If you make a booking online in April, you can get a discount of 600 yen for each person.

ウ Hakone Tour is held every month.

エ You can get on the bus in front of the Northern Hotel even if you don't stay there.

オ If you join the tour, you will be back at Shinjuku Station in eight hours.

（　　）（　　）

032 Read the passage and choose the answer which best completes sentence ①, and choose the answer which best completes each blank (1) and (2). (大阪府)

032

A report on the views of high school students about *social participation was made in 2021. [A] In this report, the words "social participation" mean any activity that students join both inside and outside school. According to the report, a *survey was done to know two things. [B] One is the *awareness of high school students about social participation. [C] These two things are used to find what kind of *characteristics there are in each country. [D] Students in the following four countries joined this survey: Japan, America, China, and Korea. They were asked 28 questions, for example, "How interested are you in *social issues outside school?", and the students answered each question by choosing one answer. The *table shows the *percentages of the answers to one of the questions: "Are you *actively *participating in classroom *discussions at your school?"

We can find some things from the table. Some students didn't answer this question, but if we compare the total percentages of the students who answered "Active" or "*Somewhat active," (1) of the four countries. The total percentages of the students who answered "Not so active" or "Not active" are higher than 30% in (2).

The percentages of the answers to the question:
"Are you actively participating in classroom discussions at your school?"

	Active	Somewhat active	Not so active	Not active	No answer
Japan	29.4%	52.6%	14.9%	2.5%	0.7%
America	27.1%	41.8%	20.4%	10.7%	0.0%
China	30.7%	45.0%	20.4%	3.9%	0.0%
Korea	32.6%	45.0%	15.4%	6.9%	0.2%

(国立青少年教育振興機構「高校生の社会参加に関する意識調査報告書」(令和3年)により作成)

(注) social participation 社会参加　survey 調査　awareness 意識
characteristic 特徴　social issue 社会問題　table 表　percentage 割合
actively 積極的に　participate in ～ ～に参加する　discussion 話し合い
somewhat やや

① The sentence "The other one is their real situation on social participation." should be put in
ア [A].　イ [B].　ウ [C].　エ [D].　(　　)

② (1) ア Japan is the highest　イ America is the highest　(　　)
ウ China is the lowest　エ Korea is the lowest

③ (2) ア Japan　イ America　ウ China　エ Korea　(　　)

重要 033 Glen 先生の英語の授業で，中学生の Taku，Nick，Misaki が，自身の中学校における読書の状況についてのグラフ (graph) を見ながら，話し合いをしています。次の英文は，話し合いと，それを聞いて Naho が授業で書いたワークシートです。下の問いに答えなさい。 （岡山県）

033

Graph 1

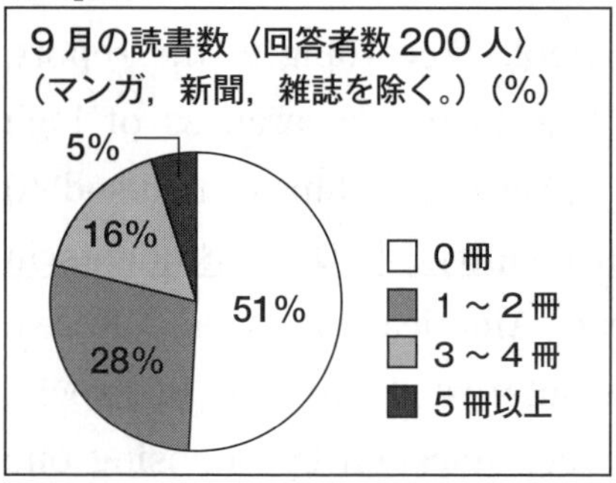

Graph 2

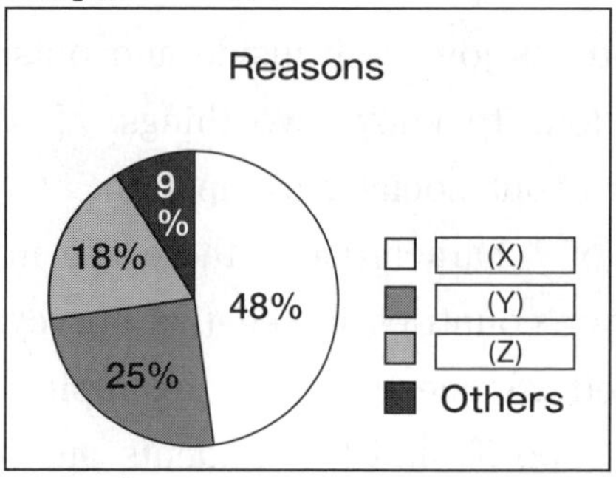

■話し合い

Mr. Glen: Look at Graph 1. This shows the results of the school *survey that you answered. I found this last week. What can we learn from this graph?

Taku: About [A] students read no books in September.

Mr. Glen: Does it mean you don't have a *reading habit?

Taku: Yes. We can see that by looking at that graph. Some students don't read books.

Nick: Really? I don't think that is true. That graph shows the number of books that we read in September. We also need to see [B].

Mr. Glen: With those *data, we can see the changes between months. It is difficult to see everything only with Graph 1. To learn your reading habit, you need more data. Do you have any other ideas?

Misaki: We also need to *consider when we answered the survey. We had our school festival in September, and we were busy then. I read books almost every month, but I didn't read any books in September.

Nick: That graph doesn't show that it was difficult for us to have time to read books then. We need to use the data carefully.

Taku: Now I understand. Mr. Glen, do you know why some students didn't read any books then? I think there are some *causes of this. If we find them, we can think about ways to improve the *situation.

Mr. Glen: OK, let's think about that. The survey asked the students why they didn't read any books in September. I made Graph 2 from the survey results. Now let's guess Reasons (X), (Y) and (Z) in Graph 2.

Taku: Maybe they're not interested in reading.

Misaki: Really? Students often say that they are too busy. They say that reading takes a lot of time.

Nick: They don't know which book to read.

Mr. Glen: Now let's check. Nick's idea is Reason (X), Misaki's is Reason (Y), and Taku's is Reason (Z).

Taku: With Graph 2, we can see why they read no books in September.

Mr. Glen: It is difficult to find the [C] causes of this situation only by guessing. To find ways to solve a problem, we can use different data and ask "Why?" or "Is that really [C]?" many times. However, there are a lot of things to consider when we use data. What do we need to think about? Please write your idea.

■ Nahoが授業で書いたワークシート

> I understand that it is important to have different data. When we use data, I think that it is also important to [D]. Some of the data may be *wrong. If it is wrong, we can't find ways to improve the situation. We should not easily believe the data that we can get.

（注） survey アンケート調査　reading habit 読書習慣　data データ
consider ～を考慮する　cause 原因　situation 状況　wrong 誤っている

① [A]に入る最も適切な数字を，次の中から選びなさい。（　　）

ア 10　イ 30　ウ 60　エ 100

② [B]に入る最も適切な語句を，次の中から選びなさい。（　　）

ア where the students often read books in September
イ how many books the students read in other months
ウ what the students thought about the survey
エ how many times the students have answered this survey

③ Graph 2の(Y)，(Z)に入る最も適切な組み合わせを，次の中から選びなさい。（　　）

ア (Y) I don't like reading.　(Z) I'm very busy.
イ (Y) I'm very busy.　(Z) I don't like reading.
ウ (Y) Books are expensive.　(Z) Reading takes time.
エ (Y) Reading takes time.　(Z) Books are expensive.

④ [C]に共通して入る英語1語を，生徒の発言から抜き出して答えなさい。（　　　　）

⑤ [D]に入る最も適切な語句を，次の中から選びなさい。（　　）

ア choose data which must be changed
イ collect data without thinking carefully
ウ check that each data is right
エ use the same data in a different situation

034 〉 次の会話は，中学３年生のかな(Kana)さんとヒル先生(Mr. Hill)との間で交わされたものです。後のグラフは，話の途中でヒル先生がかなさんに見せた，青少年のスマートフォンを使ったインターネットの利用時間に関する調査資料です。また，後のスピーチは，かなさんがスマートフォンの利用について実際に行った発表の原稿です。これらを読み，問いに答えなさい。 (鳥取県)

034

Kana: Good news! My friend, Takahiro, won *the first place at the piano contest yesterday!

Mr. Hill: That's great!

Kana: His parents were so happy. They bought a smartphone for him!

Mr. Hill: Oh, really? Kana, do you have a smartphone?

Kana: No, I don't. But my father says he will buy one for me when I'm a high school student. I can't wait!

Mr. Hill: Today, it is very important to learn how to use *information technology. A smartphone is a small computer. So it may be a good idea to have one when you are young. But when young people use smartphones, there are some problems, too.

Kana: I know. My older brother is using his smartphone too much and my mother is angry.

Mr. Hill: Look at this *graph, Kana. It shows how long Japanese students use smartphones to *access the internet in a day *on weekdays. Junior high school students use them for about 144 minutes a day.

Kana: That's a long time. Elementary school students spend *less than half of that time.

Mr. Hill: Yes. And boys are using them a little longer than girls at every *age. I especially worry about high school students because they use smartphones so much.

Kana: Wow, 208 minutes ... more than three hours a day!

Mr. Hill: What would happen if you used a smartphone for such a long time?

Kana: I get home at six o'clock after school, and go to bed at ten. If I used it for three hours each day, I would have no time to study or talk with my family.

Mr. Hill: Yes. I worry about (1)that.

Kana: Before we *graduate, maybe we need to learn more about this problem. I will choose this *topic for my speech next week.

(注) the first place 1位　information technology 情報技術　graph グラフ
access ～にアクセスする，つなぐ　on weekdays 平日に　less than ～ ～より少ない
age 年代　graduate 卒業する　topic 話題

グラフ

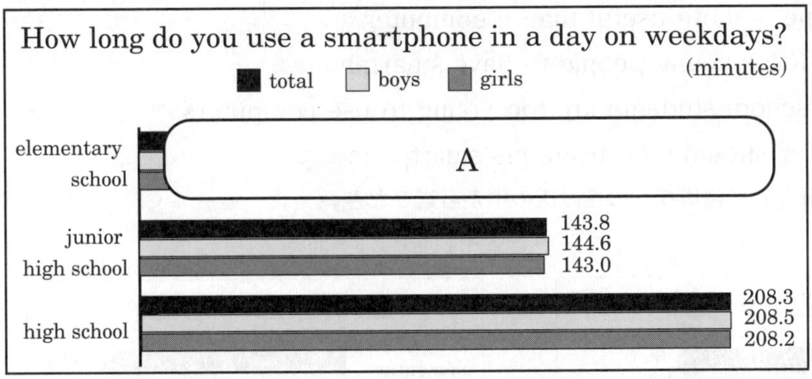

※「令和2年度青少年のインターネット利用環境実態調査」（内閣府 2021）より作成

スピーチ

Do you have a smartphone? With smartphones, we can get information easily. We can talk with friends *anytime. Playing games and watching movies on smartphones are fun!

However, what happens if we use smartphones too much? There are some problems. For example, we cannot *concentrate on studying if we send and receive messages all the time. Also, by looking at the *screens for a long time, our *eyesight will get very weak. And they keep our brains too excited at night, so we cannot sleep well. It may be bad for our health.

So, I talked with my parents and we *set three *rules. First, I will *turn off my smartphone when I study. Second, after I use it for an hour, I will stop using it (2). Third, to sleep well, I will not use it in bed. I'll *follow these rules when I get one.

A smartphone is a wonderful *tool. But if we are not careful, smartphones may make our school lives difficult. We should find a good way to live with smartphones. If we can, our lives will become more convenient and fun.

（注） anytime いつでも　concentrate on ～ ～に集中する　screen 画面
eyesight 視力　set < set （～を定める）の過去形　rule ルール
turn off ～ ～の電源を切る　follow ～を守る　tool 道具

① 2人の会話からわかることを，次の中から1つ選びなさい。　（　　）

ア Kana is very good at music.

イ Mr. Hill is looking at Takahiro's smartphone.

ウ Mr. Hill is telling Kana about Takahiro's good news.

エ Kana wants to have a smartphone.

② ヒル先生の意見として最も適切なものを，次の中から選びなさい。 (　　)

ア A smartphone is more useful than a computer.

イ It may be OK for young people to have smartphones.

ウ Junior high school students are too young to use computers.

エ Kana's brother should stop using his smartphone.

③ グラフ中のAの部分として適切なものを，次の中から選びなさい。 (　　)

ア

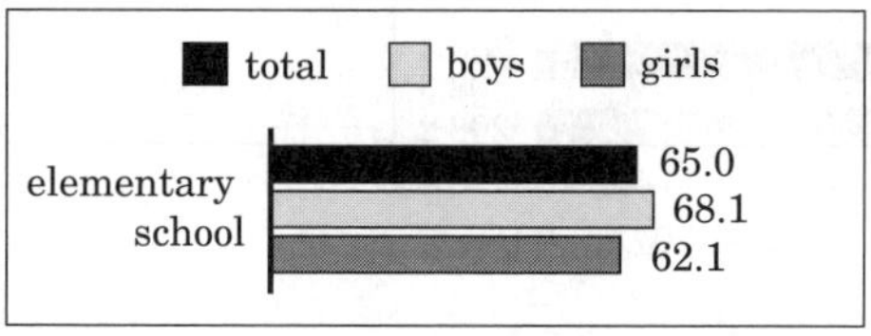

イ

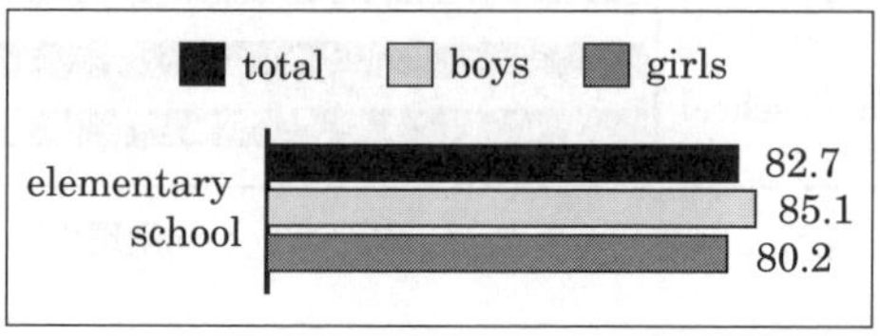

ウ

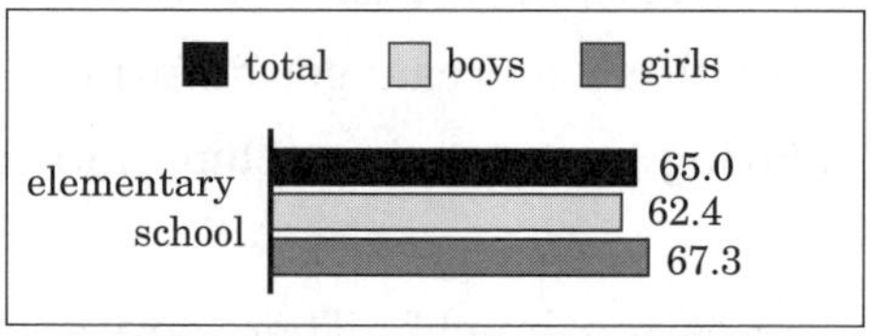

エ

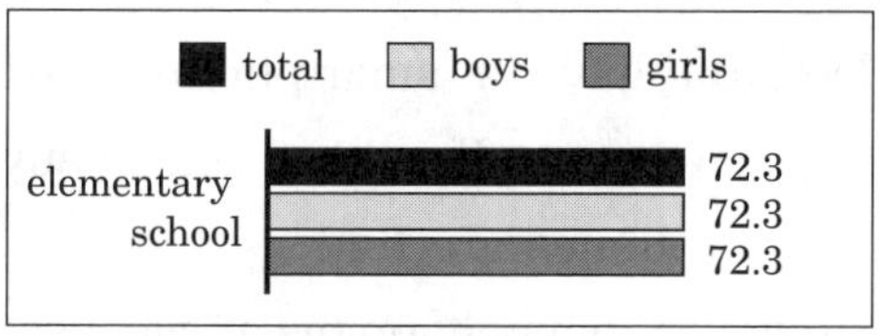

④ 下線部(1)はどのようなことを表していますか。次の(　　)に入る言葉を30字以内で答えなさい。句読点も１字に数えます。

スマートフォンを(　　　　　　　　　　　　　　)こと。

⑤ スピーチの(2)に入る最も適切なものを，次の中から選びなさい。 (　　)

ア to ask questions about my homework

イ to give my eyes some rest

ウ to make my brain excited

エ to send messages to my friends

⑥ スピーチでかなさんが伝えたい内容として最も適切なものを，次の中から選びなさい。(　　)

ア Using smartphones for a long time is good for students' health.

イ Parents should not buy smartphones for their children until they are older.

ウ Strong rules are needed when we use smartphones at school.

エ We should be good users of smartphones and enjoy our lives with them.

重要 035 次の対話は，もみじ市の高校生の京花と留学生のヘレンが，ヘレンのホームステイ先で話したときのものです。また，資料1はそのとき京花たちが見ていたウェブページの画面であり，資料2はヘレンの予定表の一部です。これらに関して，問いに答えなさい。

035

（広島県）

Kyoka: Helen, we are going to see a movie and visit the zoo this summer. Are there any other places you want to visit? [あ]

Helen: Yes. I'm interested in Japanese history, so I want to visit some *historical places here in Momiji City. Do you have any ideas?

Kyoka: Yes, I can show you a website [A] in English. Look at this! [い]

Helen: I don't know which *tour I should choose. Will you help me?

Kyoka: Of course, I'll help you.

Helen: Thanks. Here is my *schedule.

Kyoka: OK. How about this tour? It is [B] for you, because you are interested in historical places. [う]

Helen: It looks nice, but I don't like eating *meat.

Kyoka: Then how about this tour? You will visit the most historical place in the city. This is my favorite place. You will also learn about the history of our city. If I were you, I would choose this tour.

Helen: I like this tour the best, but I don't want to get tired on the last day before the second *term starts.

Kyoka: OK. Then you can join the one on Sunday. [え]

Helen: But we have plans to go out together that day.

Kyoka: We can change our plans. If you don't want to change them, you can choose this tour. You can see beautiful flowers, trees, and *stones. You will also wear traditional Japanese clothes. You are free on Tuesdays.

Helen: I like this tour too, but it's a little expensive. Is it OK to change our plans?

Kyoka: Sure. [C]?

資料1

Enjoy Momiji City!

We have some interesting tours for people from abroad. If you are interested in our one day tours, join us!

TOUR 1: Temples and Shrines

Momiji City has a lot of temples and shrines, and you can see some of them. If you are interested in Japanese history, you should choose this exciting tour.

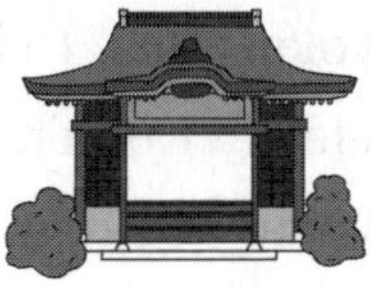

*Date: August 15 (Monday) / August 21 (Sunday)
Time: 11:00～16:00
*Fee: ¥3,000 (Lunch at a sukiyaki restaurant is *included.)

TOUR 2: Kimono Photo *Shoot

Would you like to wear a beautiful kimono? You can choose your favorite one at a kimono *rental shop. Your tour *guide will take pictures of you in a very old Japanese garden.

Date: August 16 (Tuesday) / August 23 (Tuesday)
Time: 14:00～17:00
Fee: ¥5,000 (The rental fee for a kimono is included.)

TOUR 3: Momiji City Museum and Momiji Castle

This city has a long history, and Momiji City Museum teaches it to you. You will also visit Momiji Castle. If you are interested in the history of the city, this tour is the best *choice for you.

Date: August 25 (Thursday) / August 28 (Sunday)
Time: 10:00～14:00
Fee: ¥2,500 (Lunch is not included.)

資料 2

8 August	
15 Monday	
16 Tuesday	
17 Wednesday	Practice volleyball (10:00～11:00)
18 Thursday	
19 Friday	Watch the soccer game (13:00～)
20 Saturday	Go to the summer festival with my *host family (16:00～)
21 Sunday	See a movie and have lunch with Kyoka (9:00～14:00)
22 Monday	
23 Tuesday	
24 Wednesday	Practice volleyball (10:00～11:00)
25 Thursday	
26 Friday	The beginning of the second term
27 Saturday	Go out for dinner with my host family (18:00～)
28 Sunday	Visit the zoo and have lunch with Kyoka (9:00～14:00)

(注) historical 歴史的な　tour ツアー　schedule 予定表　meat 肉　term 学期
stone 石　date 日付　fee 料金　include ～を含む　shoot 撮影
rental レンタルの　guide 案内人　choice 選択　host family ホームステイ先の家族

① [A]に入る最も適切な語を，次の中から選びなさい。　(　　)

ア write　イ wrote　ウ written　エ writing

② [B]に入る適切な 1 語を答えなさい。　(　　　)

③ 次の英文が入る適切な位置を，[あ]～[え]から選びなさい。　(　　)

There are three tours.

④ ヘレンが参加することに決めたツアーを，次の中から選びなさい。また，ヘレンがそのツアーに参加するのは 8 月の何日ですか。その日にちを数字で書きなさい。

(　　)／日にち(　　)

ア TOUR 1: Temples and Shrines

イ TOUR 2: Kimono Photo Shoot

ウ TOUR 3: Momiji City Museum and Momiji Castle

⑤ [C]に入る最も適切な文を，次の中から選びなさい。　(　　)

ア What do you want to do after seeing a movie?

イ What do you want to do after visiting the zoo?

ウ When do you want to see a movie with me?

エ When do you want to visit the zoo with me?

最高水準問題

解答 別冊 p.82

難 036 カロリー(calorie)と活動(activity)について書かれた次の英文と表を読んで，問いに答えなさい。なお，それぞれの活動とカロリー消費は比例関係にあるものとします。

(東京・国立工業高専)

036

John is a junior high school student. Ken and Tom are his brothers. Mary and Nancy are his sisters. One day, John learned about the calories in food and how many calories are *burned by walking, riding a bike, playing tennis, and *jogging. John collected some information about their activities.

Ken is an elementary school student. He walks to school every day. It is 1.5 kilometers from his home to school. However, he visited Jim's house before going to school today because Ken forgot his notebook at Jim's house yesterday. So Ken walked 900 meters more to go to school today.

John is a member of the tennis club at his school. He likes playing tennis very much. Today he played tennis for two hours after jogging for thirty minutes.

Mary is a high school student. She rides her bike three kilometers each day to go to school. She loves to talk with her friends. She went to a new cafeteria with her friend Kate after school today. Mary ate one piece of cake and talked with Kate about their favorite singers.

Nancy's university is five kilometers from her home and she always goes there by bike. This morning, she had two *slices of *buttered bread and 0.2 *liters of milk before she left her home on her bike.

Tom likes to ride his bike. He sometimes rides his bike about two kilometers after school. However, the weather was so nice today that he rode his bike six kilometers *in total.

表1

The energy in different foods	
1 piece of cake	250 *kcal
1 slice of buttered bread	100 kcal
0.2 liters of milk	120 kcal

表2

Four ways to burn 100 kcal
Walking 2 kilometers
Riding a bike 4 kilometers
Playing tennis for 15 minutes
Jogging for 20 minutes

(注) burn ～を消費する　jog ジョギングする　a slice of ～ ～の薄切り１枚
buttered バターを塗った　liter リットル　in total 合計で　kcal キロカロリー

① 本文と表から考えて，次の各文の空所に入る最も適切なものを下から1つずつ選びなさい。

(1) The calories which Ken burned by walking to school today and the calories from drinking (　　) liters of milk are the same.　(　　)

ア 0.1　イ 0.2　ウ 0.3　エ 0.4

(2) Mary has to jog for (　　) minutes to burn all the energy that was in the cakes she ate today.　(　　)

ア 20　イ 30　ウ 40　エ 50

(3) When Nancy arrived at her university this morning, she still had (　　) kcal of energy left in her body from her breakfast.　(　　)

ア 195　イ 205　ウ 215　エ 225

② 次の英文は，この調査を行ったJohnによるまとめです。空所に入る最も適切なものを下から1つずつ選びなさい。

(A) (　　)　(B) (　　)

> I found that the calories which I burned by playing tennis for two hours today and the calories from (A) were the same. The result was surprising. I also learned that the calories I burned by jogging for thirty minutes and the calories (B) were the same.

(A) ア having two pieces of cake
イ having two pieces of cake and drinking 0.2 liters of milk
ウ having two pieces of cake and three slices of buttered bread
エ having three pieces of cake and drinking 0.2 liters of milk

(B) ア Ken burned by walking to school this morning
イ Mary burned by going to school by bike this morning
ウ Nancy burned by going to university by bike this morning
エ Tom burned by riding his bike today

解答の方針

この問題では，問いを解くのに簡単な計算を求めている。英語の試験だから複雑な計算ではないが，この程度の計算を求める問題も出題されることがある，という点は知っておこう。本文の冒頭の3つの文にあるとおり，John，Ken，Tom，Mary，Nancyの5人が出てくるので，それぞれの人物が何をしてどれだけのカロリーを使ったかを，正確に計算する必要がある。なお，表2のFour ways to burn 100 kcalは「100キロカロリーを消費[燃焼]するための4つの方法」で，burnのもともとの意味は「燃やす」。体内に取り込んだカロリーは，身体の活動によって「燃やされる」ことによって消費される。

037 次の会話を読んで，問いに答えなさい。 （東京・都立新宿高）

Ayano and Hanae are high school students in Tokyo. One day, they see Mr. Green, an ALT from England, in a classroom. He is writing something on the blackboard.

037

Ayano: Hi, Mr. Green. What are you doing?

Mr. Green: You came at the right time! Can you help me?

Hanae: Sure. [A]

Mr. Green: Well, I'm practicing kanji characters because I have a Japanese language test this weekend. But I can't remember (1)one kanji.

Ayano: What does it look like?

Mr. Green: Let's see .... It has the sun on the left and the moon on the right. It also has a few numbers.

Ayano and Hanae write some characters on the blackboard.

Mr. Green: This is the one I need. The sun is between two "tens." Thank you. You've been a great help.

Hanae: You're welcome.

Ayano: We learn these four kanji parts when we are in the first year of elementary school.

Mr. Green: It's interesting for me to learn that some characters *are based on things around us. For example, I don't draw the sun like this, but it's very easy to change this Chinese character into an image in my mind. When I see different kanjis that *contain the sun, I can easily imagine that the characters are *connected to it.

Hanae: Yes. When you learn new words, you can guess their meanings if you know each part of the kanji.

Mr. Green: Kanji is similar to the affixes we have in English.

Ayano: Affixes? What are they?

Mr. Green: They are a group of letters added to the beginning or end of a word to change its meaning. For example, if you see a word starting with "re-," you know it means "again."

Hanae: Oh, yes ... and a word starting with "un-" means "not" and a word ending with "-able" means "can."

Mr. Green: True. I believe some kanji characters have such *functions. Each has its own meaning and if you know these meanings, it'll be easier to understand new words.

Ayano: Now I understand. I'm not good at learning English words because I see each word as one *unit.

Mr. Green: I see. When you try to *memorize information, it's better to connect it to something *meaningful *rather than simply *learn it by heart.

Ayano: (2)I [[1] many English words [2] was [3] have [4] trying [5] I [6] memorize [7] since [8] to [9] been] in junior high school, but my *vocabulary doesn't seem to increase. I wish I had a good memory.

Mr. Green: Do you know Ebbinghaus?

Ayano: Ebbinghaus?

Mr. Green: A German *psychologist. In 1885, he tested how well he remembered a list of three-letter words that had no meaning, over a long time. After he got the results of his *experiment, he made (3)a graph that is now known as the "Ebbinghaus Forgetting *Curve."

Mr. Green takes his smartphone out of his pocket. He searches the Internet for the Forgetting Curve.

Mr. Green: Look at this. The graph shows the *percentage of time saved to learn the words again.

Hanae: [B]

Mr. Green: For example, you needed ten minutes to memorize the words the first time. Two days later, it took seven minutes when you relearned them. How much time did you save?

Hanae: In that case, I saved 30% of the first time.

Mr. Green: Right.

Hanae: The graph shows that the percentage is 100% right after you have learned something. However, it drops quickly to 58% in just twenty minutes. It goes down to 44% in one hour, 36% in nine hours, and 34% in twenty-four hours. After that, the curve continues going down slowly.

Ayano: How can we keep memory?

Mr. Green: Ebbinghaus also found out that if you repeat or practice something a lot, the information is kept longer in your brain and the forgetting curve becomes *gentler. Using the same information sends a message to your brain to hold on to it. When the same thing is repeated, your brain says, ...

Hanae: "Oh, there it is again! [C]"

Mr. Green: That's it!

Hanae: When we see the same information again and again, we need less and less time to make the information active in our memory. Right?

Mr. Green: Yes.

Ayano: Then it becomes easier for us to pull out the information when we need it.

Mr. Green: Exactly. If you spend ten minutes *reviewing within 24 hours of getting the information, you will raise the curve to almost 100% again. A week later, when you review it for the second time, you need only five minutes to pull out the same information, and again raise the curve. In a month, for the third review, your brain will only need two to four minutes to give you the feedback.

Ayano: I don't feel I can make time to review every day.

Mr. Green: I know you are busy. But if you don't review, you will have to spend 40 to 50 minutes relearning each lesson later. [D]

Ayano: OK. I'll keep that in mind.

（注） be based on ～ ～に基づいている contain ～を含む connect ～を結びつける
function 機能 unit ひとつのまとまり memorize ～を記憶する
meaningful 意味のある rather than ～ ～よりむしろ
learn ～ by heart ～を暗記する vocabulary 語い psychologist 心理学者
experiment 実験 curve 曲線 percentage 割合 gentle 緩やかな
review 復習する

① ［ A ］～［ D ］に入る4つの英文の組み合わせとして正しいものを，下から選びなさい。 （　　）

［1］ I must keep it. ［2］ What do you mean?
［3］ I'm sick and tired of it. ［4］ What can we do for you?
［5］ You're always doing your best. ［6］ Do you have that kind of time?

ア ［A］［4］ ［B］［2］ ［C］［1］ ［D］［6］ イ ［A］［4］ ［B］［3］ ［C］［6］ ［D］［5］
ウ ［A］［4］ ［B］［6］ ［C］［3］ ［D］［5］ エ ［A］［5］ ［B］［2］ ［C］［1］ ［D］［6］
オ ［A］［5］ ［B］［3］ ［C］［6］ ［D］［4］ カ ［A］［5］ ［B］［6］ ［C］［3］ ［D］［4］

② (1)one kanji に当たる正しい文字を，次の中から選びなさい。 （　　）

ア 明 イ 胆 ウ 草 エ 朝

③ 下線部(2)の［　　］内の語句を正しく並べ替えたとき，［　　］内で2・5・7番目にくる語句の組み合わせとして正しいものを，下から選びなさい。 （　　）

I ［ ［1］ many English words ［2］ was ［3］ have ［4］ trying ［5］ I ［6］ memorize ［7］ since ［8］ to ［9］ been ］ in junior high school

ア ［2番目］［4］ ［5番目］［1］ ［7番目］［5］ イ ［2番目］［4］ ［5番目］［6］ ［7番目］［5］
ウ ［2番目］［4］ ［5番目］［8］ ［7番目］［7］ エ ［2番目］［9］ ［5番目］［1］ ［7番目］［5］
オ ［2番目］［9］ ［5番目］［6］ ［7番目］［7］ カ ［2番目］［9］ ［5番目］［8］ ［7番目］［7］

④ (3)a graph を正しく表しているものを，次の中から選びなさい。 （　　）

ア
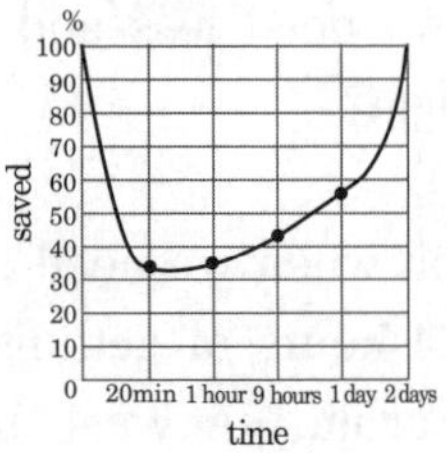

イ
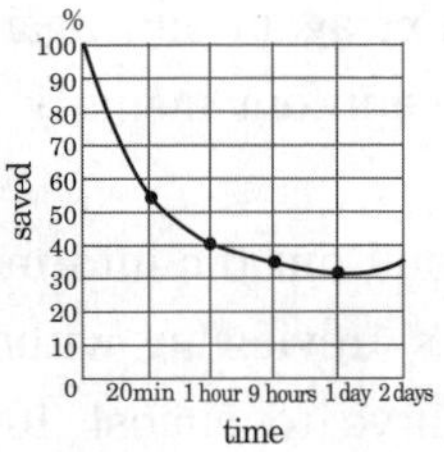

ウ
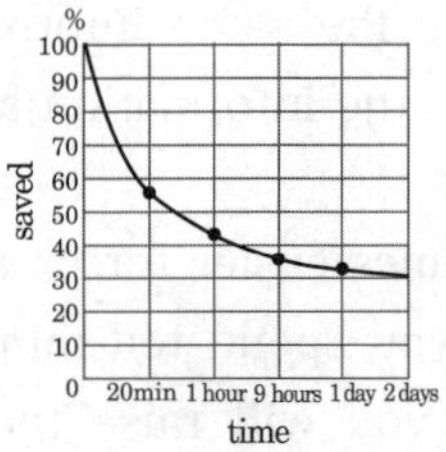

エ
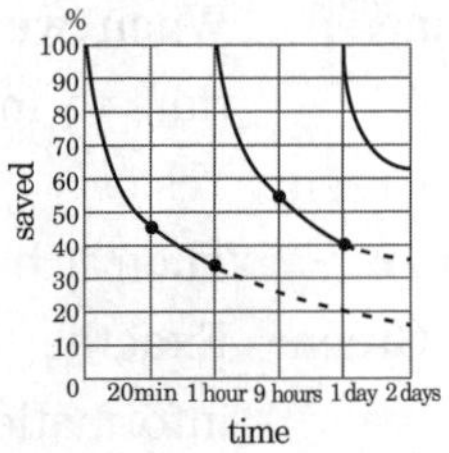

⑤ 次の英文が本文の内容に合うよう，空所に入る1語を答えなさい。 (　　　)

If you want to increase your English vocabulary, there are some ways to make it easier. One effective way is to learn affixes. Some words have small parts which have their own meaning. Knowing them will help you understand new words or guess their meanings. For example, when you see the word "(　　　)," you can guess that it means you cannot believe it.

⑥ 本文の内容に合うものを，次の中から1つ選びなさい。 (　　　)

ア It is difficult for Mr. Green to connect some kanji characters to things around him because he cannot draw pictures well.

イ Ayano wants to increase her English vocabulary, but she is worried that she does not have a good memory.

ウ Ebbinghaus asked some of his students to remember a list of three words which did not have any meaning.

エ Hanae finds out that if she practices something many times, she will be able to save 30% of the time to remember it.

オ Ayano finally accepts Mr. Green's advice to spend forty to fifty minutes reviewing each lesson every day.

解答の方針

会話中には，「漢字」の話と「記憶力」の話が出てくる。話の流れをたどりながら，3人がそれぞれの発言で何を話題にしているかを正しくつかもう。

なお，文中にkanji charactersという言葉が出てくるが，これは「漢字(の文字)」の意味。characterには「性格」「登場人物」の意味もあるが，「(表意)文字」(形が意味を表す文字)の意味でも使う。アルファベットのような単なる記号としての文字は，letterという。

④のグラフは「エビングハウスの忘却曲線」として知られる有名なグラフである。

⑤は思考力を要する良問。Mr. GreenとHanaeのやり取りのどこかにヒントがあるので探してみよう。

難 038 次の文章を読んで，問いに答えなさい。 （東京・都立青山高）

If you drive about 200 kilometers to the west from London, you will suddenly see very large stone *monuments. They are called *Stonehenge. (See Picture A.) Stonehenge is one of the world's most famous monuments. Every year more than one million people visit it. There are a lot of *mysteries about Stonehenge. The people who built it didn't leave any written records about it. Scientists have studied it for more than a century. A lot of mysteries are still left, but modern science has taught us quite a lot.

A lot of people thought the very large stone monuments were built around 2,000 or 3,000 years ago, but they were not. Around 1970, scientists used *radio-carbon dating and found they were actually built around 4,600 years ago. Look at Picture B. This picture shows what Stonehenge probably looked like around 4,600 years ago. You can see two kinds of very large stone monuments at its center. One is called the *sarsen stone circle. Thirty large sarsen stones were stood up in a circle, and then another thirty sarsen stones were put on the top of them to make a ring. It was about five meters tall and about 30 meters in *diameter. The other kind was made of *trilithons. Each trilithon was made of two standing stones and one stone on the top of them. There were five very tall trilithons built inside the circle. They were also made with very large sarsen stones. The five trilithons stood in the shape of a "U." The tallest one standing at its center was about seven meters tall. Three of them still stand today.

Picture A

Picture B

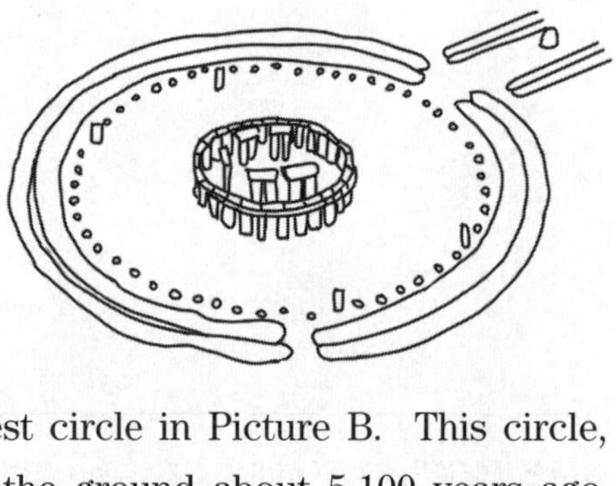

Picture C

Let's take a look at the largest circle in Picture B. This circle, about 100 meters in diameter, was *carved into the ground about 5,100 years ago. A smaller circle was then made inside it with *bluestones or *timber in holes. Now only 56 holes remain. This circle is called the *Aubrey Holes. Around 4,800 years ago, four stones called the Station Stones were added close to the circle, and a big sarsen stone, about five meters tall, called the *Heel Stone, was put up, about 25 meters outside the largest circle on the ground. A road was made from the area of the

Heel Stone to the River Avon, about three kilometers. After the two kinds of very large stone monuments at the center of Stonehenge were built, other circles and shapes were added with bluestones. As we have seen, many changes were made to Stonehenge. In 1995, modern science discovered that around 3,500 years ago, the building of Stonehenge was reaching its final stage. Stonehenge was built (1)<u>over a very long period of time</u>.

Long ago, scientists found that the large sarsen stones came from an area about 30 kilometers to the north, but it took a long time to learn where the smaller bluestones came from. In the *Ice Age, an ice sheet covered the area around Stonehenge. Some scientists thought, "Maybe the bluestones were carried there by the movement of the ice." But they were not sure because no other bluestones were found around there. Later, the bluestones of the kind used for Stonehenge were found at a place over 200 kilometers to the *northwest of Stonehenge. They believe this is the place that was the *source of Stonehenge bluestones. [A] Some scientists think the stones were put on boats and carried on the sea and on rivers.

Bluestones are very hard, and, according to some scientists, people believed those stones had the power to keep them healthy and bring them good luck. Sarsen stones are larger and softer than bluestones. The sarsen stones were carved as shown in Picture C. They were made to fit together and to stand for a long time without falling down. The stones for standing up were cut to *bulge out in the center. Because of this, Stonehenge looked strong and *impressive when it was seen from far away. Probably the people who built it knew this. Sarsen stones have a bright white color inside. When they are first cut, they look beautiful. Scientists think that the very large monuments of Stonehenge looked beautifully white when they were first built with those sarsen stones.

[B] Around 5,100 years ago, people called the *Ancient Britons lived in the area that is now the UK. Many scientists think they built Stonehenge. According to research, around 4,600 years ago, about 4,000 of the Ancient Britons from different villages lived together in a village three kilometers away from Stonehenge. Maybe these were the people who started the building of the very large monuments of Stonehenge.

In the UK, there are more than 1,000 stone circles, and the oldest ones are on an island about 1,000 kilometers to the north of Stonehenge. Stone circles probably spread across the UK from there. Scientists think the circles probably had a special meaning for people. They probably knew that the sun, the moon, and the stars move in circles and tried to show this on the ground.

Around 5,100 years ago, stone circles were simple ones made with smaller stones. But around 4,600 years ago, for some reason, the stones used for them started to get larger. [C] Around that time, the Earth was getting colder, and people had a hard time growing food. Some scientists say that they probably built the very large stone monuments to try to bring the power of the sun back.

[D] According to some scientists, it was probably used as a kind of calendar that could *predict the positions of the sun and the moon. The four stones called the Station Stones were used to predict the movement of the moon. And the circle called the Aubrey Holes and the large trilithon monuments were used to predict the movement of the sun. On the *summer solstice, if you stand in front of the tallest trilithon and look at the Heel Stone on the road, the sun will rise directly over the Heel Stone. On the summer solstice, the sun rises, and on the *winter solstice, it sets on the same line — but on the other side of the circle. For the Ancient Britons, the winter solstice probably had a special meaning. They knew that after that day, the days would become longer and longer. On that day, they probably held a special event at Stonehenge. Maybe they got together, walked on the road to Stonehenge, and saw the sunset through the space between the two standing stones of the tallest trilithon. Maybe they hoped that the power of the sun would become stronger.

Over the last 100 years or so, people have learned much about Stonehenge. In the future, as science and technology develops, scientists may learn more. Thanks to them, someday, many mysteries about Stonehenge may be understood.

(Picture A, B, C は，『まんが　新・世界ふしぎ物語 4　世界にのこるストーンヘンジのなぞ』吉川豊著（理論社）を参考に作成）

（注） monument　建造物　　Stonehenge　ストーンヘンジ　　mystery　謎
radio-carbon dating　放射性炭素年代測定法　　sarsen stone　サーセンストーン
diameter　直径　　trilithon　トリリトン（三石塔）　　carve　～を彫る
bluestone　ブルーストーン　　timber　木材　　Aubrey Holes　オーブリーホール
Heel Stone　ヒールストーン　　Ice Age　氷河期　　northwest　北西　　source　産地
bulge out　ふくらむ　　impressive　印象的な　　Ancient Britons　古代ブリトン人
predict　～を予測する　　summer solstice　夏至　　winter solstice　冬至

① 下線部(1)の内容として最も適切なものを，次の中から選びなさい。（　　）
ア　約1,100年間　　イ　約1,600年間　　ウ　約2,600年間　　エ　約3,500年間

② 本文中に述べられている次の[1]～[5]の出来事を，起きた順に並べ替えたとき，その組み合わせとして最も適切なものを下から選びなさい。（　　）
[1]　The Station Stones and the Heel Stone were put up.
[2]　Other circles and shapes were added with bluestones.
[3]　The sarsen stone circle and five trilithons were built.
[4]　The circle called the Aubrey Holes was made with bluestones or timber in holes.

［5］ A very large circle, about 100 meters in diameter, was carved into the ground.

ア ［3］→［1］→［5］→［4］→［2］　イ ［3］→［5］→［4］→［1］→［2］

ウ ［3］→［5］→［4］→［2］→［1］　エ ［5］→［1］→［4］→［2］→［3］

オ ［5］→［4］→［1］→［2］→［3］　カ ［5］→［4］→［1］→［3］→［2］

③ 本文の流れに合うよう，［ A ］～［ D ］に入る適切な文を下から1つずつ選びなさい。ただし，同じ文をくり返し使わないこと。

［A］（　　）　［B］（　　）　［C］（　　）　［D］（　　）

ア How was Stonehenge used?

イ But how were they carried so far?

ウ How did they build such very large stone monuments?

エ Who built Stonehenge?

オ What happened during those years?

④ 次のイギリスの略地図の中に示した［1］～［3］は，本文中に述べられているAサーセンストーンの産地，Bブルーストーンの産地，C最古のストーンサークル，のいずれかを表したものである。最も適切な組み合わせを選びなさい。　（　　）

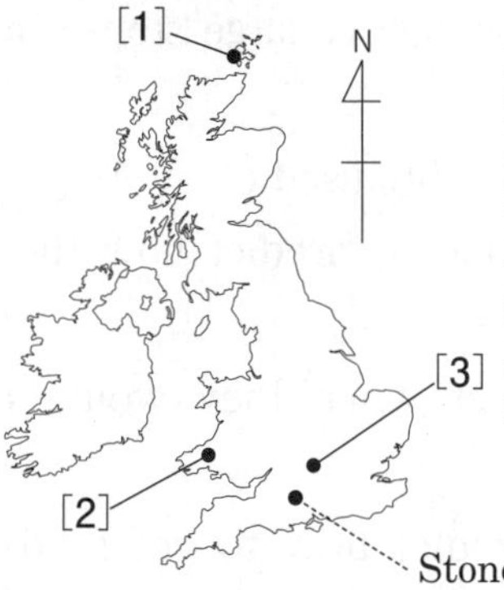

	A	B	C
ア	［1］	［2］	［3］
イ	［1］	［3］	［2］
ウ	［2］	［1］	［3］
エ	［2］	［3］	［1］
オ	［3］	［1］	［2］
カ	［3］	［2］	［1］

⑤ 下のストーンヘンジの模式図は，本文中に述べられている古代ブリトン人が冬至の日に日没を見ている様子を表したものである。その様子を最もよく表した図を，次の中から選びなさい。ただし，■は人を表し，矢印は太陽が沈む方向を示している。　（　　）

■：人 ───→：太陽が沈む方向

ア

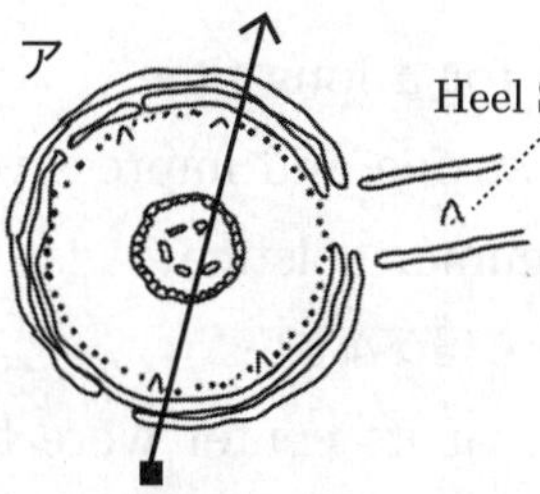

イ

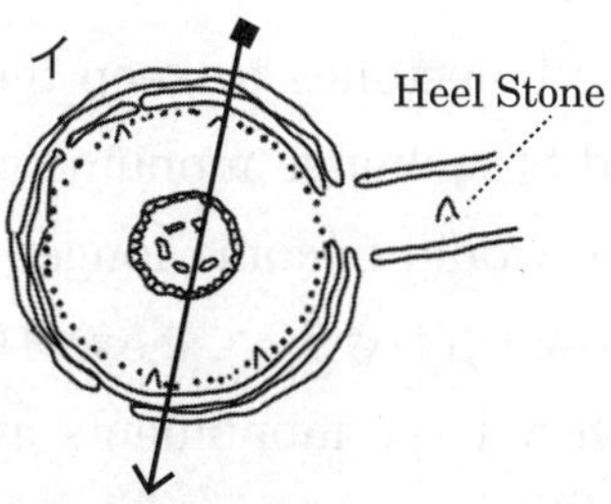

ウ

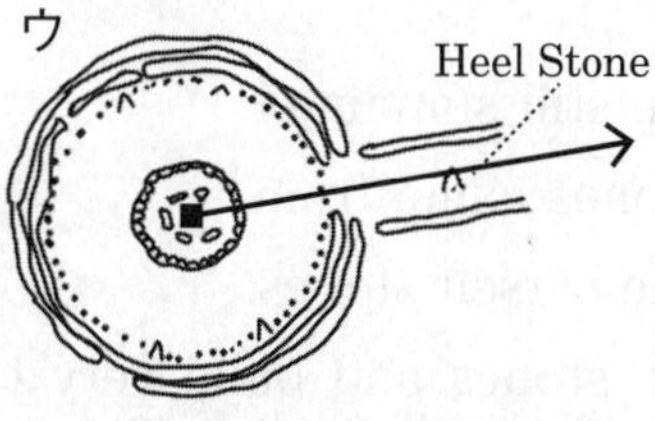

エ

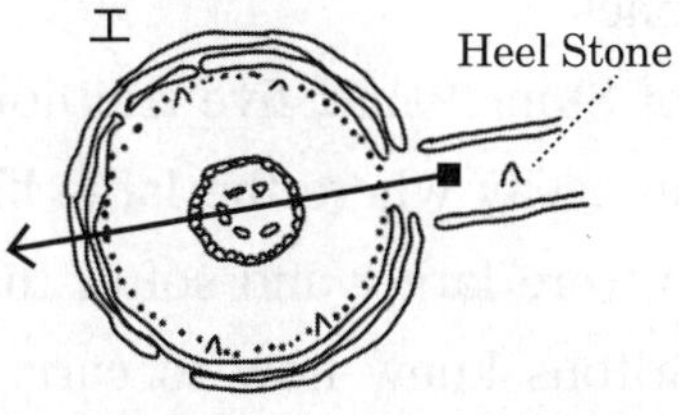

⑥ それぞれの文が本文の内容と一致するよう，空所に入る最も適切なものを選びなさい。

(1) We understand more about Stonehenge now than before because (　　).
(　　)

ア scientists have studied a lot of written records the Ancient Britons left at Stonehenge

イ scientists have seen and studied the monuments of Stonehenge for about fifty years

ウ science has developed, and scientists have studied it with modern technology

エ science has taught us how many stone circles the Ancient Britons made

(2) Scientists used radio-carbon dating and found out (　　). (　　)

ア when the very large stone monuments of Stonehenge were actually built

イ what kind of stones the Ancient Britons used to build Stonehenge

ウ that the bluestones were carried to Stonehenge by the movement of ice

エ that there are more than 1,000 stone circles with very large stones in the UK

(3) Some scientists think that the Ancient Britons probably used (　　). (　　)

ア the Station Stones and the sarsen stone circle to predict how the sun moves in circles in the sky

イ the Heel Stone and the trilithons to predict when they would have enough rain to grow food

ウ the Aubrey Holes and the bluestones to predict how to get food and survive the cold weather

エ the Aubrey Holes and the trilithons to predict the movement of the sun

(4) According to scientists, the Ancient Britons probably knew (　　). (　　)

ア that a lot of bluestones carried by the movement of ice were found near Stonehenge

イ how to carve bluestones to keep them standing for a long time

ウ how to build Stonehenge monuments that look strong and impressive

エ that the days would become longer after the summer solstice

⑦ 本文の内容に合う英文の組み合わせとして最も適切なものを，下から選びなさい。 (　　)

[1] Two kinds of very large monuments at Stonehenge at its center were built with sarsen stones.

[2] At the center of Stonehenge, five trilithons are still standing.

[3] Scientists found easily where the large bluestones came from.

[4] The bluestones were larger and softer than the sarsen stones.

[5] The Ancient Britons knew how to carry large stones and build very large

stone monuments.

[6] According to research, maybe the Ancient Britons from different villages and living in a village a few kilometers away from Stonehenge started to build the very large monuments.

[7] The stone circles were probably made to show the movement of the sun, the moon, and the stars.

[8] Scientists have solved all the mysteries about Stonehenge, and now there are no more mysteries.

ア [1][2]　イ [1][5]　ウ [2][6]　エ [3][7]　オ [5][7]
カ [1][3][5]　キ [1][4][6]　ク [3][4][7]　ケ [4][5][8]　コ [5][6][8]
サ [1][5][6][7]　シ [3][5][7][8]

解答の方針

最高レベルの難度の問題。個々の英文はそれほど複雑ではないが，内容は密度が濃く，情報を整理しながら読む必要がある。文中のキーワード(sarsen stone，trilithon など)にしるしをつけたり，箇条書きや表の形で内容をまとめるのもよい。また，問題文中の図をヒントにして，それぞれの問いがどの段落のどの箇所に関係しているかを正確につかむことも大切。全問を解くには相当な時間がかかるので，集中力を保つ練習もしておこう。

第5回 実力テスト ▶解答→別冊 p.89

時間 50 分　目標 80 点　得点　／100

美保《みほ》と光太《こうた》，アメリカ出身のアレックスが，ベーカー先生の授業で，ニュースに関するグラフ(Graph)を見ながら話をしている。次のグラフと対話文を読んで，後の問いに答えなさい。グラフ１とグラフ２のＡ，Ｂ，Ｃは，それぞれ同じ国です。（福井県）（各 20 点，計 100 点）

205

Graph 1

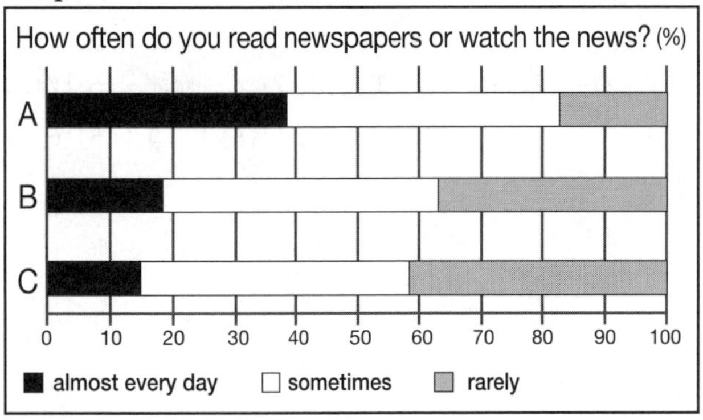

Graph 2

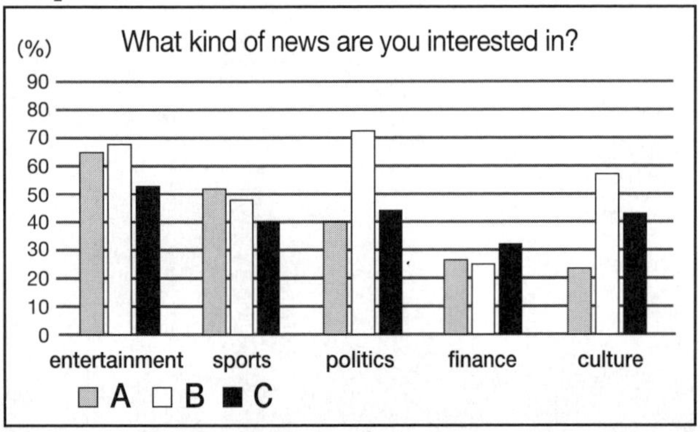

「高校生の社会参加に関する意識調査報告書—日本・米国・中国・韓国の比較—」(国立青少年教育振興機構2021.6)より日米韓の３か国を抜粋し編集。グラフ１は無回答があるため，それぞれの割合を合計しても100%にならない。グラフ２は複数回答可能のため，それぞれの割合を合計すると100%を超える。

Ms. Baker: Today we're going to talk about newspapers and news. Do you read newspapers or watch the news?

Miho: Yes, I read newspapers every morning. I often watched the news on TV before, but these days, I'm interested in reading newspapers. Our social studies teacher uses newspapers in class. We choose one interesting article and talk about it in each group. I can hear different opinions from other students. Such classes are interesting to me.

Alex: I *rarely read newspapers or watch the news, but I think it's important to know what is happening around the world.

Kota: I think reading newspapers is a better way to get a lot of information than watching the news. Newspapers include a wider variety of articles such as politics, culture, and sports.

Miho: Yes! We can become interested in things we don't know and get a lot of information about them. Also, newspapers help us learn about a lot of things in our communities such as events or volunteer activities. For example, we can learn that some people do something helpful for their own cities.

Ms. Baker: Thank you for talking about the good things about newspapers. Look at Graph 1. This graph shows how often high school students read newspapers or watch the news. What can we learn from it?

Kota: The *percentage of the Japanese high school students who said, "almost every day", is the highest of the three countries.

Alex: Almost forty percent! That's great. In Japan, about seventeen percent of the students rarely read newspapers or watch the news, but in America and Korea, about forty percent of the students rarely do that.

Kota: I'm surprised to know that. What kind of news are the high school students interested in?

Ms. Baker: Look at Graph 2. What can we learn from it?

Alex: In all the countries, more than fifty percent of the high school students are interested in the news about *entertainment such as movies or songs.

Miho: I can see that high school students are not interested in *finance. Korea has the highest percentage, but it is only about thirty percent. I think it's hard for students to understand finance.

Kota: Look! The percentage of the *American students who are interested in the news about politics is higher than the percentage in Japan and Korea. It's more than seventy percent! Japanese high school students often read newspapers or watch the news, but they are less interested in politics than American students.

Miho: Ms. Baker, when you were a high school student, were you interested in politics?

Ms. Baker: Yes, I had classes about politics in my high school. In the classes, we had to tell other students our opinions about a topic, so we needed to think about it a lot. Through the classes, I learned a lot and became interested in politics.

Miho: I see.

Alex: When people are eighteen, they can vote. It started about fifty years ago in America, but in Japan, it started just six years ago. Now

Japanese students can learn the importance of voting in social studies classes. I think more and more young people in Japan will be interested in politics.

Kota: I hope so. Now, there are many problems in our countries, so it's important for us to become more interested in them. We should read newspapers or watch the news, think about these problems, and have our own opinions about them.

Ms. Baker: That's right. Thank you, everyone. You are a member of your country. When you become eighteen, you can tell the government your opinion by voting. Each person's voice may be small, but if it is collected together, it can become a very big voice. You can change your countries for the better!

(注) rarely めったに～ない　percentage 割合　entertainment エンターテイメント
finance 金融　American アメリカ人の

① グラフ1・2の内容と合っているものを，次の中から1つ選びなさい。　(　　)

ア In each country, the percentage of the students who said, "entertainment," is the highest.

イ In each country, the students are more interested in finance than sports.

ウ Only in one country, more than fifty percent of the students are interested in culture.

エ Only in one country, more than fifty percent of the students sometimes read newspapers or watch the news.

② グラフのBの国は何か。その国名を英語で答えなさい。　(　　　)

③ 次の英文の空所に入る最も適切なものを，次の中から選びなさい。　(　　)

According to Kota, reading newspapers is better than watching the news because (　　).

ア he can read newspapers every day

イ newspapers give him more kinds of information

ウ newspapers make him interested in volunteer activities

エ students can understand international news more easily

④ 次の英文の空所に入る最も適切なものを，次の中から選びなさい。　(　　)

Alex thinks the number of the Japanese high school students who are interested in politics will grow because (　　).

ア they began to vote in elections about fifty years ago

イ they have classes that teach them how important voting is

ウ they will have a lot of classes about cultures of the world

エ they will have more time to vote after they become eighteen

⑤ 次の質問の答えとして最も適切なものを，下から選びなさい。 (　　)

What is Ms. Baker's message for the students?

ア In class, students should tell her their opinions with a big voice.

イ People in their twenties have to vote because it is their responsibility.

ウ Students have the power to change their countries for the better by voting.

エ The government should listen to a lot of opinions from young people.

□ 編集協力 ㈱シー・レップス 渡邉聖子 白石あゆみ
□ 本文デザイン CONNECT
□ 本文イラスト ㈱シー・レップス
□ 録音 高速録音㈱
□ ナレーション Ananda Jacobs Stuart O 芦澤亜希子

シグマベスト
最高水準問題集
中学英語長文

著　者 佐藤誠司
発行者 益井英郎
印刷所 株式会社天理時報社
発行所 株式会社文英堂
〒601-8121 京都市南区上鳥羽大物町28
〒162-0832 東京都新宿区岩戸町17
(代表)03-3269-4231

●落丁・乱丁はおとりかえします。

ΣBEST
シグマベスト

最高水準問題集

中学英語長文

解答と解説

文英堂

1 会話・メール

001 ① ［B］ア　［D］エ
② ⑴ **worked**　⑶ **where**
③ ウ
④ ［X］**supporting**　［Y］**for**

解説 ①会話の状況から考えて，［A］〜［E］には順にウ・ア・オ・エ・イが入る。全訳を参照。

得点アップ

①は５つの空所に５つの文を入れる問いだが，ア・エがYes. で始まっている点に着目しよう。Yes（またはNo）は「〜ですか（それともそうではありませんか）」という質問への返答だから，直前の相手の発言が一般［Yes / No］疑問文（Are you 〜?，Do you 〜? のような形）である箇所にア・エが入る。つまりア・エが入る場所は，［B］（直前の発言＝Did he?）と［D］（直前の発言＝Is that so?）である。そして問いは「［B］と［D］に入るものを答えなさい」だから，「B＝ア，D＝エ」「B＝エ，D＝ア」のどちらかの可能性しかないことになる。

② ⑴ work for 〜「〜に勤める」，⑶ know where S is「Sがどこにあるかを知っている」
③ make loud sounds「大きな音を出す」。主語がfire alarms（火災報知器）だから，voices（声），laughter（笑い），songs（歌）では意味が通らない。

得点アップ

単語同士の慣用的な結びつきを，コロケーションという。たとえば**look for**〜（〜を探す）は熟語（イディオム）として辞書の見出し語になっている。一方，「形容詞＋名詞」「動詞＋名詞」などのコロケーションの中には，辞書に見出し語として載っていないものもある。たとえば（a）**heavy rain**（大雨）や**take a bath**（入浴する）などである。コロケーションは英文を読んだり書いたりする上で非常に重要であり，できるだけ多く知っておく方がよい。この問いの場合，loud（（声や音が）大きい）との相性が最もよい名詞はvoiceであり，a loud ... という形を見たら**in a loud voice**（大声で）というフレーズが思い浮かぶのが望ましい。しかし，「声を出す」をmake a voiceとは言わない。４つの選択肢のうちで，makeとの相性が最もよい名詞はsoundである。**make a sound［noise］**は「音を出す［立てる］」という意味。この表現自体は辞書に見出し語としては載っていないが，sound［noise］の例文などとして出てくる。辞書を引くときは，見出し語の意味だけを調べるのではなく，その語が他のどんな語と結びつくか，つまり各語のコロケーションも確認するようにしよう。

④ *ll*.14-15 の The Japanese technology has supported our daily lives in America.（日本の技術はアメリカでの私たちの日常生活を支えてきた）に着目して，［X］にはsupportingを入れる。ここはandで並列されている部分なので，givingとそろえて〜ing形にすることに注意。また，*ll*.23-24 の many Japanese prepare for disasters（多くの日本人は災害に備えている）に着目して，［Y］にはforを入れる。prepare for 〜とbe ready for 〜はほぼ同じ意味を表す。このスピーチ原稿のタイトルは「日本の強み」。本文の意味は次のとおり。

「日本はとても素晴らしいです。ある日私は，アメリカから来た生徒のボブと話しているとき，新しい事実を知りました。彼はアメリカでQRコードについて知っていて，それが日本で作られたことを授業で学びました。日本の技術が他国へ広がって，人々に便利な生活を与え，日々の生活を支えているのです！

さらに，多くの日本人は災害への備えをしています。ボブは多くの日本人が災害に備えて食べ物と水を保管していることを知って驚きました…。」

精読

◆ Then fire alarms in the school make loud sounds suddenly, and let us know the drill has started.（*ll*.20-21）（それから校内の火災報知機が突然大きな音で鳴って，訓練が始まったことを私たちに知らせる）：〈let＋O＋動詞の原形〉は「Oに〜させる」の意味。Let me 〜.（私に〜させてください）の形でもよく使われる。

・**Let me know** your new address.

（あなたの新しい住所を私に知らせてください）

なお let us の短縮形は let's で，Let's go.（さあ行こう）のような使い方もする。

全訳

彩：こんにちは，ボブ。いつ故郷に帰るの？

ボブ：やあ，彩。サンフランシスコへは来月帰るよ。

彩：[A]あなたがこの学校にいた期間は早く過ぎてしまったわ[あと少し]ね。日本の学校生活はどう？

ボブ：素晴らしいよ！ ぼくは昨年からぼくたちの学校で日本について学んできたから，ホストファミリーとよくその話をするんだ。

彩：もっと詳しく聞かせて。

ボブ：そうだね，先週授業でぼくは QR コードのことを学んだ。そこでホストファミリーのおじいちゃんと QR コードの話をした。そのコードは日本で作られた，とぼくは彼に話したんだ。するとおじいちゃんは，自分が1994年に QR コードを最初に発明した日本の会社に勤めていたと教えてくれた。

彩：そうなの？

ボブ：[B]うん。QR コードはサンフランシスコでも人気がある。家族とレストランに行ったとき，お母さんが時々スマートフォンでコードを読み取って食後にお金を払っていた。とても便利だった。日本の技術はアメリカでぼくたちの日常生活を支えてきたんだ。

彩：[C]それはよかったわ。技術は日本の強みよ。他には何か話したの？

ボブ：うん，避難訓練の話をした。これは日本のもう1つの強みだと思う。日本の避難訓練はアメリカのとは違うね。

彩：そうなの？

ボブ：[D]うん。避難訓練の日に，ぼくの学校の生徒はそのことを全然知らないんだ。それから校内の火災報知機が突然大きな音で鳴って，訓練が始まったことを知らせる。

彩：日本でそういうタイプの訓練をする学校もあるわ。

ボブ：すごい！ ぼくはここにいる間に，たくさんの日本人が，火事や地震や大雨などの災害に備えていることを知ったよ。

彩：[E]なるほど。日本では毎年いろんな災害が起きるからね。私の家族も，非常用品セットを作って家に保管しているわ。

ボブ：ああ，そうなんだ。ぼくのホストファミリーはどのくらいの量の食べ物と水を保管しておくべきかを知っていて，災害の間の地元の避難所がどこにあるかも知っている。驚きだよ！

彩：うちの家族もそうよ。緊急事態に備えることは誰にとっても大切よ。

ボブ：賛成だ。アメリカへ帰った後で，うちの家族にも災害に備えて食べ物と水を保管しておくように言うよ。

語句

invent「～を発明する」 support「～を支える」
evacuation drill「避難訓練」
strong point「強み，長所」 disaster「災害」
earthquake「地震」
emergency kit「非常用品(一式)」
store「～を蓄える，保管する」 shelter「避難所」
in case of ～「～の場合に備えて」

002 ① ア　② ア　③ ウ　④ エ
⑤ (A) **jam**　(B) **events**
(C) **information**

解説 ①会話の状況から考えて，ア(ところで)が適切。イ(全部で)，ウ(たとえば)，エ(もちろん)では不自然。

②「もしぼくが(a)…と(b)それら[トマト]がどのようにして育てられたかを知っていれば安心する」という文を完成する。

ア 誰がそれらを作ったか
イ 彼はなぜそれらを育てたか
ウ それらはいつ売られたか
エ 何が値段を下げたか

かおるは直前の発言で，トマトの箱にはⓐ農家の名前とⓑ無農薬栽培であることが書かれている，と言っている。(a)はⓐ，(b)はⓑに当たる。したがって(a)に入るのはアである。

③「道の駅は地元の農家にとってよい(場所だ)，なぜなら農家は…ことができるから」という文を完成する。

ア 休憩して町の歴史について学ぶ
イ 作物を育てて訪問客の名前を見る
ウ 自分で値段を決めて自分の作物を売る
エ 他の地域の資料館を訪ねてより多くの作物を見せる

かおるの直前の発言に「祖母は自分で育てたものを使った手作り品を道の駅で売っている」という内容があるので，ウが正しい。

④「それらの(道の駅を訪ねてくる)訪問客たちは…と思う」という文を完成する。

ア 地元の産品を売るチャンスがある

イ　地元の農家が他の産品を買うのを助ける
ウ　地元の人々に他の市へ行くようにと言う
エ　地元の地域社会をより活発にする

常識的に考えてエが正解。直前のかおるの最後の発言(Local people become more cheerful.)の内容にも合う。

⑤かおるの発言を注意して読めば，空所に入る語がわかる。完成したメールの意味は次のとおり。

「お母さんへ
今日，すてきな場所を訪ねました。道の駅というところです。
地元の農家の人たちは，そこで新鮮な野菜や果物を売ることができます。(A)ジャムなどの手作りの品も年中売っています。多くの人を引き付けるために，たくさんの面白い(B)イベントが計画されるそうです。また，訪問客は観光のための役に立つ(C)情報を集めることができます。
来週他の道の駅へ行くのが楽しみです！
それでは
トム」

全訳

かおる：ここで休憩しましょう。
トム：いいよ。ここは何？
かおる：ここは道の駅よ。車のための駅なの。トイレを使ったり休んだりできるわ。
トム：見て！ ここにたくさんの野菜や果物が売られているよ。とても新鮮で，あまり高くない。
かおる：ええ，農家の人たちがここの近くの畑から持ってくるの。自分が出した品の値段を決められるのよ。
トム：いいね！ ところで，トマトの箱には何が印刷されているの？
かおる：田中さんという，農家の名前よ。その人が農薬を使わずに育てたとも書いてあるわ。
トム：なるほど。誰が作ってどうやって育てたのかがわかれば，安心できるね。
かおる：私もそう思うわ。
トム：ええと，農家の人たちは他には何か売っているの？
かおる：ええ，手作りの品も売っているわ。たとえば，私のおばあちゃんは一年中ジャムを売っているの。自分の畑で育てたブルーベリーで作るのよ。人気があって，すぐに売れるわ。
トム：それはいいね。
かおる：道の駅は，自分で値段を決められて，自分の作物を売ることができるから，地元の農家にはいい場所だわ。
トム：そう思うよ。この道の駅だけで売っているオリジナル品が買えるね。
かおる：それに，道の駅ではたくさんの人を呼ぶために催されるオリジナルのイベントも楽しめるのよ。
トム：本当？ どんなイベントがあるの？
かおる：たとえば，この道の駅では毎月刃物研ぎのイベントがあるわ。この町の会社の中には，江戸時代から高品質の刃物を作っているところもあるの。この建物の隣にそれらの品の資料館があるわ。
トム：へえ，歴史も学べるんだね。
かおる：それに，旅の便利な情報もたくさん手に入るわ。道の駅はその町の情報を広めているの。他の市から大勢の人がそこを訪れて，週末はいつも混雑しているわ。地元の人たちも活気が出るわね。
トム：そうだね。道の駅はたくさんの人を引き付ける。そこに来た人たちが地域社会をより活発にするんだね。ぼくもいろいろな道の駅を訪ねてみたいよ。
かおる：来週，別の道の駅へ行くのはどう？
トム：それはすてきだね。

語句

have a break「休憩する」
take a rest「休息をとる」 print「～を印刷する」
grow「～を栽培する」 handmade「手作りの」
product「作物，製品」
original「オリジナルの，独創的な」
next to ～「～の隣に」 spread「～を広める」
attract「～を引き付ける」

003	
① ウ　② エ　③ エ	
④ **scent**	
⑤ [1] イ　[2] ア　[3] イ　[4] イ　[5] ア	
⑥ [1] ア　[2] イ　[3] ア　[4] イ　[5] イ	
⑦ ア	

解説 ① enjoy(～を楽しむ)の後ろに動詞を置くときは，動名詞(watching)にする。
② with the leaves off は「葉が落ちた状態で」という意味(→精読)。
③ I am excited は「私は興奮[わくわく]している」という意味(→精読)。
④ has wonderful fragrance(素晴らしい香り

を持つ)を，次の文でhave excellent scent(優れた香りを持つ)と言い換えている。

⑤[1]「マユミは長野で祖父母とともに過ごしている」。マユミは長野へ行く計画をあきらめたので誤り。

[2]「クラブの会合は1月に行われる(だろう)」。マユミは会合を1月12日に行いたいと考えているので正しい。

[3]「部員たちは校舎の中に設置するために昨年花壇を作った」。マユミのメールによれば，花壇は校舎の中ではなく校舎の外(入り口の近く)にあるので誤り。

[4]「冬に庭園にバラを植えるのはよくない」。マユミのメールによれば，2月(冬)はバラを植えるのに適した時期だから誤り。

[5]「マユミはバラの庭園に関する部員たちの考えを知りたがっている」。マユミのメールの最後の文の内容に一致するので正しい。

⑥[1]「ケントは庭園を生徒にとってよい場所にするためのよい案を持っている」。ケントのメールの2文目の内容から考えて正しい。

[2]「ケントはオフィーリアとウィリアム・シェイクスピアを庭園に植えたいと思っている」。ケントが植えたいと思っているのはオフィーリアとティニーグレイスだから誤り。

[3]「人々は時にティニーグレイスをフレグラントヒル(香りの丘)と呼ぶ」。ケントのメールの最後から3文目の内容に一致するので正しい。

[4]「オフィーリアとティニーグレイスはどちらもフランス産である」。前者はフランス産だが後者は日本産だから誤り。

[5]「多くの人がそれらのバラを愛するのは，ウィリアム・シェイクスピアの劇が好きだからだ」。the roses とはオフィーリアとティニーグレイスのこと。ケントのメールの最後の文によれば，多くの人がそれらを愛するのはよい香りを持つからである。したがって誤り。

⑦マユミのメールによれば，部員たちは昨年，バラの花壇を作るために校舎の入り口のそばの土を掘り起こした。ケントのメールにもIt [=the garden] is beside the entrance(それ[庭園]は入り口のそばにある)とある。したがってアが正しい。

精読

◆Roses are sleeping now **with the leaves off** (*l*.12)(バラは今，葉を落として眠っている)：**with A B** の形は「**A** が **B** である状態で」の意味を表す(A＝名詞，B＝形容詞，分詞など)。The leaves are off. は「葉が(枝から離れて)落ちて[散って]いる」の意味。これをもとに，with the leaves off(葉が落ちている状態で)という形を作ることができる。

◆**I am excited to read** your e-mail about our new garden. (*l*.21)(ぼくたちの新しい庭園についての君のメールを読んで，わくわくしています)：excite は「(事物が)(人)を興奮させる」という意味の動詞。人が主語のときは，I am excited の形で「私は興奮させられている[わくわくしている]」という意味を表す。英語には「人に～な感情を起こさせる」という意味の動詞が多くあり，それらを受動態(**be** 動詞＋過去分詞)で使うと「(人が)～な気持ちだ」という意味を表す。その後ろにはしばしば感情の原因を表す不定詞(「～して」)を置く。

・I **was surprised to hear** the news.
(私はその知らせを聞いて驚いた)

→ surprise は「(人)を驚かせる」という意味の動詞。I was surprised は「私は驚かされた→私は驚いた」という意味になる。to hear は驚いた原因を表す。

◆I want to tell you my idea to **make the garden popular** among the students. (*ll*.21-22)(生徒の間で庭園の人気を高めるためのぼくのアイデアをお伝えしたいと思います)：make the garden だけだと「庭園を作る」の意味だが，make the garden popular は VOC(第5文型)の形で，「庭園が人気の高い状態を作る→庭園の人気を高める」ということ。このように make は，しばしば〈**make** ＋ O ＋ C[形容詞]〉の形で「O を C(の状態)にする」という意味を表す。

全訳

発信者：マユミ・サトウ
受信者：園芸部員の皆さん
日付：2022年1月3日　9時15分
あけましておめでとうございます。
休暇を楽しんでいますか。私は長野の祖父母の家に泊まる予定を立てましたが，新型コロナウイルス感染症が原因でその考えを断念しなければなりませんでした。そこで家にいて，両親と一緒にテレビを見て楽しんでいます。
クラブの会合を1月12日にしてはどうかと思っています。当日は今年の園芸計画について話したいと思います。私たちは昨年，校舎の入り口の近くにバラの花壇を作るために地面を掘り起こしました。2月は庭園にバラを植えるのに最適な季節の1つです。バラは今，葉を落として眠っていて，春が来るのを待っています。庭園に関する皆さんの考えを聞かせてください。
よろしく
マユミ・サトウ
WS園芸クラブ部長

発信者：ケント・サイトウ
受信者：マユミ・サトウ
日付：2022年1月3日　11時40分
あけましておめでとうございます。
新しい庭園についてのメールを読んで，わくわくしています。生徒の間で庭園の人気を高めるためのぼくのアイデアをお伝えしたいと思います。場所が大切だとぼくは思います。庭園は入り口のそばにあるので，校舎に出入りするときバラのそばを通るのは楽しい時間になるでしょう。庭園には2つのバラを推薦したいと思います。1つはオフィーリア，もう1つはティニーグレイスです。オフィーリアはフランス原産で，世界的に有名なバラの1つです。ウィリアム・シェイクスピアの『ハムレット』という劇の登場人物にちなんで名づけられました。一方ティニーグレイスは日本が原産です。このバラはフレグラントヒル(香りの丘)とも呼ばれます。この名前は，素晴らしい香りを持つという意味です。それらのバラはとてもよい香りなので，世界中で多くの人に愛されています。
よろしく
ケント・サイトウ
WS園芸クラブ

語句

bed「苗床，花壇」　key「秘訣，肝心なこと」
beside「～のそばに」
pass by ～「～のそばを通り過ぎる」
world famous「世界的に有名な」
be named after ～「～にちなんで名づけられる」
on the other hand「一方(では)」

004
① ウ　② エ　③ イ　④ ア
⑤ ウ　⑥ エ　⑦ エ　⑧ ウ
⑨ エ

解説 ①「どれが正しいですか。最も適切な答えを下から選びなさい」という問い。
ア　カナダの生徒たちはたいてい，1つの季節だけスポーツをすることを好む。
イ　カナダの生徒たちは，私設のクラブでスポーツをする方がよいと考えている。
ウ　カナダの生徒たちは，学校だけでなく学校外でもいくつかのクラブに入ることができる。
エ　カナダの生徒たちは多くのスポーツをやってみたいと思わない。
　ウがジョーンズ先生の最初の発言の内容に一致する。not only A but (also) B は「A だけでなく B も」の意味。
②「[A]に入る最も適切な答えを選びなさい」という問い。2つの[A]の後ろには前の発言に対する具体的な説明が続いているので，エ(たとえば)が正しい。ア(～によれば)，イ(ところで)，ウ(まず最初に)では意味が通らない。
③「[B]はどういう意味ですか。最も適切な答えを下から選びなさい」という問い。
ア　私はバスケットボール部に入っていたくない。
イ　他のスポーツをするのはよい考えではない。
ウ　バレーボールをする方がバスケットボールよりもよい。
エ　多くのスポーツを楽しむことは素晴らしい。
[B]は「あなたの意見には賛成しません[反対です]」という意味。直前のアヤノの発言から考えて，イが正解。
④「[C]に入る最も適切な文を下から選びなさい」という問い。前の I've [= I have] played が現在完了形なので，ア(私が6歳のころから(ずっと))を入れるのが適切。イ(私が小学生のとき)，ウ(私が8歳になった後)のような過去形を使った形は，現在完了形の文では使えない。またエは for(～の間に)という前置詞の後ろに文の形を置いているので，文法的に成り立たない。
⑤「[D]に入る最も適切な語を下から選びなさい」という問い。関係代名詞の that を入れると，find the sport <u>that</u> you really like は「あなたが本当に好きなスポーツを見つける」という意味になり，意味が通る。この that は目的格の

関係代名詞だから，省略することもできる。次の例も同様。

・Soccer is the sport **(that)** I like best.
（サッカーは私が一番好きなスポーツです）

⑥「[E]はどういう意味ですか。最も適切な答えを下から選びなさい」という問い。

ア　ミカは人々が自分の体をよく動かしていることを理解した。
イ　ソフトボールをすることは重要であり生活に役立つかもしれない。
ウ　1つのスポーツが上手になりたければ，他のスポーツのことを考える必要はない。
エ　他のスポーツをすることは人々にとってよいことだ。

I see. は「わかります[理解しました]」の意味。ミカは直前のアヤノの「他のスポーツから学べることがある」という発言を肯定しているので，エが正解。

⑦「[F]はどういう意味ですか。最も適切な答えを下から選びなさい」という問い。

ア　ミカと友人たちは苦しいときに一緒に練習してきたので，よい友情を築いた。
イ　新しい友人を作るために多くのスポーツをやってみることが大切だ。
ウ　私たちのよりよいコミュニケーション能力のためには，1つのスポーツに集中するのは最善の方法だ。
エ　さまざまなクラブに入ることによって，新しい友人を作りコミュニケーション能力を高めることができる。

エマは直前のアヤノの発言を受けて「わかります[理解できます]」と言っているので，エが正解。

⑧ア　私たちはよりよい選手になるために何年間も1つのスポーツに集中すべきだ。
イ　より多くのスポーツをすることは，私たちのコミュニケーション能力を高めるのに役立つことがある。
ウ　プロの運動選手になりたいとき，簡単な方法は1つもない。
エ　友人と一緒に長時間過ごすと，友情は強くなるかもしれない。

アとエはエマとミカの発言に，イはアヤノの発言に含まれている。ウのようなことは誰も言っていないので，ウが正解。

⑨完成した文章の意味は，次のとおり。

「1つのスポーツをするのと，さまざまなスポーツをするのとでは，どちらがよりよいか。今日私たちはそれについて話した。[3]よりよい選手になるためには1つのスポーツだけをすべきだと私は信じていた。[2]しかし，私たちは他のスポーツから新しいことを学べると聞いたとき，私の考えは変わり始めた。また，1つのスポーツだけをすることによって親友に会えるとも聞いた。[1]私が今日聞いたどちらの考えも正しいと思うので，どちらがよりよいかを決めるのは難しい。」

精読

◆I think that playing **more than one** sport is better.（*l.*8）（私は2つ以上のスポーツをする方がいいと思います）：**more than X** は「X より多い」の意味で，X は含まない。したがって more than one sport は「1つより多いスポーツ→2つ以上のスポーツ」という意味を表す。

全訳

ジョーンズ先生：こんにちは，皆さん。今日はスポーツとクラブ活動について話します。日本では生徒はたいてい1つのクラブに入っていて，学校で1つのスポーツをする生徒もいます。でもカナダでは，生徒はたいてい，学校や時には学校外の私設のクラブで，季節ごとに違うスポーツをします。たとえば，私は秋と冬にはバスケットボールをして，春と夏にはテニスをしました。1つのスポーツだけをするのと，さまざまなスポーツをするのとでは，どちらの方がいいですか。

アヤノ：私は2つ以上のスポーツをする方がいいと思います。私はバスケットボール部に入っていますが，他のスポーツにも興味があります。いろんなスポーツを楽しめるのは素晴らしいことです。

エマ：私はあなたに賛成しません。私は学校でバレーボール部に入っています。いい選手になりたければ，バレーボールだけを練習する必要があります。

ミカ：私もそう思います。私は6歳のころからソフトボールをしています。それに集中してきたからずいぶん上達したのだと思います。

アヤノ：でも，多くの違うスポーツをすれば，本当に好きなスポーツが見つかります。

ミカ：私はソフトボールが一番好きだから，そうする必要はないと思います。

ジョーンズ先生：あなたは本当にソフトボールが好きなんですね，ミカ。他に何か考えはありますか，アヤノ？

アヤノ：他のスポーツから数々のことを学べます。たとえば，違うスポーツをすれば，違う体の動かし方がわかります。それはソフトボールをするのに役立つでしょう，ミカ。

ミカ：なるほど。プロの運動選手でも違うスポーツをすると聞いたことがあります。

ジョーンズ先生：そのとおりです。プロの運動選手の中にはそうする人もいます。そうすれば違うスポーツ活動から多くのことを学ぶいい機会になるかもしれません。

エマ：いろんなスポーツをやってみるのはいい考えだと私も思い始めました。

ミカ：ちょっと聞いてください。長い間１つのスポーツをし続けると，チームの結束が強まります。よい友人を作ることもできます。私はソフトボール部で親友に出会いました。私たちはクラブで苦しい時間をともにして練習してきたので，お互いをとてもよく理解しています。

アヤノ：それはいいことです。でも別のクラブで他のスポーツをすれば，多くの人と友だちになれます。それに，新しい人と知り合ってコミュニケーション能力も高められます。

エマ：それはわかります。でも私もバレーボールをし続けたので，親友に出会いました。どちらがいいのかはわかりません。スポーツについてのどちらの考え方にもよい点があります。

語句

improve「上達する，〜を向上させる」
focus on 〜「〜に集中する」 athlete「(運動)選手」
united「結束して」

005 イ

解説 「カナとメアリーはいつ音楽祭に行くことになるか」。メアリーの「８月１日または３日ではどうか」という提案に対して，カナは「テニスの練習を翌日に移す」と言っている。カナは８月１日(木曜日)にはテニスの練習があり，３日(土曜日)はかもめ湖へ行く。したがってカナが変更しようとしている予定は８月１日のテニスの練習であり，２人はその日に音楽祭に行くことになるので，イが正解。

全訳

カナとメアリーは高校生である。彼女らはこの夏の予定を見ている。

カナ：こんにちは，メアリー。かもめミュージアムが７月22日から８月11日まで音楽祭を開く予定なの。一緒に行く？

メアリー：いいわね！

カナ：音楽祭の日は毎日，午前中にギターコンサートやピアノコンサートなどがあるわ。私は特に『ニューヨークの歌姫たち』という人気のミュージカルに興味があるの。そのミュージカルは，音楽祭の間，毎週火曜，木曜，土曜の午後２時に上演される予定よ。

メアリー：見たいわ！ いつミュージアムに行きましょうか。

カナ：ええと。私は７月23日か８月10日がいいわ。

メアリー：ごめんなさい，私はどちらの日も予定があるの。８月１日か８月３日はどう？

カナ：私は毎週木曜日の午後はテニスの練習よ。８月３日と４日は，かもめ湖へ行くの。

メアリー：私たちは本当に忙しいわね。両方の予定に適した日が見当たらないわ。

カナ：ええと，私がテニスの練習を翌日に移せば，その日に音楽祭に行けるわ。

メアリー：ありがとう。私は午前中のピアノコンサートにも興味があるの。その日にミュージアムで午前10時に会うのはどう？

カナ：いいわ。待ち遠しいわね！

(予定表は省略)

006

① ア
② **all his family members**
③ [1] ウ　[2] ア
④ イ　⑤ エ

解説 ①ア 彼らはそれをどう思っていますか。
イ あなたはどこで彼らと話しますか。
ウ 彼らはどのくらいの頻度で遅く帰宅しますか。
エ あなたが私に情報を与えることができるのはなぜですか。

全訳の下線部[A]を参照。they は直前の文中の my parents(太郎の両親)を指す。[A]に続いて太郎が「今晩彼ら(両親)に尋ねよう」と答えていることから，アが適切。マイクは「帰宅が遅いことをご両親自身はどう思っているのか」と尋ねている。

②「太郎は父親と一緒の時間がもっとほしいと思っており，…が同じことを願っていると彼は言う」という文を完成する。*l.*19でマイクが太郎に You want more time with your father, too, right? と尋ね，それに対して太郎が Yes, of course, and <u>all my family members</u>

wish the same. と答えているので，空所には下線の4語が入る(my は his に変える)。

③[1]「2011年には，日本の若者のうち(　)パーセントが，家族の方が大事だと考えていた」という文を完成する。2011年のグラフを見ると，「家族と仕事のどちらがより大事ですか」という質問に対して Family(家族)と回答した者が52.9パーセントいた。よってウが正解。

[2]「2017年には，人々のうち(　)パーセントが，家族は仕事ほど大事ではないと考えていた」。less は more の反対の意味を表し，A is less important than B は「AはBよりも[Bほど]大事ではない＝Bの方が大事だ」ということ。2017年のグラフを見ると，Job(仕事の方が大事だ)と回答した者は12.7パーセントだった。したがってアが正解。

④ア　物事はそれほど単純だ。
イ　物事はそれほど単純ではない。
ウ　彼らは職場で仕事をすることに満足するだろう。
エ　彼らは職場で仕事をすることに満足しないだろう。

全訳の下線部[B]を参照。マイクのこの発言は，太郎の「職場で仕事をするか家で仕事をするかを選ぶことができればいい」というアイデアに対する感想である。その後の2人のやり取りから考えて，イが適切。

⑤ア「マイクは1年前に日本に来たので，日本人が長時間働くことを知っている」。マイクの2番目の発言(I'm not sure of this)の内容に反するので誤り。

イ「太郎の母親は太郎と弟からの手助けをもっと必要としている，とマイクは思っている」。太郎によれば，母親は小さな弟の世話があるので父親にもっと家にいてほしいと思っている。マイクが太郎の母親をどう思っているかは会話の中に出てこないので誤り。

ウ「道路や橋やビルを作る仕事をしている人たちのことを多くの人が考える必要がある，と太郎は言っている」。太郎は「多くの人は働き方について考える必要がある」と言っているだけで，そのような仕事の人々のことを考えるべきとは言っていない。

エ「太郎とマイクは，家族と一緒にいたり趣味に使える時間のある仕事につきたいと思っている」。最後の2人のやり取りから考えて，これが正しい。

精読

◆ I'm **not** sure, **either**. (*l*.6) (ぼくもよくわからない)：〈否定文＋**either**〉の形は「**S** もまた～ではない」の意味を表す。

・"I don't like noisy music."　"I **don't**, **either**." (「私は騒がしい音楽が好きではありません」「私もそうです[好きではありません]」)

→返答の文は Me, neither. とも言う。I don't, too. とは言わない。

◆ I **only** talked with my father. (*l*.13) (父さんとだけ話した)：only(～だけ)は，書き言葉では修飾する語の直前に置くのが原則。この文は「父親(と)だけ」の意味だが，I talked only with my father. (または I talked with only my father.)の only を前に出した形になっている。話し言葉ではこのように only を前に出すのが普通。

[参考] I only talked with my father. は「私は父親と話しただけだ(他のことはしなかった)」の意味にも解釈できる。しかし I ónly talked with my fáther. と単語を強調して読めば，「父親とだけ(話した)」の意味になる。

全訳

マイク：ねえ，太郎。1つ質問していい？
太郎：いいよ，マイク。何を知りたいの？
マイク：ぼくが日本に来る前，日本人は長時間働くとまわりの人たちが言ったんだ。ぼくはここに来て1年になるけど，そうなのかよくわからない。君はこれをどう思う？
太郎：ぼくもよくわからない。でも両親の帰宅が遅いことはよくあるよ。
マイク：[A]ご両親はそれをどう思っているの？
太郎：そうだね，今晩聞いてみて，明日君に教えるよ。
マイク：いいね！　ありがとう，太郎。
[翌日]
太郎：やあ，マイク。少し時間はある？
マイク：いいよ，太郎。ゆうべはご両親と話したの？
太郎：父さんとだけね。でも面白い記事も見つけたんだ。
マイク：ああ，ありがとう！　お父さんは何と言ったの？
太郎：ええと，父さんは自分が長時間働いているとは思っていない。でも家から職場までは長時間かかると思っている。
マイク：へえ，お父さんの職場は君の家から遠いの？
太郎：うん，遠いよ。1時間かかる。父さんはぼくらと一緒に過ごす時間がもっとほしいと言っていた。

マイク：なるほど。君もお父さんと一緒の時間がもっとほしいんだね？

太郎：ああ，もちろん。それに家族全員が同じことを願っているよ。母さんは，特にぼくの８歳の弟の世話をしているから，父さんと一緒の時間がもっと必要だと言っている。

マイク：わかるよ。

太郎：ぼくが見つけた記事によると，近ごろの日本の若者は，仕事より家族の方が大事だと考えている。このグラフを見て。ここには2011年に3,000人を対象とした調査と，2017年に10,000人を対象とした調査の結果が載っているんだ。対象者は16歳から29歳までの人だよ。家族と仕事のどちらがより大事か，という質問だ。

(グラフは省略)

マイク：へえ，2017年には，家族の方が大事だと考えた人が63パーセント以上いたんだね。

太郎：そのとおり。2011年から約11パーセント分だけ上がっているよ。

マイク：なるほど。だから，家族の方が大事だと考える若者がますます増えていると言えるわけだね。

太郎：そう。多くの人は働き方について考える必要があると思うよ。ああ，1つアイデアがある。もし父さんが職場と家のどちらかで働くことを選べるなら，ぼくと一緒に過ごす時間を増やせるだろう。技術によってそれが可能になったよね。そうすれば働く人はみんな喜ぶんじゃないかな。

マイク：君はそう思うの？ [B]物事はそれほど単純じゃないとぼくは思うよ。

太郎：へえ，本当に？ なぜだい？

マイク：そうだね，たとえば，道路や橋やビルを作る仕事をしている人たちのことを考えてみよう。そんな仕事を家でやるのは不可能だよね？

太郎：ああ，そのとおりだ。いろんな仕事についている人たちには，いろんな働き方があるからね。実際，ぼくの母さんは看護師で，家で仕事をすることはできないと思う。母さんは患者さんを助けるために病院へ仕事に行って，自分の仕事に誇りを持っていると言っているよ。

マイク：素晴らしいね！ ぼくも君のお母さんのように自分の仕事に誇りを持てればいいと思うよ！ それに，家族と一緒に過ごしたり趣味にかける時間のある仕事につきたいとも思う。

太郎：ぼくもだ。個人の生活がより充実すれば，仕事ももっと楽しくなるね！

007 ① (1) **eating too much is bad for my[your, the] health**
(4) **would you like to[will you] come to my house tomorrow?**
(5) **I'm looking forward to tomorrow's dinner!**
② [A] イ [B] オ [C] ウ [D] エ [E] ア
③ その食べ物と結びついた快感を脳に送り，脳がその快感を覚えている
④ **lonely[alone], connected**
⑤ **remembers, memories, Making**

解説 ①(1) S is bad for my health(Sは私の健康に悪い)のSとして，eating too much(食べ過ぎること)という動名詞で始まる句を使う。
(4)「～しませんか」と相手を誘う場合には，Would you like[Do you want] to ～？やWill[Won't] you ～？を使う。
(5) look forward to ～「～を楽しみに待つ」。書き言葉では現在形(I look ...)も使うが，話し言葉では現在進行形にするのが普通。「明日のディナー」はthe dinner tomorrowでもよい。
②全訳を参照。ア How about you?「あなた(の方)はどうですか」，イ What do you mean (by that)?「(それは)どういう意味ですか」，ウ What's up?「どうした[何があった]の？」，「ごきげんいかが？(≒ How are you?)」，エ Would you like ～？「～がほしい[～はいかが]ですか」，オ You said it.「そのとおりです(自分が言おうとしていることを相手が先に言った，ということ)」
③下線部(2)の前の２つの文の内容を答える。
④完成した文の意味は，「comfort foodを食べると(あなたは)寂しい[一人だ]と感じないし，人々とつながっていると感じることができる」。この前のハンナの発言中のfeel less lonely especially when we are left aloneを手がかりにして考える。
⑤完成した文の意味は，「ドロシーは祖父母と過ごした時を覚えている。comfort foodは楽しい時についての記憶を呼び戻す。comfort foodを作ることは，彼女が自分の感情をコントロール

するのにも役立つ」。ドロシーの最後から3番目の発言，それに続くスージーの発言(Comfort food brings back happy memories from our past.)，ドロシーの最後の発言(making comfort food gives us control over our feelings)を手がかりにして考える。

精読

◆Your brain remembers those good feelings. **That's why** you will want to continue to eat comfort food.(*ll*.13-15)（脳はそれらの快感を覚えている。だから comfort food を食べ続けたくなる）：**That's why** ～は「そういうわけで～」の意味を表す頻出表現。直訳は「それが～である理由だ」(why = the reason why)。「それ」は前の内容を指す。

◆That **reminds** me **of** the words of a famous chef, "Food is like a hug."(*l*.26)（それを聞くと私は，ある有名なシェフの「料理はハグのようなものだ」という言葉を思い出す）：S **reminds** O **of** ～ は「S[物]はO[人]に～を思い出させる」という意味。Sに当たるThatは，直前のスージーの発言内容を指す。このように「S＝物，O＝人」の形の文(無生物主語構文は，「SによってOは～する」と訳すと自然な日本語になることが多い。この文の場合，「それは私に～を思い出させる→それによって私は～を思い出す」となる。なお「料理はハグ[抱擁]のようなものだ」とは，「料理を食べると作り手と抱き合っているように感じられる[作り手の愛情が伝わってくる]」のような意味を表す。

◆I also **read** (in a book) **that** making comfort food gives us control over our feelings.(*ll*.44-46)（comfort food を作ると自分の感情をコントロールできるとも本で読んだ）：read that ... は「…ということを読む」の意味。この文ではthatの前にin a book(本の中で)が加えられている。bookとthatをつなげて読まないように。thatの後ろはSVOO(第4文型)で，直訳は「comfort food を作ることは，私たちに自分の感情のコントロールを与える」。

全訳

ドロシー：チョコレートとクッキー！ まあ，それを全部食べているの？

ハンナ：そうね，今日，大事な発表を終えたところよ。ハードな仕事が終わってくつろいだとたんに，食べたくなったの。食べ過ぎるのは健康によくないとわかっているけど，やめられないわ。

ドロシー：じゃあ，それらはあなたにとって comfort foods(安らぎの食べ物)ね。

ハンナ：[A]どういう意味？

ドロシー：食べると楽しくなるもののことよ。

ハンナ：[B]そのとおりね。チョコレートとクッキーは私の気分を落ち着かせてくれるわ。だから，空腹でなくても時々食べたくなるの。

ドロシー：ええ。それは1つには脳のせいでもあると聞いたわ。理由の1つは「ドーパミン」よ。自分においしく感じられる comfort food を食べると，ドーパミンがたくさん出る。脳へドーパミンが comfort food と結びついた快感を送る。脳はそれらの快感を覚えている。だから comfort food を食べ続けたくなるの。チョコレートやクッキーは，みんな comfort food のいい例ね。

ハンナ：なるほど。

スージー：こんにちは，ドロシー！ こんにちは，ハンナ！ [C]元気にしてる？

ハンナ：こんにちは，スージー。[D]あなたも食べる？

スージー：まあ，スイーツを食べているのね！

ドロシー：こんにちは，スージー。ええと，私たちは comfort food のことを話していたの。ハンナの comfort food はチョコレートとクッキーよ。

スージー：comfort food ですって！ 私のは違うわ。私は子どものころにママが作ってくれたチキンスープを覚えていて，時々飲みたくなるの。ほら，私は一人暮らしだから。

ハンナ：ああ。有名なシェフの「料理はハグのようなものだ」という言葉を思い出すわね。特に独りぼっちのときに，料理は私たちが寂しく思うのを和らげてくれることがよくあるわ。

ドロシー：comfort food は私たちに「つながり」の気持ちも与えてくれるわ。

ハンナ：そうね。[E]あなたはどう？ あなたの comfort food は何，ドロシー？

ドロシー：ええと，ミートパイね。子どものころによく食べていた料理よ。クリスマスや私の誕生日のような特別な日に，おばあちゃんがミートパイを作ってくれて，一緒に楽しく過ごしたわ。

スージー：comfort food は子どものころの過去の経験と結びついていて，私たちは家族や世話をしてくれた人を思い出せるわ。comfort food は過去の楽しい思い出を呼び戻してくれるのね。

ハンナ：料理と記憶の結びつきはとても強いわ。脳が料理を食べているみたいに。comfort food は人それぞれね。

ドロシー：食べ物のことを話していたら，おなかがすいてきたわ！ ねえ，明日私の家に来ない？ディナーに招待するわ！ ネットでレシピを見つけたパイを作るつもりよ。デザートにはチョコレートケーキを作るわ，ハンナ，それにスージー，あなたにはチキンスープを作りましょう！

スージー：すてきね！ あなたが料理上手なのは知っているけど，いいの？ それだけの種類の料理を作るにはとても時間がかかるかもしれないわ。

ドロシー：まあ，私は本当に料理が楽しいの。料理をしているときはいやなことを忘れられるわ。comfort food を作ると自分の感情をコントロールできるとも本で読んだしね。

ハンナ：まあ，ドロシー，おいしい料理のことを考えるだけで楽しいわ。それも脳の働きよね。明日のディナーを楽しみにしています！

語句

task「仕事，任務」
calm O down「O を落ち着かせる」
partly because ...「1つには…のために」
be connected with ～「～と結びついている」
remind O of ～「O に～を思い出させる」
hug「ハグ，抱擁」 bring back ～「～を引き戻す」
recipe「レシピ，調理法」
give O control over ～「O が～をコントロールできるようにする」

008 ① ウ　② エ　③ イ　④ イ
⑤ ア　⑥ オ，ク

解説 ①ア 最も速いハトだけが群れのリーダーになれる。

イ 群れのリーダーは，0.2秒ごとに群れがどこにいるかを確認する。

ウ 群れのリーダーは，1回の飛行の間に変わることもある。

エ ハトは隣のハトを見ることによって群れになって一緒に飛ぶ。

ユウタの最後から2番目の発言で，ユウタが Was there anything you learned from pigeons?(ハトから学んだことは何かある？)とハナに尋ね，ハナは I learned that sometimes a different member of the group can lead the group.(時にはグループの違うメンバーがそのグループを率いることができると学んだ)と答えている。したがってウが正解。

②ア ゾウはあなたに多くのよい思い出を与える

イ ゾウはあなたに楽しい時を思い出させる

ウ あなたはゾウのように過去のことを好む

エ あなたはゾウのように物覚えがよい

ユウタのこの後の発言から，ゾウは昔のことを記憶する能力が高いことがわかる。したがってエが正解。

③下線部の That sounds similar (to killer whale leaders.) は「それは(シャチのリーダーに)似ているように思われる」の意味。質問の意味は「この文章によると，ゾウとシャチはどのように似ているか」。

ア どちらも冬の間は自然の中で見つけにくい。

イ 群れのリーダーが多くの経験を持つ。

ウ 雄は狩りができるので，雌よりも長生きする。

エ 群れのリーダーは一番強い雌である。

上記の文の That(それ)とは，直前の「経験豊富なリーダーを持つゾウの群れの方が多く生き残った」という内容を指す。したがってイが正解。シャチの場合もゾウと同様に，経験豊富な雌に率いられた群れの方が生存確率が高くなる。

④**全訳**の下線部(4a)～(4c)を参照。シャチは雌の方が長生きなので，経験豊富な雌をリーダーとする群れの方が生存確率が高い，ということ。

⑤下線部の the first thing to do is to get to know my group members better は，S is C(S は C だ)という構造になっている。S は「最初にすべきこと」，C は「私のグループのメンバーたちをもっとよく知るようになること」(get to *do*「～するようになる」)。つまりハナは，「私は自分のグループのメンバーをもっとよく知る必要がある」と言っている。

ア 彼女は学校外でグループのメンバーたちと一緒に1日を過ごし，よい関係を築くだろう。

イ 彼女は図書館で動物に関する本を読み，よいリーダーになる方法についてより多くのことを学ぶだろう。

ウ 彼女はグループのメンバーたちに頼りすぎるのをやめ，自分がリーダーであることを彼らに示すだろう。

エ 彼女は理科の課題についての情報をインターネット上に公開し，それについてグループのメンバーたちに話すだろう。

会話全体の内容から判断して，アが正しい。

⑥ア「全員がすべての会合に来るけれど，ハナは理科の課題がうまくいっていないと感じている」。下線部が誤り。ハナによれば，会合を休んだメンバーもいた。

イ「以前の干ばつを経験したので，群れの１つでは多くのゾウが生き延びなかった」。下線部は「群れのリーダーが経験しなかった」が正しい。

ウ「ハナはグループのためによい決定を下すための知識を持っているので，シャチのリーダーに似ている」。オリバーによれば，下線部は「ゾウのリーダー」が正しい。

エ「リーダーになりたいチンパンジーは，他の者のことの代わりに自分のことを考えてえさを分配する」。下線部が本文の内容と逆なので誤り。

オ「チンパンジーのリーダーの行動は自分の群れのメンバーに影響を与えるので，自分のメンバーを援助することが彼らにとって重要だ」。ユウタの発言内容に一致する。

カ「ハナはハトから，リーダーがいつも群れを率いることによって自分の力を示す必要があると学んだ」。下線部のようなことは述べられていないので誤り。

キ「友人たちと話した後で，ハナは全員が責任を分担すべきだと気づいたので，彼女は他の誰かをリーダーにするだろう」。下線部の内容は会話に出てこないので誤り。

ク「ハナは動物たちから多くのことを学び，自分が以前よりもよいリーダーになれると思った」。会話の最後の部分の内容に一致する。

精読

◆*she **looks like** she **has** something **on her mind***(*l*.3)(彼女は何か気になることがあるように見える)：look like は「～のように見える」の意味で，後ろには名詞を置くのが原則。くだけた表現では，この例のように(SV を含む)文の形を置くこともある(その場合は look as if とも言う)。**have O on one's mind** は「O[心配事など]が～の頭から離れない，O を気にかけている」という意味。**have O in mind**(O[計画など]を思い描いている)とは意味が違うので注意。

［参考］ on の本来の意味は「接触している」。have O on one's mind は「O が～の頭[心]にくっついている」というイメージ。in mind だと単に「頭の中にある」という意味になる。

◆I don't think that **everyone** is serious about the project.(*ll*.13-14)(全員が課題に本気になっているとは私は思わない)：「私は…ではないと思う」は，**I don't think (that) ....** と表現するのが普通。

(a) I think this book isn't interesting.
(b) I don't think this book is interesting.

２つの文が表す実質的な意味は同じだが，(b)の方がよく使われる。

［参考］ １つの理由は，英語では not をなるべく前に置く傾向があるから。もう１つは，(a)だと「その本は面白くない」と断定しているように聞こえるので，(b)(その本は面白いとは思わない)の方が穏やかな言い方になる。

次に，I **don't** think that **everyone** is serious は「みんなが真剣なわけではない[中には真剣でない人もいる]と私は思う」(部分否定)という意味を表す(**not** + **every** ～「すべての～が…というわけではない」)。「真剣な人は誰もいない」ではない点に注意(その意味なら I don't think that anyone is serious と表現する(not + anyone = no one))。

◆You've **seen** pigeons **flying** in the sky, right? I'm always surprised when **I see** a big group of pigeons suddenly **turn** in the same direction at the same time.(*ll*.19-21)(ハトが空を飛んでいるのを見たことがあるでしょ？ 大きなハトの群れが突然同時に同じ方向に向きを変えるのを見ると，いつも驚くわ)：see(見える)は次のように使う。

① **see** + **A** +～**ing**「**A** が～しているのが見える」
② **see** + **A** +動詞の原形「**A** が～するのが見える」

１文目は①，２文目は②の形。hear(聞こえる)，feel(感じる)などの感覚を表す動詞も，同様の使い方ができる。

◆I want to know how the leader of the flock can **make** the other pigeons **follow** along.(*ll*.24-25)(群れのリーダーがどうすれば他のハトを従わせることができるのか知りたいわ)：make と let は次のように使う。

・**make** + **A** +動詞の原形「**A** に～させる」
・**let** + **A** +動詞の原形「**A** に～させておく」

make は「強制」，let は「許可」を表す。

◆That's **surprising**.(*l*.38)(それは意外だわ)：surprise((人)を驚かせる)，excite((人)を興奮さ

せる)など「人に〜な感情を起こさせる」という意味で使う動詞に**ing**を加えると，「(事物が)人に〜な感情を起こさせるような」という意味を表す。たとえばexcitedは「(人が)興奮している」，excitingは「(事物が)人を興奮させるような，わくわくする」。またsurprisedは「(人が)驚いている」，surprisingは「(事物が)人を驚かせるような，意外な」の意味。

◆ **They** live longer, so **they** have more experience and know where **they** can find food. (*ll*.66-67)（雌のシャチの方が長生きだから経験も豊富で，えさをどこで見つけられるかを知っている）：代名詞は前に出てきた名詞を指すのに使う。この文では，theyは何を指すかを考える必要がある。直前のオリバーの発言にはmale killer whales usually live until they are 35 years old, but females often live until they are 60とあり，theyは下線部のどちらかを指すと考えられる。この文は「雄のシャチの寿命は35年だが，雌の寿命は60年だ」という内容だから，They live longerは「雌の方が(雄より)長生きだ」と解釈できる。つまり3つのtheyは，females [female killer whales]を指す。比較級を使った文では，比較する相手が明らかなときはthan以下を省略する。この文の場合も，They live longer = They live longer than males[male killer whales]と考えることができる。

全訳

リナ，ハナ，ユウタ，オリバーは放課後の教室にいる。オリバーはノルウェーからの留学生である。ハナは一人で席に座り，何か気になることがあるように見える。

リナ：どうしたの，ハナ？

ハナ：理科のグループ課題のことを考えていたの。うまくいっていないのよ。

ユウタ：君は課題のリーダーだよね？

ハナ：ええ，2週間後に発表しなきゃならないけど，全然準備ができていなくて。

オリバー：君たちが放課後に集まっているのをよく見かけるから，うまくいっているのかと思っていたよ。

ハナ：よく集まるけど，意見を言うのは一部のメンバーだけなの。きのうは，他に用事があると言って来なかった人もいたわ！ 全員が課題に本気になっているとは思えないの。

リナ：リーダーって大変だよね。

ハナ：私たちのグループを，ハトの群れみたいにしたいと思うことがあるわ。

ユウタ：え？

ハナ：ハトの群れ。ハトが空を飛んでいるのを見たことがあるでしょ？ 大きなハトの群れが突然同時に同じ方向に向きを変えるのを見ると，いつも驚くわ。

オリバー：どうしてハトのようになりたいの？

ハナ：グループ全員が1つのチームとして一緒に行動できるようになってもらいたいの。群れのリーダーがどうすれば他のハトを従わせることができるのか知りたいわ。

リナ：実際にリーダーがいるのかな？ ただ隣のハトがしているのと同じことをやっているだけだと思っていたよ。

ハナ：以前はそう思われていたわ。でも科学者によると，ハトは群れのどのメンバーでもなく，リーダーに従って方向を変えるそうよ。

オリバー：それはじいちゃんから聞いたことがあるよ。じいちゃんはバードウォッチングが大好きなんだ。

ユウタ：科学者たちはどうやって調べたの？

ハナ：ハトに小さなGPSをつけて，0.2秒ごとにハトがどこにいるかを確認するの。

ユウタ：ハトはどうやってリーダーを決めるの？

オリバー：普通は，一番速いハトがリーダーになるそうだ。でも，じいちゃんが面白い事実を教えてくれた。時には遅いハトが群れを率いることもあるから，その場合は1回の飛行の間でもリーダーは同じじゃないんだ。

リナ：本当？ それは意外だわ。動物の世界では，たいてい一番強い雄がリーダーになると思っていたから。

ユウタ：ぼくもそう思っていた。でも，時にはそうじゃない。たとえばゾウだ。先週見たテレビ番組では，リーダーは一番年上の雌だと言っていたよ。ところで，「ゾウのような記憶力を持つ」という表現を聞いたことはある？

ハナ：ないわ。どういう意味？

ユウタ：人がゾウのような記憶力を持っていれば，ゾウのように物覚えがいいという意味だよ。番組では，あるゾウのリーダーが，記憶力がよかったので干ばつから自分の群れを救ったという話をしていた。その群れでは多くのゾウが生き延びたのだけれど，別の群れでは半分近くが命を落としたんだ。

リナ：違いは何だったの？

ユウタ：どちらの群れにも経験豊富なリーダーがい

た。でも２番目の群れのリーダーの方が若くて，35年前の干ばつを経験していなかった。研究者たちによると，１番目の群れはリーダーが以前の干ばつを記憶していたから，生き延びることができたんだ。

オリバー：それはシャチのリーダーに似ているみたいだ。ぼくはノルウェーでよくシャチを見に行ったよ。

リナ：ノルウェーではシャチを見られるの？

オリバー：うん，特に冬の季節にね。ねえ，シャチにとっては，(4a)おばあちゃんと一緒に暮らすことが長生きの秘訣だって知っていたかい？ 研究によると若いシャチは，(4b)おばあちゃんがいなくなると命が危険になる可能性が高いそうだよ。

ユウタ：(4c)おじいちゃんじゃないのはなぜ？

オリバー：あのね，雄のシャチの寿命はたいてい35歳だけれど，雌は60歳まで生きることが多いんだ。

リナ：そんなに大きく違うなんて信じられない！

オリバー：雌のシャチの方が長生きだから経験も豊富で，えさをどこで見つけられるかを知っているんだ。

ハナ：つまり一部の動物にとっては，長生きするのに役立つ知識を持った動物に従うことが大切なのね。

オリバー：そのとおり。

ユウタ：チンパンジーもそうだね。一番小さくてもリーダーになれるんだ。

ハナ：そうなの？ どうやって？

ユウタ：力を使うやつもいるけど，頭を使ってトップに立つやつもいる。

ハナ：それで，どうやって？

ユウタ：チンパンジーがリーダーになりたければ，自分より相手のことを考えて，それから行動する。たとえば，えさを簡単に分けてやるとか。それにリーダーになった後は，他のチンパンジーがけんかをしているとき，勝ち目のない方の味方をする。

リナ：どうしてそんなことをするの？

ユウタ：自分の味方を得るためだよ。他のチンパンジーがそんな行動を見ると，彼らは安心して，リーダーに敬意を示すんだ。

オリバー：チンパンジーはとても頭がいいんだね！

ハナ：理科の課題がうまくいかなかった理由がやっとわかったわ。

オリバー：そうなの？

ハナ：原因は私よ。私はいいリーダーじゃないわ。

リナ：まあ，そんなこと言わないで。いつもとても頑張ってるじゃない。

ハナ：動物のリーダーの行動の話から，いいリーダーになる方法についてのヒントをもらったわ。

ユウタ：たとえば？

ハナ：チンパンジーから私が学んだのは，もし私がいいリーダーになりたければ，グループのメンバーのことをもっと考えて，支持を得られるように努めるべきだということよ。そうすることで，私たちはいい関係を築いてお互いを信頼できるようになるわ。

ユウタ：他に君が学んだことはある？

ハナ：知識が豊富なリーダーは，グループのためにいい決断をすることができるということね。

オリバー：ゾウやシャチみたいに？

ハナ：そう。知ってのとおり私にはそんなリーダーが持っているような経験はないけれど，それを補えるから大丈夫よ。

ユウタ：どうやって？

ハナ：グループの仲間の力を借りるわ。私たち人間は言葉でコミュニケーションをとることができるから，経験を通じて得た知識を共有することができるわ。

ユウタ：そのとおりだ！ ハトから学んだことは何かある？

ハナ：時にはグループの違うメンバーがそのグループを率いることがあると学んだわ。大切なのは，チームとして目標に到達することね。

オリバー：全員がグループの大切な一員で，ぼくたちは責任を分かち合うべきだね。

ハナ：そのとおりね！ ありがとう。理科の発表はうまくいきそうよ。

リナ：それを聞いてとてもうれしいわ！

ハナ：いいリーダーになるために私にできることはたくさんあるけど，最初にすることはグループのメンバーをもっとよく知るようになることだと思うわ。

オリバー：そこから始めるとよさそうだね！

ユウタ：理科の課題，うまくいくといいね！

語句

by oneself「一人で」 project「研究課題」
express「～を言い表す」 serious「真剣な」
follow along「後について行く」
next to ～「～の隣に」 tiny「小さな」
check「～を確認する，チェックする」
in that case「その場合は」 flight「飛行」
elephant「ゾウ」 survive「生き残る」
experience「経験，～を経験する」
similar to ～「～に似ている」
key to ～「～の秘訣」 in danger「危険な状態で」

climb「登る」 instead of ～「～の代わりに」
take action「行動を起こす」
share「～を分配する，分かち合う」
have a fight「けんかをする」
support「～を支援する，支援」
chance「可能性」 respect「尊敬」
smart「利口な」 hint「ヒント」
Like what?「たとえば？」 trust「～を信頼する」
make a decision「決断を下す」
a good place to start「よい出発点」
Good luck with ～.「～がうまくいくようお祈りします」

第 1 回　実力テスト

① [A] ウ　[B] カ　[C] エ
② **Their performance was so wonderful that I got goosebumps**
③ **It was the best music festival I have ever been to**
④ [1] イ　[2] ウ　[3] ア

解説 ①[A]like「(たとえば)～のような」。like は主に話し言葉で使う前置詞。書き言葉では such as を使う。

[B]during「～の間に」。for(～の間)は，普通，後ろに期間の長さを表す語句を置いて使う(例：for a week = 1 週間)。

[C]wait for ～「～を待つ」。wait (for) two days for ～(～を 2 日間待つ)という形で，for のくり返しを避けるために前の for を省略している。

②so ～ that ...「とても～なので…」。「鳥肌が立つ」は get goosebumps という。

③〈S is the ＋ 最上級の形容詞 ＋ A[名詞] (that) I have ever ＋ 過去分詞〉「S は私が今までに～した(ことのある)最も…な A だ」。have been to ～は「～へ行ったことがある」の意味。

④[1]「スーザンはエジンバラでの旅行中にいくつかのひどい経験をした」。彼女の最後の発言に apart from that, the trip was perfect (それ[荷物紛失の経験]以外は，旅行は申し分なかった)とあるので誤り。

[2]「エジンバラで，スーザンはホリールード宮殿へ行った」。彼女は 3 番目の発言で「エジンバラ城やコールトンヒルなどのいくつかの有名な観光スポットへ行った」と言った。ホリールード宮殿が some famous tourist spots に含まれていたかどうかは，この発言からはわからない。

[3]「スーザンはエジンバラ空港に着いたとき荷物を受け取ることができなかった」。彼女の最後から 4 番目の内容に一致する。

近年の入試では「本文の内容だけでは判断できない」ものを選ぶような問いがしばしば出題される。わざわざこのような問い方をしている以上，[1]～[3]の少なくともどれか 1 つはウだと考えるのが自然である。

なお，会話問題に限らず英文の内容を理解するためには，ある程度の一般常識を持っておく方がよい。この問いの場合，スーザンの発言中に Edinburgh，Scotland，London という地名が出てくる。これらを見たとき，頭の中の世界地図にこれらの地名(少なくとも Scotland)の具体的な場所が思い浮かぶのが望ましい。

また，スーザンが空港でどんな経験をしたかが具体的なイメージとして思い浮かぶかどうかも大切。入試や英検などの文章・会話中には，日本人にはなじみの薄い英米の習慣に即した内容(たとえば大学生の生活など)もしばしば出題される。仮に一度も飛行機に乗ったことがなくても，空港での乗客の乗り降りの手順程度の知識は持っておく必要がある。

精読

◆When I arrived at Edinburgh Airport, my baggage didn't come out. (*ll*.17-18)(エジンバラ空港に着いたとき，私の荷物が出てこなかった)：飛行機の座席にトランクなどの大きな荷物は持ち込めないので，それらは専用の格納スペースに入れられる。空港に着くとその荷物が降ろされ，受け取りカウンターへ運ばれる。乗客はベルトコンベヤーに乗って流れてくる自分の荷物を受け取る。このとき，スーザンの荷物が出てこなかった，ということ。

全訳

トモヤ：こんにちは，スーザン。夏休みはどうだった？

スーザン：こんにちは，トモヤ。最高だったわ！ 私はエジンバラへ行って，そこでとても楽しく過ごしたの。

トモヤ：エジンバラ？ それはどこにあるの？

スーザン：エジンバラはスコットランドの首都で，私はそこに1週間滞在したの。

トモヤ：へえ，スコットランドか。そこでは何をしたの？

スーザン：ええと，エジンバラ城やコールトン・ヒルなどのいくつかの有名な観光スポットへ行ったの。王立エジンバラ・ミリタリー・タトゥーもとても楽しかったわ。

トモヤ：王立エジンバラ・ミリタリー・タトゥー？ それは何？

スーザン：音楽祭よ。いろんな国の軍隊の楽団がそのイベントで音楽を演奏するの。彼らの演奏は鳥肌が立つほど素晴らしいものだったわ。

トモヤ：それはとても楽しそうだね。ぼくもいつか見に行きたいよ。

スーザン：見に行くべきよ。それは私がこれまで行った中で一番の音楽祭だったわ。でも，旅行中にひどい経験をしたの。

トモヤ：ひどい経験？

スーザン：ええ。エジンバラ空港に着いたとき，私の荷物が出てこなかったのよ。

トモヤ：何だって？ どうしてそんなことが起きたの？

スーザン：今回は羽田空港からロンドンのヒースロー空港まで飛行機で行ったの。それからロンドンで別の便に乗ってエジンバラ空港まで行ったわ。それで，言ったように，そこに着いたら荷物が見当たらないことに気がついたの。それで地上勤務員に尋ねたら，まだロンドンにあると言われて。

トモヤ：それは気の毒に。外国旅行に行くとそういうことが時々起きると聞いたことがあるよ。

スーザン：それが今回は実際に私に起きたのよ。結局，荷物がエジンバラに着くまで2日待たなければならなかったわ。だから着替えたり他の物を使ったりできなくて。

トモヤ：君はそんな大変な経験をしたんだね…。

スーザン：ええ，でもそれ以外は申し分のない旅行で，特別な休暇だったわ。

2 論説文－文化・社会

009〉① エ　② イ　③ イ　④ ア
⑤ ウ

解説 ①「段落[2]によれば，どの文が正しいか」

ア 日本ではデジタルコミックに関する多くの問題がある。

イ 書店はデジタルコミックを売ってはならない。

ウ スマートフォンはマンガ本を見つけるのには役に立たない。

エ スマートフォンでデジタルコミックを買うことができる。

エが段落[2]の4文目の内容に一致する。同文からウは間違い。他の選択肢の内容は本文に書かれていない。

②「段落[3]によれば，どの文が正しいか」

ア 日本のマンガのストーリーは，世界中の人々にとって長すぎる。

イ アメリカ型のマンガの1つは，グラフィックノベルである。

ウ バンド・デシネの店はたいていとてもまじめである。

エ 文化を学ぶよい方法は，フランスを訪ねることである。

イが段落[3]の4文目の内容に一致する。「得点アップ」も参照。

③「段落[4]によれば，どの文が正しくないか」

ア 紙のマンガを1冊読んだ後で，もっと読みたくなるかもしれない。

イ 紙のマンガを読んだ後で，それを他の人と共有すべきだ。

ウ スマートフォンでデジタルコミックを読むことができる。

エ デジタルコミックを保管するにはあまり多くのスペースは必要ない。

ア・ウ・エの内容は段落[4]に書かれているが，イのような記述はない。

④「段落[5]によれば，どの文が正しいか」

ア 紙のマンガは重いので，持ち運びにくい。

イ 小さなスマートフォンの方が大きなものよりもよいと人々は考えている。

ウ デジタルコミックを持ち運ぶのは難しい。

エ 誰でもスマートフォンでマンガを読むのを好む。

アが段落[5]の2文目の内容に一致する。

⑤「この文章の最も適切なタイトルは何か」

ア 最も人気の高いデジタルコミック

イ ある有名なマンガ家

ウ マンガを読む1つの新たな方法

エ デジタルコミックの歴史

正解はウ。本文は「導入(段落[1])→本論(段落[2]～[5])→結び(段落[6])」という構成になっており，本論ではデジタルコミックの利点が語られている。したがって本文のテーマはデジタルコミックであり，ウはそれを「マンガを読む１つの新たな方法」と表現している(紙のマンガは別の(昔からある)方法である)。

得点アップ

本文の内容は理解できているのに，選択肢を読み間違えて失点するようなミスをしないことが大切。③の設問文中のNOTを見落とすようなケースがその典型で，本文の内容に一致しない文を選ぶ必要がある。また，誤りの選択肢は本文の単語を別の語と入れ換えて作られていることも多い。たとえば②のウ The stores of Bandes Dessinées are usually very serious. は，本文の stories(ストーリー)を stores(店)に置き換えたものである。単語のつづりにも注意して選択肢を読むよう心がけよう。

全訳

[1]あなたはマンガを読むだろうか。もし読むなら，紙のマンガとデジタルマンガのどちらだろうか。数年前は紙のマンガの人気の方が高かった。しかし(新型コロナウイルス)感染症の広範囲の流行以来，この状況は一変した。人々は家にこもり，インターネットでデジタルコミックを読むことが多くなり始めた。2020年には，日本のマンガ本の売上の半分以上がデジタルコミックだった。デジタルコミックの人気が高まっているのだ。

[2]デジタルコミックにはいくつかのよい点がある。人々はデジタルコミックをどこでも買える。書店に行く必要はない。自宅のソファに寝転がりながら，スマートフォンでほしいマンガを見つけて買うことができる。買った後は，すぐに読み始めることができる。

[3]もう１つのよい点は，世界中のあらゆる種類のマンガを買えることだ。たとえば，日本式のマンガは人気が高い。そのストーリーや登場人物は，世界中の人々に愛されている。グラフィックノベルは，アメリカ型のマンガの一種である。ストーリーが長くシリアスなので，ボリュームがあり，たいていは大人が読む。バンド・デシネは，別のタイプのフランスのマンガだ。ほとんどはフルカラーで，ストーリーもたいていとても詩的なので，一種の芸術だと考える人もいる。外国のマンガを読むことは，言語や文化を学ぶための優れた方法である。

[4]第３のポイントは，あまりスペースを必要としないことだ。マンガを読んだ後，また別のマンガを読みたくなるかもしれない。紙のマンガ本をたくさん買うと，大きな本棚が必要になる。デジタルコミックを読むなら，スマートフォンさえあればいい。置き場所に困らないし，部屋も整頓しておける。

[5]第４のポイントは，簡単に持ち運べることだ。たくさんの紙の本はとても重いので，運ぶのは重労働である。一方，デジタルコミックを読む場合は，本を運ぶ必要がない。もちろん，スマートフォンの小さな文字は読みにくいという人もいる。そういう人は，タブレット端末の方がいい。紙のマンガと同じくらいの大きさなので，楽に読める。

[6]デジタルコミックを選ぶ人が以前よりも増えている。それらは紙のマンガより便利である。どこでも買えるし，世界中のあらゆるマンガを読んでみることができる。たくさん買えて，本棚は必要ない。スマートフォンに入れて楽に持ち運べる。将来はデジタルコミックを選ぶ人がさらに増えるだろう。

010
① 自分がほしいもののためにお金を使うよう言われた人々(25字)
② イ
③ **on experiences makes you happier than spending it on things**
④ [A] イ　[B] ア　[C] ウ
⑤ **happiness**　⑥ ア，エ

解説 ①この段落の４文目(*ll*.8-9)に，Half of them were told to use it for something they wanted, and the other half were ...「半数の人々はそれ[研究者たちにもらったお金]を自分のほしいもののために使うよう言われ，残りの半数は…」とある。「第１のグループ」とは，この下線部の人々を指す。

得点アップ

「○○字以内で」という字数制限のついた問いでは，その文字数を超えた答案は０点になる可能性が高い。また，答案用紙の所定の解答欄(下線やマス目など)をはみ出して書いたり，後

で解答欄の外側に1文字書き加えたりするのも不可。面倒でも全部を消して，書き直そう。なお，たとえば「30字以内」という字数制限の場合は，少なくとも20字(できれば25字)以上書くことが必要。字数が少なすぎると，想定された正解とは違う(たとえば情報不足である)とみなされて減点される可能性が高い。

② You may worry that spending money on yourself isn't good. Don't worry.「自分のためにお金を使うのはよくない，とあなたは心配するかもしれない。心配しなくてよい」に続く言葉としては，イの It is. が適切。この It は下線部を指しており，It is good. の good が省略されている。つまり It is. は「自分にお金を使うことはよいことだ」という意味になる。

③ A makes you happier than B.(B よりも A の方があなたを幸せにする[満足させる])という形を作る。A は Spending it on experiences (それ[お金]を体験に使うこと)，B は spending it on things(それを物に使うこと)。

④[A][B]については，直前の文に spend a small amount of money on smaller experiences more often(少額のお金をより小さな体験により頻繁に使いなさい)とある。次の文にはその具体例が書かれていると考えて，Talking with your friends at a coffee shop every weekend makes you happier than going abroad every year.「毎年外国へ行くよりも，毎週末に喫茶店で友人と話す方があなたを幸せにする」という文を作る。[C]は直前の文に buy something which helps to make experiences more meaningful「体験をより意味のあるものにするのに役立つものを買いなさい」とある。その例として「よいカメラを買うこと」と対になるものとしては，getting a new bicycle「新しい自転車を買うこと」が適切。get はくだけた表現では buy(買う)の意味で使う。

⑤文章全体の趣旨から考えて，空所には *l*.7に出てくる happiness(幸福)を入れるのが適切。

⑥ア 他人にすてきなものを買ってあげること
イ 自分がほしいものを全部買うこと
ウ 他人のためだけにお金を使うこと
エ 体験を他人と共有すること
オ 何を買うべきかを選ぶために多くの時間を費やすこと

第2段落によれば，他人のためにお金を使った(たとえば弟に絵本を買ってやった)人の方が，自分のほしいものを買った人よりも幸福度が高かった。その内容から考えて，筆者は読者にアをすすめていると考えられる。イは本文に書かれていない。ウは *ll*.17-18の内容に一致しない。エは *l*.23 (First, ...)以下の内容に一致する。オは本文に書かれていない。したがって，ア，エが正解。

精読

◆A study showed that (A)people who spent money on others felt happier than (B)people who bought themselves something [they wanted].(*ll*.4-5)(ある研究によると，自分がほしいものを買った人よりも，人のためにお金を使った人の方が幸福感が強かった)：A study showed that(ある研究は…ということを示した)の後ろは，A felt happier than B(A は B よりも幸せに感じた)という形。2つの who は関係代名詞で，それぞれ who 以下が前の people を修飾している。something (that[which]) they wanted は「彼らがほしかったもの」。下線部(目的格の関係代名詞)を補って考えることができる。

◆Half of **them** were told to use **it** for something they wanted, and **the other** half were told to spend it on **someone else**.(*ll*.8-9)(半数の人は自分のほしいもののために使うよう言われ，残りの半数は他の人のために使うよう言われた)：代名詞を多く含む文では，それぞれの代名詞が何を指すかを考えながら読むことが大切。**them** は前に出てきた複数の名詞を，**it** は単数の名詞を指す。この文の場合，them = the people， it = the money である。the other half は「残りの半分(の人々)」。**the other (A)** は「他[残り]の全部(の **A**)」の意味で使う。

・She is 15, and (all) **the other** members of the club are 14.(彼女は15歳で，クラブの他のメンバーは(全員)14歳だ)

「他の(不特定の)**A**」は，1つ[1人]なら **another A**，複数なら **other As** で表す。ただし，**-thing** や **-one[body]** で終わる語に「他の」の意味を加えるときは，後ろに **else**(他の)を置く。

・I don't know. Ask **someone else**.
(知らないな。誰か他の人に聞いて)

◆S[The amount of money they got] did not affect how they felt.(*ll*.15-16)(もらったお金の額は，人々の感じ方に影響しなかった)：主語はThe amount of money (that[which]) they got(彼らが手に入れた[もらった]お金)で，目的格の関係代名詞(that[which])が省略された形。このようにSが関係詞節を含む文を日本語に直す場合は，「後ろから訳す」必要がある。この文の場合も，「お金の額は…」と訳し始めるとうまくいかない。

・The book our teacher told us about was interesting.(先生が私たちに話してくれたその本は面白かった)

→下線部を先に訳す。「その本は…」と訳し始めないこと。この文は，The book was interesting.(その本は面白かった)＋Our teacher told us about it.(先生がそれ[その本]について私たちに話した)と考えればよい。

◆Second, **don't spend** a lot of money on special experiences **but spend** a small amount of money on smaller experiences more often.(*ll*.27-29)(第2に，特別な体験に大金を使うのではなく，少額のお金をより小さな体験により頻繁に使いなさい)：don't spend 〜は「〜を費やしてはいけない」という意味の命令文。命令文は普通，動詞の原形を文の最初に置くが，この文のように，動詞の原形の前に副詞(句)が置かれて，命令文であることがわかりづらくなっていることがある。

・If you want to be a good player, **practice** hard every day.(いい選手になりたければ，毎日熱心に練習しなさい)

また，don't spend 〜 but spend ... が **not A but B**(AではなくB)の形になっている点に注意。この形のbutは「〜を費やすのではなく…を費やしなさい」と訳す(「しかし」とは訳さない)。

全訳

ずっとほしかったすてきなバッグを買うと，幸せに感じる。有名なレストランでおいしいディナーを食べると，幸せに感じる。しかし，もっと幸せになれるお金のよりよい使い方がある。

ある研究によると，自分がほしいものを買った人よりも，人のためにお金を使った人の方が幸福感が強い。その研究で，人々は5ドルまたは20ドルの入った紙袋を受け取る。人々に紙袋を渡すとき，研究者たちは本人に幸せの度合いを尋ね，その日にお金を使うように言う。半数の人は自分のほしいもののために使うよう言われ，残りの半数は他の人のために使うよう言われた。その晩に研究者たちは各人に電話をかけ，幸せの度合いとお金の使い方を尋ねた。第1のグループの人々は，飲み物，ケーキ，服を買った。第2のグループは，弟に絵本を買ってあげたり，貧しい子どもたちにおもちゃを買ってあげたり，慈善団体にお金を寄付したりした。その実験の後，彼らがどんな気持ちだったかをあなたは想像できるだろうか。驚くかもしれないが，第1のグループより第2のグループの人々の方が幸せだった。もらったお金の額は，人々の感じ方に影響しなかった。

自分のためにお金を使うのはよくない，とあなたは心配するかもしれない。心配しなくてよい。それはよいことである。しかし，お金は体験のために使いなさい。物にお金を使うよりも，体験に使う方が幸せになれるのだ。物を買うときは幸せな気分になるが，物が与えてくれる幸せはそれを何度も使った後で消えてしまう。しかし体験が与えてくれる喜びや思い出は，心の中により長くとどまることができる。ここでは，体験にお金を使うときの助言をしよう。第1に，友人や家族，あるいは見知らぬ人と一緒にイベントに参加しなさい。そうすればその人たちと思い出を共有することができる。また，よい関係を築くことができて，より幸せになれるだろう。友人たちと一緒に高い山に登るのがよい例だ。そのときはつらく感じても，後で友人たちと話せば気分がよくなる。第2に，特別な体験に大金を使うのではなく，少額のお金をより小さな体験により頻繁に使いなさい。毎年外国へ行くよりも，毎週末に喫茶店で友人と話す方が幸せになれる。体験をよりよいものにしたいなら，体験をより意味のあるものにするのに役立つものを買いなさい。よい例は，よいカメラを買ったり新しい自転車を買ったりすることだ。

もう，お金の使い方と幸せにはつながりがあるとわかっただろう。あなたは明日，どのようにお金を使うだろう？ 自分の答えを見つけなさい。

011 ① エ ② イ ③ ア ④ エ
⑤ ウ ⑥ エ ⑦ [1] エ [2] ア
⑧ ウ，カ ⑨ ア ⑩ D

解説 ①S is said to have been invented by 〜で「Sは〜によって発明されたと言われている」という意味を表す(→精読)。

②ブッシュ大統領が手の向きを間違えて観客に不

快感を与えた，という状況だから，イのUnfortunately(残念なことに)が適切。ア(たぶん)，ウ(成功して，うまく)，エ(最後に，結局)では文脈に合わない。

③直後にand is used to insult people(人々を侮辱するために使われる)とあるので，アが正解。

④point out ～は「～を指摘する」という意味。

⑤空所の前は「親指を立てるジェスチャーは絶対に使わない方がよい」，空所の後ろは「けんかを売られるかもしれない」という内容だから，後者は前者の理由と考えられる。したがってウのbecause(…だから)が適切。

⑥下線部(6)の文の修飾語を(　)に入れて考えると，children (using it to call adults) (sometimes) had their fingers broken (as a punishment)となる。usingはwho usedの意味。前から訳すと，「子どもたちは(←大人を呼ぶためにそれを使った)＋時々＋指を折られた＋罰として」となる。〈have + one's X ＋過去分詞〉は「自分のX[持ち物など]を～される」という意味。

⑦[1]「2本指のジェスチャーを『平和』のサインとして使い始めたのは誰か」。*ll.*5-6 (But people ... ‘peace.’)から考えて，エの「ベトナム戦争に反対した人々」が正解。

[2]「下のどれがイギリスに当てはまるか」。

ア 人々は「よくやった」を表すために親指を立てるサインを使う。

イ 親指を立てるサインを使うとトラブルを引き起こすことがある。

ウ 人々が誰かを呼ぶときに人差し指を立てるのは礼儀正しいことだ。

エ 人々がピースサインをするとき手の甲を観客に向けるのはよい習慣だ。

*ll.*19-20(In England ... ‘job well done.’)から考えて，アが正解。

⑧ア「ピースサインはもともと『平和』を意味する」。ピースサインはもともとチャーチル首相が「勝利」のサインとして使ったものだから誤り。

イ「日本の多くの子どもたちは，勝利を意味するのにピースサインを使う」。本文に書かれておらず，常識的に考えても誤り。

ウ「親指を立てるサインはアラブ諸国ではトラブルになることがある」。*ll.*22-23(In particular ... a fight!)の内容に一致する。

エ「初代ブッシュ大統領がピースサインを考案したと言われている」。ピースサインを考案したのはチャーチル首相だから誤り。

オ「フィリピンでは，親指を立てるサインは人を呼ぶのに時々使われる」。親指を立てるサインを説明した第4段落中にフィリピンは出てこないので誤り。

カ「同じジェスチャーが国ごとに違う意味を持っている」。これが本文のテーマだから正しい。

⑨イ，エは最後の段落，ウは最初の段落に出てくる。アは最後の段落に関係しているが，イギリスやアメリカでは人差し指だけを使うイのジェスチャーが使われる。

⑩全訳の下線部を参照。

精読

◆(A1)The ‘peace sign,’ (A2)the two-fingered gesture that many Japanese children make when they are being photographed, **is said to have been invented** by (B1)the British Prime Minister, (B2)Winston Churchill. (*ll.*1-3)(日本の多くの子どもたちが写真を撮られるときにする「ピースサイン」というジェスチャーは，イギリスの首相ウィンストン・チャーチルによって考案されたと言われている)：〈X, Y〉のように名詞(のかたまり)を2つ並べて，「XであるY」「X，つまりY」のように，一方が他方を説明する場合がある。これを「同格(関係)」と言う。この文では，A1とA2，B1とB2がそれぞれ同格である。文全体は，S is said to have been invented by ○.(Sは○によって考案されたと言われている)という形。次の例を参照。

(1) **It is said** that he is a great soccer player.

→ He **is said to be** a great soccer player.
(彼は偉大なサッカー選手だと言われている)

(2) **It is said** that he was a great soccer player.

→ He **is said to have been** a great soccer player.
(彼は偉大なサッカー選手だったと言われている)

(1)の最初の文では，動詞がどちらもis。このときはto beを使って言い換えられる。(2)では前がis，後ろがwas。このように時間のずれがあるときは，〈**to have**＋過去分詞(been)〉の形を使って言い換える。本文では，「〜だと言われている」のは現在のこと，「考案された」のは過去のことだから，(2)と同様にto be inventedの下線部が〈have＋過去分詞(been)〉の形になる。

◆In the United States that **doesn't matter** very much.(*ll.*9-10)(アメリカ(合衆国)ではそれはあまり問題にはならない)：matterは名詞では「問題，ことがら」，動詞では「問題だ，重要である」という意味を表す。動詞の**matter**は，否定文で「(大した)問題ではない，どうでもよい」という意味を表すことが多い。主語のthat(そのこと)は，前の文のheld his hand the wrong way round(自分の手を間違った向きに保った)を指す。heldはholdの過去形で，holdはここでは「〜の状態に(固定)しておく」という意味。the wrong way (a)roundは「間違った向きに」の意味。the other way (a)round(逆向きに)もよく使うので覚えておこう。

［参考］ roundはイギリス英語，aroundはアメリカ英語。このようにイギリスとアメリカとで少し違うつづりを使うことがある。たとえば「〜の方へ」は，イギリス英語ではtowards，アメリカ英語ではtowardを使う。

◆**few** people know that Churchill also used the gesture the wrong way round (*ll.*13-14)(チャーチルも間違った向きのジェスチャーを使ったことを知る人はほとんどいない)：fewとa fewの違いに注意。これらは複数形の名詞の前に置き，(peopleはpersonの複数形)，**few**は「ほとんどない」，**a few**は「少しはある」という意味を表す。

・There were **few** passengers on the bus.
（バスにはほとんど乗客がいなかった）

→話し言葉では，fewの代わりにonly a few(少しの〜しかない)もよく使う。

・There were **a few** passengers on the bus.
（バスには少し［2，3人の］乗客がいた）

［参考］ たとえばバスに3人の乗客がいた場合，それを「少ししかいなかった」と(否定的に)考えればfewを，「少しはいた」と(肯定的に)考えればa fewを使う。

一方，数えられない(単数形の)名詞の前では，fewの代わりに**little**を使う。

・There is **little** milk left in the fridge.
（冷蔵庫にミルクはほとんど残っていない）

・There is **a little** milk left in the fridge.
（冷蔵庫にミルクが少し残っている）

全訳

日本の多くの子どもたちが写真を撮られるときにする「ピースサイン」というジェスチャーは，イギリスの首相ウィンストン・チャーチルによって考案されたと言われている。チャーチルは第二次世界大戦中，それを「勝利を表すV」の意味で使った。ベトナム戦争の後，ニクソン大統領もこのジェスチャーを勝利を意味するのに使った。しかしベトナム戦争に抗議する人々は，このジェスチャーを「平和」を意味するために使い始めた。

1990年代にオーストラリアを訪問中に，初代ブッシュ大統領は，空港で彼を出迎えたオーストラリア人の群衆にピースサインを出そうとした。残念ながら，彼は手を間違った向きに出してしまった。アメリカでは，それはあまり問題にはならない。しかしイギリスやオーストラリアでは，手の甲が観客の方を向いていると，そのジェスチャーは非常に不快なものとなり，人を侮辱するために使われる。オーストラリアの人たちはとてもショックを受けた！

ブッシュ大統領の間違いの写真は広く出回ったが，チャーチルも第二次世界大戦の初期に間違った向きのジェスチャーを使ったことを知る人はほとんどいない。しかし，人々は素早く彼のミスを指摘したので，チャーチルはそれを裏返して，ピースサインとして知られるようになったジェスチャーを考案した。

欧米でよく見られる「サムズアップ(親指を立てる)」サインのジェスチャーも，誤解されることがある。イギリスやアメリカでは，それは「すべて順調」あるいは「よくやった」という意味を表す。しかしラテンアメリカ，西アフリカ，ギリシャ，ロシア，南イタリアではそれは非常に不快なジェスチャーであり，「親指を立てる」のは避けた方がよい。特にアラブ諸国では，けんかを売られるかもしれないので絶対に使わない方がよい！

トラブルの元になるジェスチャーがもう1つある。日本やフィリピンでは，人を呼ぶとき手のひらを下向きにして手を伸ばし，上下に手を振る。イギリスやアメリカでは，手を上に向けて人差し指だけを使う。日本人がこのジェスチャーで気分を害することはない。しかしフィリピンでは，指を1本立てて人を呼ぶのはとても不快感を与える。それは犬にしか使わないジェスチャーである。昔は，大人を呼ぶのにそれを使った子どもは，罰として指を折られることもあったという。

語句

two-fingered「２本指の」
make a gesture「ジェスチャー[身振り]をする」
photograph「～の写真を撮る」
invent「～を発明する，考案する」
British「イギリスの」 Prime Minister「首相」
World War II「第二次世界大戦」
victory「勝利」 the Vietnam War「ベトナム戦争」
President「大統領」
the first President Bush「初代ブッシュ大統領(ブッシュは父子の２人が大統領を務めた。その父親の方を指す)」
welcome「～を歓迎する」
back of one's hand「手の甲」 face「～に向く」
offensive「不快な，侮辱的な」
insult「～を侮辱する」 reverse「～を裏返す」
thumb「親指」
misunderstood < misunderstand「～を誤解する」
job well done「上手に行われた仕事」
Greece「ギリシャ」 in particular「特に」
challenge ～ to a fight「～に戦いを挑む」
cause「～を引き起こす」
call ～ over「～を呼び寄せる」
the Philippines「フィリピン」
extend「～を広げる」 palm「手のひら」
face downwards「下を向く」
wave one's hand「手を振る」
upset「動揺して，怒って」
held up ～ < hold up ～「(指)を立てる」
adult「大人」 as a punishment「罰として」

012
① [A] イ [B] オ [C] エ [D] ウ [E] ア
② [1] ウ [2] ア [3] エ [4] ア [5] ウ [6] イ
③ (1) **poor** (2) **group** (3) **high** (4) **on** (5) **loss**
④ **different**
⑤ (1) **doubt** (2) **trust**

解説 ①**全訳**の下線部[A]～[E]を参照。

②[1]「ユヌスが地元のジョブラ村へ学生たちを連れて行ったのはなぜか」
ア 教授資料を捨てたかった。
イ 彼らにジョブラで作られた製品を使って経済学を教えたかった。
ウ 彼らにバングラデシュの実生活を見せたかった。
エ 現地調査を通じてソフィアと仲よくしたかった。
ll.7-9よりウが正しい。

[2]「ソフィアの生活はどのようなものだったか」
ア 高利のローンのために貧困から抜け出すことができなかった。
イ 家族を養えるだけの金を稼いでいた。
ウ 稼ぎはわずか２セントで，その金を全部家族のために使った。
エ 手作りの製品を作ることによって自立した。
ll.16-18よりアが正しい。

[3]「ユヌスはジョブラの女性たちのために何をしたか」
ア 手作りの製品を生産するための原材料を彼女らに与えた。
イ 少額の金を高金利で貸した。
ウ 低金利で少額の金を彼女らに貸すために，地元の業者を紹介した。
エ 貧しい女性たちが竹製の腰かけなどを作るための原材料を買う手助けをするために，自分の金を彼女らのために使った。
ll.19-20よりエが正しい。

[4]「ユヌスによれば，貧しい女性は男性とどのように違っていたか」
ア 得た金を家族のために直接使った。
イ 利益を使って自分自身の服を買った。
ウ 夫がやらないので，自分が子どもを教育した。
エ 男性よりも教育と娯楽にずっと多くの金を使った。
ll.37-38よりアが正しい。

[5]「グラミン銀行の何が特別だったか」
ア グラミン銀行は貧しい人々に金を貸すことによって大金を稼いだ。
イ グラミン銀行は世界経済に大きな影響を与えた。
ウ グラミン銀行は貧しい人々の生活水準を改善し続けた。
エ グラミン銀行は60億ドル以上を貸し出し，それによって有名になった。
ll.41-42よりウが正しい。

[6]「ユヌスの努力によって何が起きたか」
ア ユヌスの低金利ローンによって世界中の女性が完全に救われた。
イ 世界中の多くの銀行がユヌスの銀行モデルを導入した。

ウ 貧しい人々は怠け者だから貧しいのではないことにほとんどの人が気づいた。

エ ユヌスとその銀行自身が，利益を得ないで多くの金を人々に与えたためにノーベル平和賞を受賞した。

ll.46-47よりイが正しい。

③完成した英文の意味は次のとおり。

「『グラム』はベンガル語で村を意味し，それはその銀行の起源を反映している。グラミン銀行は，(1)貧しくても熱心に働く意志を示す人々に対して少額の個人融資を行う。5人が(2)グループを作り，ローンを返済するためにお互いに協力する。その結果，グラミン銀行から金を借りた人々は驚くほど(3)高い率でローンを返済した。これは，ローンを返済するという社会的なプレッシャーが，メンバーたちが期限(4)内に返済することを可能にするからである。しかし，たとえ誰かが未払い金を返済できなくても，仲間のメンバーがそれを返済する必要はない。その銀行は，未払金を(5)損失とみなす。その方針が，貧しい人々が自立するのに役立った。」

④空所には different を入れ，「貧しい人々と金持ちの間に（労働意欲の面で）違いはない。違う家庭に生まれただけだ」という内容にすれば文脈に合う。

⑤完成した英文の意味は次のとおり。

「この話は印象的だった。ムハマド・ユヌスと彼のグラミン銀行は，誰にとっても模範例だった。両者は私たちに，銀行にとってさえ金もうけがただ1つの目標ではないことを示した。江戸時代には，日本にも類似の5家族による近隣制度（5人組）があった。しかし当時の村人たちは，税の不払いに対する責任を取らねばならなかった。言い換えれば，それは他の村人たち(1)を疑うためのシステムとして働いた。他人を信じる余地はほとんどなかった。一方，ムハマド・ユヌスと彼のグラミン銀行は，貧しい人々の善意に期待することによって彼らを救おうとした。両者は(2)信頼の力を示した。その意味で，ノーベル平和賞を受賞する価値があった。」

精読

◆During that period, (A)a worried young professor at Chittagong University, (B)Muhammad Yunus, **was disappointed that** S[**all he could do** to help society] **was** C[**to teach** economics]. (*ll*.4-6)（当時，チッタゴン大学の悩める若き教授ムハマド・ユヌスは，社会の役に立つために自分にできるのは経済学を教えることだけであることに落胆していた）：(A)と(B)は同格の関係，「**A**である**B**」の意味。was disappointed that ... は「…ということ（のため）に失望していた」。disappoint は「（人）を失望させる」という意味で，人が主語のときは（surprise や excite と同様に）**be disappointed** の形で「失望させられる→失望する［している］」という意味を表す。このような感情を表す語に続く **that** は，**because**（…なので）の意味を表す。

［参考］ surprised（驚いている），excited（わくわくしている），disappointed（失望している）などは，形容詞と考えてもよい。

that に続く部分の基本構造は S was C（S は C だった）。all の後ろには that（関係代名詞）を補って考える。直訳すると「社会に役立つために彼がすることのできたすべてのことは，経済学を教えることだった」となる。このように S **is** C の S に **all** が含まれた文は，「すべては～だ→～しかない」という否定的な意味を表す。

◆she only made 2 cents **a day** from her work (*ll*.11-12)（彼女は自分の仕事から1日に2セントしか稼いでいなかった）：made 2 cents は「2セントをもうける」の意味（make [earn] money「金をもうける」）。a day は「1日につき」。**a[an]** が「～につき」の意味を表すことがある（in a day とは言わない）。

・She goes to the gym twice **a week**.
（彼女は週に2回（スポーツ）ジムへ行く）

◆So, he lent O_1[42 poor women] O_2[the 27 dollars he had with him] **to buy** raw materials **to make** their bamboo seats, etc. (*ll*.19-20)（そこで，彼は持っていた27ドルを42人の貧しい女性たちに貸し，竹製の腰かけなどを作るための原材料を購入させた）：lend（貸す）は SVO_1O_2（第4文型）で使うと，「O_1［人］に O_2［物・お金］を貸す」という意味を表す。この文では，「O_1＝42人の貧しい女性たち」「O_2＝自分が持っていた27ドル」である（with him は「そのとき手元にあった」の意味）。to buy は「買うために」（目的）の意味を表すが，「買う」のはユヌス教授ではなく女性たちである（for them to buy「彼女たちが買うために」の下線部を省略した形）。また to makeは形容詞的用法の不定詞で，前のmaterialsを修飾している。したがってto buy以下を正確に訳すと，「(その女性たちが)竹の腰かけなどを作るための原材料を買うために」となる。

◆**To get** a loan, S[**all** you need to show] **is** C[**that** you are poor and you have the will to work hard]. (*ll*.29-30)(融資を受けるには，自分が貧しく，一生懸命働く意志があることを示しさえすればよい)：文の最初に置かれた不定詞は，「〜するために(は)」(目的)の意味と考えてよい。all以下はS is C.の形。allの後ろにはthat(関係代名詞)を補って考える。直訳は「あなたが示す必要があるすべてのことは，あなたが貧しく，一生懸命働く意志を持っているということだ」。

◆**Not only** do they repay their loans, **but** they **also** clothe, educate and feed their children with their profits. (*ll*.38-39)(彼女らはローンを返済するだけでなく，得た利益で子どもたちに衣服を与え，教育を受けさせ，食事をさせる)：**not only A but (also) B**は「**A**だけでなく**B**も」の意味。下線部はVSの倒置形(疑問文と同じ形)になっている。否定の意味を含む副詞(句)(この文ではnot only)を文頭に置くと，その後ろはVSの形になる。

・**Never** have I seen such a beautiful rainbow.
(こんなに美しい虹は今まで見たことがない)

◆They just happen **to have been** born into different families. (*ll*.48-49)(彼らはたまたま生まれた家庭が違うだけである)：happen to *do*は「偶然〜する」の意味。「生まれた」のは過去のことだから，They just happen to was born ... と書きたいところだが，不定詞のtoの後ろには動詞の原形を置かねばならない。そこでwas(過去形)の代用品として，have been(完了形)を使う(haveは原形だからtoの後ろに置ける)。このように〈**to have**＋過去分詞〉(完了(形)不定詞)は，V(述語動詞)よりも前の時点の出来事を表す。

全訳

1974年，バングラデシュで大洪水が深刻な食糧不足を引き起こした。バングラデシュ全土で，その後数年の間に約100万人が餓死した。

当時，チッタゴン大学の悩める若き教授ムハマド・ユヌスは，社会の役に立つために自分にできるのは経済学を教えることだけであることに落胆していた。彼は，同胞のためにより多くのことをしたいと思った。彼は経済学の理論や教科書をわきへ置き，バングラデシュの貧しい人々の実生活を知りたいと考えた。その思いを抱いて，彼は学生たちを連れて地元のジョブラ村へ現地調査に行った。

ジョブラで教授と学生たちは，小さな竹製の腰かけを作って生計を立てているソフィアという女性に出会った。彼女の1日の仕事の稼ぎがわずか2セントであることがわかって彼らはショックを受けた。その金のほとんどは，彼女にとって必要な原材料を買うためにかつて利用した高利のローンの返済に充てられていた。ジョブラでの彼らの調査によって，ソフィアと全く同じような生活を送るはるかに多くの貧しい人々がいることがわかった。

[A]従来の銀行は，貧しい人々が金を返済すると信用せず，彼らには金を貸そうとしなかった。そのため，ソフィアのような村人たちは，恐ろしく高い金利を取る地元の業者から金を借りるしかなかった。みんなが高金利のローンを返さねばならなかったので，村人たちは誰も貧困から抜け出せるだけの金を稼ぐことができなかった。

[B]もしこれらの人々がもっと手ごろな利子で金を借りることができれば，大いに助けになるとユヌスは理解した。そこで，彼は持っていた27ドルを42人の貧しい女性たちに貸し，竹製の腰かけなどを作るための原材料を購入させた。これらの貧しい女性たちが返済してくれることを信じることが重要だった。もし返済してくれなければ，彼にできることは何もなかった。

ユヌスが返済利率を下げたことによって，その女性たちは生活できるだけの収入と利益を得ることができた。彼は純粋に信頼だけに基づく貧者のための銀行システムを継続し，まもなくそれはいくつかの村で成功した。そこでユヌスは1983年に，「最貧困層」に金を貸すというただ1つの目的で，自らの銀行であるグラミン銀行を設立することに決めた。「グラム」という語はベンガル語で村を意味し，銀行の起源を反映している。

[C]グラミン銀行は独自のシステムを持つ。融資を受けるには，自分が貧しく，一生懸命働く意志があることを示しさえすればよいのだ。そして，5人で1つのグループを作り，各人が少額の個人融資を受ける。その銀行から金を借りた人は，ローンを返済することによって，自分に与えられた信頼に報いる。その結果，記録的な数の返済が行われた。

[D]もしグループの1人がローンを返済できなければ，グループの残りのメンバーはプレッシャーを感じる。この社会的なプレッシャーが，メンバーが

ローンを期限内に返済することを促す。しかし，残りのメンバーは未返済のローンの返済義務はなく，グラミン銀行はそれを損失として受け入れる。これらの人々を信頼して少額の融資を行うことによって，ユヌスは彼らの自助努力を可能にしたのだ。

［E］グラミン銀行の借り手の約97%が女性であるというのは，興味深い事実である。貧しい女性は，男性よりも直接的に家族のためにお金を使うとユヌスは信じている。彼女らはローンを返済するだけでなく，得た利益で子どもたちに衣服を与え，教育を受けさせ，食事をさせる。

ここ数年，従来の銀行の強欲さと間違いが，世界経済に大きな問題を引き起こしている。その一方で，グラミン銀行は世界の貧しい人々の生活を少しずつ改善し続けている。従来の銀行とグラミン銀行との対比は明らかである。従来の銀行は金もうけのために働き，グラミン銀行は貧しい人々を助けるために働いている。

グラミン銀行は，これまでに約64億ドルを740万世帯に融資し，今では世界中の多くの金融機関がムハマド・ユヌスのシンプルなモデルを模倣している。貧困層は怠け者だから貧困なのではない，ということは覚えておく価値がある。彼らは富裕層と何も変わらない。ただたまたま生まれた家庭が違うだけなのだ。2006年，ユヌスとグラミン銀行の功績が認められ，両者にノーベル平和賞が授与された。

語句

serious「深刻な」 flooding「洪水」
shortage「不足」 throughout「～じゅうで」
period「期間」 worried「心配した」
professor「教授」
be disappointed「失望している」
economics「経済学」
fellow countrymen and women「同国人(の男女)」
put away ～「～をわきへ置く，片付ける」
theory「理論」
find out about ～「～について(事実を)知る」
with this in mind「このことを心に抱いて」
field trip「現地調査」
bamboo seat「竹製の腰かけ」
for a living「生活のために」
pay back ～「～を返済する」
high-interest「高金利の」
loan「貸付金，～を貸し付ける」
dealer「業者，商人」 interest rate「利率」
escape「～を逃れる」 poverty「貧困」
trust O to *do*「O が～するのを信用する」
allow O to *do*「O が～するのを可能にする」
live on「暮らしていく」
based purely on ～「純粋に～(だけ)に基づいて」
single「ただ1つの」 purpose「目的」
reflect「～を反映する」 origin「起源」
repay「～を返済する」 as a result「その結果」
in record numbers「記録的な数で」
social「社会的な」
encourage O to *do*「O が～するのを促す」
rest「残り」 unpaid「未払いの」
accept O as ～「O を～として受け入れる」
trust O with ～「O を信頼して～を預ける」
tiny「小さな，わずかな」 directly「直接に」
clothe「～に衣服を与える」 feed「～に食事を与える」
cause「～を引き起こす」 economy「経済」
contrast「対比，違い」 so far「今までのところ」
billion「10億」 copy「～を模倣する」
worth ～ing「～する価値がある」
lazy「怠け者の」 recognize「～を認める」
the Nobel Peace Prize「ノーベル平和賞」
borrower「(ローンの)借り手」 unique「独特の」
reasonable「手ごろな」 rate「割合，率」
throw away ～「～を捨てる」
get along with ～「～と仲よくやっていく」
What is S like?「S はどのようなものか」
get out of ～「～から抜け出す」
amusement「娯楽」
have an impact on ～「～に影響を与える」
standard of living「生活水準」
fully「十分に，完全に」
introduce「～を導入する」
cooperate with each other「お互いに協力する」
surprisingly「驚くほど，意外に」 policy「方針」
shining example「模範例」 goal「目標」
similar「似ている」 neighborhood「近所」
tax「税(金)」 in other words「言い換えれば」
room for ～「～の(ための)余地」 good will「善意」

013 ① ウ　② ウ

③ **can influence what people think about**

④ ア　⑤ 全訳の下線部(5)を参照。

⑥ (a) **fast**　(b) **victory**　⑦ B

⑧ 揚げ物しか売っていない店だと客に思われたくなかったから。

⑨ イ

解説 ①この後に「Ford, Toyota, Tata などは創業者の名前を持つ」と書かれているので，people(人)を入れるのが適切。

②この後に「BMW は Bavarian Motor Works を表す」とある。つまり BMW は3つの単語の頭文字(initials)を並べた社名だ，ということ。

③ A name が主語だとすると，その後ろには動詞が必要。「名前は考える」では意味的に不自然なので，「名前は影響を与える(ことができる)」と考えて，最初に can influence を置く。その後ろに what people think about (a company or a product)(人々が(会社や製品を)どう思うか)と並べれば意味が通る。

④直後の and 以下の内容から考えて，boring (退屈な)を入れるのが適切。

⑤文全体は，(Perhaps) S is C.((もしかしたら)S は C だ)という構造。S と C のそれぞれが〈名詞 + that で始まる関係詞節〉という形になっている。S は the most important factor [that a company must consider]([会社が考慮しなければならない]最も重要な要素)，C は the emotion ... [that people will feel when ...]([人々が…するときに感じる]感情)。

⑥(a)と(b)を含む2つの文の意味的な関係に着目する。(a)を含む文によれば，Nike という社名はギリシャ(神話)の(1)勝利の女神に由来する。一方 Reebok は，「とても(a)走るアフリカの大きな動物」に由来する。(b)を含む文は，「それらの会社は，客が自社のシューズを買う際に(b)と(2)スピードを思い浮かべてほしいと思っている」の意味。(1)から考えて(b)に入る語は victory(勝利)であり，(2)から考えて(a)に入る語は fast(速く)である。

⑦全訳の波線部を参照。「商品名の選択は音に関係することもある」という一般的な説明に，「たとえば…」という具体例を続けると文脈に合う。

⑧前後の文の内容から考えて，Kentucky Fried Chicken が KFC に社名を変更したのは，Fried という語が「揚げ物しか売っていない」という印象を客に与えるのを避けたかったからだとわかる。

⑨文脈から考えて，ValuJet 社が社名を変更したのは，墜落事故のことを客に忘れてほしかったからである。

精読

◆ *Green Moon* or *Crazy Cow* **would** not be good names for shoes(*l*.18)(Green Moon(緑の月)とか Crazy Cow(狂った牛)は，シューズの名前としてはよくないだろう)：下線部を is[are] not と表現すると，「よくない」と断定することになる。その代わりに would not be を使うことで，「よくないだろう」という穏やかな響きになる。この would は，仮定法過去の助動詞である。仮定法過去は，「実際にはそうではない[そうなる可能性は低い]が，もし〜なら」という仮定を表す。この文の場合，「シューズに Green Moon とか Crazy Cow のような名前をつけることはまずないだろうが，もしそういう名前をつけたなら」という仮定の意味をこめて，仮定法過去の would を使っている。このように，実現する可能性の低いことを仮定する気持ちを込めて「〜だろう」「〜かもしれない」と言いたいときは，仮定法過去の助動詞(**would**, **could**, **might** など)を使って表現する。これらは日常的に非常によく使われるので，覚えておこう。

・It **would** be difficult for him to pass the exam.
(彼がその試験に合格するのは難しいだろう)

→「彼がその試験をもし受けたら[たとえ受けても]」と仮定した発言。彼がその試験を受けることがすでに確定している場合は It will be 〜. を使う。It is 〜. だと「難しい」とさらに断定することになる。

全訳

会社や製品の名前の由来はさまざまである。古い会社は人間から名前をもらうことが多い。自動車会社はよい例である。Ford, Toyota, Tata など多くの自動車メーカーにはすべて，その会社を始めた人の名がついている。また SAAB, FIAT, BMW など他の自動車メーカーは，頭文字の社名を持つ。たとえば BMW は，Bavarian Motor Works を表す。今日では，ほとんどの新しい会社はこのような名前を選ばない。そうした会社はより興味深い名前を求めるが，それは社名や製品名が非常に大切だと知っているからである。

新しい会社は，社名を慎重に選ばねばならない。また製品に名前をつける際にも慎重に考えねばならない。名前は，人々が会社や製品をどう思うかに影響を与えうる。人々はよい名前を覚えるものだ。名前のせいでその会社や製品を選ぶ場合もある。これは，よい名前を持つ会社や製品には多くの広告は不要かもしれないことを意味する。それによって会社は多くのお金を節約することができる。

会社は名前を選ぶ際に多くのことを考慮する。客がその会社や製品に結びつけるような名前がほしいと考える。会社がランニング用のシューズを作るなら，足や靴に関係のある名前を考えるべきである。Green Moon(緑の月)とかCrazy Cow(狂った牛)は，シューズの名前としてはよくないだろう。よい名前は，覚えやすいことも必要である。しかし，名前は平凡すぎてはいけない。Best Shoes(最高の靴)とかThe Shoe Company(靴の会社)のような名前を選ぶのは，おそらくよい考えではない。これらの名前は退屈であり，その会社が他社とどう違うのかを示していない。

(5)もしかしたら会社が考慮しなければならない最も重要な要素は，人々がその社名を聞いたときに抱く感情かもしれない。その名前を聞いて人々はどう思うだろうか。オンライン企業のAmazonは，最初は本だけを売っていた。創業者がこの名前を選んだのは，アマゾン川が広大で力強いからだ。それは世界で一番大きな川である。彼は自分の会社を世界最大の書店にしたかったのだ。

よい名前はストーリーを伝える。靴の会社がFast Feet(速い足)のような名前を選べば，それが客への商売の説明になる。靴と会社の目的との間に明確な関係があるが，その名前は少し平凡である。ランニングシューズを作る2つの会社は，より興味深い名前を選んだ。それはNike(ギリシャの勝利の女神)とReebok(とても速く走るアフリカの大きな動物)である。これらの名前はよいストーリーを伝える。両社は客が自社のシューズを買う際に勝利とスピードを思い浮かべることを望んでいる。

電子機器やテクノロジー製品の名前も，製品への反応を示すよい例である。これらの製品の名前は，人々に現代の科学技術を思い浮かべさせるものがよい。この選択は音に関係することもある。たとえばe-mailやiPhoneのようにe-やi-で始まる単語は，人々にテクノロジーを連想させる。英語では，x-ray(レントゲン)のようにxで始まったり終わったりする単語は，非常に科学的・技術的な響きを持つことがよくある。商品名のよい例はXerox(ゼロックス)である。これは技術的な響きの強い語だが，同時に覚えやすい。もう1つの好例は，Googleという社名だ。この名前は，10の100乗という非常に大きな数を意味するgoogolという語に由来する。その会社の元の名前はBack Rub(背中のマッサージ)だったが，成長するにつれてよりよい社名が必要だと役員たちは判断した。彼らが(Googleという)新しい名前を選んだのは，その名前が会社に科学的で力強い響きを持たせるからである。今日，Google社は大成功を収めている。

最後に，企業が新しい名前を見つけようとすることもある。Kentucky Fried Chickenは多くのフライドチキンを売っている。今日，多くの客は脂肪の摂りすぎを心配している。Kentucky Fried Chickenは，客に揚げた料理だけを思い浮かべてほしくなかった。同社は社名をKFCに変更することに決めた。KFCは客に揚げ物以外の商品も思い浮かべてほしかったのだ。また，会社は悪いことが起きたときに名前を変えるかもしれない。たとえば，1997年にフロリダで飛行機の墜落事故があった。その事故で多くの人が亡くなった。その飛行機を所有していたValuJet社は，墜落事故を客に忘れてもらいたかったので，社名をAirTranに変更した。

名前を選んだり変えたりすることは，どんなビジネスでも重要な一部である。名前は客に強い影響を与えうる。客からの反応がよければ，会社は売上を増やせる。反応が悪ければ，会社は大きな損をするかもしれない。

語句

origin「起源」
stand for ～「(略語などが)～を表す」
advertisement「広告，宣伝」 ordinary「平凡な」
factor「要因，要素」 emotion「感情」
vast「広大な」 powerful「力強い」
connection「関係」 electronic「電子(機器)の」
response「反応」 crash「墜落」
own「～を所有する」

014
① イ
② [A] エ [B] イ [C] ア [D] オ
③ イ ④ エ ⑤ エ
⑥ [1] ウ [2] ウ [3] イ
⑦ [1] ア [2] ウ [3] ウ [4] イ

解説 ① this(これ，このこと)は，直前の内容を指すことが多い。この This も，前の段落の最後の2つの文(They didn't judge him.... They judged him....)を受けて「このことは…」はと言っている。

②[A]直後の文に「会話に関心がない」という内容があるので，エの「私は何も意見を持っていない」が入る。

[B]前に contradict someone(誰かを否定する)とあるので，相手を否定するような内容の発言を選ぶ。イの「あなたは間違っている」がそれに当たる。

[C]直前に「相手の意見に満足していない」とあり，その発言は perfectly good to ask(尋ねるのは完全によい)だと書かれていることから，アの「ええ，でも X についてはどうですか」が入る。

[D]「日本人の先生は授業中にあまり生徒に質問せず，たとえ質問しても深くは尋ねない」という内容にすれば文脈に合う。したがって，オの「それはとても面白いね」を入れる(これに対してアメリカ人の先生は，「なぜそう思うのか」とさらに深く尋ねる)。

余る選択肢はウの「気にしないで」。

③この This も直前の内容を指す。話題になっていることについて何も知らない場合は，「あなたの方はどう思いますか」と相手に質問すればよい，ということ。

④下線部の理由は直後の文に書かれている。「ただ相手に同意するだけでは，自分の意見がないと思われてしまう」ということ。

⑤「(アメリカ人の)教師は生徒が自分に質問することを好む。それは…ということを示すからだ」という文脈から考えて，エの「彼ら[生徒]が積極的に考えている」が入る。ア「彼らが教師に同意していない」，イ「彼らが教師の考えを理解していない」，ウ「彼らが英語をとても上手に話せる」は不適切。

⑥[1]「日本人はたいてい…」

ア 他人をその意見の内容で判断する
イ 他人の意見に興味がないときだけ黙り続ける
ウ 何の疑問も持たずに他人の意見を受け入れる
エ 積極的に注意を払っていることを示すために多くの質問をする

*ll.*7-8 に it was usual for Japanese people to accept the opinions of others (他人の意見を受け入れることは日本人にとって普通だった)とあるので，ウが正しい。

[2]「アメリカ人の考え方は…ということだ」

ア 他のメンバーとは違う意見を持つ人々はグループを去るべきだ
イ 全員がグループの一員であり，同じように考え同じように感じている
ウ 全員が独自の存在であり，自分自身の意見を持つべきだ
エ 正しい答えを見つける前に話し始めるべきではない

*ll.*13-14 に American people's idea is that "you and I are different persons, and therefore you and I are original."(アメリカ人の考え方は「あなたと私は違う人間だ。したがって私たちは独自のものだ」ということである)とあるので，ウが正しい。

[3]「アメリカ人は…と考える」

ア 社会的地位の高い人に反対意見を述べるのは行儀が悪い
イ 誰かの考えに同意しないことはその人を尊重していないことを意味しない
ウ 誰かの意見を疑問に思うと友情が壊れるだろう
エ 生徒は教師の言うことをすべて受け入れねばならない

*ll.*37-38 に disagreeing with an idea does not show disrespect for the person (ある考えに反対することはその人に対する無礼を示すわけではない)とあるので，イが正しい。

⑦[1]「生徒はあらゆる話題について自分の意見を言い表す準備をしておかねばならない」。第4段落(But he ...)の最後の文の内容から考えて，これはアメリカ人の考え方に基づくと言える。

[2]「生徒は同じように考え感じるために小さなグループを作るべきだ」。本文にはこのようなことは書かれていない。

[3]「生徒たちが何も意見を持っていないなら，教師は話題を変えなければならない」。本文にはこのようなことは書かれていない。

[4]「教師はたいてい質問をしないで生徒の意見を受け入れる」。最後から2番目の段落(But for Japanese ...)の内容から考えて，これは日本人の考え方に基づく。

精読

◆They judged him (A)by content, (B)by things that he **had to say**.(*l*.6)(彼らは内容，つまり彼が言いたいことで彼を判断した)：things を X に置き換えて考えると，he had X to say(彼は言うために X を持っていた)→X that he had to say(彼が言うために持っていたX)となる。つまり things はもともと had(持っていた)の目的語だから，had to say を「言わねばならなかった」と解釈するのは誤り。「彼が言うために持っていたこと」とは「彼が言いたかったこと[彼自身の意見]」ということ。英文中の下線部(B)は(A)の具体的な説明であり，「(A)，つまり(B)」という意味(一種の同格と考えてもよい)。

◆This made a real problem for him, because A[it was usual for Japanese people to accept the opinions of others, **either** C[by agreeing with everything they said], **or** D[by continuing to be silent]], **and** B[he mostly did so in Japan].(*ll*.7-9)(これは彼には大問題だった，なぜなら日本人にとっては，他人が言うことにすべて同意するか，または黙っていることによって相手の意見を受け入れるのが普通であり，彼もたいてい日本ではそうしていたからである)：長い文中に and(や or)が出てきた場合，**A and B** の **A・B** を正確にとらえることが大切。A と B に当たる部分を[ ]で囲んだり，下線を引いたりして考えてもよい。この文の A・B は，上に示したとおり。さらに A の中には，either C or D(C と D のどちらか(一方))の形が含まれている。

◆Teachers like students who **don't** easily believe **but** ask questions about X[things that teachers say in class](*ll*.39-40)(教師は，授業で教師の言うことを簡単に信じるのではなく質問する生徒を好む)：**not A but B** は「**A**ではなく**B**」の意味で，**B, not A** とも言う。この文では下線部が A・B であり，X は両方の目的語になっている。つまり「X を簡単に信じるのではなく，X について質問する」ということ。**but** を「しかし」と訳してはいけない点に注意。

全訳

アメリカに 2，3 か月滞在した日本人のある大学生は，言いたいことがはっきり伝わりさえすれば，アメリカ人は彼の英語がどのくらい上手か下手かには関心がないことを知って驚いた。

(アメリカの)人々が興味を持ったのは，主に彼の個人的な考えや意見とそれを持つ理由だった。彼らは形式，つまり彼が英語をどれだけ上手に話せるかによって彼を判断することはなかった。内容，つまり彼が言いたいことで彼を判断したのだ。

これは彼には大問題だった，なぜなら日本人にとっては，他人が言うことにすべて同意するか，または黙っていることによって相手の意見を受け入れるのが普通であり，彼もたいてい日本ではそうしていたからである。日本人の考え方は「あなたと私は集団の一員だ。したがって私たちは同じように考え，同じように感じる」ということである。

しかしアメリカでこのような行動をとると，人々は自分のことを利口ではなく頭が悪いと考える，ということが彼にはすぐにわかった。アメリカ人の考え方は「あなたと私は違う人間だ。したがって私たちは独自のものだ」ということである。話題に上るあらゆることについて自分の意見を持つだけでなく，いつでもその意見を表現できるよう準備しておくことが大切なのだ。

自分がその問題について考えていることを示せば，自分の意見が正しいか間違っているかは問題ではない。すべての答えを知る必要はなく，最終決定をする必要もない。しかし「X をどう思うか」と聞かれて，本当はそれについて何も知らない場合に，「わかりません」とか「意見は何もありません」としか答えないのはよい考えではない。それは失礼に響く。なぜなら「自分は会話に興味がない」と言っているように相手が思うかもしれないからだ。

そんな場合は，「X をどう考えるべきかわかりません。あなたはどう思いますか」のように，いつでも質問を返すことができる。そうすれば，自分が少なくともその問題について考える用意があると伝わる。そして相手がアメリカ人なら，喜んで話してくれるだろう。

しかし，彼が自分の考えをあなたに話した後，あなたはただ同意するべきではない。「ああ，なるほど」とか「ええ，そうですよね」と言うだけでは，自分の意見を持てないほど愚かだと思われてしまうだろう。

アメリカでは，意見を言わないことは自分の意見を持っていないことを意味する。自分の脳が働いており，積極的に注意を払っていることを示さねばならない。そのために，相手に同意する自分なりの理由を述べたり，相手の意見に関する質問をしたり問題点を見つけたりする。

お互いの意見に疑問を持つことはアメリカ人に

とって非常に自然なことなので，たいていの場合彼らは自分がそうしているとさえ思わない。アメリカ人は，たとえ相手が社会的地位の高い人でも，その人の考えに疑問を持つことが失礼だとは考えない。考えはそれを表現する人とは別だとみなされるので，ある考えに反対することはその人に対する無礼を示すわけではない。

教師は，授業で教師の言うことを簡単に信じるのではなく質問する生徒を好む。その態度は生徒が積極的に考えていることを示すからである。生徒は教師の言うことをすべて受け入れる必要はない。だからアメリカ人の教師によい印象を与えたければ，たくさんの質問をしなさい。

もちろん，「いや，それは正しくない」とか「君は間違っている」のようなことを言って反論すれば，失礼に響くこともありうる。しかし「なぜそう思うのですか」と尋ねたり，「ええ，でもXについてはどうですか」と言って相手の意見に満足していないことを示すのは，いつでも全く問題ない。

日本で教えるアメリカ人教師は，英会話の授業で不満を感じる。彼らは生徒からの疑問を，独自の意見や考えを生み出す方法として楽しむ。

しかし日本人にとって，相手の意見を問題にするという考えは非常に失礼に思える。日本人教師は，授業で生徒の意見をあまり求めない。また生徒の意見を求めるときも，その意見についてあまり質問せず，「とても面白い意見だね」のような返事をするだけである。

しかしアメリカ人教師は，常に生徒に意見を求める。そして生徒が意見を言うと，教師は必ず「なぜそう思うのですか」と尋ねる。この質問がとても意外なので，日本の生徒は自分が「間違った」答えをしたと感じるのである。

語句

hold「～を(心に)抱く」 content「内容」
silent「黙っている」 mostly「普通は，たいてい」
therefore「したがって」 stupid「愚かな」
original「独創的な，独自の」
come up「現れる，生じる」
sound「～に聞こえる」 impression「印象」
feel frustrated「欲求不満を感じる」
respond「反応する」

015 ① イ　② ア　③ エ　④ ア
⑤ ウ　⑥ エ，カ

解説 ①「金継ぎに関して正しくないものは次のうちのどれか」

ア 人々は単語を組み合わせることによって金継ぎという言葉を作った。
イ 金継ぎは美しく壊れやすい焼き物を作る日本の伝統である。
ウ 金継ぎは美しい方法でものを修理する技術である。
エ 人々は金継ぎで焼き物の壊れた部分を見せる。

第1段落の内容に着目する。金継ぎは壊れた焼き物を修理する技術だから，イは正しくない。

②「16世紀半ばより前の日本の壺や椀について正しいものはどれか」

ア それらはとても壊れやすいため簡単に割れたので，日本人は壊れた焼き物をゴミとして捨てることを気にしなかった。
イ それらを大事に(世話)することが日本の伝統だったので，それらはとても慎重に扱われた。
ウ 壊れた焼き物を修理する費用が高すぎたので，日本人はそれらを修理することを決して考えなかった。
エ 日本人は美しい壺や碗をとても愛好していたので，壊れたかけらさえ長い間持ち続けていた。

第2段落の3～4文目(However, ...)によれば，壺や碗は壊れやすく，ほとんどの持ち主は壊れた品をすぐに捨てていた。したがってアが正しい。

③「金継ぎの方法で，人々が壊れた焼き物を修理するために接着剤に金粉を入れるのはなぜか」

ア 金粉を使って，焼き物の割れた部分を隠すことができる。
イ 金粉を使って，割れた焼き物はより丈夫で使いやすくなる。
ウ そのようにして人々は，壊れやすい焼き物を修理するのはとても難しいと示そうとしている。
エ そのようにして人々は，壊れた部分を示して割れた焼き物をより美しくすることができる。

第2段落の最後から3文目と2文目(By doing this ...)に「碗や壺が修理されたことを明確に示していた」「修理することでよりいっそう美しいものを作れることを示していた」とあるので，エが正しい。

④「下線部の『金継ぎは大きな発想である』とはどういう意味か」

ア 金継ぎの発想は人間の心を修復するのに使う

ことができる。

イ 金継ぎの発想はどんな壊れた碗や壺でも直すことができる。

ウ 金継ぎの発想は人間の折れた骨を直すのに使うことができる。

エ 金継ぎの発想は，あなたが他人を好きでないときにその人の気持ちを変えることができる。

下線部に続く内容から考えて，アが正しい。第4段落の最初の文(However, you can ...)によれば，金継ぎの発想は自分の心の修復に使えるのであって，他人の心を変えるわけではないからエは誤り。

⑤「あなたが誰かを傷つけたとき，金継ぎの流儀はどのようにあなたを助けるか」

ア あなたが申し訳なく感じて，心の中で「ごめんなさい」と言うのを助けることができる。

イ ひどいことは何も起こらなかったとあなたが考えようとするのを助けることができる。

ウ あなたが自分の感情を修復して状況を改善するのを助けることができる。

エ あなたが「金粉」を使ってそのひどい出来事を忘れるのを助けることができる。

第4段落の2～4文目(For example, ...)によれば，口論をした相手に謝ることで自分の気持ちと相手との人間関係を修復することができる(この謝るという行為が金継ぎに当たる)。したがってウが正しい。

⑥「本文に従って，2つの正しい文を次の中から選びなさい」

ア「金継ぎが生まれる前には，日本人は割れた焼き物のすべてのかけらを使って新しい壺や碗を作っていた」。金継ぎが生まれる前には，日本人は割れた焼き物をすぐに捨てていた。したがって誤り。

イ「接着剤だけを使って割れた焼き物を修理するのは，金粉を使って修理するよりも難しかった」。本文にはこのようなことは書かれていない。

ウ「人の心は焼き物のように壊れやすいので，人々は他人の感情を傷つけるべきではない」。筆者が言いたいのは「他人の感情を傷つけた場合に金継ぎの発想が利用できる」ということだから，誤り。

エ「金継ぎの方法は友情を以前よりも強くすることができる」。最後の段落の1～2文目(When you ...)の内容に一致する。

オ「親に対する私たちの感情は，友人に対する感情よりも簡単に修復することができる」。本文にはこのようなことは書かれていない。

カ「たとえ他人の感情を傷つけても，金継ぎの方法を使うことによって相手との関係を修復することができる」。これが本文の中心的なテーマなので正しい。

精読

◆Normally, if something is broken, you feel it is **not** useful **anymore**.(*ll.*5-6)(普通は，何かが壊れればもう役に立たないとあなたは思うだろう)：〈not + any = no〉という関係がある。not ～ anymore[any more]は「もう(それ以上は)～ではない」の意味で，no more ～とも言う。次の例も同様。

I do**n't** know **anything** about baseball.
= I know **nothing** about baseball.
(私は野球については何も知りません)

→英語では否定語(not，noなど)をなるべく前に置く傾向があるので，1つ目の文の方が好まれる。

◆they were also showing that they could create **even more beautiful** things by fixing them(*ll.*20-21)(彼らは修理することでよりいっそう美しいものを作れることも示していた)：〈**even** + **X**の比較級〉は「今でも(十分に)**X**なのだが，さらにいっそう～」という意味を表す。

◆It is **not just** the physical breaking of bones or hurting the body. Breaking can **also** happen if ...(*ll.*24-26)(それは単に物理的に骨を折ったり体を傷つけたりするだけではない。壊れることは…の場合にも起こりうる)：justはonlyの意味で，この2文は**not only A but also B**(**A**だけでなく**B**も)の変形と言える。この連語はさまざまな形で文中に出てくるので，見逃さないようにしよう。

全訳

金継ぎ

あなたは以前に「金継ぎ」という言葉を聞いたことはたぶんないだろう。それはあまり意外なことではない。金継ぎは日本語である。その言葉は2つの日本語の単語から作られたものだ。1つ目の部分はgolden(金の)を意味する「金」，2つ目の部分はfixing(直すこと)を意味する「継ぎ」である。この2つの言葉を組み合わせると，壊れたものを美しく修理するという意味になる。普通は，何かが壊れればもう役に立たないとあなたは思うだろう。あなたはそれを捨てて，新しいものを買いたいと思うかもしれない。しかし，金継ぎの流儀はそうではない。

金継ぎは，ずっと昔に日本で始まった。昔の日本人は壺や碗を愛好し，美しい品を作る伝統を持っていた。しかしそれらの壺や碗はとても壊れやすいので，簡単に割れてしまった。ほとんどの持ち主は割れたものをすぐに捨て，新しいものを買った。しかし16世紀の中ごろ，美しい壺，碗，鉢をゴミとして捨てるべきではないと考える人たちが現れた。彼らはそれらを修理してみるべきだと考えた。この発想は当時の日本人の間で次第に広まった。人々は壊れた焼き物を修理し始めた。最初は接着剤だけで壊れたかけらをつなぎ合わせて直していたが，そのうち接着剤に金粉を混ぜて使うようになった。これはどの部分が修理されたのかがはっきりとわかることを意味した。こうすることで，その椀や壺が以前は壊れていなかったと偽《いつわ》るのではなく，修理されたものであることを明確に示していた。彼らはその事実を受け入れてもかまわないこと，また修理することでよりいっそう美しいものを作れることを示していた。これが金継ぎの流儀である。

金継ぎは大きな発想である。それは割れた椀を直すというとても小さなことから始まったが，同じ発想がもっと大切なことを考えるのにも使える。たとえば，人はとても繊細なので，簡単に壊れてしまう。壊れるとは，物理的に骨を折ったり体を傷つけたりするだけではない。本当に怒ってひどいことを言ったり，不親切なことをしたりした場合にも壊れることがある。このようなことが起こると，自分の中のよい点が損なわれたような気になる。他の人々はもう自分のことはいらないだろうという気分になることもある。

しかし，あなたは金継ぎの流儀で自分を治すことができる。たとえば，自分がひどいことをしたときに申し訳ないと思い，相手に謝る。それは一種の修理である。あなたは自分の気持ちと相手との関係を修復しているのだ。あなたはひどいことが起きたのを忘れておらず，その悪いことを言ったりしたりしていないと偽ってはいない。同時に，あなたは状況を改善して問題を解決しようと努めている。このように，あなたは金継ぎとちょうど同じように，「金粉」を使って最善を尽くしているのだ。

誰かと仲直りすると，2人の関係は以前よりよくなる場合もある。仲直りした後は，口論は友情の終わりを意味するのではなく，口論を通じて友情が深まることもあると確信することができる。たとえば，時には親に腹を立てることもあるだろう。しかし，何が問題なのかを説明し，話し，耳を傾ければ，お互いをもっと理解することができる。そうすれば親との関係は以前よりもよくなる。私たちの気持ちは修復できるものだと知っておくことは役に立つ。自分が他人の気持ちを傷つけることもあれば，相手が自分の気持ちを傷つけることもある。それは決して楽しくはない。しかし金継ぎの発想を心に留めておけば，物事をよい方法で修復できることを覚えておこう。

語句

put ～ together「～を組み合わせる」
normally「通常は，普通は」
not ～ anymore「もはや～ではない」
ancient「古代の」 pot「壺」
delicate「繊細な，壊れやすい」
right away「すぐに」 bowl「鉢」
waste「ゴミ，廃棄物」
mix O with ～「O を～と混ぜる」
damage「～に(損)害を与える」
relationship「(人間)関係」
keep ～ in one's mind「～を心に留めておく」

016
① **mother**
② (a) ア (b) ウ (c) ウ
③ **she wasn't home in time for dinner**
④ 全訳の下線部(4)を参照。
⑤ ア ⑥ **please** ⑦ C，D

解説 ①ミーガンは何でも完璧にこなそうとする女性だったことから考えて，空所にはmotherを入れて「よい妻でありよい母親であろうとした」という内容にするのが適切。

②「自分に援助を求めてくるいとこからの電話に，ミーガンは最近出ない」という状況だから，(a)はミーガン，(b)(c)は彼女のいとこである。

③be in time for ～は「～に間に合って」の意味。並べ替えた部分は「彼女は夕食に間に合うよう帰って来られなかった[帰宅が遅れて夕食のしたくができなかった」という意味になる。

④A is about B. の形で「Aの最も重要な目的はBだ，Aの本質はBにある」という意味を表す。ここではnotがあるので，セミコロン(;)の後ろと連動して「Aの最も重要な目的はBではなく～だった」という意味になっている。

［参考］ about はもともと「～のまわりに」の意味だから，この形は「A は B のまわりにある」，つまり「中心は B だ」と考えればよい。

⑤ア 彼らはあまり気にしていないようだった
イ 彼らは彼女に別の頼みごとをするつもりだった
ウ 彼らは実際には彼女に好感を持っていなかった
エ 彼らはそれまでに彼女がしたことにとても感謝していた
オ 彼らはもう二度と彼女に頼みごとをしないという態度をとった

「相手の頼みを断っても，ミーガン自身が思っているほど相手は気にしない。それを知ってミーガンは気が楽になった」という状況だと考えるのが自然だから，アを入れるのが適切。

⑥ she felt less pressured to ( ) others（彼女は他人を…するというプレッシャーを感じることが減った）という文を完成する。下線部は不定詞だから，空所には動詞の原形が入る。前の段落の最後の文に pleasing があるので，これを原形にした please（～を喜ばせる）が正解。

⑦全訳の下線部［A］～［J］を参照。

精読

◆At age thirty-five, she was married and had two young children.（*l*.4）（35歳の彼女は既婚者で，2人の幼い子どもがいた）：下線部は she の説明になっており，「彼女は（そのとき）35歳だった」ということ。「彼女は35歳で結婚した」という意味ではない。

◆**The more** Megan talked, **the clearer it became that** she was a woman who couldn't say no.（*ll*.9-10）（ミーガンが話せば話すほど，彼女はノーと言えない女性であることがはっきりした。）：〈**The** ＋比較級＋ SV, **the** ＋比較級＋ SV.〉の形は，「～すればするほど（その分だけ）…」という意味を表す。コンマの後ろは，it became clear that ...（…ということが明らかになった）という形をもとにして，下線部を the clearer に置き換えて前に出したもの。it は形式主語で，後ろの that 節を指す。形式主語の it を使った主な構文には，次の２種類がある。

(A)〈**It is** ＋形容詞＋ **(for A) to *do*.**〉「…することは（**A** にとって）～だ」

・**It is difficult** (for me) **to solve** this puzzle.
（このパズルを解くことは（私には）難しい）

(B)〈**It is** ＋形容詞＋ **that ....**〉「…ということは～だ」

・**It is well-known that** smoking is bad for your health.（喫煙が健康に悪いということはよく知られている）

◆Parents of her Girl Scout troop sometimes **relied on her to drive** their children home（*ll*.11-12）（ガールスカウトの親たちは，時々自分の子を車で家まで送ることを彼女に頼った）：〈V ＋ O ＋ **to *do***〉がひとまとまりの意味を表すことがある。この文では，**rely on** O **to *do***（O が～するのを頼る［当てにする］）を１つの表現としてとらえるのがポイント。このような形で使う動詞をまとめて覚えておくとよい。たとえば allow（許す）は，この形で使う主な動詞の１つ。文中に allow が出てきたら，〈allow ＋ O ＋ to *do*〉（O が～するのを許す［可能にする］）の形を予想しながら読み進める必要がある。

・The teacher **allowed** us to go home.
（先生は私たちが帰宅するのを許した）

◆some sort of last-minute problem, **ranging from** being short on cash **to** needing help with a home improvement project（*ll*.16-17）（金が足りないという問題から家の修繕作業の手伝いが必要だという問題に至るまでの，切羽詰まった問題）：上記と同様に，range という動詞を見たら，**range from A to B**（（範囲が）**A** から **B** まで及ぶ）という形が思い浮かぶようにしたい（下線部が A・B に当たる。to は前置詞だから，後ろには動名詞 needing が置かれている）。なお ranging は現在分詞で，which ranged で置き換えて考えることができる（ranging 以下は前の problem を詳しく説明している）。このように〈コンマ＋分詞で始まる句〉が前の名詞に説明を加える形がある。

・*Botchan*, **written**［=which was written］**by Natsume Soseki**, is a popular novel.
（夏目漱石によって書かれた『坊ちゃん』は人気の高い小説だ）

◆Lately, Megan **had stopped** answering her cousin's phone calls（*ll*.17-18）（最近，ミーガンはいとこからの電話に出るのをやめていた）：〈**had** ＋過去分詞〉の形を，過去完了形という。過去完了形は，過去のある時点（X）を基準にして，X

より前に完了していた出来事や，Xまで続いていた状態などを表す。ここでは，ミーガンが「私」の治療を受けた(過去の)時点を基準にして，「それより前に電話に出るのをやめていた」という意味を表す。

◆So **each time** her cousin asked for a favor or her sister asked her to babysit, she automatically said yes.(*ll.*21-22)(だから，いとこが彼女に頼みごとをしたり，妹が彼女に子守を頼んだりするたびに，彼女は自動的にイエスと答えていた)：**each time** SVは「SがVするたびに」の意味で，each timeは接続詞として使う。timeを含むその他の接続詞には，**every time**(…するときはいつも)，**the last time**(最後に[最も最近]…したとき)，**the next time**(次に…するとき)などがある。

・I'll return this book **the next time** I come here.
(今度ここに来るときにこの本を返します)

◆When I asked her [**what impact that had on her husband and children**] (*ll.*22-23)(それが彼女の夫と子どもたちにどんな影響を与えるかを私が彼女に尋ねたとき)：that(それ，そのこと)は前の文の内容を指す。[ ]の部分は，That had a X impact on her husband and children.(それは彼女の夫と子どもたちにXな影響を与えた)という文を元にして考える(have a X[形容詞] impact on ～「～にXな影響を与える」)。この文の下線部をwhat impactで尋ねる疑問文にして間接疑問にすると，[ ]の形になる。

◆S[Just admitting that out loud] **helped** Megan **begin** to realize [why saying yes to extended family meant she was saying no to her immediate family].(*ll.*24-26)(そのことを口に出して認めるだけで，近親者にイエスと言うことが肉親にノーと言うことになるのはなぜかをミーガンは理解し始めた)：[ ]の部分が意味のまとまりを作っている。基本構造は，S helped Megan begin to realize ...(Sはミーガンが…と理解し始めるのに役立った)。**help O (to) *do***は「Oが～するのを助ける」という意味。この文ではbeginの前のtoが省略されている。Sは「単にそのことを口に出して認めること」(admit O out loud「Oを口に出して認める」)。why以下は，why S meant (that) ...(Sはなぜ…ということを意味するのか)という形になっている。

◆**Once** she changed [**the way** she thought about people pleasing], she was able to begin changing her behavior.(*ll.*34-35)(人を喜ばせることに関する考え方を変えたとたんに，彼女は自分の行動を変え始めることができた)：この文の**once**は，「ひとたび…すれば，…するとすぐに」の意味の接続詞として使われている。**the way** SVは「SがVする方法」。

・I like **the way** this announcer speaks.
(私はこのアナウンサーの話し方が好きです)

people pleasingは「人を喜ばせること」(bird watching「バードウォッチング＝鳥を見ること」と同様の形)。

◆**It took some practice for Megan to begin** saying no to people.(*l.*36)(ミーガンが人々に対してノーと言い始めるには，いくらかの練習が必要だった)：**it takes A for B to *do***は「～するのにBはAを要する」の意味。it takes B A to *do*ともいう。この形のAは，「時間の長さ」を表す名詞(句)であることが多い。

・**It took 20 minutes for us to walk** to the station.
＝**It took us 20 minutes to walk** to the station.
(駅まで歩くのに私たちは20分かかった)

一方，本文のsome practiceのように，Aに「労力，努力」などを表す名詞を置くこともできる。

全訳

ミーガンは，ストレスに押しつぶされそうになっていたので，助けを求めて私の治療院へ入って来た。彼女は，する必要があることを全部やり遂げるための時間が1日のうち十分にないと言った。

35歳の彼女は既婚者で，2人の幼い子どもがいた。彼女はパートで働き，日曜学校で教え，ガールスカウトの団長をしていた。彼女はよい妻でよい母親であろうと努力したが，十分な仕事ができていないように感じていた。家族に対して怒りっぽく不機嫌になることが多く，彼女にはその理由がよくわからなかった。

ミーガンが話せば話すほど，彼女は[A]ノーと言えない女性であることがはっきりした。教会のメンバーは土曜日の夜に彼女に電話をかけてきて，日曜日の朝の教会の礼拝のためにマフィンを焼いてほしいと頼むことがよくあった。ガールスカウトの親たちは，仕事で身動きがとれない場合，自分の子を車で家まで送ることを彼女に頼むことが時々あった。

ミーガンは，妹がシッターにお金をかけなくてもよいよう，しばしば妹の子の子守をしていた。また彼女には頼みごとをしてくるいとこもおり，そのいとこは金が足りないという問題から家の修繕作業の手伝いが必要だという問題に至るまで，いつも切羽詰まった問題を抱えているようだった。最近，ミーガンはいとこからの電話に出るのをやめていた。彼女が電話をかけてくるたびに，何か必要なものがあるとわかっていたからだ。

ミーガンは私に，自分の一番のルールは家族に対して決して[B]ノーと言わないことだ，と言った。だから，いとこが彼女に頼みごとをしたり，妹が彼女に子守りを頼んだりするたびに，彼女は自動的に[C]イエスと答えていた。それが夫や子どもたちにどんな影響を与えるのかと私が尋ねると，帰宅が夕食や子どもの寝かしつけに間に合わないことがある，と彼女は私に言った。そのことを口に出して認めるだけで，近親者に[D]イエスと言うことが肉親に[E]ノーと言うことになるのはなぜかをミーガンは理解し始めた。彼女は近親者を大切にしていたが，夫と子どもが最優先だったので，それに従って彼らを扱い始める必要があると決めた。

私たちは，みんなに好かれたいという彼女の願望も見直した。彼女が最も恐れていたのは，他人に利己的だと思われることだった。しかし数回の面談治療を経て，常に好かれたいという自分の欲求は，実は誰かに[F]ノーと言うよりもはるかに利己的だと彼女は認識し始めた。(4)(彼女が)他人を助ける本当の目的は，その人の生活を向上させることでは決してなかった。彼女は自分がより高く評価されたいから，他人のために尽力していたのだ。人を喜ばせることに関する考え方を変えたとたんに，彼女は自分の行動を変え始めることができた。

ミーガンが人々に対して[G]ノーと言い始めるには，いくらかの練習が必要だった。実際，彼女はどのようにして[H]ノーと言えばよいかさえよくわからなかった。言い訳が必要だと思っても，うそはつきたくなかった。しかし私は，長々とした理由は説明せず，「いいえ，それはできません」のようなことをただ言えばいいと彼女に勧めた。彼女は[I]ノーと言う練習をし始め，断れば断るほど断りやすくなると自分でわかった。断れば相手は自分に対して怒るだろうと彼女は想像していたが，実際はあまり気にしないことに彼女はすぐ気づいた。家族と過ごす時間が増えるほど，彼女のいらだちは減った。ストレス度も下がり，何度か[J]ノーと言った後，彼女は人を喜ばせるというプレッシャーをだんだん感じなくなった。

語句

stressed out「ストレスで参っている」
accomplish「～を成し遂げる」
Girl Scout troop leader「ガールスカウトの団長」
bake「～を焼く」 muffin「マフィン」
church service「教会の礼拝」
drive ～ home「～を車で家まで送る」
stuck「身動きがとれない」
babysat < babysit「子守りをする」
sought < seek「～を探し求める」
favor「好意，親切」 last-minute「どたん場の」
be short on cash「(現)金が足りない」
home improvement project「家の修繕作業」
lately「最近」 number one「第一の，最優先の」
ask for a favor「願いごとをする」
automatically「自動的に」 impact「影響，衝撃」
put O to bed「O を寝かしつける」
admit「～を認める」 value「～を重視する」
top priority「最優先(のこと)」 treat「～を扱う」
accordingly「(それに)従って」
review「～を見直す」
selfish「利己的な，わがままな」
recognize「～を認識する，わかる」
behavior「振る舞い，行動」 excuse「言い訳」
encourage O to *do*「O に～するよう促す」
simply「単に」
something like ～「～のようなもの[こと]」
provide「～を提供する」 lengthy「長ったらしい」
notice「～に気づく」 decrease「減る」
pressure「～にプレッシャーを与える」

第 2 回 実力テスト

① **attention**
② **suggest they are smarter than their younger siblings**
③ **younger, any other child**
④ エ → イ → ウ → ア
⑤ [1] 親密な(3字) [2] 周囲の人々に自分の個性を示す(14字) ⑥ D
⑦ (a) イ (b) オ (c) エ (d) ウ (e) ア

解説 ①「きょうだいは互いの物を取り合い，親の…を求めてけんかをする」という文を完成する

(fight for 〜「〜を求めて争う」)。本文の後半は，一番上の子と一番下の子は親の関心を引きやすいが，真ん中の子はそうではない，という内容になっている。たとえば *l*.20 には，parents usually give more attention to first-born children(親はたいてい長子により多くの関心を寄せる)とある。この文脈から考えて，空所には attention(関心，注目)を入れるのが適切。

②(some studies) suggest they are smarter than their younger siblings(いくつかの研究は，彼ら[長子]が年下のきょうだいたちより利口であることを示唆している)と並べれば意味が通る。suggest (that) ... は「…と(いうことを)示唆する，示す」の意味で，この文では that が省略されている。

③「彼は家族のすべての子どもたちのうちで一番若かった」という文を，「彼は家族の他のどの子よりも若かった」と言い換える。〈比較級 + than any other X〉は「他のどの X よりも〜」の意味。X には単数形の名詞を使う点に注意。

［参考］ any の本来の意味は「たとえどの１つを選んでも」。smarter than any other child は「他のどの１人の子を選んでも，その子よりも利口だ」ということだから，単数形の child を使う。

④全訳の下線部(4)を参照。アの個人名は，ウの some great members の具体例になっている。またエの they は，この４つの文の前にある the poor kids in the middle(真ん中のかわいそうな子たち)を指している。「真ん中の子」とは，３人以上のきょうだいの中で一番上でも一番下でもない子のこと。彼らが「かわいそう」なのは，長子や末子ほど親の関心を引かず，いつも一番好かれるわけではないからである。

⑤下線部(5)を含む文とその次の文の内容を，適切な日本語で表す。全訳の下線部(5)を参照。

⑥全訳の下線部[D]を参照。直前の文をふまえて訳すと，「人々はかつては，一人っ子として育つのは悲しいことだと考えていた」となる。

⑦全訳の＿＿部(a)〜(e)を参照。(e)はbe different from 〜(〜とは異なる)の形を作る。

精読

◆But brothers and sisters are often with us for almost all our lives **for better or for worse** ....(*ll*.2-3)(しかし兄弟姉妹は，私たちの人生の大半をともにすることが多い。よくも悪くもではあるが…)：for better or for worse は「よくも悪くも，好もうと好むまいと，どんなことがあろうと」。「親とは死別してもきょうだいの付き合いは，仲がよかろうと悪かろうと一生続く」ということ。文の最後が .... のは，for better or for worse が「もっとも…ではあるが」という(余分な)付け足しの情報だからである。

◆Why **can** this **be**?(*l*.19)(なぜこのようなことがありうるのか)：多くの助動詞は，推量・可能性の意味を持つ。たとえば，

・**must**「(1)〜しなければならない，(2)〜に違いない」
・**may**「(1)〜してもよい，(2)〜かもしれない」
・**can**「(1)〜できる，(2)〜でありうる」

それぞれの(2)が「推量・可能性」の意味である。「〜でありうる」の意味の can は，しばしば否定文・疑問文で，can(not) be の形で使う。

・This story **cannot be** true.(この話は本当ではありえない[本当のはずがない])

◆Her parents didn't have to worry about **her being seen as** "special" or different from any siblings.　She didn't steal attention away from anyone.(*ll*.38-40)(彼女の両親は，彼女が「特別」だとか，きょうだいとは違うとみなされることを心配しなくてよかった。彼女は誰からも注目を盗まなかった)：下線部は「彼女が〜として見られること」の意味。about(前置詞)の後ろには名詞または動名詞を置く必要があるので，be seen(見られる)の be を動名詞(being)にする。her は動名詞の意味上の主語で，次の文と同じ形。

・Do you mind **me[my] sitting** here?
(私がここに座ってもかまいませんか)

ll.38-40の２つの文で筆者が言いたいことは次のとおり。「彼女にもしきょうだいがいて，彼女だけが女優になったら，他のきょうだいが彼女と比較されるかもしれない。しかし一人っ子なら，親はそういう心配をする必要がない。また彼女は，親の関心を他のきょうだいと競って取り合う必要もなかった[他のきょうだいに向けられるはずの親の関心を自分が「盗む」という事態は起きなかった]。」

◆"Please, it's not us.　It's me!"(*l*.44)(お願いします，「私たち」じゃありません。「私」なんです！)：Please は「わかって[ちゃんと見て]ください」というニュアンス。双子はたいてい２人１組で見られるが，本人たちはそれを嫌い「私をきょうだ

いとは違う1人の人間として扱ってください」と周囲に訴えねばならない，ということ。

全訳

配偶者や子どもは，私たちの人生の後期に現れる。親はあまりにも早く私たちの元を去る。しかし兄弟姉妹は，私たちの人生の大半をともにすることが多い。よくも悪くもではあるが…。

同じ屋根の下で2人以上の子どもを育てると，苦労することが多い。きょうだいは互いの物を取り合い，親の関心を求めてけんかをする。実際，最近のイングランドでの調査によれば，31％の子どもがきょうだい同士でよくけんかするために不満を持っている。

しかし，こうしたけんかは私たちにとってよいこともある。けんかは感情的に安全な環境で問題に直面するチャンスである。朝食時のけんかは，昼食時までに忘れられる。イギリスの詩人ディラン・トマスはかつて，「私が雪だるまを作って，兄がそれを倒して，私が兄を倒して，それから一緒にお茶を飲んだ」と言った。

特に姉妹がいると私たちにとって助けになるようだ。イギリスのアルスター大学の研究によると，きょうだいに女の子がいると，家族の中で正直なコミュニケーションが増える。これは私たちの心の健康に(a)よい。

では，もう1つの家族の問題について考えてみよう！ バラク・オバマ，ベン・アフレック，JK・ローリングに共通するのは何だろうか。彼らはみんな金持ちで，成功者で，長子[最初に生まれた子]である。実際，アメリカ大統領やノーベル賞受賞者の半数以上が長子である。USA TODAYという新聞の調査によると，大企業の社長の43％も長子だった。なぜこのようなことがありうるのか。

さて，親はたいてい，長子により大きな関心を寄せ，彼らに大きな期待を抱く。その結果，こうした子は(b)責任感を持ち，自信に満ちていることが多い。彼らは学校の成績がよく，年下のきょうだいたちより利口であると示唆する研究もある。しかし，長子は弱点も持ちうる。彼らは時に，自分に期待しすぎたり，完璧であろうとしすぎたりする。そのため彼らは，心配性でミスをするのを(c)怖がることもある。

末子[最後に生まれた子]，つまり「一家の赤ちゃん」も，たいてい多くの注目を浴びる。彼らは愛情深く，社交的で，魅力的であることが多い。年上のきょうだいよりも自由で，変わったことや(d)危険なことをする可能性が強い。ポーランドの科学者コペルニクスのように，彼らはしばしば規則を破る。彼は家族の中で一番年下だった。1543年に，彼は地球が太陽のまわりを回っているという本を書き，世界中に衝撃を与えた。当時は，太陽が地球のまわりを回っていると誰もが信じていたので，一部の人々はコペルニクスに間違っていると言われて非常に腹を立てた。

真ん中の気の毒な子どもたちはどうだろう？ (4)研究によると，彼らは長子や末子ほど注目されず，いつも一番好かれるわけではない。しかし，もしあなたが真ん中の子でも心配しなくていい。あなたの仲間の中には素晴らしい人々がいる。ビル・ゲイツも，ジョン・F・ケネディも，マドンナも，みんな真ん中の子である。

一緒に遊ぶ兄弟姉妹がいない一人っ子として育つのは悲しいことなのか。[D]昔はそう考えられていた。しかし最近の多くの研究によると，一人っ子は幸せで成功することが多い。女優のナタリー・ポートマンはかつて，「両親が私に女優になることを許してくれたのは，私が一人っ子だったからだ」と語った。彼女の両親は，彼女が「特別」だとか，きょうだいとは(e)違うとみなされることを心配しなくてよかった。彼女は誰からも注目を盗まなかった。彼女は自分のやりたいことを全部できて満足することができた。

最後に，多子出産という問題がある。双子であることはどんな感じだろうか。(5)双子は極めて親密な関係を持つことができ，それは彼らが人生を生き抜く助けになる。しかし双子は時に，自分自身の個性を示すのが難しいことがある。彼らは周囲の人々にこう思い出させなければならない。「お願いします，『私たち』じゃありません。『私』なんです！」

語句

appear「現れる」 later「後で」
almost「ほとんど」 bring up ～「～を育てる」
two or more ～「2つ[人]以上の～」
roof「屋根」 trouble「苦労，トラブル」
face「～に直面する，立ち向かう」
environment「環境」 poet「詩人」
knock ～ down「～を(打ち)倒す」
have ～ in common「～を共通に持つ」
successful「成功した」
give attention to ～「～に注意を払う」
as a result「結果として」
confident「自信を持った」 smart「利口な」
expect O of ～「Oを～に期待する」
loving「愛情深い」 sociable「社交的な」
Polish「ポーランド(人)の」

Copernicus「コペルニクス」
shock「～に衝撃を与える」
be sure that ...「…と(いうことを)確信している」
What about ～?「～についてはどうだろうか」
actress「女優」
worry about ～「～のことを心配する」
steal「～を盗む」 lastly「最後に」
extremely「極めて，非常に」
close「親しい，親密な」
relationship「(人間)関係」
get through life「人生を生き抜く」
character「性格，個性」
remind「～に思い出させる」

3 論説文－科学・技術

017 ① (A) カ (B) ア (C) ウ
② (1) **No, they didn't.**
(2) **(They put it) On the three corners (of it).**
③ エ，オ

解説 ①全訳を参照。完成した表は次のようになる。

段落	見出し
[1]	私たちの日常生活の中の2次元コード
[2]	(カ)バーコードを使うことの問題点
[3]	(ア)日本の技術者たちによって発明された新しい種類の2次元コード
[4]	(ウ)新しい種類の2次元コードの別の使い方
[5]	世界中の人々のための2次元コード

その他の選択肢の意味と，これらを選ばない理由は次のとおり。

イ 作業員たちの状況を改善することのできるバーコード(下線部は「2次元コード」が正しい)

エ アメリカのいくつかの2次元コードの使い方(段落[3]に関係しているが，この段落の要約としては不適切)

オ 携帯電話のカメラを使い始めた会社(段落[4]に関係しているが，正しくは「携帯電話のカメラに2次元コード(の読み取り)を使い始めた会社」である)

②(1)「日本の自動車部品メーカーの技術者たちは，アメリカの2次元コードを使ったか」。Yes か No かで答える形の疑問文だから，段落[3]の内容から No, they didn't[did not]. と答える。

(2)「新しい種類の2次元コードを発明したとき，技術者たちはどこに特殊な目印を入れたか」。*ll*.22-24 (They thought, "If ... angle.") を参照して，(They put it) On the three corners (of it).(彼らはそれ[＝新しい種類の2次元コード]の3つの隅にそれ[＝特殊な目印]を入れた)と答える。

③ア「日本のある自動車部品メーカーがバーコードを発明した」。バーコードがどこで発明されたかは本文に書かれていない。

イ「自動車部品メーカーはより多くの車を売るためにバーコードを使った」。本文にこのようなことは書かれていないし，部品メーカーの仕事は車を売ることではないから常識的に考えても誤り。

ウ「バーコードは2次元コードより多くの情報を含むことができる」。段落[3]の内容とは逆だから誤り。

エ「特殊な目印の入った2次元コードは，素早く読み取ることができる」。日本の自動車部品メーカーがそのようなコードを発明した，と段落[3]に書かれているので正しい。

オ「ある携帯電話会社は，利用者がより簡単にホームページを見るのに役立つよう，新しい種類の2次元コードを使った」。段落[4]の内容に一致するので正しい。

カ「日米の技術者たちは，新しい種類の2次元コードを発明するために協力した」。段落[3]に関係しているが，本文にはこのようなことは書かれていない。

精読

◆The engineers at the car parts maker did not use these types. (*ll*.19-20) (その自動車部品メーカーの技術者たちは，これらのタイプを使わなかった)：下線部の解釈に注意。この段落の最初の文に，The engineers at a car parts maker in Japan ...(日本のある自動車メーカーの技術者たちは…)とある。「その自動車部品メーカー」とは，このメーカーのことである。彼らはアメリカで使われていた種類の2次元コードを使わず，独自のアイデアを思いついた。

全訳

[1]隅に特殊な目印がある2次元コードを見たことがあるだろうか。たとえば，教科書に2次元コードを見つけることができる。2次元コードをタブレット端末で読み取ると，写真を見たり動画を見たりすることができる。今日では，世界中の多くの人がさまざまな方法で2次元コードを利用している。この種の2次元コードは，日本の自動車部品メーカーの技術者たちによって発明された。

[2]自動車が生産される際には，多くの種類の部品が必要とされる。自動車部品メーカーは，その部品をすべて管理しなければならない。30年ほど前，自動車会社はより多くの種類の自動車を生産する必要があり，自動車部品メーカーはそれぞれの車に対して多くの異なる種類の自動車部品を管理しなければならなかった。当時は自動車部品を管理するのにバーコードを使っていたが，1つのバーコードに多くの情報を入れることはできなかった。そこで，彼らは多くのバーコードを使った。作業員たちは多くのバーコードを読み取らねばならなかった。ある自動車部品メーカーの作業員は，1日に約1,000回バーコードを読み取る必要があった。それらを読み取るには長時間を要した。作業員たちは自らの状況を改善するために何らかの支援を必要としていた。

[3]日本のある自動車部品メーカーの技術者たちは，作業員たちの状況を知っていた。2次元コードにはバーコードよりも多くの情報を含むことができるため，彼らは2次元コードについて学び始めた。アメリカにはすでにいくつかの種類の2次元コードがあった。1つのタイプは多くの情報を含むことができたが，そのタイプを読み取るには長い時間がかかった。別のタイプは，読み取るスピードはとても速いが，他のタイプよりも含まれる情報量が少なかった。その自動車部品メーカーの技術者たちは，これらのタイプを使わなかった。彼らはこの2つの長所の両方を持つ新しい種類の2次元コードを作り出すことに決めた。技術者たちが，素早く読み取れるこの新しいタイプを作り出すには長い時間を必要とした。ついに彼らは，あるアイデアを思いついた。「2次元コードの3つの隅に特殊な目印があれば，どの角度からでもとても素早く読み取ることができる」と彼らは考えた。こうして，特殊な目印を持つ新しい種類の2次元コードが，日本のある自動車部品メーカーの技術者たちによって発明された。

[4]どのようにして世界の人々がその新しい種類の2次元コードを使い始めたのか。自動車部品メーカーがそれを使い始めた後，他の企業もそれに注目し始めた。たとえば，ある携帯電話会社は，人々が自分の携帯電話のカメラを使って直接ホームページを見るのに役立つよう2次元コードを利用し始めた。携帯電話で2次元コードを読み取ることによって，利用者は多くの情報を素早く簡単に得ることができる。この技術によって，人々はその新しい種類の2次元コードが非常に便利であることを知った。

[5]今日では，日本のある自動車部品メーカーの技術者たちによって発明された2次元コードは，世界中の人々の生活の面で人気が高まっている。2次元コードは作業員たちを手助けするために技術者たちによって発明されたものだが，今では世界中の人々に大いに役立っている。

018 ① ウ　② ア　③ ウ　④ ア　⑤ エ

解説 冒頭の指示文は，「文章を読んで①～⑤のそれぞれの文を最も適切に完成する答えを選びなさい」の意味。

①「（ 1 ）に入れるべき語は…である」
ア よりよい　イ 便利な
ウ 危険な　エ 間違っている，悪い
この後に続く内容から考えて，正解はウ。

②「宇宙の問題の1つは…である」
ア 人工衛星を破壊するかもしれないさまざまなゴミ
イ 私たちの日々の生活のために働いている多くの種類の人工衛星
ウ 速く動いて深刻な事故を引き起こす人工衛星
エ 私たちの活動を助けるスペースデブリの数
第2段落の内容から考えて，正解はア。

得点アップ

設問文を正確に読もう。この問いでは，One of the **problems** ...(問題の1つは…)がヒントになる。problemとは「解決すべき問題」であり，それ自体がネガティブな意味を含む。したがってイやエは正解の候補から外して考えてよい。

③「スペースデブリの問題を解決するために試されていない計画は…である」
ア スペースデブリを発見し監視すること
イ 人工衛星をより長く働かせること
ウ ロケットと人工衛星の数を減らすこと

エ スペースデブリを宇宙から取り除くこと

第3段落で，スペースデブリの問題を解決するための3つの試みが説明されている。アは第1，イは第2，エは第3の試みである。ウは本文に書かれていない。

④「(2)『両方』という語は…について語っている」

ア 私たちの日々の生活と地球環境

イ 私たちの活動と通信

ウ 世界中の科学者と多くのチーム

エ スペースデブリと人工衛星

Bothは直前の文の最後の部分(our daily lives and the global environment)を受けている。「両方とも守られるべきだ」という文脈から考えても，アが正しい。

⑤「本文によれば，…」

ア「古い人工衛星は作動していないのでスペースデブリではない」。*ll*.7-8(For example, ... all space debris.)によれば，古い人工衛星はスペースデブリである。したがって誤り。

イ「世界の科学者と多くのチームが，ロケットと人工衛星からスペースデブリを切り離そうと努めている」。ロケットや人工衛星とスペースデブリがつながっているわけではないから誤り。

ウ「日本チームによって作られた機械は，回転しているスペースデブリを捕らえることができる」。*ll*.24-25(Some kinds of ... space debris.)に「回転しているスペースデブリを捕らえるのはその機械には難しすぎる」とあるので誤り。

エ「スペースデブリの数は増え続けているので，近い将来スペースデブリが人工衛星に衝突する回数は増えるかもしれない」。*ll*.11-12(Now, the number ... near future.)に「スペースデブリの数は増え続けている」「近い将来事故が増えるかもしれない」と書かれているので正しい。

全訳

私たちの日々の生活は，宇宙にある多くの人工衛星に支えられている。現在，地球のまわりには約4,300基の人工衛星がある。2030年までには約46,000基が宇宙に存在することになるだろう。これらの人工衛星は私たちの活動や通信に役立つ。たとえば気象情報，インターネット，携帯電話は，この人工衛星技術を使って利用できる。

しかし，スペースデブリが人工衛星の状況を危険なものにしている。スペースデブリとは，宇宙の中のゴミである。たとえば作動していない古い人工衛星や，ロケットから切り離された部品はすべてスペースデブリである。スペースデブリの大きさや形はさまざまである。スペースデブリは地球のまわりを高速で飛び回っている。その速いスペースデブリが人工衛星に衝突するとどうなるだろうか。それは人工衛星を破壊するかもしれない。現在，スペースデブリの数は増え続けている。これは，近い将来に事故が増えるかもしれないことを意味する。何もしなければ，そうした事故が私たちの日々の生活に影響を与えるだろう。

今，世界中の科学者や多くのチームが，この問題を解決するために3つのことを試みている。1つ目は，スペースデブリの発見と監視。2つ目は，新しいスペースデブリの数を減らすこと。つまり，ロケットから切り離される部品の数を減らす技術の向上である。使用期間の長い人工衛星を作ることも有効だ。3つ目は，すでに宇宙にあるスペースデブリの除去である。

多くの人が3つ目の点は難しすぎると考えてきたが，日本のチームが現在それを試みている。そのチームはどのようにしてスペースデブリを除去するのか。そのチームは磁石の力を利用する機械を発明した。回転していないスペースデブリを発見した後，その機械はそれを追いかけて捕らえる。ある種のスペースデブリは回転しているので，その種のスペースデブリを捕らえるのはその機械には難しすぎる。回転するスペースデブリを捕らえるために，チームは機械の改良を続けるだろう。

「ゴミを減らそう。」これは私たちの日々の生活と地球環境を考える上で重要なテーマになっている。どちらも守られるべきだが，今日では私たちは宇宙の環境も守らねばならない。私たちは地球と宇宙の両方の環境を守る責任があるのだ。

019 ① ウ　② ウ

③ 人造肉の生産には費用がかかりすぎること／人造肉の安全性に不安があること

④ ア　⑤ イ，エ

⑥ [A] **less**　[B] **population**

[C] **enough**　[D] **bad**

[E] **growing[increasing, using]**

解説 ①「これらの事実のために，牛肉の生産は時に悪いこととみなされる」という文脈から考えて，「これらの事実」とはその前に書かれている内容のこと。具体的には，牛肉を生産するために多くの土地とえさと水が必要なこと，牛が温室効果ガスを出すため環境に悪いということである。それに最も近いのは，ウ「牛肉を生産することは多くの点で地球によくない」。他の選択肢は，ア「牛は多くの温室効果ガスを必要とする」，イ「牛肉を生産するのは私たちにとって簡単だ」，エ「私たちは将来の生活の中で牛肉を見ることができないだろう」。

② such projects（そのような研究）は，この段落の２文目に出てくる new projects を指している。具体的には，牛肉を使わずに牛肉に似た食品を作ることである。したがって，ウの「牛肉と全く同じように楽しめるもの[食品]を生産しようとする」が最も近い。他の選択肢は，ア「豆腐を使って食肉用の動物を育てようとする」，イ「温室効果ガスを出さずに動物を育てようとする」，エ「牛肉に似た食品を作るために豆腐のより簡単な作り方を見つけようとする」。

③後ろに書かれている内容から考える。この段落の３文目（The technology is ...）には「人造肉は生産のコストがかかりすぎる」という内容が，また６文目（Also, ...）には「人造肉の安全性を不安視する人々もいる」という内容が書かれているので，これらを簡潔にまとめる。

④ア それは私たちの食品の生産方法を変える大発明の１つかもしれない

イ 肉ではなく他の種類の食品が実験室で生産できる

ウ 私たちは人造肉の生産を止めるために熱心に働くべきだ

エ 農場産の肉は人造肉ほどおいしくないことに誰もが気づくだろう

第４段落以降では人造肉が中心的な話題になっている。「人造肉が食品として万人に受け入れられるには時間がかかるだろう。しかし私たちは…と言うことができる」という文脈から考えて，アが最も適切。

得点アップ

文章の最後の文なので，締めくくりとしてふさわしい内容のものを選ぶ。イは細かすぎる内容，ウやエはネガティブな内容だから，よりよい未来のための新技術について述べている文章の最後に置くには不適切だと想像がつく。

⑤ア「牛肉は生産するのが難しく，世界で生産される牛肉の量は減りつつある」。前半は正しいが，「牛肉の生産量が減りつつある」という内容は本文中に出てこないから誤り。

イ「実験室で肉を生産する技術は，患者を助けるのに使われるのと同じ技術に由来する」。*ll*.23-24（This technology ... medical care.）に「この（人造肉製造の）技術は医療で使われている技術と同じだ」とあるので正しい。

得点アップ

「本文中の該当箇所を別の表現で言い換えた文が正解」というケースがよくある。この問いの場合も，イの the same one [=technology] used to help patients（患者を助けるのに使われるのと同じ技術）は，本文中では医療（medical care）で使われている技術と表現されている。

ウ「人造肉は，実験室で豆腐から作られる種類の肉である」。第４段落に「人造肉を作るために科学者は牛の細胞を使う」とあるので誤り。

エ「人造肉を食べることを不安に思う人々もいる」。第６段落の６文目（Also, ...）に「その[人造肉の]安全性を心配する人々もいる」とあるので正しい。

オ「すでに人造肉を販売し始めたいくつかの企業がある」。第６段落の７文目（Some governments ...）によれば，近い将来企業に人造肉の販売許可を与えると言う政府もある。しかし現時点で人造肉を販売している企業があるとは本文に書かれていないから誤り。

⑥完成した文章の意味は次のとおり。

「牛肉は現在では多くの人にとって非常に重要な種類の食品である。しかし，将来私たちは今よりも[A]少ない牛肉で暮らさなければならないかもしれない。これは，世界の[B]人口が増え，すべての人にとって[C]十分な牛肉がなくなるかもしれないからだ。また，牛を育てるのは環境に[D]悪い可能性がある。すでに豆腐を使って肉を作った企業もある。また，細胞を[E]育てる[増やす，使う]ことによって，実験室で肉を生産することができる。世界中でそれを販売する前に，いくつかの問題が解決されなければならない。」

なお，[E]にcowを入れることはできない。「牛の細胞を使って」の意味は，with cow cellsまたは(by) using cow cellsで表す。

精読

◆In the last ten years, researchers and companies around the world **have been using** these technologies **to produce** lab-grown meat products.(*ll*.28-29)(ここ10年，世界中の研究者や企業が，これらの技術を使って人造肉の製品を製造してきた)：have been usingは現在完了形と進行形を組み合わせた形(**have been ＋～ing**)で，「過去から今までずっと～し続けている」という意味を表す。

・They **have been playing** tennis for two hours.
(彼らは2時間ずっとテニスをしている)

to produceは「製造するために」の意味(目的を表す副詞的用法の不定詞)。**use O to *do***は「～するためにOを使う」だが，日本語に直すときは「Oを使って～する」のように前から訳してよい。次の例も同様。

・I went to Nagano **to stay** with my uncle.
(私はおじの家に泊まるために長野へ行った[長野へ行っておじの家に泊まった)

全訳

人々が食べる牛肉の量は年々増えている。ハンバーガーやステーキのような食品は，かつてないほど人気が高い。これは大きな驚きではない。牛肉はおいしいだけでなく，私たちの体によい成分を含む。しかし，私たちは今食べているほど牛肉を食べ続けることができないかもしれない。

牛肉は最も生産しにくい種類の食品の1つである。牛肉を作るにはもちろん牛が必要だが，牛を育てるには多くの土地とえさと水が必要である。また，牛は地球温暖化の原因となる温室効果ガスを大量に発生させる。これは世界で最も深刻な解決すべき問題の1つになっている。これらの事実のために，牛肉の生産は時に悪いこととみなされる。牛肉は多くの人々にとって大切な食べ物だから，そんなにすぐに生産をやめることはできない。しかし世界の人口は増え続けており，2050年には約97億人になるかもしれない。これは近い将来より多くの牛肉が必要となり，状況は悪化するだろうということを意味する。

このような事実から，近い将来に牛肉なしで暮らさなければならなくなると心配する人々もいる。そこで一部の企業や科学者は，新しい研究に取り組み始めた。たとえば，見た目も味も牛肉に似ているけれど原料が牛ではない食品を製造する会社がある。その1つは，豆腐を原料とする。豆腐ハンバーガーや豆腐ミートボールは，多くの国で人気がある。近い将来，このような研究に取り組もうとする企業や科学者はますます増えるだろう。

実は，牛肉にも新しい生産方法がある。その肉は農場ではなく実験室で作られる。この種の肉は，人造肉[実験室産の肉]と呼ばれる。この肉の生産には新しい技術が使われる。この技術は医療で使われている技術と同じである。人造牛肉を作るために，科学者は牛の細胞を使う。その細胞を特殊な液体の中に入れると，細胞の数が増え始める。十分な数になると，細胞同士がつながり始める。こうして科学者たちは少しずつ牛肉を生産することができる。

ここ10年，世界中の研究者や企業が，これらの技術を使って人造肉の製品を製造してきた。2013年には，人造肉を使って作られたハンバーガーが世界に公開された。その後，アメリカの企業が人造の鶏肉を作った。2021年2月にはイスラエルの企業が特殊な3Dプリンターを使って，人造肉で初めて分厚いステーキを作ったと発表した。それはステーキそっくりの人造肉を作ることができる。

人造肉を生産する技術は素晴らしいものだ。しかし，その肉を人気にするのは難しいと言う人々もいる。その技術は新しいので，低コストで人造肉を作る方法はまだない。2013年に人造肉で最初のハンバーガーを作るには，約32万5千ドルかかった！ だから科学者や企業はコストを下げようとしている。また，人造肉の安全性を心配する人々もいる。一部の政府は，人造肉は安全であり，近い将来企業に販売の許可を与えると言っているが，それだけでは人々の考えを変えるのに十分ではない。科学者たちはさらに研究を進める必要がある。

現在では人造肉に注目し始めた企業が増えている。まだ解決しなければならない問題があるので，人造肉が食品として万人に受け入れられるには時間がかかるだろう。しかし，人造肉は食品の生産方法を変える大発明の1つかもしれないと言うことができる。

語句

amount「量」 steak「ステーキ」
project「研究課題」
lab-grown meat「研究室で育てられた肉，人造肉」
medical care「医療」 little by little「少しずつ」
announce「～を発表する」 thick「厚い」
at a low cost「安いコスト[費用]で」
pay attention to ～「～に注意を払う」
accept「～を受け入れる」

020
① 全訳の下線部(1)を参照。
② ア
③ 現実で目覚まし時計が鳴っても，電話や玄関のベルが鳴って起き，それに答える夢を見るということ。(46字)
④ [A] キ [B] ウ ⑤ エ
⑥ イ

解説 ①〈not + always〉は「常に～だというわけではない」という意味を表す。it は後ろの不定詞を指す形式主語。what happened in our mind は，次の2通りの解釈ができる。
(1)私たちの頭の中で何が起きたか(ということ)(間接疑問)
(2)私たちの頭の中で起きたこと(what は the thing(s) that の意味の関係代名詞)
②この段落の前半は「夢を見ている間は体の働きが鈍くなる」という内容になっている。目覚めるとそれが元に戻る，と考えて，ア の normal(正常な(状態))を入れるのが適切。rise to normal は「(体温や血圧が)正常な状態まで上がる」，become normal は「正常になる」ということ。
③下線部(3)は「夢は私たちが騒音に耐えて眠るのを助けることができる」という意味。その直後の文(For example ...)に具体的な説明があるので，その部分を日本語で表現すればよい。
④完成した文は，(This means that) some of the things <u>that happen in dreams</u> (could happen when we are awake.)となる。下線部が前の things を修飾する形(that は主格の関係代名詞。which も使える)。
⑤「私たちは one thing(1つのこと)を覚えておかねばならない」の one thing の具体的な内容は，次の2文(Dreams ... the future.)に書かれている。したがってエ(夢は決して未来を語れない)が正しい。ア(夢の中には現実になるものもある)，イ(他の夢は現実にならない)，ウ(夢は未来を語るのに使われる)は誤り。
⑥ *ll*.6-7(When we sleep ... holding area.)の内容に一致するイが正解。アは「翌日の活発な運動が必要」が誤り。ウは「夢を見ている時」ではなく「夢を見ていない時」が正しい。エは後半が *ll*.24-25(Dreams also ... to them.)の内容に反する。

精読

◆The brain also slows down **so that** we **can't** think or act consciously.(*l*.15)(脳も，私たちが意識的に考えたり行動したりすることができないよう活動が鈍る)：**so that** S **can[will]** ～は「Sが～できる[する]ように」(目的)の意味を表す。この文では can't が使われているので，「私たちが～できないように，私たちが～しないために」という意味になる。slow down は「スピードが落ちる，動きが鈍くなる」。ここでは脳の働きが不活発になるということ。

◆**Some** dreams are realistic **while others** are not.(*l*.26)(夢には，現実になるものもあればそうでないものもある)：**some** ～**, (and) others ...** は「(ある集団の中で)いくつかは～であり，別のいくつかは…だ」ということ。「～なものもあれば…なものもある」「～な人もいれば…な人もいる」と訳せることが多い。and の代わりに **but**(しかし)，**while**(一方では)，セミコロン(;)などを使うこともある。

全訳

私たちは睡眠とは何かについては多くのことを知っているが，何が睡眠を引き起こすかは知らない。睡眠は休んでいる状態である。睡眠をとると，私たちの体は日中の活動によって生じた疲労から回復する。よく眠ると，私たちは再び活動的になり毎日の活動の準備ができる。

科学者たちは，睡眠が学習の過程でも重要であることを発見した。私たちが眠るとき，脳は日中に受け取った新しい情報を保持領域へ運ぶ。それから，その情報はより永続的な記憶装置へ移動し，記憶の奥深くに保存される。

⑴朝起きたとき，私たちは寝ている間に頭の中で何が起きたか[起きたこと]をいつも思い出せるわけではない。夢は覚えているかもしれないが，それ以外の睡眠時間は一種の暗闇であり，何も起きなかったように思える。

眠りが深くなるにつれて，私たちの身体にはいくつかのことが起こる。筋肉が弛緩する。心拍が遅くなる。体温と血圧が下がる。脳も，私たちが意識的に考えたり行動したりすることができないよう活動が鈍る。しかし夢を見ることはできる。最初に目を覚ますと，体温と血圧は上昇して正常に戻る。心拍や呼吸も正常になり，さらに完全に目覚める。そして，眠っている間に見た夢のほとんどを忘れることが多い。

夢とは何か。それは眠っているときに起こる頭の活動である。夢はいくつかの理由で重要だと思われる。1つは，夢は私たちが騒音に耐えて眠るのを助けることができるということだ。たとえば目覚まし時計が鳴っても，私たちの頭は，電話や玄関のベルが鳴っていて，自分が目覚めてそれに答えている夢を見させる。また夢は，自分の問題について多くのことを明らかにし，それに対する解決策を提供することもできる。

夢には，現実になるものもあればそうでないものもある。つまり，夢の中で起きることの一部は，目が覚めているときにも起こりうる。一方，そうではないものもある。しかし覚えておかねばならないことが1つある。夢は未来を知る手段としては使えない。夢が未来を語ることは絶対にできないのだ。

語句

cause「～を引き起こす」 rest「休息」
ready for ～「～の準備ができている」
process「過程，プロセス」 receive「～を受け取る」
holding area「(記憶)保持領域」 rest「残り」
darkness「暗闇」 take place「起こる」
muscle「筋肉」 relax「弛緩する」
heartbeat「心拍」 temperature「体温」
slow down「活動が鈍くなる」
breathing「呼吸」 ring「鳴る」
cause O to *do*「Oが～する原因となる」
doorbell「玄関のベル」 solution「解決法」
simply can never ～「絶対に～できない」

021 ① ア　② ウ
③ **Germany's government**
④ エ　⑤ (X) 2022　(Y) 2050
⑥ ウ

解説 ①空所の前のコロン(:)は，具体的な説明や例などを示す際にしばしば使われる。ここでは直前のan important part of the climate crisis(気候危機の重要な部分)の具体的な説明が(A)に入る。

ア 気候危機は大人より若者に与える影響の方がずっと大きいだろう
イ 気候危機は世界中の自然環境を破壊するだろう
ウ 気候危機はその国[ドイツ]が多くの金を失う原因となるだろう
エ 気候危機は記録破りの高い気温を引き起こすだろう(result in ～「～の結果になる，～を引き起こす」)

直後の2文(That's because ... become adults.)の内容から考えて，アが正解。若者たちが訴訟を起こした理由は，「大人が気候危機を深く考えなかったために，自分たちの世代が責任を負うことになる」という不満である。

②ア 2019年にドイツ政府がカーボンニュートラルを実現することに関する新法を作った。
イ ドイツ最高裁は気候危機が解決困難な問題だと言った。
ウ ドイツの最高裁判所は気候変動対策をとることによって若者の基本的な権利が保護されるべきであるということに同意した。
エ 新しい気候保護法はドイツ憲法に従っていなかった。

thatは前の内容を指し，that's official nowは「そのこと[気候保護が私たちの基本的な権利だということ]が今(最高裁判所に認められて)正式のものになった」ということ。したがってウが正しい。

③文脈から考えて，itは直前の「ドイツ政府」を指す。

得点アップ

〈X＋接続詞＋Y〉の形でYのS(主語)が代名詞のときは，接続詞が何であっても「XのS＝YのS」であることが多い。

・John gave his son a present when he came home.(ジョンは帰宅したとき息子にプレゼントをあげた)

この文の下線部は，「息子が帰宅したとき」ではなく「ジョンが帰宅したとき」(he = John)と解釈するのが普通。X when Y の X の S が John なら，Y の S も John のはずだからである。本文の場合も，X[Germany's government has said] **that** Y[it will quickly begin ...]. の X の S はドイツ政府だから，Y の S に当たる it もドイツ政府のことだと予想できる。

④ Germany's lawmakers 以下は「ドイツの立法者たちは，自分たちが（ B ）を作り出すとき，若者の気候に関する未来を考慮する可能性が高くなるだろう」という意味。この文脈から考えて，（ B ）にはエの laws(法律)を入れるのが適切。なお，lawmakers(立法者)とは(国会)議員たちのこと。

⑤完成した英文の意味は次のとおり。

「ドイツの最高裁判所は，政府が((X)2022年)の末までに気候保護法を変更し，新法が((Y)2050年)までに気候変動対策をより慎重に計画するよう命じた。」

⑥ア「ドイツの最高裁判所の裁判官たちは，2019年の気候保護法が若者の未来を十分に守っていることに同意した」。「若者たちが訴訟に勝った」という文章のタイトルから考えても明らかに誤り。

イ「若者たちは4つの分野で気候保護法に異議を申し立てたが，裁判官たちはそのうちどれにも同意しなかった」。*ll*.22-24 (The judges didn't ... their challenges.)の内容に反する。

ウ「最高裁判所の判決は，同国の若者の気候に関する未来のための政府の行動に影響を与えるだろう」。最後から2番目の段落(Germany's government ...)の内容に一致する。

エ「Fridays For Future という気候活動団体は，世界中の若者と話し合って，政府を相手に訴訟を始めた」。下線部のような記述は本文中にない。ドイツ政府を相手に訴訟を起こしたのは9人の若者であり，気候活動団体ではない。

精読

◆Germany's top court has reached **a decision** [**that** parts of the country's 2019 climate action law must be changed] (*ll*.1-2)(ドイツの最高裁判所は，同国の2019年の気候保護法の一部が変更されねばならないという決定に達した)：〈**X**[名詞] + **that ...**〉が「…という**X**」の意味を表すことがある。このような that 節は同格節と呼ばれ，意味的に〈X = that 節〉の関係が成り立つ。この文の a decision that ...(…という決定)には，「決定は…ということだ(った)」の意味が含まれている。事実・情報・思考・可能性などを表す名詞は，後ろに同格節を置くことができる。たとえば**the fact [news] that ...** は「…という事実[知らせ]」，**the idea that ...** は「…という考え」。また，〈V + **that** 節〉の V を名詞に変えて，その後ろに同格節を置くこともある。本文の **a decision that ...** はその例で，decide that ...(…と(いうことを)決定する)がもとになっている。believe that ...(…と信じる)→ **the belief that ...**(…という信念)なども同様。

◆young people will **be left to handle** them as they become adults(*l*.8)(若者は大人になったときにこの問題の扱いを任されることになる)：〈be 動詞 + 過去分詞 + to *do*〉の形にはいくつかのパターンがあるが，〈V + O + to *do*〉の O が主語になった受動態の文がよく見られる。この文は，they[=the adults] will **leave** young people **to handle** them ...(彼ら[大人]は若者にそれら(の問題)を扱うことを任せる)という文の下線部を主語にした受動態と考えればよい(leave O to *do*「O が～するのに任せる」)。次の例も同様。

・I **was asked to clean** this room.

(私はこの部屋を掃除するよう頼まれた)

→ Someone **asked** me **to clean** this room.(誰かが私にこの部屋を掃除するよう頼んだ)の me を主語にした受動態の文。

◆it was **putting** their future lives **in danger**(*ll*.14-15)(それ[政府]は彼らの将来の生活を危険にさらしていた)：put O in danger は「O を危険にさらす」の意味だが，この表現を知らなくても，単語の本来の意味に立ち返って「彼らの将来の生活を危険の中に置く」という意味に解釈できる。またこの文の lives[laivz] は，名詞の life(生活，命)を複数形にしたもの。動詞の live(生きる)

に3単現のsを加えた形と同じなので，文脈に応じてどちらの意味かを考える必要がある。

◆The judges didn't agree with **all** of the challenges.(*ll*.22-23)(裁判官たちは，その異議申し立ての全部に同意したわけではない)：「全部」「完全に」などの意味を表す語(**all, every, always**など)の前に**not**があるときは，「全部が[完全に]～だというわけではない」という意味(部分否定)になる。「裁判官たちはその異議申し立ての全部に同意しなかった[全部退けた]」と誤解しないこと。

・Good players **don't always** become good coaches.(よい選手がいつもよいコーチになるとは限らない)

全訳

ドイツで若者が気候変動裁判に勝利

ドイツの最高裁判所は，同国の2019年の気候保護法の一部が，若者の保護に有効ではないため変更されねばならないという決定に達した。この結果は，訴訟を起こした9人の若者にとって大きな勝利となった。

この裁判は，気候危機の重要な部分，つまり気候危機が大人よりも若者に対してずっと大きな影響を与えるだろうという点に，大きな関心を寄せている。それは，近い将来地球温暖化の影響がより深刻になるからである。大人たちがこの問題に関心を持ってこなかったために，若者は大人になったときにこの問題の扱いを任されることになる。

2019年にドイツでは新法が可決され，政府はその法律で2050年までに同国が二酸化炭素の排出をゼロにすると約束した。その法律は2030年までの行動計画を立てた。しかしその法律には，2031年から2050年の間に行う気候変動対策についての明確なルールや計画がなかった。

15～24歳の9人の若者のグループが，その法律について政府を相手に裁判を起こした。政府が慎重な計画を立てなかったために，自分たちの将来の生活が危険にさらされていると彼らは言った。政府の計画では，自分たちが大人になったとき最も困難な排出量の課題に直面することになると彼らは感じた。

2021年4月29日，ドイツの最高裁判所の裁判官たちは若者らに同意し，ドイツの法律の一部はドイツ憲法に従っていないと述べた。政府が気候変動対策を行わなければ，よりよい未来を手に入れるという若者の基本的な権利を奪うかもしれない，と裁判官たちは言った。

若者たちは4つの分野で政府の法律に異議を唱えた。裁判官たちは，その異議申し立ての全部に同意したわけではない。彼らは若者たちの異議申し立ての一部だけに同意した。しかし，彼らの訴訟の一部でも大きな勝利と考えられる。

ルイーザ・ノイバウアーは，政府を相手に裁判を起こした若者の1人だった。彼女は気候活動団体であるFridays For Future(未来のための金曜日)で活動している。ノイバウアーは，「気候保護は私たちの基本的な権利であり，それが今正式なものとなりました。これは気候変動運動にとって大きな勝利です。それは多くの変化をもたらします」と語った。

裁判所はドイツ政府に対して，法律を修正するための期間として，2022年末までの1年間を与えた。気候法は今では，ドイツの汚染を削減し，2050年までに同国の二酸化炭素の排出をゼロにするために，2030年以降に取られる行動のための以前よりずっと慎重な計画を持つ必要がある。

ドイツ政府は，必要とされる変更を行うための作業を速やかに開始すると述べている。このような高裁判決の重要な点の1つは，それが将来の判断の指針や手本となることである。つまり，今後ドイツの立法者たちは，法律を作る際に若者の気候に関する未来を考慮する可能性が高くなるだろう。

世界中の他のグループの若者たちも，政府を相手に訴訟を起こしている。昨年，ポルトガルの6人の若者グループが，ヨーロッパ33か国を相手に，欧州人権裁判所への訴訟を開始した。最近では，オーストラリア，ブラジル，イギリスの若者たちも，気候変動対策について各国政府を相手に裁判を起こしている。

語句

win a case「訴訟に勝つ」
decision「決定，判決」 victory「勝利」
give[pay] attention to ～「～に注意を払う」
impact「影響，衝撃」 adult「大人」
handle「～を扱う」 pass a law「法律を通過させる」
aged ～「～歳の」
take ～ to court「～を告訴する，裁判にかける」
face「～に直面する」
challenge「難題，異議申し立て」
take away ～「～を取り去る，奪う」
basic「基本的な」 right「権利」 area「分野」
movement「運動」 fix「～を修正する」
pollution「汚染」
lead O to *do*「Oを～する方へ導く」
act as ～「～(として)の働きをする」 guide「指針」
lawmaker「立法者，立法府[議会]の人々」

022 ① エ　② ウ

③ **which lead to the parts of Pager's brain that control movements**

④ **Pager** の脳が腕や手を動かすために使っている信号。

⑤ **Pager** の脳からの信号を，彼の手が実際に行っている動きと照合すること。

⑥ **was, connected**

⑦ 全訳の下線部(7)を参照。　⑧ ア

解説 ① *ll*.6-7(Neuralink is working ... brains.)によれば，この会社は人が脳だけで物を動かせる装置の開発に取り組んでいる。その文脈から考えて，空所にはエの mind を入れて，the monkey is playing the video game with just its mind(そのサルは頭だけを使ってビデオゲームをしている)という意味にするのが適切。mind はここでは「思考(力)」の意味。

②前の文に「脳だけを使って物を動かす」とある。これはいわゆる超能力のように思えるので，ウを入れて a science fiction movie(SF[空想科学]映画)という意味にするのが適切。ア「アクション(映画)」，イ「冒険(映画)」，エ「サスペンス(映画)」では文脈に合わない。

③完成した文は，These devices are connected to 2,048 wires [which lead to the parts of Pager's brain [that control movements of the arms and hands]]. となる(下線部が並べ替えた部分)。「これらの装置は2,048本のワイヤーにつながれている」という(完成した形の)文の後ろに wires を修飾する関係詞節(which ... hands)が続いている。さらにその中にも，the parts of Pager's brain を修飾する関係詞節(that ... hands)が含まれている。which 以下は「(それらのワイヤーは)ペイジャーの脳の部分につながっている＋(その脳の部分は)腕と手の動きを制御する」ということ。

④「これらの信号」とは，直前の文中の the signals his brain was using to control his arms and hands を指す。

⑤「これ」とは，直前の文中の to match up (A)the signals from Pager's brain to (B)the movements that his hands were actually making を指す。match up A to B で「A を B に対応させる，A を B と照合する」という意味。A は「ペイジャーの脳からの信号」，B は「彼の手が実際に行っている動き」(make a movement「動きをする，動く」)。つまり科学者たちは，ペイジャーの脳から出る1つ1つの信号が，手のそれぞれの動きにどう対応しているかを分析した。次の段落では，その結果を使って，ペイジャーに(手を動かさずに)脳の信号だけでビデオゲームを操作させようとしたのである。

⑥文脈から考えて，even though it was not connected to the computer(それ[ジョイスティック]はコンピューターに接続されていなかったけれど)とするのが適切。ペイジャーは最初のうちは今までどおりジョイスティックを手で動かしていたが，すぐに頭の中だけでゲームができるようになった，という状況が説明されている。even though は though(～だけれど)とほぼ同じ意味。let Pager keep moving the joystick は「ペイジャーにジョイスティックを動かし続けさせておく」の意味。〈let ＋ O ＋動詞の原形〉は「O に～させておく，O が～するのを許す」，keep ～ing は「～し続ける」。

⑦文全体は，S wants to make it possible for A to *do*.(S は A が～するのを可能にしたがっている)という形になっている。make it possible は「it を可能にする」という VOC(第5文型)の形。it は形式目的語で，後ろの不定詞を指す。A に当たるのは humans who have lost the ability to control their bodies(体を動かす能力を失った人間)。その後ろの不定詞(to communicate and connect with the world around them)は「自分のまわりの世界とコミュニケーションをとってつながること」。and は communicate と connect を結びつけており，with 以下はその両方とつながっている。

⑧ its system will allow O to *do* は「その(会社の)システムは O が～することを可能にするだろう」の意味。この下線部にそれぞれの選択肢を入れて考えてみよう。

ア 体がまひした人々が再び腕や脚を使うこと

イ (どんな動物であれ)動物がスマートフォンを使ってコミュニケーションをとること

ウ よりよいビデオゲームが開発されること

エ イーロン・マスクが AI(人工知能)を使ってロ

ボットを作ること

文脈から考えてアが適切。①で説明したとおり，Neuralink社は人が脳だけで物を動かせる装置の開発に取り組んでいる。現在のところサルを使った実験は成功しているので，将来は人間にも応用できるだろう，というのが本文の結論である。

精読

◆S[**what** makes the video even stranger] **is** C[**that** the monkey is playing the video game with just its mind] (*ll*.2-4)（その動画がさらに奇妙なのは，このサルが頭だけを使ってビデオゲームをしていることである）：全体はS is C（SはCだ）という構造。**what**はthe thing that（…すること[もの]）の意味の関係代名詞。その後ろにV（makes）+O（the video）+C（even stranger）（その動画をさらに奇妙にする）の形が続いている。thatは「…ということ」の意味の接続詞。S **is that …**（Sは…ということだ）という形はよく見られる。

◆**At first**, Pager controlled the video game using a joystick, which is a normal gaming controller. (*ll*.17-18)（最初のうちは，ペイジャーはジョイスティックという普通のゲーム用コントローラーでビデオゲームを操作していた）：at firstは「最初は～だったが，その後変化が起きた」という場合に使う。whichは関係代名詞だが，前にコンマに注意。このように関係代名詞をコンマの後ろに置く使い方を，非制限[継続]用法という。この用法の関係代名詞は，先行詞に補足的な説明を加える働きをする。この文はコンマの前の部分（最初ペイジャーはジョイスティックでビデオゲームを操作していた）だけで意味が完結しており，which以下は先行詞のjoystickがどういうものかを補足的に説明している。

・I have a cousin **who** lives in Osaka.
（私には大阪に住むいとこがいる）

→ 下線部はcousin（いとこ）の意味を限定している。このような（前にコンマのない）関係代名詞の使い方を，制限[限定]用法という。この文の場合，「私」のいとこは1人とは限らない。たとえばI have a cousin who lives in Osaka and a cousin who lives in Hakata.（私には大阪にいるいとこと博多に住むいとこがいる）という場合もありうる。

・I have a cousin, **who** lives in Osaka.
（私にはいとこが1人おり，そのいとこは大阪に住んでいる）

→ I have a cousinで文の意味が完結するので，「私」のいとこは1人しかいないことになる。

◆S[The final step] was C[**to have** a computer **make** moves in the video game **as if** Pager had actually moved the joystick]. (*ll*.25-26)（最終段階は，まるでペイジャーが実際にジョイスティックを動かしたかのように，コンピューターにビデオゲーム中での動きをさせることだった）：この文もS is C. の構造であり，Cには「～すること」の意味の不定詞が置かれている。S **is to *do*.**（Sは～することだ）もよく使われる形なので頭に入れておこう。have a computer make movesは「コンピューターに動きをさせる」。〈**have** ＋ O ＋動詞の原形〉で「Oに～させる」という意味を表す。このように，後ろに〈O ＋動詞の原形〉を置いて「Oに～させる」の意味を表す動詞には**make**・**let**・**have**の3語があり，これらをまとめて使役動詞という。**as if**は「まるで～であるかのように」の意味。「まるで（それ以前に）～した[だった]かのように」という意味のときは，後ろを過去完了形（この文ではhad moved）にする。

・He spoke English very well **as if** he had lived in the U.S.（彼はまるで以前アメリカに住んでいたかのようにとても上手に英語を話した）

◆The next step **would** be to allow them to control a computer. (*ll*.37-38)（その次の段階は，彼らがコンピューターを操作できるようにすることだろう）：willでなくwould（仮定法過去）が使われている理由を考えてみよう。前の文に「体がまひした人でも，手を使っている人よりも速くスマートフォンを操作できるようになるだろうとマスク氏は信じている」とある。この内容を受けた上の文には，「もしマスク氏の予想どおりになれば，その次の段階は…」という仮定の意味が含まれている。

全訳

Neuralinkという名の会社が，サルがビデオゲームをしている場面に見える動画を公開した。それはかなり珍しいことだが，その動画がさらに奇妙なのは，このサルが頭だけを使ってビデオゲームをしていることである。

Neuralinkは，自動車会社のTeslaやロケット会社のSpaceXを所有するイーロン・マスクが所有する会社だ。同社は人が脳だけを使って物を動かせる装置の開発に取り組んでいる。SF映画に出てきそうな話だが，同社はすでにブタなど他の動物を使った同様の研究で成果を上げている。

動画に登場するサルはペイジャーという名で，脳の中にNeuralink社の特殊な「リンク」装置を2つ持っている。その装置は，外科医によってペイジャーの脳に移植された。これらの装置は，ペイジャーの腕と手の動きを制御する脳の部分につながる2,048本のワイヤーに接続されている。科学者たちはペイジャーにビデオゲームのやり方を教えた。彼らはバナナのスムージーを特別なごちそうとして使って，彼がゲームを正しくプレーしたときにほうびを与えた。やがてペイジャーは，より多くのスムージーをもらうために，上手にプレーしたがった。

最初のうちは，ペイジャーはジョイスティックという普通のゲーム用コントローラーでビデオゲームを操作していた。しかしペイジャーがプレーする間，彼の「リンク」装置は，彼の腕と手を動かすために脳が使っている信号に関する情報をワイヤレスで送信した。Neuralink社の科学者たちは，これらの信号のすべてを記録した。

それから彼らはコンピューターを使って，ペイジャーの脳からの信号を，彼の手が実際に行っている動きと照合した。これは難しい作業であり，科学者たちはペイジャーの脳の信号を解読するのに人工知能(AI)の助けを借りなければならなかった。

最終段階は，まるでペイジャーが実際にジョイスティックを動かしたかのように，コンピューターにビデオゲーム中での動きをさせることだった。もしペイジャーがジョイスティックを上に動かそうと思えば，コンピューターはビデオゲームに「上」の信号を送ることになる。最初のうち研究者たちは，ジョイスティックがコンピューターに接続されていないにもかかわらず，ペイジャーが手でジョイスティックを動かし続けるのをそのままにしておいた。しかしそのうちペイジャーは，脳だけを使ってゲームをすることができるようになった。

今のところNeuralink社の研究は動物とビデオゲームに集中しているが，その背後には非常に重大な目的がある。(7)Neuralink社は，自分の身体を動かす能力を失った人が周囲の世界とコミュニケーションをとってつながることを可能にしたいと考えている。

マスク氏によると，近い将来Neuralink社は，体がまひした人が考えるだけでスマートフォンを操作できるようにしたいと考えている。その人々は手を使っている人よりも速くそれができるだろうと彼は信じている。その次の段階は，彼らがコンピューターを操作できるようにすることだろう。

人の体がまひしているときは，脳が体のさまざまな部分に信号を送る能力を失っているためであることが多い。Neuralink社は，いつの日か将来，同社のシステムによって，体がまひした人が再び腕や脚を使えるようになることを願っている。

語句

share「～を共有する，インターネット上に公開する」
fairly「かなり」 unusual「普通でない，独特の」
control「～を制御する，動かす」 brain「脳」
sound like ～「～のように聞こえる[思われる]」
plant「～を植え付ける，移植する」
surgeon「外科医」 wire「ワイヤー，電線」
smoothie「スムージー(砕いた果物や野菜を氷やミルクなどと混ぜた飲み物)」
treat「ごちそう」 reward「～にほうびを与える」
correctly「正確に」
be eager to *do*「しきりに～したがる」
at first「最初(のうち)は」
wirelessly「ワイヤレスで」
send out ～「～を送り出す」 signal「信号」
record「～を記録する」
match up ～「～を組み合わせる，適合させる」
challenging「難しい」
artificial intelligence「人工知能」
decode「～を解読する」
make a move「動きをする」
even though ～「～だけれども」
right now「ちょうど今」
focus on ～「～に集中する」 purpose「目的」
behind「～の背後に」
communicate (with ～) 「(～と)コミュニケーションをとる」
connect with ～「～とつながる」

023 ① イ ② ウ ③ ア
④ **how it looks** ⑤ エ
⑥ **human activity** ⑦ エ

解説 ①全訳の下線部①を参照。空所イの次の文中のhowever(しかし)に着目する。イにこの文を入れることで，この文中のhave usually taken a long time(たいてい長い時間を要した)と，次の文中のover a very short period of time(非常に短い期間にわたって)とが意味的に対比されるので文脈に合う。

②「この変化はなぜ起きたのか」という問いかけに対する適切な答えを選ぶ。「この変化」とは，前の段落に書かれている「peppered mothの色が黒くなり始めたこと」を指す。

ア　工場地帯の近くの森の木の樹皮に生える多くの地衣類が死に，樹皮がもとの黒い色を失ったから。

イ　工場地帯の近くの森の木の樹皮をおおう地衣類が，多くの工場がそこに建てられた後に増えたから。

ウ　工場地帯の近くの森の木の樹皮の色が，樹皮に生える多くの地衣類が死んだ後で黒くなったから。

エ　工場から出る煙が工場の近くの森の木の樹皮をおおい始め，木の色が明るくなったから。

この段落の3文目(The air pollution caused ...)の内容から考えて，ウが正しい。樹皮の上に明るい色の(コケなどの)地衣類が生えていた時代には，peppered mothの体は一種の保護色として明るい色だったと考えられる。

③表のreleasedは放たれた蛾《が》の数，caught againはそのうちで再び捕らえられた(つまり他の生物に捕食されずに生き延びた)蛾の数を表す。表の前の段落の終わりから2文目には，「工場地帯では黒い色のpeppered mothの方がより多く生き残れたことがわかる」とある。表を見ると，(a)と(b)ではdark mothsの方が生存率が高く，(c)ではlight mothsの方が生存率が高い。したがって，(a)と(b)が工場地帯，(c)が田園地帯である。

④「peppered mothとちょうど同じように，ある植物種《しゅ》はごく短期間で…を変えた」という文の空所を補う。第2段落の[ウ]の直前にsome species have changed how they look over a very short period of time(ごく短期間で姿を変えた種もある)とあり，その1つの例がpeppered mothだと説明されている。「peppered mothとちょうど同じように」はこの箇所を受けていると考えられるので，下線部のhow they look(外見がどのように見えるか)の形を利用する。ここでは主語がa species of plantなので*l*.36にあるhow it looksとすることに注意。

⑤全訳の下線部⑤を参照。Dのthis question(この問い)が大きな手がかりになる。この選択肢を使うとしたら，this questionはBの疑問文を指していると考えられる。そこでB→Dと並べてみると，Dが並べ替えた3つの文の最後にくるとは考えられない。直後にWhy has this happened?という別の疑問文があるからだ。それなら「B→D→？」の順だろう。Bは「人間は明るい色と暗い色のどちらの植物の方が見つけやすいだろうか」という内容だから，直前の「暗い色の方が目立ちにくい」という内容と自然につながる。これに続くDは「その答えは簡単だ(明るい色の方が見つけやすい)」ということ。その後にA(しかし以前と同じくらい明るい色のままの植物もある)を続ければ，その後の「これが起こったのはなぜか(＝それらの植物の色が暗くならなかったのはなぜか)」という文脈が完成する。したがってエが正解。

⑥「今日では…がそれ[地球上の生命の進化のしかた]に与える影響は以前より大きい」の空所を補う。第1段落の4文目(They call ...)にあるhuman activity has a great influence on the Earth's environment(人間の活動は地球の環境に大きな影響を与える)という箇所に着目して，空所には下線部の「人間の活動」を入れるのが適切。the influence that human activity is having on it(人間の活動がそれに与える影響)という形を作るのがポイントになる。このthatは目的格の関係代名詞で，human activity is having an influence on it(人間の活動がそれに影響を与えている)という形がもとになっている(have an influence on ～「～に影響を与える」)。

⑦[1]「一部の科学者たちは20世紀が始まった直後に『人新世』という名前を使い始めた。なぜなら彼らはそれが新しい種類の人間の時代だと思ったからだ」。第1段落の2文目(The Anthropocene is ...)によれば1つ目の下線部は「21世紀の初めに」が正しい。また，第1段落の4文目(They call ...)によれば，2つ目の下線部は「人間の活動が地球環境に大きな影響を与えている」が正しい。

[2]「私たちはpeppered mothの例を見ることによって，人間が人新世において短期間で一部の種の動物の色の変化の速度を下げ始めたと言える」。reduce the speedは「速度を下げる」の意味。本文の内容は逆で，人新世ではpeppered mothやFritillaria delavayi

の色の変化の速度は上がっている。

[3]「田園地帯に住む peppered moth の色は，他の地域で建設される工場の数が増えた後も変化しなかった。なぜならそこでは木の樹皮の色が以前と同じままだったからだ」。本文の内容に一致する。第 4 段落の最後の文に，「田園地帯に住む peppered moth は明るい色のままだ」とある。これは，工場のない田園地帯では周囲の環境が変化しなかったので，peppered moth は体色を変える必要がなかったからである。

[4]「一部の科学者たちは peppered moth の遺伝子を研究しているので，イングランドの工場地帯の多くの peppered moth が自らの環境を変えた理由が将来わかるだろう」。下線部が本文の内容と異なる。peppered moth は周囲の環境に合わせて自らを変化させたのであり，「環境を変え」たわけではない。

[5]「peppered moth の捕食者は鳥ではなく人間だから，人間は Fritillaria delavayi よりも peppered moth により直接的な影響を与えていると言える」。下線部は正反対である。人間は蛾を捕食しない。Fritillaria delavayi は植物であり，第 8 段落(Fritillaria delavayi ...)によれば中国の人々は昔からそれを利用して薬を作っていた。

[6]「Fritillaria delavayi は花と葉に薬草成分を持つため，中国の人々はそれが健康のために重要な植物だと長い間考えてきた」。下線部が誤り。第 8 段落の 3 文目に，It has a herbal component in its bulbs(それは球根に薬草成分を持つ)とある。

[7]「人々が場所を訪れるのがどれだけ簡単かが，これらの場所に生える Fritillaria delavayi の次の世代の色を決める」。最後から 3 番目の段落の後半(If nobody comes ...)の内容に一致する。この植物は，人間が行きやすい場所に生えるときは(摘まれるのを避けるために)色を変え，そうでない場所ではもとの色を保つ，と説明されている。

[8]「Fritillaria delavayi を研究する科学者の数は近い将来増えるだろう，なぜならさまざまな場所へ移動した他の植物はほとんどないからだ」。下線部が誤り。最後から 2 番目の段落によれば，この植物の研究を希望する科学者が増えているのは，それが色の急速な変化を経験した植物の数少ない例の 1 つだからである。

精読

◆it is easy for white moths to hide themselves from **their predators, birds** (*ll*.23-24)(白い蛾は捕食者である鳥から身を隠しやすい)：下線部は「それら[白い蛾たち]の捕食者である鳥」ということ。A，B が「A つまり B」の意味を表す形(同格)だが，their predators, which are birds と補って考えるとわかりやすい。

・I was born in Sendai, (which is) the capital of Miyagi Prefecture.(私は宮城県の県庁所在地である仙台で生まれた)

◆S[**Where** the peppered moth lives and **how** it looks] is very important for the species to survive. (*ll*.35-37)(peppered moth がどこに住み，どんな外見であるかは，この種が生き残るために非常に重要である)：疑問文をより大きな文の一部として使った形を間接疑問という。間接疑問は名詞の働きを持ち，SVO の O として使うことが多い。間接疑問内の語順は SV になる。

・Do you know [where he comes from]?
(彼がどこの出身か知っていますか)

→［ ］は Where does he come from? という疑問文を間接疑問にした形。下線部は SV の語順。

また，間接疑問が S(主語)の位置に置かれることもある。本文の S は，Where does the peppered moth live?(peppered moth はどこに住んでいるのか)と How does it look?(それはどのように見えるか)という 2 つの疑問文を間接疑問にして，and で結びつけた形である。

全訳

私たちは今「人新世」に生きていると言う人々がいる。人新世とは，21 世紀の初めに一部の科学者が使い始めた時代の名前である。Anthropo は英語で「人間」，cene は「新しい」という意味を表す。人間の活動が地球環境に大きな影響を与えていることから，地球の歴史の中で最も新しい時代を彼らは人新世と呼ぶ。もちろん動物はその一例である。

すべての動物種は，自らの環境で生き残るために何十億年もの間進化してきた。たとえば，それぞれの種が進化する過程が各動物の外見を決めてきた。そのおかげで，それぞれの種は捕食者から身を守り，周囲の環境の中で生き残りやすくなる。①地球の歴史の中で，このような進化はたいてい長い時間を要した。しかし人新世が始まってから，ごく短期間で姿を変えた種もある。この時代には，人間の活動が急速な変化を引き起こしている。その1つの例は，peppered moth（オオシモフリエダシャク）という種類の蛾である。

peppered mothはヨーロッパに生息している。体は白く，羽には霜降り模様がある。かつてイングランドに生息していた蛾の多くは，同じような明るい色だった。しかし19世紀後半に，特に工場地帯ではpeppered mothの色が黒くなり始めた。

この変化はなぜ起きたのか。19世紀初頭には工場がどんどん建設された。これらの工場から出る黒煙が引き起こした大気汚染で，工場の近くの木の樹皮に生えていた（コケなどの）地衣類が大量に死滅し，樹皮の色が黒くなった。peppered mothは，昼間はこれらの木の上で休む。地衣類が樹皮に生えて木が明るく見えると，白い蛾は捕食者である鳥から身を隠しやすい。しかし地衣類が樹皮をおおわず木が黒っぽいと，鳥は黒っぽいpeppered mothを見つけにくい。この変化した環境の中では，黒い色の蛾の方が生き残る確率が高い。実際に，工場から離れた田園地帯に住む同類のpeppered mothは，明るい色のままである。

1953年と1955年にあるイングランド人研究者が，黒色のpeppered mothの方が鳥から身を隠しやすいことを示す実験を行った。彼のグループは，工場地帯の近くの森と田園地帯の森の両方に多くのpeppered mothを放った。それから，しばらくして生き残った蛾を捕らえた。その結果は次ページの表に示されている。表中の数字は，明るい色の蛾と黒い色の蛾の放たれた数と捕らえられた数を示している。工場地帯では黒い色のpeppered mothの方がより多く生き残れたことがわかる。peppered mothがどこに住み，どんな外見であるかは，この種が生き残るために非常に重要なのだ。

（表は省略）

しかし一部の科学者は，他の要因が黒いpeppered mothの増加に影響しているかもしれないと言っている。実際に科学者たちは今これらの蛾の遺伝子について研究しているので，いつかはさらに詳しいことがわかるだろう。これはまだ研究中だが，環境の変化が蛾の色の変化に何らかの点で関連していることは明らかである。これは，人新世の間に人間の活動が以前にも増して動物の生活に影響を与えていることを示す一例である。

実際，人新世には人間の活動が動物だけでなく植物にも影響を与えている。peppered mothとちょうど同じように，ある植物種はごく短期間で見かけの姿を変えた。peppered mothの場合，人間が環境を変え，その後一部の蛾が捕食者から身を隠すために黒い色になった。しかしこの植物の場合，捕食者は人間である。つまり，人間の活動がより直接的にこの植物に影響を与える。この植物の名は，Fritillaria delavayiという。

Fritillaria delavayiは中国に自生している。かつては，花の色は鮮やかな黄だけ，葉の色は鮮やかな緑だけだった。球根に薬草成分を含むので，人々は少なくとも2,000年前からそれを摘んで薬を作ってきた。しかし20世紀後半には，中国だけでなく他の国でもこの薬の需要が増え始めた。それ以来，中国では人々がその植物を摘む頻度が以前より増えた。このために，この植物に奇妙なことが起こり始めた。

Fritillaria delavayiに何が起こったのか。答えは，花や葉の色が黒ずんだのだ。灰色になったものや，茶色になったものもある。なぜだろうか。その植物は山地の岩や石の近くに生えるので，灰色や茶色などの暗い色の方が目立ちにくいのだ。⑤B捕食者である人間がそのような場所で明るい色の植物と暗い色の植物を見つけるのは，どちらの方が簡単だろう。Dこの問いに答えるのは簡単である。Aしかし中には，以前と同じ明るい色のものもある。これはなぜ起こったのか。

中国で6年にわたって行われた調査によると，山の頂上付近の非常に高い場所など，人間の手が簡単には届かないところに生える植物は明るい色のままであり，人間の手が届きやすいところに生える植物は暗い色になりつつある。誰も摘みに来なければ，次の世代は自分を目立たちにくくする必要がないので，明るい色のままになるだろう。しかし人間の近くに生える植物の次の世代は，自分を目立ちにくくするために暗い色になるだろう。ここでもまた，Fritillaria delavayiがどこに生えてどのような外見なのかは，その種が生き残るためには非常に大切である。

これらの色の変化を引き起こした要因は，他にあるかもしれない。この植物の遺伝子の研究を始めた研究者はまだいないが，色の急速な変化を経験した植物の数少ない例の1つなので，Fritillaria delavayiの研究を望む科学者は増えている。

多くの要因が地球上の生命の何十億年にもわたる進化の過程に影響を与えてきたが，今日では人間の活動が与える影響は以前より大きい。一部の人々はこの時代を「人新世」と呼ぶが，地球は人間だけのためにあるのではなく，そこに住むすべての生物のためにある。将来人新世の時代からよりよい時代へ移行するために，私たちはあらゆる努力をすべきである。それがいつ実現できるかはわからないが，すぐにでも実現する方がよいことは確実に言える。

語句

the Anthropocene「人新世」
billions of ～「何十億もの～」
protect oneself from ～「～から自分(の身)を守る」
pattern「模様」 wing「羽，翼」
experiment「実験」 hide「～を隠す」
pick「(花など)を摘む」 grey「灰色の」
sooner than later「なるべく早く，すぐにでも」

第3回　実力テスト

①ア　②エ　③イ　④ウ
⑤イ

解説 文章のレベルは標準的。主題がロボットであることもわかりやすい。文章中にsurgeons, medical students, nursesなど医療関係の語が多く出てくるので，全体は医療用ロボットの説明だとわかる。文章構成は，第1段落が総論(テーマの導入)，第2段落以降が具体例である。医療には，手術などの物理的な問題だけでなく，最後の段落に書かれている患者の精神的なケアという側面もある。医療に関する文章では，後者がテーマになっているものもよく見られる。

①「ロボット手術について本文中に書かれていないのはどれか」
ア　ロボット手術はあまり費用がかからない。
イ　ロボットは集中力を失ったり疲れたりしない。
ウ　ロボット手術は患者へのダメージが少ない。
エ　医師は手術室にいる必要がない。

イ・ウ・エの内容は第2段落に書かれているが，アは書かれていない。

②「医学生が模造人体を使ってできることに関して正しいのはどれか」
ア　遠隔手術のやり方を直接見ることができる。
イ　人々を1つのベッドから別のベッドへ移す練習をすることができる。
ウ　実際の状況でのロボットの使い方を学ぶことができる。
エ　直面するかもしれない緊急事態への備えをすることができる。

第3段落の最後の3つの文(Because they are ...)の内容から考えて，エが正しい。

③「ロボットは看護師の代わりに何をすることができるか」
ア　手術の後で患者の痛みを軽減すること。
イ　疲れずに肉体的な仕事をすること。
ウ　毎日患者の病状を記録すること。
エ　入院する予定の人のためにベッドを移動すること。

第4段落の最初の3つの文(Robots can help nurses, ...)から考えて，イが正しい。

④「ロボットパンツについて正しいのはどれか」
ア　患者がまひから回復するのを助ける。
イ　患者の車いすへの乗り降りを手伝う。
ウ　患者を身体と感情の両面で支える。
エ　体がまひした患者が高くジャンプするのを可能にする。

最終段落(Finally, ...)の内容から考えて，ウが正しい。

⑤「この文章に最も適したタイトルは何か」
ア　遠隔手術の大きな改善
イ　医療を改善するさまざまなロボット
ウ　優れた医療機器を持つ医師たち
エ　患者のためのロボット，マネキン，特別なパンツ

本文では，さまざまなロボットが外科医，医学生，看護師など医療関係者に役立つことが説明されている。したがってイが正しい。

得点アップ

冒頭の文にrobotという語が出てくることからわかるとおり，この文章は基本的にロボットの話である。だからrobotという語を含まないアやウは最初から除外できる。またエのように具体的な言葉を並べただけのようなタイトルはあまりない。文章のタイトルは，抽象的すぎても具体的すぎてもいけない。たとえばこの文章のタイトルとして，Robotsは抽象的すぎて適切とは言えない。

精読

◆Although it might seem scary to **have a robot performing** an operation on you, robotic surgery has many benefits. (*ll*.7-8)
(ロボットに手術されるのは怖いと思われるかもしれないが，ロボット手術には多くの利点がある)：下線部はVOCの形。〈**have**＋O＋～**ing**〉は「O

に～させる」の意味で，「Oが～している状態を持つ」と考えてもよい。

[参考]〈V＋O＋分詞句〉の形は「分詞句が前の名詞を修飾している」（この文で言えばperforming＝which performs）場合もある。どちらの解釈がベターかはケースバイケースで考える。

◆They can "**suffer**" from almost any emergency situation possible (*ll*.20-21)（それら[ロボット患者]はほとんどあらゆる緊急事態を「患う」ことができる）：ロボット患者(human simulators)は，医学生が人体について学ぶのに利用される。実際にはロボットが病気などを患う[にかかる]わけではないが，「(いわば)患う(ような反応を示す)」という意味をこめて，sufferを引用符で囲んでいる。一般に引用符は，ある語句を読む人に注目させたい場合に使われる。たとえば，その語句を本来の意味とは違う意味で使うときや，「いわゆる[世間一般で言う]～」という意味を表したいときに使う。

・The number of young "freeters" is increasing.
　（若い「フリーター」の数が増えている）

→「フリーター」は和製英語であり，英語にはfreeterという言葉はない。そこで引用符で囲み，「(日本の人々が言う)いわゆるフリーター」という意味を表している。

◆Because they do not get tired, they can **help prevent** injury (*l*.27)（それら[ロボット]は疲れないので，けがを予防するのに役立ちうる）：〈help ＋ O ＋ (to) *do*〉は「Oが～するのを助ける，Oが～するのに役立つ」の意味。toはしばしば省略される。さらにOを省略して，**〈help ＋ (to) *do*〉**（～するのに役立つ）という形でも使う。下線部はその形(toが省略されている)。

全訳

国際ロボット連盟によると，「ロボット」という言葉は1920年代に初めて使われ，現在では世界中で数百万台のロボットが利用されている。健康産業では，ロボットの活用が日々進んでいる。

外科医が遠隔手術(telesurgeryともいう)にロボットを使うケースが増えている。言い換えれば，患者の手術を行うのに外科医が物理的に同じ場所にいる必要はなく，実際に遠く離れたところにいる場合もある。ロボットに手術されるのは怖いと思われるかもしれないが，ロボット手術には多くの利点がある。ロボットは，くり返しの作業に気が散ったり飽きたりすることはない。さらに，ロボットの方がずっと正確である。その結果，患者は手術中に感じる痛みが少なく，回復も早いかもしれない。

医学生もロボットを使って，人体について学ぶ。彼らは「模造人体」という最新技術を使ったマネキン人形で練習する。この装置は外見が本物の人間に似ているだけでなく，人間のように活動する。それは泣いたり，汗をかいたり，唾液を出したり，目を開いたり閉じたりすることができる。呼吸音や心音を出し，血を流し，薬に反応することもできる。このマネキンには，男性，女性，10代の若者，さらに妊婦，赤ちゃんなどさまざまな型がある。このロボット患者は本物の人間に非常によく似ているので，未来の医師たちが仕事の中で直面する可能性のある現実的な状況に備えることができる。それらは心臓発作やてんかん性発作のような，ほとんどあらゆる緊急事態を「患う」ことができる。このリアルな「緊急事態」を体験することは，残念ながらよくありがちな医療過誤を防ぐのに役立つかもしれない。

ロボットは看護師も手助けすることができる。病院でよくある問題は，看護師が絶えず患者を1つのベッドから別のベッドに移したり，抱き上げたり，車いすに乗せたりしなければならないことである。ロボットは力が強いので，このような疲れる作業の手助けができる。ロボットは疲れないので，けがを予防するのに役立ち，さらに怒ったり退屈したりいらついたりすることは決してない。

最後に，ロボットは運動機能を失った人々の生活を向上させることもできる。ロボットパンツは，体がまひした患者が車いすに縛られずに自立して動き回ることを可能にする。このパンツの利点は，身体的なものだけではない。ある患者は「また歩けるようになるとは夢にも思っていませんでした。歩くのがどんな感じか忘れていました」とコメントした。彼はさらにこう続けた。「私には3歳の娘がいます。私が歩いているのを娘が初めて見たとき，彼女は最初の数分間は黙っていて，それから『パパは背が高いね』と言いました。それを聞いて私は，まるで空を飛んでいるようないい気分になりました。」

語句

(be) in use「使われて(いる)」
federation「連盟，連邦」
robotics「ロボット工学」　increasingly「ますます」
remote surgery「遠隔手術」
physical「物理的な，身体的な」　location「場所」
human simulator「模造人体」

equipment「装置，機器」 sweat「汗をかく」
breathing「呼吸」 heartbeat「心臓の鼓動，心拍」
respond to ～「～に反応する，～の影響を受ける」
male「男性の」 female「女性の」
version「型，バージョン」 pregnant「妊娠した」
lifelike「生きているような，実物そっくりな」
prepare O for ～「O に～の準備をさせる」
real-life「現実の」 scenario「状況」
career「職業」 emergency situation「緊急事態」
heart attack「心臓発作」
realistic「現実的な，リアルな」
all too common「(あまりにも)よくありがちな」
constantly「絶えず」 pick ～ up「～を持ち上げる」
wheelchair「車いす」 tiring「(仕事などが)疲れる」
injury「けが」 frustrated「いらいらした」
mobility「機動性，(体を動かすための)運動機能」
independently「独立して」
like「まるで～であるかのように」

4 物語・随筆

024〉
① ウ
② [A] エ [B] ア [C] ウ [D] イ
③ う ④ エ
⑤ お互いの役割をまだ決めていなかったから。
⑥ キ，オ，ア ⑦ イ
⑧ 質問する役割，レポートを書く役割，写真を撮る役割
⑨ オ，カ

解説 ①⑴ A and B の形では，A と B の形をそろえる。この文では A[talked together] and B[decided to go ～]で，下線部をどちらも過去形にする。⑵ stop ～ing「～することをやめる」。stop(～をやめる)の後ろには動名詞を置く。

②[A] as「～として」(前置詞) [B] wait for ～「～を待つ」 [C] look down「下を見る，うつむく」 [D] like「～に似て(いる)」(前置詞)

③メアリーたち4人は，織物工場に行った時点ではお互いの役割分担を決めていなかったが，グリーン氏の話を聞いて，お互いが協力することの大切さを知った。この話の流れから考えて，与えられた「しかし彼女らはうれしかった」は文章の後半に入ると考えられる。(う)の空所にこれを入れれば，前の文と合わせて「1時間かかって少しの布しか作れなかったが，彼女たちはうれしかった」という意味になるので文脈に合う。

④全訳の下線部⑶，⑸，⑹を参照。

得点アップ

文章中のいくつかの空所に入る文を選ぶ問いでは，消去法で考えるのもよい。④の場合，b. の His name was Mr. Green.(彼の名前はグリーン氏だった)がわかりやすい。この文はグリーン氏が初めて登場する場面で使われるはずだと推測できるので，少なくとも⑹に入ることはない(この段落の最初の文に Mr. Green が出てくるから)。では⑶と⑸のどちらに入れるべきか？ と考えると，⑶が適切だとわかる。このように，わかりやすいものから順に入る位置を決めていけば，効率的に問題を解くことができる。

⑤③で説明したとおり，メアリーたちが happy でなかったのは，その時点では4人の役割分担が決まっていなかったからである。具体的には，第1段落の最後の部分から，4人のうち2人が写真を撮る係を希望し，質問をする係とレポートを書く係を希望する者はいなかったことがわかる。

⑥完成した形は，(At) first they didn't say a single word(最初は彼女らは一言も話さなかった)となる。at first「最初(のうち)は」，not ～ a single ...「1つの…も～ない」

⑦直前の文が「1本の糸は短くて弱い」という意味なので，イの「しかし，たくさんの糸を組み合わせることによって丈夫な布を作ることができる」を入れると意味が通る。他の選択肢は，ア「だからたくさんの糸を組み合わせるのは不可能だ」，ウ「しかし，たくさんの糸を組み合わせずに丈夫な布を作ることができる」，エ「だから多くの糸を組み合わせるために多くの服を買うべきだ」。

⑧第1段落で先生は，One student will ask questions. Two students will write a report and one student will take pictures. と生徒たちに指示している。下線部を日本語に直せばよい。

⑨ア「メアリーの先生は，メアリーと友人たちに織物工場へ行くように言った」。第1段落の5文目によれば，メアリーと友人たちは話し合って織物工場へ行くことを決めた。先生に指示されたわけではないから誤り。

イ「メアリーは織物工場を訪ねる前にそれに関するレポートを書きたかった」。本文にはそのようなことは書かれていないので誤り。

ウ「グリーン氏が『何か質問はあるかい』と言ったとき，メアリーはいくつかの質問をした」。第2段落の最後の2文から，グリーン氏の質問には誰も答えなかったことがわかる。したがって誤り。

エ「メアリーと先生は，一緒に小さな布を作った後で喜んだ」。織物工場へ行ったのはメアリーと友人たちであり，先生については述べられていないので誤り。

オ「グリーン氏は，お互いが助け合うことが大切だと言った」。第3段落のグリーン氏の発言中（*l*.29）に Working together is important.（一緒に働くことが大切だ）とあるので正しい。

カ「メアリーと友人たちは，仕事に関して多くのことを学んだ」。本文の最後の文の内容に一致するので正しい。

全訳

メアリーは中学生だった。ある日先生が「今度の金曜日には仕事について学ぶ予定です。どの場所を訪ねたいか考えなさい。4人のグループを作ってそれについて話し合いなさい」と言った。メアリーと友人たちは話し合って，学校の近くの織物工場に行くことに決めた。先生は「グループのメンバーとして何をするか決めなさい。1人の生徒が質問をして，2人はレポートを書き，1人は写真を撮ることになります」と言った。「私はレポートを書きたくない。誰がレポートを書くの？」とメアリーは尋ねた。誰も答えなかった。メアリーの友人が「私は写真を撮りたい」と言った。もう1人の友人が「私も」と言った。「質問をするのは難しいわ」と彼女の友人が言った。誰も質問をしたくなかったので，4人はその話をするのをやめた。

数日後にメアリーと友人たちは織物工場を訪れたが，自分たちが何をすべきか決められなかった。織物工場では1人の男性が彼女らを待っていた。(3)彼の名前はグリーン氏だった。彼は「おはよう」と言った。「おはようございます」と彼女らは言ったが，うれしくなかった。彼は布について多くのことを教えてくれた。「昔は布は多くの人にとって貴重なもので，布を作るのは大変な作業だった。お互いに助け合う必要があった」と彼は言った。(5)彼は布の作り方や，織物工場で何種類の布を作っているかも見せてくれた。「何か質問はあるかい？」と彼は尋ねた。みんな下を向いて，彼に答えなかった。

グリーン氏は「では，布の作り方を学ぼう。まず私たちは，強い糸を作らねばならない。1本の糸は短くて弱いけれど，数本の糸をより合わせることによって強い糸を作ることができる」と言った。女の子たちはやってみたが，難しかった。メアリーはそれを1人ではできなかったが，友人たちが手伝ってくれた。(6)彼女らは一緒にたくさんの強い糸を作った。グリーン氏は「次はこの糸を使って布を作ろう」と言った。彼女らは一緒にやってみた。彼女らは最初は一言もしゃべらなかったが，やがて友人の1人が「メアリー，この糸を引っ張ってくれる？」と言った。「いいわ」とメアリーは言った。別の友人は「布を作るのは難しいけど，楽しいわ」と言った。メアリーと友人たちは笑顔になった。彼女らは1時間作業したが，ほんの小さな布しか作れなかった。しかし彼女らはうれしかった。グリーン氏はメアリーと友人たちに「1本の糸は短くて弱い。(8)しかし，たくさんの糸を組み合わせることによって丈夫な布を作ることができる。君たちはこの布のようなものだ。力を合わせることが大切なんだ。将来何かするときは，このことを思い出してください」と言った。それからメアリーは友人たちに「ごめんなさい。私がレポートを書くわ」と言った。「いいえ，メアリー。一緒に書きましょう」と彼女らは言った。

次の日，メアリーと友人たちはレポートについて話した。彼女らは「私たちは布を作ることについてたくさんのことを学んだし，私たちにとって大切なことも学んだわ」と言った。

語句

location「場所」　cloth「布」
combine「～を組み合わせる」

025 ① その付近には何もなく，自分がたまたまそばを通らなければその女性はそこで立ち往生していただろうと思ったから。

② 彼は２週間前に失業して(まだ次の仕事が見つからず)，その時点では収入がなかったから。

③ 彼女はレストランに着く前に(車がパンクして困っているところを)知らない男性に助けてもらったので，今度は自分が(妊娠中でも懸命に働いている)そのウエイトレスを助けてあげたい[男性に渡すはずだったお金をウエイトレスに渡すことで男性へのお礼の代わりになる]と思ったから。

解説 ①直後の There is nothing around here. から，その付近には(民家などが)何もなかったことがわかる。したがってポールは，「自分が見つけなければ，エドナはパンクを直すことができないままいつまでもそこにいなければならなかっただろう」と考えたと推測できる。

②彼が「本当にそのお金を必要としていた」のは，そのとき彼にはお金がなかったから。その理由はなぜか？ と考えると，第２段落の He lost his job ... two weeks ago ... という文がその答えになる。

③エドナは食事代のおつりを受け取らず，さらにもう100ドルをテーブルに置いて行った。100ドルはチップとしては高額であり，ウエイトレスには自分がそんなお金をもらう理由がわからなかったが，エドナにはそれなりの理由があった。問いの「レストランに着く前に起きたことをふまえて」という文をヒントにして考えると，エドナは「自分はさっき困っているところを見知らぬ男性に助けてもらった。だから今度は(妊娠中で苦労しているように見える)この見知らぬ女性を自分が助けてあげよう」と思ったのだ，と推測できる。

精読

◆How did that woman know she needed that money right now?(*l*.49)(自分が今すぐにそのお金を必要としていることをどうしてあの女性[エドナ]は知っていたのだろう)：そのウエイトレスの女性がお金を必要としているのは，夫のポールが失業中で家計が苦しいから。このストーリーをていねいに要約すると次のようになる。一口で言えば「善行は報われる」という話である。

「ポールは見知らぬ女性[エドナ]を助けた。失業中の彼は金に困っていたが，(困っている人を助けるのは当然だという理由で)お礼のお金を受け取らなかった。エドナは，本来ポールに渡すはずだったお金を，(彼女の目には苦労しているように見えた)ウエイトレスに渡すことで，自分もポールが自分にしたのと同じような善意を彼女に施そうとした。そのお金は結果的にウエイトレスの夫であるポールに届いた。」

全訳

12月の寒い夜が更けようとしていた。風が強く，雨が降り出した。１人の男が車を運転していた。彼はとても疲れており不安だった。

彼は２週間前に工場が閉鎖されたとき失業したので，新しい仕事を探さなければならなかった。

今日の午前中に彼は仕事の面接を受けるために車で町へ行ったが，遅すぎた。すべての職はすでに占められていたので，彼は追い払われた。彼は一日中町を歩き回って何らかの種類の仕事を探したが，１つも見つからなかった。すぐに仕事を見つけなければ，彼はどうすればよいかわからなかった。

暗くなって，とても遅い時間になった。男の前方の道端に車が見えた。彼はそばを通り過ぎながら見てみようとしてスピードを落とした。その車は新しくて値段が高そうだった。年配の女性が車のそばに立って，手を振っていた。男は車を道の片側に寄せ，車から降りた。「どうしたのですか」と男は尋ねた。

女性は何も言わなかった。彼女は怖くて，この男を信用できるかどうかわからなかった。女性は自分が金持ちに見えることを知っていた。彼女は高価なコートを着て，いい車の横に立っていた。しかし彼女は寒くて雨に濡れてもいた。彼女はこの男を信用するしかなかった。

「タイヤがパンクしてるんです。レッカー車に電話をかけてみたのですが，ここは携帯電話の電波が届かないのです」と彼女は言った。

「ああ，わかりました。でも心配しないで。ぼくがタイヤを交換してあげましょう」と，その男は笑顔で言った。

「ところで，ぼくの名前はポールです」と彼は言った。

「私はエドナです」と女性は言った。「助けてくれてありがとうございます。誰も来ないかと不安でした。」

「どういたしまして。あなたは運がいい。このあたりは何もないところです」とポールは言った。彼は予備のタイヤと道具をエドナの車から取り出した。「ぼくの車で待って暖まってはどうですか」と彼は提案した。

エドナはうなずいて車に乗り込んだ。車内は暖かかった。まもなくポールはタイヤ交換を終えた。エドナは彼の車から降りて，彼にお礼を言った。「感謝の言葉もありません」。彼女はポールにいくらかの金を渡すために財布を開けた。ポールはその金のことを少し考えた。彼は本当にその金が必要だったが，首を振った。「心配ないと言ったじゃないですか」と彼は笑顔で言った。エドナは再び彼に感謝して，彼らは自分の車へ戻り，夜道を走り去った。

1時間ほどして，エドナの目に町が見えた。彼女は疲れてきたので，コーヒーを飲んで何か食べるために小さなレストランに立ち寄った。

ウエイトレスが注文を取りに来た。彼女はとても疲れているようだった。エドナは，おなかの大きさからそのウエイトレスが妊娠8か月ほどだとわかった。しかし彼女はそれでも明るい笑顔を浮かべていた。彼女はエドナの注文を受けるときとても愛想がよかった。

エドナは食事をしてコーヒーを飲んだ。彼女はそのウエイトレスが他の客の給仕をする姿を見つめた。彼女は注文を取りながら，みんなと親しげに世間話をした。立ち止まって休むことは少しもなかった。食事が終わると，エドナはウエイトレスに食事代として100ドル札を渡した。ウエイトレスがおつりをレジに取りに行くと，エドナは立ち上がって静かにドアの外へ出ていった。ウエイトレスが戻ってくると，エドナはいなくなっていた。彼女は急いでドアから出てエドナを捕まえようとしたが，エドナはすでに去っていた。エドナのテーブルを片付けるために彼女が中に戻ると，テーブルの上にもう1枚の100ドル札が見えた。そのチップは，そのウエイトレスのためのものだった。彼女はそれを取り上げた。信じられなかった。あの女性はどうして，自分が今すぐにそのお金が必要だと知っていたのだろうか。

ウエイトレスは仕事を終えた。彼女は車に乗って家へ帰った。彼女は満面の笑みを浮かべていたが，それはいつもとは違う笑顔だった。家に帰ると，彼女の夫はソファに座ってテレビを見ていた。彼女は駆け寄って彼に抱きついた。彼は驚いて彼女を見た。

「ねえポール，今日仕事で何があったか，あなたは想像もつかないでしょうね！」と彼女は言った。

語句

slow down「スピードを落とす」
wave one's arms「腕を振る」
trust「～を信用する」 call for ～「～を電話で呼ぶ」
I can't thank you enough.「あなたに感謝してもしきれません[お礼の言葉もありません]」
stomach「おなか，腹」
for a second「少しの間」 quietly「静かに」
guess「～を推測する」

026 ① エ ② **never** ③ ア
④ イ ⑤ オ，カ

解説 ①全訳の下線部(1)を参照。直後の文に「その猫を手放したくなかった」とあることから考えて，エの「どうして飼い主が彼女を十分に見張っておかなかった[猫から目を離した]のかを私は理解できない」が適切。他の選択肢の意味は次のとおり。

ア 私はできるだけ早く飼い主を見つけて，猫をその人に戻さなければならない。
イ 私は今から学校の図書館へ新聞を調べに行かねばならない。
ウ 私は友だちがそんなかわいい猫をなぜ私にくれたのを本当に知りたい。

②形の上から考えると，I ( ) said a word about it to my parents. の空所には何も入れなくても文として成り立つ。したがって空所には修飾語(副詞)が入る。内容的には，話の流れから「町内新聞の告知のことは両親には言わなかった」という状況と考えられる。しかし空所にdidn'tを入れることはできない(それだと後ろの語がsayのはずだから)。そこでneverを入れれば，I never said a word about itが「私はそれについて決して一言も言わなかった」という意味になる。

③Snow noticed (that) something was wrong. は「何か具合が悪いと(いうことに)スノウは気づいた」という意味。

ア スノウは何かが起きそうだと感じた。
イ スノウは自分がひどいミスをしたと思った。
ウ スノウは自分が私を気の毒に思うべきだと思った。
エ スノウは私たちがもっと注意深く考えるべきだと感じた。

話の流れから，筆者の不安がスノウに伝わったという状況と考えられる。したがってアが正解。

④全訳の下線部(4)を参照。I could say to her, "(　)" But it was too late ...(私は彼女に『…』と言うことができた。しかし手遅れだった)という状況から，筆者は実際にはその言葉を言わなかったことになる。

ア　こんにちは，ようこそ。ドアを開けてください。

イ　すみませんが住所をお間違えです。

ウ　すみませんが，ルーシーについては何も知りません。

エ　どちらさまですか。母がすぐにまいります。

筆者はその女性に会いたくなかった(彼女がスノウの飼い主ならスノウはいなくなってしまうから)。その状況から考えて，イが適切。この時点では筆者はスノウの本当の名前がルーシーだとは知らなかったのだから，ウは不適切。

⑤ア「リサは毎日小さな友だちと一緒に中学へ歩いて通っている。彼女は30分ほどかけて登校する」。*l*.8にa small friend was following me(小さな友だちが私の後をついて来ていた)とあるが，この「小さな友だち」とはスノウのこと。筆者は毎日スノウを連れて登校していたわけではないから誤り。

イ「最初リサの両親は，リサがまだ子どもで猫を飼わない方がいいと思ったので，リサにその猫を飼い主のもとへ返すようにと言った」。下線部が誤り。*ll*.14-15(My parents love ... her back.)から考えて，両親は猫がいなくなった飼い主のことを最優先に考えるべきだと思っていた。

ウ「結局，リサは自分の猫を探していた女性に会うことに同意したので，母親がその女性に電話をかけた」。下線部が誤り。*ll*.45-46にI started to push the numbers on my phone(私は電話でその(女性の)番号を押し始めた)とあるので，電話をかけたのは筆者自身である。

エ「やって来た女性は，猫の飼い主だった。彼女は『ありがとう』と言い，リサの両親にお金を渡した」。下線部が誤り。*ll*.66-69(She opened ... shook their heads.)によれば，女性はお金を渡そうとしたが，リサの両親はそれを受け取るのを断っている。

オ「子猫は真っ白だったのでリサによってスノウと呼ばれていたが，同じ猫は車の中の少女によってルーシーと呼ばれていた」。前半は*ll*.36-37(She was all white ...)の内容に一致する。また後半は*ll*.75-76(The girl said, "Come here, Lucy!")に一致する。

カ「車の中の少女にとって，その猫は町で唯一の友だちだった。彼女はその町に来たばかりだったので，そこには他に友だちはいなかった」。*ll*.77-79(My family moved ... lonely every day.)，*l*.83(Lucy is ... new place.)の内容に一致する。

精読

◆However, that was **the last** thing I wanted to do.(*l*.17)(それは私が一番やりたくないことでした)：the last thing (that) I want to doは「私がやりたかった最後のこと→私が最もやりたくなかったこと」の意味。〈**the last X**＋関係詞節(または**to *do***)〉の形は「最も～ではないX」という意味になる。

◆I hoped a miracle would happen.(*l*.51)(私は奇跡が起こることを願いました)：文脈から考えて「奇跡」とは，たとえば「訪ねて来る女性がスノウの飼い主ではないとわかる」というようなこと。

◆She has been **a joy**.(*ll*.69-70)(その猫と一緒にいられてずっと楽しかったです)：sheはスノウのことだが，「スノウは喜んでいた」という意味ではない。一般に〈S is C[名詞].〉の形では，S＝Cの関係が成り立つが，「スノウ＝喜び」とは言えないから，このjoyは「喜び(という感情)」ではなく「喜びの種，喜びを与えるもの」という意味である。つまり「スノウは(私たちに)喜びを与えてくれるものだった→スノウといて私たちはずっと楽しかった」ということ。

◆When I saw the car going away, the smile on my face was real.(*l*.86)(車が去って行くのを見たとき，私の顔の笑顔は本物でした)：*ll*.64-65にI wanted to run away with Snow. Instead, I smiled a little(私はスノウと一緒に逃げ出したいと思った。その代わりに少し笑顔になった)とある。このときの笑顔は作り笑いであり，スノウが去るときの笑顔は自然に出たものだった，ということ。

全訳

こんにちは，私の名前はリサ・スミスです。友だちからはリサと呼ばれています。私は15歳です。両親と兄と一緒にカナダの小さな町に住んでいます。

先日，大事なことが起こり，ペットの動物には特別な力があると知りました。ペットの動物には特別な力があると私が思うのはなぜか？ その理由を説明します。

私は中学生です。私は毎日歩いて学校へ通っています。私は歩くのを楽しみ，30分ほどかかります。ある春の暖かい日，学校からの帰り道で，小さな友だちが私の後をついて来ていました。この友だちは，他の友だちとは違いました。彼女はとても小さかったのです。「なんてかわいい子猫だろう！」その猫には，身元を示す何のしるしもありませんでした。「のら猫かな？」と思いました。猫はずっと私の後をついて来ました。家に着くと，猫は私のすぐ後ろにいました。

その夜，両親が仕事から帰って来たとき，彼らは子猫を見て驚いていました。友だちがくれた，と私は言いましたが，それはうそでした。両親は私がうそを言っているとわかっていました。両親は猫が大好きですが，飼い主を見つけて返すべきだと私に言いました。私は飼い主のことを考えるべきだと両親は言いました。「どうすればいいんだろう？」と私は思いました。町内新聞に告知を出すことも考えました。しかし，それは私が一番やりたくないことでした。「町内新聞に告知を載せたら，飼い主が現れるかもしれない」と思いました。とてもかわいい子猫でした。「⑴どうして飼い主が目を離したのか理解できない」と私は思い始めました。私はその猫を手放したくありませんでした。

その子猫はたぶん生後6か月くらいだろう，と兄は言いました。猫はすぐに私たちになつきました。夕食の後私の脚の上によじ登って，私たちと一緒にテレビを見ました。そのころにはこの猫を飼いたいと私は両親に頼んでいました。

その週の終わりまでに，新しい猫は私たちの家族の一員になっていました。猫はとても賢く，私によくなついていました。両親の猫への気持ちも変わり始めました。父は私にこう言いました。「リサ，この猫を探している人はいないと思うよ。だからもう，君が別の命に責任を持つべき時だ。これは君にとって大切なことを学ぶいい機会になるだろう。君は将来親になったときに必要なことを学ぶだろう」。

翌週，何気なく町内新聞を見ました。1つのとても小さな告知が，私の目に飛び込んできました。それを見て，私は驚きました。私の家の近くに住む女性が，迷子の猫を探していました。私の手は震えていました。その女性に電話すべきだとわかってはいても，電話機を取ることができませんでした。その代わりに，私はその告知を見なかったことにしようとしました。新聞はすぐに自分の部屋の押入れに入れて，私は宿題を続けました。それについて両親には一言も言いませんでした。

私たちは子猫に名前をつけました。全身が雪のように真っ白だったので，スノウと呼ぶことに決めました。私が机に向かって勉強しているとき，スノウは静かにしていました。でも私が庭に出ると，ついて来て一緒に遊ぼうとせがみました。私が皿洗いをしていると，手(あるいは前足と言うべきでしょうか)を貸そうとしてそこにいました。

この完璧なイメージには，1つだけ問題がありました。私は町内新聞に掲載された告知を忘れられませんでした。ある日，私は本当にどうすべきかを考え始めました。心の中では，その女性に電話すべきだと思っていました。その人は本当に自分の猫に再会したがっているとわかっていました。「うちのスノウが，その女性が会いたがっている猫だろうか？」と私は思いました。その夜はよく眠れませんでした。

翌朝，私は両親に告知のことを話し，ついに電話で番号を押し始めました。心の中では誰も出なければいいと思っていましたが，誰かが出ました。「もしもし」。それは若い女性の声でした。私が猫のことを説明すると，彼女は多くの質問を私にしました。ぜひ行きたい，と彼女は言いました。電話の後で，私はとても不安でした。一緒にいてくれるよう，私は両親に頼みました。

私は両親と一緒に台所のテーブルにいました。私は奇跡が起こることを願いました。スノウはずっと私の足元に座っていて，時々そのきれいな瞳で私を見上げました。スノウは何かおかしいと気づきました。

数分もしないうちに，その女性は玄関にいました。私は窓から彼女を見ました。彼女は手に地図を持ってそこに立っていました。彼女は玄関のドアをノックしました。「失礼ですが，スミスご夫妻のお宅でしょうか」と彼女は尋ねました。彼女がまたドアをノックしたとき，私の頭の中を無数の思いがよぎりました。私は彼女に「⑷すみませんが住所をお間違えです」と言うこともできました。しかしもう手遅れで，母がドアを開けました。私も，恐怖と向き合うためにそこに行きました。

その女性はスノウを見て，表情が変わりました。満面の笑みを浮かべているのが見えました。「ほら，ルーシー」と彼女は呼びました。「こっちへいらっしゃい」。そのとき私はその猫が女性にルーシーと呼ばれていることがわかりました。女性の声を聞いて，猫はとてもうれしそうでした。猫がその女性のものであることは明らかでした。

私は泣いていました。何もできませんでした。スノウと一緒に逃げ出したいと思いました。そうせずに私は少し笑顔になり，両親は若い女性に入るよう言いました。

その若い女性は，もうスノウを両腕で抱きかかえていました。彼女は財布を開いて，両親にお金を渡そうとしました。

「ご迷惑のおわびに」と彼女は言いました。

両親は首を横に振りました。母は，「いえいえ，いただけません。その猫と一緒にいられてずっと楽しかったです。私たちこそお金を払わないと」と言いました。それを聞いて，その女性は笑顔でまたスノウを抱きしめました。

スノウはその女性と再会できて本当に喜んでいました。私は女性とスノウはそろそろ家に帰る時間だとわかっていました。私は玄関のドアを開けました。女性が立ち去ろうとしたとき，小さな女の子が父親と一緒にいるのに私は気づきました。その子は車の前の座席に座っていました。その子が子猫を見たとき，満面の笑みを浮かべているのが見えました。その子は「おいで，ルーシー！」と言いました。

私が何か言う前に，その女性は説明を始めました。「私の家族は，先月この町に引っ越して来ました。車の中の女の子は私の娘です。彼女はこの町に知り合いが誰もいなくて，毎日とても寂しい思いをしていました。夫と私は娘が猫好きだと知っていたので，娘にルーシーをあげたのです」。

女性は続けて「ルーシーがいなくなったとき，娘はとてもショックを受けました。娘は一日中泣いていました。ずっと自分の部屋にいました。毎日，ルーシーにまた会いたいと言っていました。ルーシーはこの新しい場所での娘の唯一の友だちです。娘はその子猫と特別なきずなで結ばれているのです」。

突然，私は自分のことばかり考えていたことに気がつきました。私はその少女に同情しました。車が去って行くのを見たとき，私の顔の笑顔は本物でした。私は自分が正しいことをしたと思いました。子猫はまさに正しい場所にいるとわかっていました。私はその猫から大切なことを学びました。

語句

owner「持ち主」 appear「現れる」
right away「すぐに」
climb on to ～「～によじ登る」 smart「利口な」
something tells me ...「…のような気がする，何となく…のような感じがする」
jump out at ～「～に向かって飛び出す(ここでは「私に向かって飛び出してきた→私の目に突然入った」ということ)」
shake「震える，揺れる」 closet「押入れ」
continue「続ける」 do the dishes「皿洗いをする」
lend a hand「手を貸す，手伝う」
explain「説明する」 nervous「不安な，緊張して」
front door「玄関」
face「～に直面する，立ち向かう」 fear「恐怖」
realize「～に気づく，悟る」
be in tears「泣いている」
run away with ～「～と一緒に逃げる」
trouble「迷惑」 exactly「まさしく，正確に」

027
① 全訳の下線部(1)を参照。
② エ
③ [A] エ [B] ア [C] オ [D] イ [E] ウ
④ **would, for** ⑤ エ
⑥ **trophy** ⑦ ウ

解説 ①he'd は he would の短縮形で，would は「～したものだ」(過去の習慣)の意味。ask O to *do* は「O に～するよう頼む」，an hour before ～は「～の1時間前に」。

②直後の文に着目する(→精読)。「新しいシューズの話題は私にとっていつも難題だった」とは，新しいシューズを買うお金がなかったということ。

③[A]look at ～(～を見る)の at の前に over を加えた形。over は「(何かを越えて)向こうへ」という意味の副詞で，ここでは遠くにあるシューズに対して(その間にあるものを飛び越して)視線を向けた状況を表している。[B]「私から(見て)数ヤード先のスタンド席」の意味。なお，1 yard は約90センチだから，a few yards は2～3メートル程度の距離と考えられる。[C]精読を参照。[D]in his new shoes は「(自分の)新しいシューズを履いて」の意味。この in は「～を身につけて」(着用)を表す。[E]「みんなの注目(attention)がテイラー(の上)に集まった」と考えて on を入れる。on は基本的に「(表面に)接触している」という意味を表すので，人々の注目の視線がテイラーに注がれていると考えればよい。

④insist on ～は「～と言い張る，主張する」で，下線部は「彼は(自分が)テイラーに～を買ってやると言い張った」という意味。これを He firmly said that he would buy ～.(彼は自分が～を買うつもりだときっぱり言った)と言い

換える(前のsaidとの時制の一致で，willが過去形のwouldになる)。buy O for ～は「～(のため)にOを買ってやる」。この意味ではtoは使えない。

⑤前の内容から考えて，「スポーツマンシップ賞」が入る。他の選択肢は，ア「年間(最優秀)コーチ[監督](賞)」，イ「(年間)新人賞」，ウ「最優秀シューター賞」。

⑥*ll.*58-59に，Tyler's team had come in second place, and each player received a trophy.(タイラーのチームは2位になり，各選手がトロフィーを受け取った)とある。この時点でタイラーはトロフィーを1つもらっている。*ll.*71-72には，... Tyler walked over and picked up his second trophy(タイラーは歩いて行って2つ目のトロフィーを受け取った)とある。これは彼に贈られたスポーツマンシップ賞のトロフィーのこと。だから彼は「今では[これで]トロフィーの1つはママの家用に，もう1つはパパの家用にある」と言ったのである。なおこの文は，*ll.*6-7のBecause then I could have a basketball at my mom's house and at my dad's house(そうすればママの家とパパの家にバスケットボールを持てる)に対応している。

⑦ア come down は「降りてくる」，イ run down は「走って降りる」，エ throw up は「～を放り上げる」などの意味であり，文章の内容に合わない。ウ show up には「(はっきりと)見えるようになる」の意味があるので，これが正解。Showing Up というタイトルは，今まで目立たなかったタイラーの長所が，賞を取ったことでみんなに認められた，という状況を表している。

精読

◆Because then I **could have** a basketball at my mom's house and at my dad's house(*ll.*6-7)(そうすれば，ママの家にもパパの家にもバスケットボールを持てるから)：couldは仮定法過去。then(そのとき，そうすれば)は，if I got another basketball(もし別のバスケットボールが手に入ったら)の意味。この仮定法過去には，「無理かもしれないけれど，もし手に入ったら」とタイラーが母親に対して遠慮する気持ちがこめられている。

◆I closed my eyes tightly, **wishing** that his last sentence would just go away.(*ll.*15-16)(私は目をぎゅっと閉じて，彼の最後の言葉がただ消えてほしいと願った)：下線部は省いても文が成り立つので，修飾語である。分詞で始まる句の働きは，(A)前の名詞を修飾する働き，(B)それ以外の働き，の2つに大別できる。(A)の例は次のとおり。

・The dog **barking over there** is my pet.
(向こうで吠えている犬は私のペットです)

一方，上の文の下線部は，(前に名詞がないから)(B)の例である。このようなものを分詞構文と言う。分詞構文は「～しながら」「～なので」「～するとき」「そして～」などの(接続詞を使った文に近い)意味を表す。この文のwishing that ... は「…と願いながら」の意味だと考えてよい。

◆**Being** a single mom, the topic of new shoes was always difficult for me.(*ll.*16-17)(私はシングルマザーだったので，新しいシューズの話は私にとっていつも難題だった)：この文のBeing a single momは，Because[As] I was a single mom(私はシングルマザーだったので)に近い意味を表す。

◆I **shared** (**with him**) O[**how** I thought that Tyler played somewhat cautiously].(*ll.*36-37)(タイラーのプレーは少し慎重すぎると思う，と私は彼に打ち明けた)：**share**は「(自分の考えなど)を隠さずに話す，打ち明ける」の意味で，share O with him(Oを彼に打ち明ける)の形からwith himを前に出した形。Oに当たるhow I thought that ... は「私が…と思っているということ」。このhowは**that**(…ということ)と同じ意味を表す。

◆I remembered O[**how** (earlier in the season,) Tyler had mentioned that he thought he needed better shoes].(*ll.*38-39)(シーズン初めに，もっといいシューズが必要だと思うとタイラーが言ったのを私は思い出した)：このhowも，thatで言い換えられる。earlier in the season(シーズン初めに)はhad mentionedを修飾する副詞句。had mentioned(過去完了形)を使っているのは，「私が思い出した時点」から見て「タイラーが言った時点」の方が過去だから。このように「過去から見たさらに過去」の出来事を表すには過去完了形を使う。

◆話の筋をふまえて説明を加えておく。本文中に書かれているとおり，タイラーの母親はsingle mom(シングルマザー)であり，息子と2人で暮らしている。彼女と離婚した夫との仲は今でも良好とは言えないが，タイラーは夫(つまり彼の父親)の家にも時々行く(だから2つの家にバスケットボールとトロフィーを持てるのを喜んだ)。両親はタイラーの試合を見に来たが，(お互いに話したくないので)数ヤード離れて座った。そしてタイラーが賞を取ったとき，2人はWe actually smiled at one another. という行動をとった(*l.*70)。このactuallyという副詞は，「(意外に思えるだろうが)実は」という意味でしばしば使われる。つまり，今まであまり良好な仲ではなかったタイラーの両親は，このとき初めて「(意外なことだが実は)お互いにほほえみ合った」，つまりタイラーが2人に和解のきっかけを与えたのである。

全訳

息子がバスケットボールを始めたのは10歳のときだった。私が彼の父親の家に車で迎えに行くと，息子はよくバスケットボールをしていた。そんなある日，息子は私の車に駆け寄って「ママ，お願い，もう1つバスケットボールをもらえる？」と言った。

「どうしてバスケットボールが2つ必要なの，タイラー？」と私は尋ねた。

「そうすれば，ママの家にもパパの家にもバスケットボールを持てるから」と彼は答えた。

特にタイラーが話すのはバスケットボールのことばかりだったので，それはいい考えだと思った。(1)時々彼は，練習が始まる1時間前に体育館へ連れて行ってくれと私に頼んだものだ。タイラーは新しいチームメイトと合うのが楽しみで，バスケットボールの練習を楽しいと思っていた。練習が終わった後，私は体育館から出るよう彼を説得しなければならないことがよくあった。彼はたいてい，ぶらぶらしていつまでもバスケットボールをしたがっていた。

タイラーと私はいつも，私が彼の部屋へ入っておやすみを言うときに最も特別な話をしてきた。ある夜，彼はバスケットシューズについての不安を打ち明けた。もっといいシューズが必要かもしれない，と彼は私に言った。私は目をぎゅっと閉じて，彼の最後の言葉がただ消えてほしいと願った。シングルマザーだったので，新しいシューズの話は私にとっていつも難題だった。私はきれいにたたんだユニフォームの隣に置いてある彼の「履き古した」シューズに目をやった。それは私には全く問題ないように見えた。私はすぐに話題を変えた。

そしてついにシーズン初戦の日が来た。体育館は驚くほど混雑していた。タイラーの所属するチーム，ホーネッツは，マジックと対戦していた。父親が私から数ヤード離れたスタンド席に座っているのを見て，息子の目にうれしそうな表情が浮かぶのが見えた。

チームメイトに加わったとき，タイラーは決意の表情をしていた。他の子どもたちがコートをあちこち走り回るのを見つめながら，私の目には息子がベンチに座っている姿が見えた。第4クオーターまでにタイラーはボールに触ることさえなく，チームは試合に勝った。

それに続く試合もほとんど同じだった。チームは勝ち続けたが，タイラーはほとんどボールに触らなかった。彼はコートにいるとき懸命に走ったが，ボールを持つとすぐにチームメイトに投げるのだった。私は胸がどきどきする思いでその場に座っていた。

ある試合からの帰り道で，私は「タイラー，今でもバスケットボールは楽しい？」と尋ねた。

彼は「バスケットボールは大好きだよ。でも，ぼくより上手な子もいることは知っているから，ぼくはボールを持ったらその子たちに投げるだけだよ」と答えた。

翌日私は，若いころバスケットボールをしていた旧友に偶然会った。タイラーのプレーは少し慎重すぎると思う，と私は彼に打ち明けた。

「彼はいいシューズを持っているの？」と彼は尋ねてきた。シーズン初めに，もっといいシューズが必要だと思うとタイラーが言ったのを私は思い出した。タイラーの履き古したシューズのことを考える私の表情に，友人も気づいたに違いない。いつの間にか，私たちはシューズを買いに行っていた。タイラーにきれいで上質のバスケットボールシューズを買ってあげる，と彼は言い張った。それはどんなシングルマザーにも，特に息子を持つ母親に，深い感謝の念を抱かせるような素振りだった。

タイラーを寝かしつけるとき，彼はずっと前から新しいバスケットシューズがほしかったと私に言った。タイラーはそのシューズをとても気に入った。それは最高のシューズだった。新しいシューズが試合で役立つことを彼は願った。

タイラーのバスケットボールへの果てない熱意と没頭の数週間があっという間に過ぎ去った。タイラーはもう一度，自分はチームで最高の選手ではないけれど，バスケットボールが大好きだからかまわない，と私に言った。彼は懸命にプレーし，練習を続けた。私は彼が上達するのを見守った。彼は決してくじけなかった。新しいシューズの方が履き心地がいいと言い，もう一度私に礼を言った。彼は自分が思いついた新しいプレーを詳しく説明してくれた。こんないいチームにいることを誇りに思う，と彼は私に言った。それまで彼らは無敗だった。

チームはプレーオフに進出した。満席の観衆の前で，タイラーは大接戦の熱戦の最後に8点を取った。

シーズンが終わり，表彰式の時が近づいていた。タイラーは，最優秀選手賞，最優秀の守備選手，最も上達した選手，最優秀万能選手の各賞をどの子が受賞するのかを予想していた。タイラーのチームは2位になり，各選手がトロフィーを受け取った。セレモニーの終わりのころ，責任者が立ち上がってみんなにお礼を言った。それから彼はこう言った。「まだ終わりではありません。最後にもう1人，とても特別な選手のための特別な賞があります。彼は全試合に積極的な態度で臨みます。審判や他の選手と口論したこともなく，遅刻もせず，練習も試合も休んだことはありません。彼はプレー中の自分の立場を知っており，チームメイトたちは彼を賞賛します。彼がプレーする理由は明らかに試合が大好きだからであり，常に懸命に走り，ベストを尽くします。スポーツマンシップ賞は，タイラー・マースデンに与えられます！」

突然，すべての注目がタイラーに集まった。チームメイトや友人たちは，彼とハイタッチをしたり背中をたたいたりしていた。私は目に涙があふれるのを感じた。スタンド席の数ヤード先を見ると，彼の父親も同じように涙を浮かべていた。私たちは実際，お互いにほほえみ合った。

タイラーが歩いて行って2つ目のトロフィーを受け取ったとき，他の子どもたちはまだ彼を祝福していた。他の親たちが「彼は今夜の一番感動的な賞を取ったね」と言っているのが聞こえた。

タイラーは誇らしげにこう言った。「これでママの家のトロフィーとパパの家のトロフィーができたよ！」

語句

pick O up「Oを車で迎えに行く」
reply「返答する」
convince O to *do*「Oを説得して～させる」
hang around「ぶらつく」 express「～を言い表す」
concern「懸念，不安」 tightly「きつく」
next to ～「～の隣に」 fold「～を折りたたむ」
surprisingly「驚くほど」 determination「決意」
up and down「～のあちこちへ，～を行ったり来たり」
quarter「クォーター(試合時間を4分割したうちの1つの時間帯)」
pretty much the same「かなりよく似ている」
barely「ほとんど～ない」
somewhat「やや，いくぶん」
cautiously「警戒して，用心深く」
mention that ...「…ということを話す」
worn-out「(使いすぎて)すり切れた」
high-quality「高品質の」
inspire「(気持ち)を呼び起こす」 gratitude「感謝」
single mom「シングルマザー」
put O to bed「Oを寝かしつける」
awesome「素晴らしい，最高の」
unending「終わりのない」
enthusiasm「情熱」 devotion「献身，没頭」
fly by「(時間が)飛ぶように過ぎ去る」
discouraged「落胆して」 detailed「詳細な」
description「説明，描写」 undefeated「全勝の」
make it to ～「～に到達する」
play-off「プレーオフ，優勝決定戦」
standing-room-only「立見席以外満席の」
close「(試合が)接戦の」
come to a close「終わる」 award「賞」
come up「近づいてくる」
Most Valuable Player「最優秀選手(MVP)」
defense「守備」
all-around player「オールラウンド[万能]の選手」
come in second place「2位になる」
trophy「トロフィー」
toward the end of ～「～の終わりごろに」
director「責任者」 get up「立ち上がる」
show up for ～「～に現れる」
positive「積極的な，前向きの」 attitude「態度」
argue with ～「～と口論する」 referee「審判」
speak highly of ～「～をほめる」
obviously「明らかに」 attention「注意，注目」
give ～ a high-five「～とハイタッチをする」
slap「平手で(ぴしゃりと)たたくこと」
well up「(涙が)こみ上げる」
congratulate「～を祝福する」
pick up ～「～を受け取る」
overhear「～をふと耳にする」
impressive「印象的な，感動的な」

028 ① ア ② エ ③ イ ④ ア
⑤ **the center of the table**
⑥ イ ⑦ [1] ウ [2] カ [3] ケ
⑧ **butter** ⑨ カ，キ

解説 ①食堂の準備をしていた1人の男が，誤ってテーブルの上の像を壊してしまったという状況。He looked ～.(彼は～に見えた)の空所に入る適切な形容詞は，アのpale((顔色が)青ざめて)。

イ(喜んで)，ウ(利口な)，エ(怒って)は文脈に合わない。

②「伯爵はその美しい〜がなければとても怒るだろう」という文の空所に入る適切な名詞は，エのstatue((彫)像)。「壊れた像がテーブルになければ」ということ。この文のwouldは仮定法過去で，withoutは「もし〜がなかったら」という意味を表す。像はその時点では(壊れて)なくなっているが，「もし(万一)夕食が始まるまでに代わりの像を用意できなければ」という気持ちをこめて仮定法過去を使っている。ア(石)，イ(テーブル)，ウ(夕食)は文脈に合わない。

③「男はなぜ笑ったのか」という問い。男の直後の発言から考えて，適切な答えはイの「その少年が1時間で像を作るとは信じられなかったから」。他の選択肢の意味は次のとおり。

ア 男はその少年が像を作るのは素晴らしいアイデアだと思ったから。

ウ 男はその少年が像と同じくらい美しいと思ったから。

エ 男はその少年がとても勇敢だと知ってただ驚いたから。

④直前に「他の人々はみんな，その少年が像を作るのが上手だと知っていたので」とある。したがって，アの「彼ならできる！ 彼ならできる！」が適切。イは「そうだ，(私たちが)やろう！ そうだ，(私たちが)やろう！」，ウは「彼は(うまく)やった！ 彼は(うまく)やった！」，エは「ご注意ください[お知らせします]！ ご注意ください[お知らせします]！」(アナウンスなどで相手の注意を引くために使われる言葉)。

⑤「男はそれ[バターで作った像]をits place(その像を置くべき場所)へ運んだ」という状況。*ll*.24-25に，I have broken a statue that should stand at <u>the center of the table.</u>(テーブルの中央にあるべき像を壊してしまった)とあるので，下線部が像を置く場所である。

⑥伯爵はこの時点で初めて，テーブルの上のバターの像を見ている。その後の話の流れを考えると，「実を言うと〜」に続く伯爵の言葉として適切なのは，イの「私は君たち全員と同じくらい驚いている」。ア「壊れた像を見て私は悲しい」，ウ「私はなぜここにバターがあるのかを知っている」，エ「新しい像を見てショックを受けている」は文脈に合わない。

⑦並べ替えた文は，(I have no teacher but I) learned <u>from</u> my grandfather <u>how</u> to carve sculptures <u>out</u> of (stone).(私には先生はいないが，祖父から石で像を彫る方法を学んだ)となる。

⑧He carved stone, not [E]は，「彼は[E]でなく石を彫った」という意味(A, not B「BでなくA」)。少年は晩餐会ではバターを彫って像を作ったが，本格的に彫刻を学ぶ際には石を彫った，ということ。したがって[E]にはbutterが入る。

⑨ア「アントニオは他の少年たちと一緒に外で遊ぶのを楽しんでいたが，あまり丈夫な子ではなかった」。前半が*l*.5のHe didn't like to play with other boys of the town(彼は町の他の少年たちと遊ぶのが好きではなかった)と一致しない。

イ「アントニオの祖母は毎晩お話を語り，アントニオは石の上にその絵を描いた」。*ll*.12-13にAntonio tried to make some of those pictures in stone(アントニオはそれらの絵[イメージ]を石で作ろうとした)とある。彼は石の上に絵を描いたわけではない。

ウ「アントニオと祖父母は，キッチンで手伝いをするためにしばしば伯爵の家へ行った」。第4段落によれば，祖母は伯爵の家へは行っていないし，しばしば行っていたのも祖父だけである。

エ「キッチンで像が壊れたとき，担当の者たちは伯爵が怒るだろうと思った」。第6段落によれば，像が壊れたのは食堂である(アントニオはキッチンでその音を聞いた)。

オ「像を壊した男はアントニオのところへ行き，バターの像を作るよう頼んだ」。本文によれば，男はアントニオが像を作れるわけがないと思っており，*l*.32でアントニオがMay I make one for you?(あなたに作ってあげてもいいですか)と頼んでいるので，男がバターで像を作るようアントニオに頼んだわけではない。

カ「大きなバターのかたまりを彫ってライオンの形にするのに，アントニオは数分しかかからなかった」。*l*.44にIn a few minutes, he made it into the shape of a sitting lion. とあり，この内容と一致する。make O into 〜は「Oを〜に加工する」の意味で，intoの後ろにはOが変化した結果を置く。

同様にcarve O into ～も「Oを彫って～に加工する」という意味を表す。また，〈It takes A[人]＋時間＋to *do*〉は「Aが～するのに…の時間がかかる」という意味。

キ「伯爵のパーティーの客たちは，その素晴らしいライオンの像を作ったのが誰なのかを知りたがった」。*ll*.51-52にthey asked the Count to tell them the name of the artist(彼らはその(バターのライオン像を作った)芸術家の名前を教えてくれるよう伯爵に頼んだ)とあり，この内容と一致する。

精読

◆his grandfather cut stone [**to make** statues [**to sell** to rich people]](*ll*.3-4)(彼の祖父は石を削って像を作り，金持ちに売っていた)：厳密に考えると，「彼の祖父は石を切った」＋「像[←金持ちに売るための]を作るために」となる(to makeは目的を表す副詞的用法の不定詞，to sellはstatuesを修飾する形容詞的用法の不定詞)。ただし不定詞はもともと「～する方へ向かって」という意味を持つので，「祖父は石を切った＋像を作る方へ向かって＋金持ちに売る方へ向かって」のように前から意味をつなげて考えてよい。

全訳

アントニオ・カノーヴァは，イタリアに住む幼い少年だった。両親は亡くなっており，貧しい祖父母と暮らしていた。祖母は夫と少年の世話をし，祖父は石を削って像を作り，金持ちに売っていた。

アントニオはあまり丈夫ではなかった。彼は町の他の少年たちと遊ぶのが好きではなかったが，像を作れるほど丈夫で美しい大きな石を探すために，祖父と一緒によく出かけていた。アントニオは祖父と一緒に仕事をするのがとても楽しかったので，すぐに祖父のように像を作る方法を覚えた。「この子はいつか立派な石彫作家になるだろう」と祖父は言った。

毎晩仕事が終わると，アントニオの祖母は彼に歌を歌い，すてきで美しいもののイメージで頭がいっぱいになるような話を聞かせてくれた。そして翌日，石を探しに戻ったアントニオは，そのイメージのいくつかを石で作ろうとした。

同じ町に金持ちの男がおり，伯爵と呼ばれていた。彼はよく晩餐会を開き，他の町から金持ちの友人たちが訪ねて来た。そんなときはしばしばアントニオの祖父が，料理も得意だったのでよく台所で手伝いをした。

ある日，また大きなパーティーが予定されていたので，アントニオは祖父と一緒に伯爵の大邸宅へ行った。少年は料理を作れず，客に料理を出せる年齢でもなかったが，鍋やフライパンを洗うことはできたし，頭がよくて素早かったので，いろんな仕事を手伝うことができた。

夕食が始まる直前に，食堂で大きな音がして，1人の男がキッチンに駆け込んできた。彼は青ざめていた。

「どうしよう？ どうしよう？」と彼は叫んだ。「テーブルの中央に置く像を壊してしまった。その像がないとテーブルの見栄えが悪くなってしまう。伯爵は何と言うだろう？」

そしてアントニオのまわりの人々はみんな困ってしまった。この晩餐会は失敗するのだろうか。食卓は豪華でなければならなかった。美しい像がなければ，伯爵はとても怒るだろう。「ああ，困った！ どうしよう？」とみんながお互いに言い合った。

そこで幼いアントニオ・カノーヴァは，像を壊した男のところに行った。

「ぼくが像を作れます。あなたに作ってあげてもいいですか」

「ぼうや」と男は言った。「新しい像は，私が壊した像と全く同じ大きさでなければならないんだ」

「わかりました。問題ありません」とアントニオは言った。「壊れた像と同じくらい美しい像をたぶん作れます」

男は笑った。「君は何者だい，ぼうや。なぜ1時間で像を作れると言えるんだ？」

「ぼくの名前はアントニオ・カノーヴァです」と少年は言った。

他の人々はみんな，その少年が像を作るのが上手だと知っていたので，「彼ならできる！ 彼ならできる！」とみんなが言った。

キッチンのテーブルの上に，巨大な四角い黄色いバターがあった。重さは100キロ近くあった。アントニオは包丁でこのバターを切って彫り始めた。彼は数分で，バターを座ったライオンの形に作り上げた。

「なんてきれいなんだ！」と彼らは叫んだ。「壊れた像よりずっときれいだ」

それが完成すると，男はそれを所定の場所へ運んだ。

伯爵と彼の友人たちが夕食に入って来たとき，彼らが最初に見たのは黄色いライオンだった。

「何と美しい芸術品だろう！」と彼らは叫んだ。「こんな像を彫ることができるのは立派な芸術家だけだが，バターで作るとは面白いじゃないか！」それから彼らは，その芸術家の名前を教えてくれと伯爵に頼んだ。

「実は私も，君たちみんなと同じくらい驚いている。

この素晴らしい像を作ったのは誰なんだ？ 誰か知っているか？」

キッチン担当の少年の1人が「ほんの1時間前に，キッチンにいた小さな男の子が彫りました」と言った。

これには客たちも大いに驚き，伯爵はその少年を部屋に呼び入れた。

「ぼうや，君がこんな素晴らしい作品を作ってくれたのか」と伯爵は言った。「君は何という名で，君の先生は誰だ？」

「ぼくの名前はアントニオ・カノーヴァです」と少年は言った。「それから先生はいませんが，祖父から石で像を彫る方法を習いました」

このパーティーで未来の素晴らしい芸術家に会えたことに客たちはみんな喜び，誇りにも思った。そして彼らはアントニオと夕食を共にしたがり，アントニオはとても喜んでテーブルについた。

翌日，伯爵はアントニオの祖父に，アントニオを自分の家に来させるように頼んだ。そしてアントニオが伯爵の家に住むよう頼まれたので，祖父は大変喜んだ。アントニオに彫刻の技術を教えるために，国一番の芸術家たちが伯爵の家に住み始めた。彼はバターではなく石を彫り，数年後にアントニオ・カノーヴァは世界最高の石彫作家の1人になった。

語句

statue「(彫)像」 rush into ～「～に駆け込む」
square「四角い」 weigh「～の重さがある」
carve「～を彫る」 delighted「喜んで」

029 ① 全訳の下線部(1)を参照。
② ア ③ **tail**
④ 探し始めてすぐに，デューイが自分の勝ちだとでも言いたげに現れたから。(34字)
⑤ [A] ウ [B] ア [C] イ
⑥ ウ ⑦ エ ⑧ ウ，カ

解説 ① I know won't の部分を見て「I know / won't」という意味の切れ目を発見することが大切。the dictionary (which) I use(私が使っている辞書)などと同じ形で，Most of the librarians (who(m)) I know(私が知っている司書のほとんど)という意味を表す。won't は will not の短縮形で，「～しないだろう」ということ。

②「デューイはタイミングをつかむ…な感覚を持っていた」という文を完成するために適切な形容詞を考える。それぞれの形容詞の意味は，ア「驚くほどの，素晴らしい」，イ「ひどい」，ウ「普通の」，エ「狭い」。*ll*.8-9 のデューイの行動から，正解はア。

③「彼[デューイ]は自分が…を持っているのを忘れているように見えた」という文を完成する。「頭だけを本棚に押し込んで隠れたつもりになっているが，体の後ろ半分は見えている」という状況だから，空所には tail(しっぽ)が入る。

④ fair は「公平な，公明正大な」(日本語でも「フェアプレー」などと言う)。「それは公平ではない[不公平だ]よ，デューイ。君は私に20秒しか与えなかった」とは，筆者が時間をかけて探し出す前に，デューイが「ほら，見つけられなかっただろう」とでも言いたげに現れた，という状況を表している。

⑤ 全訳 の下線部[A]～[C]を参照。本文によれば，筆者はコンピューターに向かって仕事をしながら，時々息抜きにデューイとかくれんぼ遊びをする。そのとき筆者は，まず探す役になり，次は隠れる役になる。ウの You win!(君の勝ちだ)は[A]～[C]のどこに入れても意味が通じるが，1つの文は1回しか使えないので，他の文との関係で[B]に入れる。

⑥ The weight was lifted. は「重しが持ち上げられた」の意味から転じて，「肩の荷が下りた」という状況を表す。as they say は「人々が言うとおりに→いわゆる，俗に言う」の意味。直前に「悩みが消えていた」という内容があるので，筆者の気持ちに近いのはウの relaxed(くつろいだ，落ち着いた)。ア(興奮した)，イ(興味を持った)，エ(感銘を受けた)は誤り。

⑦「天井が私の上に崩れ落ち始めた」は比ゆ的な表現。この後に tears in my eyes(目に涙をためて)とあることなどから，筆者の気分が落ち込んでいる状況を表している。したがってエが正解。この段落の最初の文に，「デューイとのかくれんぼ遊びで私は多くのつらい夜を通り抜けた[乗り切った]」とあるので，筆者の気分が沈むのはデューイのせいではない。したがってアやウは誤り。

⑧ウとカは，それぞれ 全訳 の　　　　の内容に一致する。アは，デューイが暗い図書館を怖がっていたという記述は本文にない(そもそも猫は夜行性だから暗闇を怖がることはない)。イは，*ll*.32-33より，後をつけたりするのはデューイの方な

ので誤り。エは，最後から２つ目の段落によればデューイは，筆者が望むときはいつも筆者のそばにいてくれた。オは，*l*.57にIt wasn't just love. とあるから誤り。

精読

◆Have you ever been in a library after closing? Of course **not**! (Or at least I hope **not**.) (*ll*.1-2) (閉館後の図書館にいたことがあるだろうか。もちろんないはずだ(あるいは少なくとも私はそう願いたい))：同じ言葉のくり返しを避けるために，notだけを残して他の言葉を省略することがある。２文目は (you have) not (ever been in a library after closing) の(　)内を省略した形で，「あなたはもちろん閉館後の図書館にいたことはないだろう」ということ。３文目はOr at least I hope (you have) not (ever been in a library after closing). の(　)内を省略した形で，「あるいは少なくとも私は，あなたが閉館後の図書館にいたことがないことを願っている」ということ。

◆While I worked, Dewey sat on top of my computer screen, **slowly moving his tail**. (*ll*.8-9) (私が仕事をしている間，デューイは私のコンピューター画面のてっぺんに座り，ゆっくりとしっぽを動かしていた)：下線部は分詞構文で，「ゆっくりとしっぽを動かしながら」の意味。文の最後に置かれた～ingで始まる分詞構文は，「～しながら」または「そして～」の意味を表すことが多い。

・I stayed at home **playing video games** today. (今日はビデオゲームをしながら家にいた[家にいてビデオゲームをしていた])

◆Where **could** that cat **be**? (*l*.28) (あの猫はどこにいるんだろう？)：意味的にはWhere is that cat? と同じ。**could be**は「(もしかしたら)～かもしれない」の意味で，「あの猫は(いったい)どこにいる可能性があるのだろうか」というニュアンス。「could＝できた」ではない。

全訳

閉館後の図書館にいたことがあるだろうか。もちろんないはずだ！(あるいは少なくとも私はそう願いたい。)ちょっと教えてあげよう。閉館後の図書館は寂しい場所だ。とても静かで，ずらりと並んだ棚が人を不安にするようなたくさんの暗いものかげを作っている。(1)私の知り合いの司書のほとんどは，日が暮れてから図書館に一人でいようとはしないだろう。しかし私はスペンサー公立図書館で，他のみんなが帰宅した後，ほとんど毎晩働き，少しも怖くなかった。私は強かった。私は頑固だった。そして何より，私は一人でいたことは一度もなかった。私にはデューイがいた。

私が仕事をしている間，デューイは私のコンピューター画面のてっぺんに座り，ゆっくりとしっぽを動かしていた。私が仕事をやめると，彼はいつもキーボードの上に飛び降りた。「もう十分だ」と彼は言ったものだ。「遊ぼうよ」。デューイはタイミングをつかむ驚異的な感覚を持っていた。

「わかったよ，デューイ」と私は彼に言った。「お先にどうぞ」

デューイの遊びはかくれんぼだったので，私が合図するとすぐに飛び跳ねて行って(本棚の)角を曲がったものだった。私はよく，長い毛のオレンジ色の猫の後ろ半分をすぐに見つけた。デューイにとって，隠れるとは本棚に頭を押し込むことであり，自分にしっぽがあることを忘れているようだった。

「デューイはどこかな」と，私はこっそり彼に近づきながら大声で言った。「ワッ！」２，３フィートの距離まで近づくと，私は叫び，デューイを走らせた。

彼はもっと上手に隠れることもあった。私ははずれの棚をいくつか歩き回り，角を曲がると，デューイがうれしそうに私の方へ意気揚々と歩いてくるのが見えた。

「見つけられなかっただろう！　やーい！」

「ずるいよ，デューイ。たった20秒しかくれないなんて」

時には彼はとても狭い場所で静かにしていた。私は５分ほど探してから，彼の名前を呼び始めた。「デューイ！　デューイ！」その暗い図書館は少し怖かったが，私はデューイが２，３フィートだけ離れて隠れ，私を笑っているのをいつも想像していた。

「わかった，デューイ，もういいよ。[A]君の勝ちだ！」

そこには何もなかった。あいつはどこにいるんだろう？　あきらめかけたそのとき，振り向くとそこに彼はいた。通路の真ん中に立って，私を見ていた。

「ああ，デューイ，君は賢い子だ。[B]今度は私の番だよ」

私が走って本棚の陰に隠れると，いつも２つのうちのどちらかが起きた。私が隠れる場所に着いて振り向くと，デューイがちょうどそこに立っていた。彼は私を追いかけてきていたのだ。

「見つけた。簡単だったよ」

彼のもう１つのお気に入りの方法は，(ウ)棚の反対側を走って回って，私より先に私の隠れ場所に着くことだった。

「やあ，君はここに隠れようと思っていたのかい？ だって，まあ，わかっていたけどね」

私は笑って，彼の耳の後ろを優しくなでてやった。「よくやった，デューイ。ちょっと走ってみようか」

私たちは棚の間を走り，通路の端で落ち合う。15分もすると，私は悩みをすっかり忘れたものだ。私を悩ませていたものはすべて消えた。いわゆる，重荷が降りたのだ。

「よし，デューイ。[C]仕事に戻ろう」

デューイは決して文句を言わなかった。私がいすに戻ると，彼はコンピューターのてっぺんによじ登って戻り，画面の前でしっぽを動かし始める。私が次に彼を必要とするとき，彼はそこにいた。

デューイとのこのかくれんぼ遊びで，私は多くのつらい夜を乗り切った。私が泣いている間，デューイが私のひざの上に頭をのせてかぼそい声で鳴いていたとか，私の顔の涙をなめてくれたとか，そんなことも語るべきかもしれない。しかし，想像はつくだろう？ そしてそれはほとんど真実であり，時々，天井が崩れて私の上に落ち始め，私が目に涙を浮かべて膝を見下ろすと，私がまさにいてほしいそこにデューイはいた。

デューイは愛情深い猫だった。しかし彼はそれでも猫だったので，自分だけの空間を好んだ。ただ彼はいつも，私がいつ暖かい体を必要とするかを知っており，私にとって一番よいのが愚かで無心になれるかくれんぼ遊びであるのはいつなのかを知っていた。

彼は私が必要とするものを何でも与えてくれた。何も考えず，見返りを求めず，そして私が頼まなくても。それは単なる愛ではなかった。愛以上のものだった。敬意だった。共感だった。そしてそれは双方向のものだった。そんなつながりをデューイと私は会ったときに感じていただろうか。(カ)図書館で私たちだけで夜を一緒に過ごすうちに，それは決して切れないきずなに変わった。

語句

lonely「寂しい」 create「〜を作り出す」
nervous「不安な」 above all「とりわけ，特に」
tail「尾」 onto「〜の上に」
give the word「合図を送る」
take off「飛び跳ねて行く」 back half「後ろの半分」
push O into 〜「O を〜の中に押し込む」
bookshelf「本棚」 say out loud「大声で言う」
shout「叫ぶ」 within「〜以内に」
hidden < hide「〜を隠す」 second「秒」
spot「場所」 frightening「怖い」
turn around「振り向く」
the other side of 〜「〜の反対側に」
completely「完全に，全く」
trouble「悩み，〜を悩ます」 complain「不平を言う」
climb back「よじ登って戻る」
get O through 〜「O に〜を切り抜けさせる」
tears「涙」 ceiling「天井」 fall in「崩れる」
loving「愛情深い」
personal space「個人的な空間，縄張り」
silly「愚かな」 mindless「頭を使わない」
in return「お返しに」
turn O into 〜「O を〜に変える」
unbreakable「壊すことのできない」 bond「きずな」

030 ① [1] ア [2] ウ [3] イ [4] エ [5] ウ
② ア ③ ウ，エ ④ ア
⑤ エ，キ，ケ

解説 ①[1]「ケビンが(1)アンディはおなかがすいちゃうよと言ったのはなぜか」

ア アンディの間違いをからかいたかったから。
イ アンディが手を動かして叫び始めたから。
ウ アンディが自分のピザをもらえないと思ったから。
エ アンディが自分の選んだピザをもう食べてしまったから。

直後に Kevin joked(…とケビンは冗談を言った)とある。これは「10分の1のピザではアンディは満腹にならならないだろう」ということ。したがってアが正解。

[2]「アンディが先生の質問に『10分の1』と答えたのはなぜか」

ア 10人のクラスメイトにピザを分けたかったから。
イ ケビンが最初に3分の1と答えたので，アンディはもう一方を選んだ。
ウ 3分の1は10分の1よりも小さいと思ったから。
エ 彼のクラスには3人より多くの生徒がいたから。

l.9に Ten is the bigger number, so that's what he picked.(10の方が大きい数字なので，彼が選んだのはそれ[10分の1]だった)

とある。したがってウが正解(→精読)。

[3]「アンディが『休み時間のベルが鳴ればいいのに』と思ったのはなぜか」(→精読)

ア 全部の問題を簡単に解き終えたから。
イ クラスメイトたちが彼のことを笑ったとき恥ずかしかったから。
ウ 他の子たちと一緒に遊びたかったから。
エ 早く昼ごはんを食べたかったから。

直前に「クラス中が笑っていた」とある。この時点ではアンディは自分が笑われている理由を理解できなかっただろうが,「みんなに笑われて恥ずかしい」とは思っただろう。したがってイが正解。

[4]「数学の教科書の問題はどのように解くのか」

ア 分数の間に20個の円を描く。
イ 20個の分数を順番に並べる。
ウ めまいがするような推理クイズをする。
エ それぞれの問題でどちらの分数の方が大きいかを見分ける。

*ll.*18-21(Each problem ... each circle.)から,エが正解。各問いは「1/2 ○ 1/3」のような形で出題され,生徒は○(空白の円)の中に「>」と「<」のどちらかの記号を書き込むことになる。

[5]「アンディは写真の中でどんな姿をしているか」

ア アンディは自分のチームのユニフォームを着て名札をつけている。
イ アンディはホームランを打ったバットを持っている。
ウ アンディはホームランを打てそうに見える。
エ アンディは制服を着てクラスメイトたちと一緒にいる。

*ll.*30-32(Andy sent ... a home run.)から,ウが正解(→精読)。

②下線部(3)の直訳は「彼[ジョーイ]の返答で(パソコンの)画面が明るくなる前に長い時間がかかったように思われた」(lit up < light up「明るくなる」)。「ジョーイがアンディの宇宙人の質問に答えるのにそれほど長い時間がかかったのはなぜか」という問いの答えを考える。

ア ジョーイはアンディの質問に対してすぐにいい答えを見つけることができなかった。
イ ジョーイのパソコンが故障した。
ウ ジョーイは自分の写真を撮っていた。
エ ジョーイが地球からのメッセージを受け取るのに時間がかかった。

文章全体の流れから考えて,アが正解。ジョーイは自分が障がい者であることをアンディに知られたくなかったから,事実とは違うことを語ったという状況。

③「インターネットがジョーイの生活で果たした役割は何か」

ア 多くの情報を得るための道具。
イ 友人たちとつながるための道具。
ウ 自分の病状を改善するための道具。
エ 自分を他の人と違う存在にするための道具。

*ll.*63-65(He is not ... new friends.)に,アとイの内容が書かれている。ウのような記述は本文になく,エは*ll.*71-72でジョーイ自身がwhen I'm on the Internet, they think I'm just another kid(インターネット上では彼らはぼくを普通の子どもだと思う)と語っているから誤り。

得点アップ

たとえば選択肢が4つあり,「当てはまるものをすべて選びなさい」と指示されていれば,選ぶべき選択肢は2つ以上あると考えてよい。わざわざ「すべて」と指示しておいて,正解は1つしかないという意地悪な問いが出る可能性は少ない。

④下線部の最初のBoyは,「わあ」「へえ」など喜びや驚きなどを表すのに使う言葉。「どこへ行くにもぼくと一緒に行ってくれる友だちがいてとてもうれしい」という言葉から読み取れるアンディの気持ちを表すために,「アンディはうれしかった,なぜなら彼は…ことができるだろうから」という文を完成する。

ア いつも親友と一緒にいる
イ 新しい学校で新しい友だちを作る
ウ 初めて訪ねる市で新しい生活を始める
エ 再び祖母と一緒に暮らす

話の流れから考えて,アンディは新しい学校になじめるかどうかを心配しているが,インターネット上でいつでも親友のジョーイに会えることを喜んでいる。したがってアが正解。

⑤ア「アンディはジョーイと直接会ってはいない」。本文の冒頭の文にthey've never actually met(彼らは実際に会ったことは一

度もない)とあるので正しい。

イ「ジョーイは地元の学校へ行く代わりに家で勉強している」。*ll.*3-4にJoey doesn't go to school. He chooses to get his education at home.(ジョーイは学校に通っていない。彼は家で教育を受けることを選んでいる)とあるので正しい。

ウ「アンディはベッカー先生が出した数学の小テストで小さい方のピザを選んだ」。アンディは1枚のピザの10分の1と3分の1のうちから前者を選んだのだから正しい。

エ「ジョーイの写真はついに送られてきたが，画像が不鮮明でアンディには見えづらかった」。ジョーイから写真は届かなかったので誤り。

オ「ジョーイは他の子どもたちよりも宇宙のことをずっとたくさん知っていた」。*ll.*47-48(*Is this why ... outer space?*)から考えて正しい(→精読)。

カ「アンディの家族は彼の祖母と一緒に暮らすことを計画していた」。正しい。*ll.*51-54(We'll move to ... live with them.)より，一家はデンバーに引っ越して祖母と暮らす予定だった。

キ「父親がデンバーへの引っ越しを発表したとき，アンディの家族全員がうれしかった」。両親は喜んだが，*ll.*54-55にBut Andy just felt confused.(しかしアンディは戸惑うばかりだった)とあるので，アンディは喜んではいなかった。したがって誤り。

ク「デンバーへ引っ越すことについて聞いたとき，アンディは新しい友人たちと仲よくできるかどうか不安だった」。*ll.*56-58(That night ... *to know me.*)の内容から，アンディは新しい学校での友だち作りに不安を感じていることがわかる。したがって正しい。

ケ「ジョーイが他の惑星から来たことをアンディは最初から知っていた」。誤り。ジョーイはフロリダに住む人間の子どもである。

コ「テレビでジョーイを見た後，アンディは彼がどんな姿でも気にしないと決めた」。*ll.*78-79(He decided ... *It doesn't matter what Joey looks like.*)の内容に一致するので正しい。

以上から，本文の内容と異なるのは，エ，キ，ケである。

精読

◆Ten is the bigger number, so that's **what he picked.**(*l.*9)(10の方が大きい数字なので，それ[10分の1]が彼の選んだものだった)：文中のwhatには，(1)疑問詞(「何」)，(2)関係代名詞(「～する[である]もの[こと]」)の2つのケースがある。この文のwhatは後者。(2)のwhatは，the thing(s) thatで言い換えることができる。

◆***I wish that the recess bell would ring***, thought Andy.(*ll.*13-14)(休み時間のベルが鳴ればいいのに，とアンディは思った)：**I wish ....**は「…ならいいのに(実際はそうではないのが残念だ)」という意味を表し，wishの後ろの動詞は過去形(仮定法過去)にする。この文では(ベルはまだ鳴っていないから)will ringのwillを過去形にして，would ringを使っている。

・**I wish** I were[was] five centimeters taller.
(もう5センチ背が高ければいいのになあ)

この例のように，仮定法過去のbe動詞は，主語が何であっても**were**を使うのが原則(口語では，主語がyou以外の単数の人やものならwasも使う。I wish I am ... とは言えない)。

◆Andy, do you see how **the more** you divide the whole pizza, **the smaller** the pieces become?(*ll.*15-16)(アンディ，ピザを分ければ分けるほど，1切れは小さくなるのがなぜなのかわかるかな？)：howはこの文ではwhyに近い意味を表す。**〈the＋比較級 ～, the＋比較級 ...〉**は「～すればするほど(それだけいっそう)…」。

◆***Is this why he knows so much*** *more than other kids about spaceships ant outer space?*(*ll.*47-48)(だから彼は宇宙船や宇宙空間について他の子よりあんなにずっと詳しいんだろうか)：Is this why .... の直訳は「このことが…の理由だろうか」。thisはジョーイが語った内容(自分は宇宙人だということ)を指す。why以下は「…である(ことの)理由」という意味で，the reason whyともいう。**This is why ....**は「これが…の理由だ，こういうわけで…だ」ということ。whyを「なぜ」と訳すと意味が通じないので注意。また，he knows (so) much more than ～は「～よりもあんなにずっと多くのことを知っている」の意味。muchを比較級の前に置くと，2つのものの差の大きさを強調して「～よりずっと

[はるかに]…」という意味になる。so(それほど)は，アンディがそれまでにジョーイから宇宙について多くのことを学んでいたことを示している。

◆ ***The other kids*** *treated me differently for a while until they got to know me.*(*l*.58)(他の子たちは，ぼくと知り合うまで，しばらくの間ぼくを特別扱いした)：〈**the other** ＋複数名詞〉は「他[残り]の全部」の意味だから，「(自分以外の)他の子たちは全員ぼくを違うように扱った」ということ。**get to *do*** は「～するようになる」の意味で，come to *do* とも言う。

◆ When other kids **see** me, they just **see that** I'm different.(*l*.70)(他の子がぼくを見たら，ぼくを変わっていると思います)：1つ目の see は「(目で)見る，(目に)見える」の意味。一方，2つ目の see のように **see that ...** の形で使うと「…ということを(頭で)理解する」の意味になる(I see.「わかります，なるほど」の see と同様)。同様に **hear** も，that を続けると「(耳で)聞こえる」ではなく「(誰かから)聞いて知る」という意味になる。

・I **hear[heard] (that)** Ken is in the hospital.
(ケンは入院しているそうだ)

◆ **It doesn't matter where** Joey came from(*l*.78)(ジョーイがどこから来たのかはどうでもいい)：〈**It doesn't matter** ＋疑問詞〉は「たとえ～でも問題ではない[どうでもよい]」という意味(matter は「重要である」という意味の動詞)。疑問詞は who，when などを使うこともある。

◆ I am so glad to have a friend [who goes with me **everywhere** I go](*l*.82)(どこへ行くにも一緒に行ってくれる友だちがいてとてもうれしい)：who 以下の関係詞節が a friend を修飾している。**everywhere** は「～するところならどこ(へ)でも」の意味で接続詞的に使われている(wherever とも言う)。次の文も同様。

・My aunt gives me something nice **every time** [＝whenever] she comes to my house.(おばはうちに来るときはいつでも私に何かいいものをくれる)

◆ Andy has his bat which he hit a home run with.(問①[5]イ)(アンディはホームランを打ったバットを持っている)：hit(～を打つ)は，hit-hit-hit と活用する(過去形・過去分詞も hit)。前の has は現在形だが，hit が現在形なら hits となるはず。したがってこの hit は過去形であり，「(ホームラン)を打った」という意味になる。このように現在形と過去形が同じ形の動詞(hit，cut，put など)は，いつの時点でのことかに注意しよう。

◆ Andy **looks like** he can hit a home run.(問①[5]ウ)(アンディはホームランを打てそうに見える)：look like((外見が)～のように見える)の後ろには名詞を置くのが原則だが，くだけた表現では文の形を置くこともある(look as if ともいう)。

全訳

インターネットに宇宙人がいる

アンディの親友はジョーイだが，彼らは実際に会ったことは一度もない。彼はジョーイとインターネットで知り合った。ジョーイから太陽系についてあらゆることを学んだので，スターウォーズのゲームが楽しくなった。ジョーイは学校に通っていない。彼は家で教育を受けることを選んでいる。ジョーイがここポートランドのぼくたちの学校に来ればいいのに，とアンディは思った。

先週，アンディの担任のベッカー先生が黒板に大きな円を描いて，それがピザだと言った。

「アンディ，このピザを分けるとしたら，3分の1と10分の1のどちらがいい？」と先生は尋ねた。10の方が大きい数字なので，彼が選んだのはそちらだった。

ケビンが手を振り始めて，自分は3分の1の方を選ぶと叫んだ。ベッカー先生は円に線を引き，ケビンはアンディのピザより自分のピザの方が大きいことを示した。「アンディはおなかがすいちゃうよ」とケビンは冗談を言った。

そのとき，クラス中が笑っていた。休み時間のベルが鳴ればいいのに，とアンディは思った。

ベッカー先生の大きくて力強い声で，部屋は静かになった。「アンディ，ピザを分ければ分けるほど，1切れは小さくなるのがなぜなのかわかる？」

「はい，ベッカー先生」とアンディはうそをついた。休み時間のベルはそれから30分たっても鳴らず，その間にベッカー先生は算数の教科書の問題を20問出した。どの問題も分数が2つあり，その間に空白の円があった。生徒たちはそれぞれの円の中に，＞(～より大きい)または＜(～より小さい)の記号を入れることになっていた。それらすべての分数と円を見ていると，アンディはめまいがしてきた。彼はどちらが正しいかを当てる確率は半々だと決めて問題を解いたが，しばしば答えを間違えた。

放課後，アンディはジョーイとネットでつながったとき，「今日，数学の小テストで失敗したんだ。分数とかどっちの方が大きいかとかがわからない」と入力した。

ジョーイは「いい手があるよ」と返信した。そして彼は，画板へ行きアンディにやり方を示した。

次の週，ベッカー先生が分数のテストをすると，アンディだけが満点を取った。ジョーイのおかげで，クラスのみんなはアンディのことをもうそれほどばかだとは思わなくなった。

ある日，アンディは郵便で写真を交換しようと言った。アンディは野球のユニフォームを着て，バットを肩にかついでホームランを打とうとしているかのような写真を送った。それから，アンディはジョーイに写真は届いたかと聞くと，ジョーイは「君の写真は届いたよ。感動した。ありがとう！」と返信してきた。

「よかった！」とアンディは答えた。「それなら，ぼくにももうすぐ君のが届くはずだ」。しかし，ジョーイの写真は来なかった。

不思議だった。ジョーイからは写真もコメントも来ない。彼はただ話題を変えただけだった。それからある日，彼らが星や宇宙人の話をしているとき，アンディは彼に「地球には変装した宇宙人がいると思う？」と尋ねた。返事がスクリーンに映し出されるまで，長い時間がかかったような気がした。

「君は秘密を守れる？」

「たぶん」とアンディは答えた。

「約束する？ 本当に大事なことなんだ！」

「わかった。約束するよ」

「ぼくは異星から来たエイリアンなんだ。だから君に写真を送れない。ぼくの姿はフィルムには写らないんだ」

アンディはパソコンを見つめながら，ショックでその場に座っていた。「これはジョーイのいつもの冗談だろうか？ それならどうして写真を送ってくれなかったんだろう？ だから彼は宇宙船や宇宙空間について他の子よりあんなにずっと詳しいんだろうか？ なぜ彼は自分のことをあまり話したがらないんだろう？」と彼は思った。

夕食のとき，お父さんがこう発表した。「いい知らせだ！ 転勤願いが受理されたんだ。今月末にデンバーの本社に移ることになった。会社が家を見つけてくれたんだ。アンディのためにいい学校も近いし，おばあちゃんも一緒に住めるくらいの広さの家だ」。アンディのお母さんは，自分の母親がデンバーに住んでいて最近脚を骨折したため，同居してもらいたいと思っていたのでうれしかった。しかしアンディはただ戸惑うばかりだった。

その夜，アンディはベッドの中で，新しい学校で新入りになることについて考えた。「ここに引っ越してきたときの気持ちを思い出す。新しい友だちを作るのは大変だった。他の子たちは，ぼくと知り合うまで，しばらくの間ぼくを特別扱いした」

翌朝，アンディが台所のテーブルで朝食をとっていると，母親がテレビである番組を見ていた。ニュースキャスターがフロリダの女性にインタビューしていた。「ジョーイの生活でインターネットが果たしている役割について教えてください」とニュースキャスターは尋ねた。

「そうですね，インターネットは彼に今まで知らなかった自由を与えてくれています。彼は車いすから情報にアクセスできるだけでなく，何よりも大切なことに，新しい友人たちができました」

続いてニュースキャスターは，「ジョーイ，君のインターネットの友だちのことを話してくれるかい」と尋ねた。

カメラは，パソコンの前に座っている車いすに乗った子に移動した。彼は少しやせていて，足が不自由だった。頭が片方に傾いていて，答えるときの言葉も聞き取りにくかった。彼はその言葉を発するために大きな努力をしなければならなかった。「他の子がぼくを見たら，ぼくを変わっていると思います。ぼくにとっては，話すことも理解してもらうことも大変です。でもインターネット上では，姿が見えないから普通の子だと思われます。ぼくはいろんな人と友だちになっています」とジョーイは説明した。

学校で一日中，アンディの頭の中はさまざまな思いでいっぱいだった。考えたのは，ネットの友だちのジョーイ，宇宙人のジョーイ，テレビの中のジョーイ，デンバーでの新しい友だち作り，そしておばあちゃん。彼は家に帰るとすぐにパソコンの前に走って行き，スイッチを入れた。

彼はこう決めた。ジョーイの出身地が別の星だろうとフロリダだろうと関係ない。ジョーイがどんな姿をしているかは関係ない。ぼくはジョーイが誰だか知っている。ジョーイはぼくの友だちだ。

アンディはコンピューターにこう入力した。「ジョーイ，あのね。ぼくらはデンバーへ引っ越すんだ。ねえ，どこへ行くにも一緒に行ってくれる友だちがいてとてもうれしいよ」

語句

alien「宇宙人」 the solar system「太陽系」
education「教育」 circle「円」
one-third「３分の１」 one-tenth「10分の１」
wave one's hand「手を振る」 whole「全体の」

recess「休憩時間」 empty「空っぽの，空白の」
be supposed to *do*「～することになっている，～しなければならない」
dizzy「めまいがして」 fifty-fifty「五分五分の」
guess wrong「推測を間違える」 quiz「小テスト」
trick「芸，わざ」 drawing board「画板，製図板」
trade「～を交換する」 impressive「印象的な」
change the subject「話題を変える」
lit up < light up「明るくなる」
image「像，姿」 spaceship「宇宙船」
outer space「(外)宇宙」
confused「困惑して，戸惑って」
treat「～を扱う」 allow「～に与える」
freedom「自由」
have access to ～「～を入手できる」
wheelchair「車いす」 shift「移動する」
thin「やせた」 disabled「障がいのある」
hung < hang「垂れる」
just another「ありふれた，平凡な」
switch O on「Oのスイッチを入れる」
embarrassed「恥ずかしい，ばつが悪い」

第4回 実力テスト

① エ　② イ　③ B　④ イ
⑤ 彼女は(中学3年生の初めには)完全に目が見えなくなって，動き回るのが怖くて部屋に一人でいるようになっていたから。
⑥ ウ　⑦ エ　⑧ ア

解説 ①ア「彼女は日本盲導犬訓練センターで生まれた物静かな犬だった」。ラッキーはセンターで生まれたわけではないから誤り。
イ「彼女は花の香りと庭で走ることが好きだった」。彼女が好きだったのは，芝生の上で横になることと虫の動きを見ること。したがって誤り。
ウ「彼女は夕食の時間になると興奮する騒がしい犬だった」。ラッキーは夕食のとき自分の順番をじっと待っていた。したがって誤り。
エ「彼女は自分のまわりで何が起きているかを理解するがまん強い犬だった」。*l*.6の patiently (がまん強く)と *ll*.19-21(She was always very focused on the surroundings ...)から考えて正しい。

② be concerned about ～は「～を心配している」の意味。イの be worried about ～も同じ意味を表す。他の選択肢は，ア「～を楽しんだ」，ウ「～を変えた」，エ「～に誇りを持っていた」。

③ 全訳 の下線部を参照。この文を[B]に入れれば，意味の通じる文章になる。

④ surroundings は「周囲の状況，環境」の意味。最も近い意味を表すのは，イの environment (環境)。他の選択肢は，ア「感情」，ウ「知らない人」，エ「音」。

⑤下線部の意味は「学校へ行くことは彼女[ルミ]にとって難しかった」。その理由を短く言えば，彼女は(全く)目が見えなかったからである。

得点アップ

この問いでは「詳しく述べなさい」という指示があるので，下線部(3)の前に書かれている内容を解答欄に収まる範囲で詳しく答える必要がある。解答欄をはみ出して書くのはNG。

⑥ confident は「自信がある」という意味の形容詞。最も近い意味を表すのは，ウの positive (前向きな，積極的な)。他の選択肢は，ア「貴重な」，イ「創造的な」，エ「好奇心の強い」。

⑦「ルミの友人たちはルミをどう思っているか」という問い。
ア ラッキーの支援は不十分であり，自分たちも彼女を積極的に助ける必要がある，と彼女たちは信じている。
イ ルミの勇気への注目がもっと集まり，彼女とラッキーがもっと有名になってほしい，と彼女たちは願っていた。
ウ ルミはラッキーと一緒の時間を楽しんでいるので，彼女は支援をほしがっていない，と彼女たちは感じ始めた。
エ ルミはラッキーに助けてもらってとても多くのことができるので，ルミが障がいを持っていることに彼女たちは気づかなかった。

l.37に Rumi's friends forget that Rumi sometimes needs help(ルミの友人たちは彼女が時々助けを必要とすることを忘れる)とあるので，エが正しい。

⑧「これは何についての話か」という問いに対し

て，「～についての話である」と答える文を完成する。

ア　ある盲導犬の能力がどのようにある人の人生を改善することができるか

イ　ある盲導犬が耳の不自由な人々を助けるためにどのように訓練されたか

ウ　目の悪いある少女と，彼女がどのようにして一人で生きていくことができたか

エ　どのような点で犬は人間の持てる最高のペットであるか

この文章は，ラッキーという犬が盲導犬になり，ルミという少女の支えとなったというエピソードである。したがってアが正しい。

全訳

幼い子犬のころ，ラッキーは兄弟姉妹たちとは違っていた。他の犬たちは遊びの時間にはたいてい庭で走り回っていたが，彼女は芝生の上で静かに横になっていた。彼女はまわりの世界に興味を持ち，花から花へ飛び回る虫の動きを追うのが好きだった。夕食の時間になっても，他の犬たちのように跳びはねたり吠えたりしないで，じっと座って自分の番を待っていた。

飼い主たちはラッキーの行動を心配していた。ラッキーは他の人たちとの遊び方を知らないし，おとなしくて内気すぎると彼らは思っていた。しかしそれは，1つの出来事を経て変わった。ある日，飼い主の友人たちが，1歳になるケントという子を連れて遊びに来ていた。ケントは最近初めて歩けるようになったので，長時間歩けずに倒れた。ケントが立ち上がろうとすると，ラッキーがそばに行ってその子を支える役をした。一歩ずつ，ケントがバランスをとるのを手助けするために，彼女は一緒に移動した。そのとき，ラッキーの飼い主たちは，ラッキーが単なるペットではなく，盲導犬として目の不自由な人を助けることができると気づいた。

彼女と別れるのは飼い主たちにとってつらい決断だったが，それが正しいことだと彼らは知っていた。彼らはラッキーを日本盲導犬訓練センターへ連れて行った。6か月の間，ラッキーはプロの訓練士たちに訓練を受けた。訓練士たちはラッキーに，命令の聞き方や道の歩き方を教えた。ラッキーはいつもまわりをよく見て，遠くから危険を感知することができた。盲導犬であることは大変な仕事だが，ラッキーはそれを楽しんでいるようだった。訓練士が首輪をつけるといつも，ラッキーは仕事の時間になってうれしいと言いたげにしっぽを振り始めた。

6か月の訓練の後，ラッキーは目の不自由な最初の飼い主に会う準備ができた。彼女は，石田家のルミという15歳の娘を助けるために派遣された。ルミは幼いころ珍しい目の病気にかかり，中学に入ってから徐々に視力が低下し始めた。3年生の初めには，彼女の目はもう何も見えなくなった。そのため彼女は動き回るのを怖がり，部屋に一人でいるようになった。学校へ行くのは彼女にとって難しかった。ルミに初めて会ったとき，ラッキーはルミのところまで自然に歩み寄って，ケントにしてやったのと全く同じように彼女のそばに立った。

そのときから，両者のきずなはどんどん強くなった。ルミは自信がわいてきて，ラッキーを横に連れて家の外へ短い散歩に出かけるようになった。やがて彼女は，ショッピングモールに行ったり，遊園地に行ったり，他の十代の子と同じことができるようになり，そばにはいつもラッキーがいた。実際，ルミとラッキーはとても上手に動き回ることができたので，ルミの友人たちは彼女が時々助けを必要とすることを忘れてしまうほどである。

そのコンビにとって，それは素晴らしい旅の始まりにすぎない。これから先，彼女たちは多くの問題に直面するかもしれないが，ラッキーが飼い主のそばにいて，先へ続く道を導いてくれるだろう。

語句

puppy「子犬」　run around「走り回る」
calmly「静かに」　flew < fly「飛ぶ」
turn「順番」　behavior「行動，振る舞い」
quiet「静かな，無口な」　shy「内気な」
take one's first step(s)「第一歩を踏み出す」
fall down「転ぶ」
keep one's balance「バランスをとる」
guide dog「盲導犬」　tough「難しい，つらい」
be focused on ～「～に集中している」
sense「～に気づく」
from far away「遠くから」　tail「尾」
blind「目の不自由な」　rare「珍しい，まれな」
disease「病気」　no longer「もはや～ない」
naturally「自然に」
walk over to ～「～のところへ(はるばる)歩いて行く」
next to ～「～の隣に」　amusement park「遊園地」

5　ビジュアル読解

031　イ，オ

解説　ア「乙女口バス乗り場でツアーガイドに会う

はずだ」。経路図の下の文によれば，ツアーガイドがいるのは御殿場駅の案内所だから誤り。

イ「4月にオンラインで予約すれば，1人600円の割引を受けることができる」。冒頭に「オンラインで予約すれば10%の割引が受けられる」とある。日程表によれば4月の1人当たり料金は6,000円だから，その10%は600円。したがって正しい。

ウ「箱根ツアーは毎月開かれている」。日程表によれば12月にはツアーがないので誤り。

エ「ノーザン・ホテルに泊まらなくても，そのホテルの前でバスに乗ることができる」。経路図の1行目のNorthern Hotel in Shibuyaの下に[guests only]とある。これは「8時30分のバスに乗れるのはホテルの宿泊客のみ」という意味。したがって誤り。

オ「ツアーに参加すれば，8時間後に新宿駅に戻ることになる」。経路図によれば，ツアーは新宿駅を8時に出発して，16時に新宿駅に戻って終了となる。したがって正しい。

得点アップ

案内文や広告などによく使われる語句や表現形式を知っておこう。たとえば本文の最初に出てくるBook Online & Get 10% OFFは，形としては命令文になっている(& = and)。直訳すると「オンラインで予約して10%の割引を手に入れなさい」。OFFが全部大文字になっているのは，「割引」を強調したいから。日程表のPrice per personは「1人当たり料金」。**per**は「～につき」の意味の前置詞である。表の下の〈X included〉は「Xが含まれる」ということ。tax included = including tax(税込み)という言葉もよく使われる。

精読

◆ Children of five and under: FREE(日程表の下)(5歳以下のお子様は無料)：「5歳の子とそれより下の年齢の子」ということ。under[over] Xは「Xより下[上]」の意味で，Xの数字は含まない。したがって，children under fiveだと「5歳より下の子 = 4歳以下の子」の意味になる。freeは「無料の」。アピール効果を高めるために，全部大文字で書かれている。

全訳

箱根ツアー

オンライン予約で10%オフ[割引]

箱根の自然美を楽しむハイキングツアーのご案内です。多くの楽しい活動をお試しいただけます。

☆ツアーの経路

(経路図は省略)

ツアーガイドが御殿場駅の案内所でお待ちしております。

☆ツアーの日程と時期

月	1人当たり料金
1～3月	4,000円
4～6月	6,000円
7～9月	6,500円
10～11月	5,000円

(バス料金，昼食，ガイド料を含む)

5歳以下のお子様：無料

語句

fun「楽しい」 information counter「案内所」
per「～につき」 fare「運賃」
fee「(サービス)料金」 included「含まれて」
free「無料の」

032〉① ウ　② ア　③ イ

解説 冒頭の指示文は，「文章を読んで①の文を最も適切に完成する答えと(1)～(2)を最も適切に完成する答えを選びなさい」の意味。

①「『もう1つは社会参加に関する高校生の実態である』という文は，…に入れられるべきである」という文を完成する。正しい位置は[C]。[B]の直前にto know two things(2つのことを知るために)とある。これを受けて，次の文のOne is ～.とこの(補うべき)文のThe other one is ～.とが，「1つは～だ」「もう1つは～だ」という意味を表している。全訳の下線部を参照。

②「『積極的』または『やや積極的』と答えた生徒合計の割合を比較すると，4か国のうちで…」という文を完成する。選択肢はそれぞれ，ア「日本が最も高い」，イ「アメリカが最も高い」，ウ「中国が最も低い」，エ「韓国が最も低い」。表のActiveとSomewhat activeの欄の数字を合計すると，日本は82.0%，アメリカは68.9%，中国は75.7%，韓国は77.6%。したがってアが正しい。

③「『あまり積極的でない』または『積極的でな

い』と答えた生徒の合計の割合は，…では30%を超えている」という文を完成する。表のNot so activeとNot activeの欄の数字を合計すると，30%を超えているのはアメリカだけである。

全訳

高校生の社会参加に関する意見をまとめた報告書が2021年に作成された。この報告書では，「社会参加」という言葉は，生徒が学校の内外で参加する活動全般を意味する。報告書によると，2つのことを知るために調査が行われた。1つは高校生の社会参加に対する意識である。もう1つは社会参加に関する高校生の実態である。この2つは，各国にはどのような種類の特徴があるかを知るのに使われる。調査には，以下の日本，アメリカ，中国，韓国の4か国の生徒が参加した。たとえば「あなたは学校外の社会問題にどの程度関心がありますか」のような28の質問をし，学生はそれぞれの質問に1つの回答を選んで答えた。表は，「あなたは学校で，教室での話し合いに積極的に参加していますか」という質問に対する回答の割合を示している。

表からいくつかのことがわかる。質問に答えなかった生徒もいるが，「積極的」または「やや積極的」と答えた生徒の合計の割合を比較すると，4か国のうちで日本が最も高い。「あまり積極的でない」または「積極的でない」と答えた生徒の合計の割合は，アメリカでは30%を超えている。

（表のタイトル）

「あなたは学校で，教室での話し合いに積極的に参加していますか」という質問に対する回答の割合

（表は省略）

語句

view「意見」 compare「～を比較する」

033 ① エ　② イ　③ イ
④ **true**　⑤ ウ

解説 ①「約…人の生徒が9月には1冊も本を読まなかった」という文を完成する。グラフ1によれば，9月に読んだ本が0冊だと答えた生徒が51%いる。回答者数は200人だから，その生徒の実数は約100人である。

②「私たちは…も確かめる必要がある」という文を完成する。

ア 9月に生徒たちがしばしばどこで本を読んだか

イ 他の月に生徒たちが何冊の本を読んだか

ウ 生徒たちがそのアンケート調査をどう思ったか

エ 生徒たちがこのアンケート調査に何回答えたことがあるか

直後のグレン先生の発言に「そのデータがあれば，月々の変化がわかる」とあるので，イが正しい。9月には51%の生徒が本を1冊も読まなかったが，他の月にはその割合は違っていた(たとえばほぼ全生徒が1冊以上の本を読んでいた)かもしれない。もしそうなら，ニックの言うとおり，タクの2番目の発言中のSome students don't read books.((習慣的に)本を読まない生徒もいる)という説明は正しくないことになる。

③グラフ2のReasonsというタイトルは，グレン先生の4番目の発言によれば，「(51%の生徒が)9月に1冊も本を読まなかった理由」という意味である。これについて3人は順に下のように述べ，グレン先生は5番目の発言で「(X)，(Y)，(Z)はそれぞれニック，ミサキ，タクの考えだ」と言っている。したがって，

タク「読書に興味がない(から)」→(Z)

ミサキ「忙しすぎる(から)，読書は時間がかかる(から)」→(Y)

ニック「どの本を読めばいいかわからない(から)」→(X)

となる。選択肢の意味は次のとおり。

ア (Y)「読書が好きではない」，(Z)「とても忙しい」

イ (Y)「とても忙しい」，(Z)「読書が好きではない」

ウ (Y)「本は高価だ」，(Z)「読書は時間がかかる」

エ (Y)「読書は時間がかかる」，(Z)「本は高価だ」

以上から，正解はイである。

④空所の前後の語句から，空所には形容詞が入ると推測する必要がある。find the [C] causesは「…な理由を見つける」，Is that really [C]?は「それは本当に…であるのか」という意味になる。両方に共通して入れることのできる形容詞は，ニックの最初の発言中に出てくるtrue(本当の，正しい)である。

⑤「…(する)ことも大切だと私は思う」という文を完成する。

ア 変えられなければならないデータを選ぶ

イ 注意深く考えずにデータを集める

ウ それぞれのデータが正しいことを確認する
エ さまざまな状況で同じデータを使う

直後の文に「データの一部が間違っているかもしれない」とあるので，ウを入れるのが適切。

全訳

(グラフは省略)

グレン先生：グラフ1を見てください。これは，君たちが回答した校内アンケート調査の結果を示しています。私は先週これを見つけました。このグラフから何がわかりますか。

タク：約100人の生徒が，9月には1冊も本を読みませんでした。

グレン先生：それは読書習慣がないという意味ですか。

タク：はい。そのグラフを見ることによってそれがわかります。本を読まない生徒もいます。

ニック：本当に？ それは正しくないとぼくは思います。そのグラフはぼくたちが9月に読んだ本の数を示しています。生徒が他の月に何冊の本を読んだかも調べる必要があります。

グレン先生：そのデータがあれば，月々の変化がわかりますね。グラフ1だけですべてを理解するのは困難です。読書習慣を知るためには，もっと多くのデータが必要です。他に意見はありますか。

ミサキ：いつその調査に答えたかを考慮する必要もあります。9月には文化祭があったので，私たちはそのころ多忙でした。私はほぼ毎月本を読みますが，9月は1冊も読みませんでした。

ニック：そのグラフは，そのころぼくたちが本を読む時間を持つのが難しかったことを示してはいません。データを注意深く使う必要があります。

タク：今わかりました。グレン先生，9月に本を1冊も読まなかった生徒がいたのはなぜだかわかりますか。それにはいくつかの原因があると思います。それを見つければ，状況を改善する方法について考えることができます。

グレン先生：よろしい，それについて考えましょう。アンケート調査では，なぜ9月に1冊も本を読まなかったのかを生徒に尋ねました。その調査結果から，私はグラフ2を作りました。では，グラフ2の理由(X)，(Y)，(Z)を推測しましょう。

タク：その人たちは読書に興味がなかったからかもしれません。

ミサキ：本当に？ 生徒は忙しすぎるとよく言います。読書には多くの時間がかかると彼らは言います。

ニック：彼らはどんな本を読めばいいのかわからないのです。

グレン先生：では確認しましょう。ニックの考えは理由(X)，ミサキの考えは理由(Y)，タクの考えは理由(Z)ですね。

タク：グラフ2を使えば，彼らが9月に1冊も本を読まなかったのはなぜかがわかります。

グレン先生：推測だけでこの状況の本当の原因を知るのは困難です。問題を解決する方法を見つけるために，さまざまなデータを使って，「なぜ」あるいは「それは本当に正しいのか」と何度も尋ねることができます。しかし，データを使う際に考慮すべき多くのことがあります。何について考える必要がありますか。自分の考えを書いてください。

■ナホが授業で書いたワークシート

さまざまなデータを持つことが大切だとわかりました。データを使うときは，それぞれのデータが正しいことを確かめるのも大切だと思います。データの一部が間違っているかもしれません。もしそれが間違っていれば，状況を改善する方法を見つけることができません。私たちは入手できるデータを簡単に信じるべきではありません。

034 ① エ　② イ　③ ア
④ 長時間使いすぎると，勉強や家族との会話の時間がなくなる(27字)
⑤ イ　⑥ エ

解説 ①ア かなは音楽がとても得意だ。
イ ヒル先生はタカヒロのスマートフォンを見ている。
ウ ヒル先生はタカヒロのよい知らせについてかなに話している。
エ かなはスマートフォンを持ちたがっている。

かなの3番目の発言から，エが正しい。

② ア スマートフォンはコンピューターよりも役に立つ。
イ 若者がスマートフォンを持つのは問題ないかもしれない。
ウ 中学生はコンピューターを使うには若すぎる。
エ かなの兄はスマートフォンを使うのをやめるべきだ。

ヒル先生の3番目の発言中のSo it may be a good idea to have one when you are young.(若いうちに1台持つのはいい考えかもしれない)から考えて，イが正解。前の文でA smartphone ... と言っているので，同じ語のくり返しを避けるためにone[=a smartphone]を使っている。

③２人の会話の内容から，[1]「小学生がスマートフォンを使う時間は中学生の半分にも満たない」，[2]「どの年代でも男子の方が女子より長くスマートフォンを使っている」ことがわかる。[2]の条件からウ・エは誤り。中学生のグラフと比較すると，[1]の条件からイは誤り。残るアが正解となる。

④ that(そのこと)は直前のかなの発言(If I … my family.)を指しているので，この部分を日本語に直せばよい。

⑤ア　私の宿題について質問するために

イ　私の目に休息を与えるために

ウ　私の脳を興奮させるために

エ　友人たちにメッセージを送るために

かなは，第２段落でスマートフォンを使いすぎることの問題点として，[1]勉強に集中できない，[2]視力が低下する，[3]寝不足になる，の３つを挙げている。第３段落でかなが決めた３つのルールは[1]～[3]にそれぞれ対応しているので，この空所には[2]に関係する内容が入る。したがってイが正解。

⑥ア　スマートフォンを長時間使うことは，学生の健康によい。

イ　親は子どもの年齢がもっと高くなるまでスマートフォンを買ってやるべきではない。

ウ　私たちが学校でスマートフォンを使うときは，強力なルールが必要である。

エ　私たちはスマートフォンを上手に使って，スマートフォンのある生活を楽しむべきだ。

スピーチの最後の段落の内容から考えて，エが正しい。

全訳

かな：いい知らせがあります！　友だちのタカヒロが，きのうピアノのコンクールで１等賞を取りました！

ヒル先生：すごいですね！

かな：ご両親もとても喜んでいました。彼にスマートフォンを買ってあげたそうです！

ヒル先生：わあ，そうですか。かな，君はスマートフォンを持っていますか。

かな：いいえ。でも高校生になったら父が買ってくれると言っています。待ちきれません！

ヒル先生：今日では，情報技術の使い方を学ぶことはとても大切です。スマートフォンは小さなコンピューターです。だから，若いうちに１台持つのはいい考えかもしれません。でも，若者がスマートフォンを使うとき，いくつかの問題もあります。

かな：知っています。兄はスマートフォンを使いすぎていて，母は怒っています。

ヒル先生：このグラフを見てください，かな。これは日本の学生が平日の１日にどのくらいの時間スマートフォンを使ってインターネットにアクセスしているかを示しています。中学生は１日に約144分間使っています。

かな：長時間ですね。小学生はその時間の半分も使っていません。

ヒル先生：ええ。それにどの年代でも，男子の方が女子よりもスマートフォンを使う時間が少し長くなっています。高校生はスマートフォンをとてもよく使うので，私は特に彼らが心配です。

かな：わあ，208分…１日３時間を超えています！

ヒル先生：そんなに長時間スマートフォンを使えば，何が起きるでしょうか。

かな：私は放課後，６時に帰宅して，10時に寝ます。もし私が毎日３時間スマートフォンを使ったら，勉強したり家族と話したりする時間が全くなくなります。

ヒル先生：ええ。私はそれが心配です。

かな：卒業する前に，私たちはこの問題についてもっと考える必要がありそうです。来週私のスピーチでこの話題を選ぼうと思います。

(グラフは省略)

(スピーチ)

皆さんはスマートフォンを持っていますか。スマートフォンがあれば，私たちは簡単に情報を得ることができます。友だちといつでも話ができます。スマートフォンでゲームをしたり映画を見たりするのは楽しいですね！

しかし，スマートフォンを使いすぎるとどうなるでしょう？　いくつかの問題があります。たとえば，いつもメッセージの送受信をしていると，勉強に集中できません。また画面を長時間見ることで，視力がとても低下します。そして夜は脳が興奮しすぎて，よく眠れません。それは健康に悪いかもしれません。

そこで私は両親と話して，３つのルールを決めました。第１に，勉強するときはスマートフォンの電源を切ります。第２に，１時間使ったら，目を休ませるために使うのをやめます。第３に，よく眠るために寝床では使いません。スマートフォンを手に入れたら，私はこれらのルールを守ります。

スマートフォンは素晴らしい道具です。でも注意しないと，スマートフォンのせいで私たちの学校生活は難しくなるかもしれません。私たちはスマートフォンと上手に付き合う方法を見つけるべきです。それができれば，私たちの生活はもっと便利で楽しいものになるでしょう。

035 ① ウ　② **good**　③ い
④ ウ，**28**　⑤ エ

解説 ①a website (which[that] is) written in Englishで「英語で書かれている(ウェブ)サイト」という意味を表す。

②「それ[＝このツアー]はあなたにとって…，なぜならあなたは歴史的な場所に興味があるから」という文の空所に入る適切な語は，good(よい)。「歴史が好きなあなたには，このツアーが向いている」ということ。suitable(適している)でもよい。

③「3つのツアーがあります」という文は，それらのツアーの具体的な紹介の前に置くのが適切。この文を[い]に置けば，その後ろの「どのツアーを選べばよいかわからない」というヘレンの発言と自然につながる。

④京花はヘレンに，TOUR 1→TOUR 3→TOUR 2の順で勧めている。2人の対話をたどって確認しよう。

・京花は4番目の発言(OK. ...)でヘレンに1つ目のツアーを勧めている。ここにhistorical places(歴史的な場所)という言葉が出てくるが，TOUR 1(寺と神社)にもTOUR 3(もみじ城)にもそれに当たる場所がある。しかしヘレンが「肉は食べたくない」と答えているので，京花が最初に勧めたのはすき焼き料理店での昼食が含まれるTOUR 1だとわかる(資料1を参照)。

・京花が5番目の発言(Then how about ...)で勧めた2つ目のツアーでは，the most historical place in the city(市内で一番歴史的な場所)を訪ねることになっている。これはもみじ城のことと考えられる。つまりTOUR 3である。

・京花が7番目の発言(We can change ...)で勧めた3つ目のツアーでは，美しい花や木や石を見て，着物を着ることになっている。これはTOUR 2である。これに対してヘレンは「値段が少し高すぎる(から選びたくない)。予定を変更してもいいか」と京花に尋ねている。

以上から，ヘレンは最後に勧められたTOUR 2は選ばなかったと考えられる。彼女が「変更してもいいか」と京花に尋ねた予定とは，その前の2人の発言から，日曜日に一緒に外出する予定だとわかる。つまりヘレンは，外出の予定を日曜日以外の日に変更して，日曜日のツアーに参加しようとしている。資料1を見ると，8月21日(日)にはTOUR 1が，28日(日)にはTOUR 3が予定されている。しかしTOUR 1の方は「肉(すき焼き)は食べたくない」という理由で最初に断っているので，ヘレンが最終的に決めたのは28日(日)のTOUR 3である。

⑤ア　映画を見た後で何をしたい？
イ　動物園を訪ねた後で何をしたい？
ウ　いつ私と一緒に映画を見たい？
エ　いつ私と一緒に動物園を訪ねたい？

ここでは2人が「スケジュールを変更する」ことについて話しているので，ウとエのどちらかが答えになる。資料2から，ヘレンがTOUR 3に参加する28日(日)に，2人はもともと一緒に動物園へ行く予定だったことがわかる。したがってエを入れるのが適切。

全訳

京花：ヘレン，私たちはこの夏に映画を見に行って動物園へ行く予定よ。他にどこか行きたいところはある？

ヘレン：ええ。私は日本の歴史に興味があるから，このもみじ市の歴史的な場所をいくつか訪ねたいの。何かアイデアはある？

京花：ええ，英語で書いてあるサイトを紹介できるわ。これを見て！ 3つのツアーがあるの。

ヘレン：どのツアーを選べばいいかわからないわ。手助けしてくれる？

京花：もちろん，手助けするわ。

ヘレン：ありがとう。これが私の予定表よ。

京花：そうね。このツアーはどう？ あなたは歴史的な場所に興味があるから，これがいいわ。

ヘレン：よさそうだけど，お肉は食べたくないの。

京花：じゃあ，このツアーはどう？ 市内で一番歴史的な場所へ行けるわ。ここは私の一番好きな場所よ。私たちの市の歴史も学べるし。私があなたなら，このツアーを選ぶわ。

ヘレン：このツアーが一番気に入ったけど，2学期が始まる前の最後の日に疲れたくはないわね。

京花：わかった。じゃあ，日曜日のに参加したらどう。

ヘレン：でもその日は一緒に出かける予定でしょ。

京花：予定を変更すればいいわ。変更したくなければ，このツアーが選べるわ。きれいな花や木や石が見られて，伝統的な日本の着物も着られるから。火曜日は予定が空いているわよね。

ヘレン：このツアーもいいけれど，ちょっと高いわ。私たちの予定を変えてもいい？

京花：もちろん。私と一緒に動物園へ行くのはいつにしたい？

（資料１）

もみじ市を楽しんでください！

当市では海外から来られた皆さんに興味深いツアーをいくつか用意しています。１日ツアーに興味のある方は，ご参加ください！

ツアー１：寺と神社

もみじ市には多くの寺と神社があり，そのいくつかを見ることができます。日本の歴史に興味をお持ちなら，このわくわくするツアーをお選びください。

日付：８月15日（月）／８月21日（日）

時間：11時～16時

料金：3,000円（すきやき料理店での昼食代を含む。）

ツアー２：着物で写真撮影

美しい着物を着るのはいかがですか。着物レンタル店でお好きな着物をお選びいただけます。ツアーガイドがとても古い日本庭園であなたの写真をお撮りいたします。

日付：８月16日（火）／８月23日（火）

時間：14時～17時

料金：5,000円（着物のレンタル料を含む。）

ツアー３：もみじ市立博物館ともみじ城

当市は長い歴史を持ち，もみじ市立博物館がそれを教えてくれます。もみじ城へも行きます。当市の歴史に興味をお持ちなら，このツアーがベストの選択です。

日付：８月25日（木）／８月28日（日）

時間：10時～14時

料金：2,500円（昼食代は含みません。）

（資料２）

8月	
15日（月）	
16日（火）	
17日（水）	バレーボールの練習（10時～11時）
18日（木）	
19日（金）	サッカーの試合観戦（13時～）
20日（土）	ホームステイ先の家族と一緒に夏祭りに行く（16時～）
21日（日）	京花と一緒に映画を見て昼食（９時～14時）
22日（月）	
23日（火）	
24日（水）	バレーボールの練習（10時～11時）
25日（木）	
26日（金）	２学期の開始
27日（土）	ホームステイ先の家族と一緒に夕食に出かける（18時～）
28日（日）	京花と一緒に動物園へ行って昼食（９時～14時）

036 ① (1) イ　(2) エ　(3) ア
② (A) ウ　(B) エ

解説 ①(1)「ケンが今日学校へ歩いて行くことによって消費したカロリーと…リットルのミルクを飲むことで得られるカロリーは同じである」。第２段落（Ken is ...）によれば，ケンが今日学校まで歩いた距離は2.4km（1.5km＋900m）である。表２によれば2km歩くと100kcal（つまり1km当たり50kcal）を消費するから，2.4kmでは120kcalの消費になる。これは表１の0.2リットルのミルクに含まれるカロリーの量と同じである。したがってイが正しい。

(2)「メアリーは彼女が今日食べたケーキ中のすべてのエネルギーを消費するために…分間ジョギングしなければならない」。第４段落（Mary is ...）によれば，メアリーは今日ケーキを１つ食べた。それによって彼女は250kcalを摂取したことが表１からわかる。表２によれば20分間のジョギングで100kcalを消費するから，250kcalの全部を消費するには2.5倍の時間がかかる。したがってメアリーは，50分間（＝20分×2.5）ジョギングする必要がある。

(3)「ナンシーがけさ大学に着いたとき，朝食から取った…キロカロリーのエネルギーがまだ体に残っていた」。第５段落（Nancy's university is ...）によれば，彼女が朝食から取ったエネルギーは，表１から200kcal（２枚のパン）＋120kcal（0.2リットルのミルク）で合計320kcalである。彼女は大学まで５キロ自転車に乗ったことによって，表２から125kcal（＝100kcal × 5/4）を消費したことがわかる。したがって彼女の体内には，差し引き195kcalが残っていた。

②「今日[1]２時間テニスをすることによって消

費したカロリーと，（　A　）から得るカロリーは同じだとわかった。その結果は意外だった。[2]30分間ジョギングすることによって消費するカロリーと（　B　）カロリーが同じであることも知った」という文章を完成する。表2から，[1]は800 kcal，[2]は150kcal である。選択肢の意味と，その活動で消費されるカロリーは次のとおり。

(A)ア　ケーキを2個食べる(500kcal)

イ　ケーキを2個食べ，0.2リットルのミルクを飲む(500＋120＝620kcal)

ウ　ケーキ2個とバターを塗ったパン3枚を食べる(500＋300＝800kcal)

エ　ケーキ3個を食べ，0.2リットルのミルクを飲む(750＋120＝870kcal)

したがってウが正解。

(B)ア　ケンがけさ学校まで歩くことによって消費した(120kcal)

イ　メアリーがけさ自転車で学校へ行くことによって消費した(75kcal)

ウ　ナンシーがけさ自転車で大学へ行くことによって消費した(125kcal)

エ　トムが今日自転車に乗ることによって消費した(150kcal)

したがってエが正解。

全訳

ジョンは中学生だ。ケンとトムは彼の兄弟で，メアリーとナンシーは彼の姉妹である。ある日，ジョンは食べ物のカロリーと，歩いたり自転車に乗ったりテニスをしたりジョギングしたりすることによって何カロリーが消費されるかについて学んだ。ジョンは彼らの活動に関する情報を集めた。

ケンは小学生だ。彼は毎日歩いて学校に通う。家から学校までは1.5キロメートルである。しかしケンはきのうジムの家にノートを忘れたので，今日は学校に行く前にジムの家を訪ねた。そのためケンは今日，学校に行くために900メートル多く歩いた。

ジョンは学校のテニス部員である。彼はテニスをするのが大好きだ。今日彼は30分ジョギングした後で2時間テニスをした。

メアリーは高校生だ。彼女は毎日3キロの距離を自転車で通学している。彼女は友人たちと話すのが大好きだ。彼女は今日，放課後に友人のケイトと新しいカフェテリアへ行った。メアリーはケーキを1つ食べ，ケイトと大好きな歌手の話をした。

ナンシーの大学は家から5キロ離れていて，彼女はいつも自転車で通っている。けさ，自転車に乗って家を出る前に，彼女はバターを塗ったパンを2枚食べ，ミルクを0.2リットル飲んだ。

トムは自転車に乗るのが好きだ。彼は時々放課後に2キロほど自転車に乗る。しかし今日はとても天気がよかったので，彼は合計で6キロ自転車に乗った。

表1

さまざまな食品中のエネルギー	
1個のケーキ	250 kcal
1枚のバターを塗ったパン	100 kcal
0.2リットルのミルク	120 kcal

表2

100キロカロリーを消費する4つの方法
2キロ歩くこと
4キロ自転車に乗ること
15分間テニスをすること
20分間ジョギングすること

037 ① ア　② エ　③ オ　④ ウ　⑤ **unbelievable**　⑥ イ

解説　①全訳の下線部[A]～[D]を参照。[A]に入る What can we do for you? の直訳は「私たちはあなたのために何ができますか」。we を I に置き換えた文は，店員が客に対して「いらっしゃいませ」と言うときの決まり文句。[B]に入る What do you mean (by that)? も「(それは)どういう意味ですか」の決まり文句として覚えておこう。[C]には I must keep it.(私はそれをキープして[保存して]おかねばならない)が入る。その前の文の there it is は「(探し物などが)ほら(そこに)あった」という状況などで使う言葉で，ここではくり返し入ってくる情報に対して脳が「またた」と反応する様子を比ゆ的に表現している。[D]に入る Do you have that kind of time? の直訳は「あなたはその種の時間を持っていますか」。「その種の時間」とは，前の文を受けて「復習に使う40～50分もの(必要以上に長い)時間」ということ。使わない選択肢は[3](それには飽き飽きしている)と[5](君は常に最善を尽くしている)。

得点アップ

4つの選択肢を入れた後で，余った2つの選択肢が4つのどれかの代わりに入る可能性はないかを考えるのがよい。その結果「どこにも入らない」と判断できれば，最初に選んだ4つが正しい答えだと確認できる。

②全訳を参照。グリーン先生は「左側に日，右側に月がある」「日が2つの十の間にある」と言っている。

③正しく並べ替えると，(I) have been trying to memorize many English words since I was (in junior high school) となる(私は中学生のころからずっと多くの英単語を暗記しようとしてきた)となる。〈have been＋過去分詞〉(現在完了進行形)で「(以前から今まで)ずっと～し続けている」という意味を表すのがポイント。

④全訳の④＿＿＿を参照。ハナエのこの説明に合うのは，ウのグラフである。イは2日後の方が1日後よりも割合が高くなっているので誤り。エは *ll.*69-74の内容を示すグラフなので誤り。

⑤完成した文の意味は次のとおり。

「英語の語いを増やしたいなら，それをより簡単にするいくつかの方法がある。1つの効果的な方法は接辞を学ぶことだ。単語の中には，それ自体が意味を持つ小さなパーツを持つものがある。それらを知ることは，新しい単語を理解したりその意味を推測するのに役立つ。たとえばunbelievableという単語を見たとき，それが『信じられない』という意味だと推測することができる。」

全訳の⑤＿＿＿を参照。unbelievableは，un-(～ではない)＋believ(信じる)＋-able(～できる)のようにパーツに分けて考えることができる。

⑥ア「グリーン先生は絵が上手に描けないので，一部の漢字と身の回りのものを結びつけるのが難しい」。下線のような記述は会話の中に出てこない。

イ「アヤノは英語の語いを増やしたいと思っているが，自分の記憶力がよくないことを心配している」。下線部(2)を含むアヤノの発言内容から考えて正しい。

ウ「エビングハウスは，何の意味も持たない3つの単語のリストを覚えるように生徒たちの何人かに頼んだ」。下線部が誤り。正しくは「3つの文字から成る単語のリスト」である。

エ「ハナエは，何かを何度も練習すれば記憶する[思い出す]時間を30%節約できるとわかる」。30%という数字はグリーン先生とハナエのやり取りの中に出てくるが，ハナエが理解したのはこのような内容ではない。

オ「アヤノは結局，毎日それぞれの授業の復習に40～50分使うというグリーン先生の助言を最終的に受け入れる」。2人の最後のやり取りの内容から考えて誤り。グリーン先生は「授業の復習に40～50分使いなさい」という助言はしていない。

全訳

アヤノとハナエは東京の高校生である。ある日，彼女らはイングランドから来たALTのグリーン先生と教室で会う。彼は黒板に何かを書いている。

アヤノ：こんにちは，グリーン先生。何をしているのですか。

グリーン先生：いいときに来てくれたね！ 手助けしてくれるかい？

ハナエ：いいですよ。[A]何をしましょう。

グリーン先生：あのね，私は今週末日本語のテストがあるから，漢字を練習しているんだ。でも1つの漢字が思い出せない。

アヤノ：どんな形の字ですか。

グリーン先生：ええと…。左側に日，右側に月がある。数字も少し入っている。

アヤノとハナエは黒板にいくつかの文字を書く。

グリーン先生：これが私のほしい文字だ。日が2つの「十」の間にある。ありがとう。とても助かったよ。

ハナエ：どういたしまして。

アヤノ：私たちは小学1年生のときこの4つの部首[漢字のパーツ]を習います。

グリーン先生：私たちのまわりのものに基づく漢字もあると知るのは，私にとって面白いことだ。たとえば，私は日をこのようには書かないけれど，この漢字を頭の中でイメージに変えるのはとても簡単だ。日を含むいろんな漢字を見ると，それらの字が日に結びついていることが簡単に想像できるよ。

ハナエ：はい。新しい言葉を学ぶとき，漢字のそれぞれのパーツを知っていれば意味が推測できます。

グリーン先生：漢字は英語の接辞に似ているね。

アヤノ：接辞？ それは何ですか。

グリーン先生：単語の意味を変えるために最初または最後に加えられるひとまとまりの文字だよ。たとえば，re-で始まる単語を見たら，「再び」の意味だとわかる。

ハナエ：ああ，そうですね…それに⑤un-で始まる語は「～ではない」の意味だし，-ableで終わる語は「できる」の意味です。

グリーン先生：そのとおり。漢字の中には，そんな働きを持つものもあると思う。それぞれが独自の意味を持っていて，その意味を知っていれば新しい単語を理解しやすくなるね。

アヤノ：今わかりました。私はそれぞれの単語が1つのまとまりに見えるので，英単語を覚えるのが苦手です。

グリーン先生：なるほど。情報を記憶しようとするときは，それをただ暗記するよりむしろ，意味のあるものと結びつける方がいい。

アヤノ：私は中学のころからずっとたくさんの英単語を暗記しようとしてきましたが，私の語いは増えないようです。記憶力がよければいいのに。

グリーン先生：エビングハウスを知っているかい？

アヤノ：エビングハウス？

グリーン先生：ドイツの心理学者だ。1885年に，彼は無意味な3文字の単語のリストを，長い時間をかけてどれだけうまく記憶できるかをテストした。そして実験の結果が出た後，現在では「エビングハウスの忘却曲線」として知られているグラフを作った。

グリーン先生はポケットからスマートフォンを取り出す。彼はインターネットで忘却曲線を検索する。

グリーン先生：これを見てごらん。このグラフは，単語を覚え直すために節約された時間の割合を示している。

ハナエ：[B]どういう意味ですか。

グリーン先生：たとえば，最初に単語を覚えるのに10分必要だった。2日後には，その単語を覚え直すとき7分かかった。どれだけの時間が節約されたかな？

ハナエ：その場合，最初の回の30%が節約されました。

グリーン先生：そのとおり。

ハナエ：④グラフによれば，何かを覚えた直後の割合は100%です。でも，ほんの20分後に58%にまで急減します。1時間後に44%に，9時間後に36%に，24時間後に34%にまで下がります。その後，曲線はゆっくり下がり続けます。

アヤノ：どうすれば記憶を保つことができますか。

グリーン先生：エビングハウスの発見によれば，何かをたくさん反復したり練習したりすれば，情報はより長い間脳内に保たれて，忘却曲線はより緩やかになる。同じ情報を使うと，それを持ち続けるよう脳にメッセージが送られる。同じことをくり返すと，脳はこう言うんだ…。

ハナエ：「ほら，また来た！[C]取っておかなくちゃ」

グリーン先生：そのとおり！

ハナエ：同じ情報を何度も見ると，記憶の中でその情報が活発に働くのに必要な時間がだんだん短くなる。そういうことですね？

グリーン先生：そうだね。

アヤノ：それなら私たちは，必要なときに情報を引き出しやすくなりますね。

グリーン先生：そのとおり。情報を得てから24時間以内に10分を費やして復習すれば，再びほぼ100%まで曲線を引き上げられる。1週間後に2度目の復習をするときは，同じ情報を引き出すのに5分しかかからず，また曲線を引き上げる。1か月後の3回目の復習では，脳は反応を返すのに2分から4分しか必要としない。

アヤノ：毎日復習する時間は作れそうにありません。

グリーン先生：忙しいのはわかる。でも，復習しなければ，それぞれの授業を後で学び直すには40分から50分を使う必要がある。[D]そんな時間があるかい？

アヤノ：わかりました。頭に入れておきます。

語句

character「(漢字などの)文字」
be similar to ～「～に似ている」 affix「接辞」
letter「(アルファベットなどの)文字」
save「～を節約する」
right after ～「～した直後に」
repeat「～をくり返す」 brain「脳」
hold on to ～「～を離さずに持っておく」

038
① イ　② カ
③ [A] イ　[B] エ　[C] オ　[D] ア
④ カ　⑤ エ
⑥ (1) ウ　(2) ア　(3) エ　(4) ウ
⑦ サ

解説 ① *ll*.21-22(This circle ...)に「このサークルは約5,100年前に地面に彫られた」とある。一方，*ll*.31-32(In 1995 ...)に「約3,500年前にストーンヘンジの建造が最終段階を迎えていた」とある。ストーンヘンジが作られたのはこの期間だと考えられるので，イの「約1,600年間」が正解。

②[1]ステーションストーンとヒールストーンが立てられた。

[2]他のサークルと形がブルーストーンを使って加えられた。

[3]サーセンストーンのサークルと5つのトリリ

トンが建てられた。

[4]オーブリーホールと呼ばれるサークルが，穴を掘ってブルーストーンや木材が入れられて作られた。

[5]直径約100メートルの巨大なサークルが地面に彫られた。

これらの内容が文中のどの箇所に出てくるかは，全訳の＿＿部[1]～[5]を参照。これらの番号を本文に出てくる順に並べ，本文中に示された建造時期を示すと次のようになる。

[3]	約4,600年前
[5]	約5,100年前
[4]	[5]の後
[1]	約4,800年前
[2]	[3]の後

したがって，起きた年代が古い順に並べると[5]→[4]→[1]→[3]→[2]となり，正解はカ。

③全訳の＿＿部[A]～[D]を参照。直後の内容から，空所にどんな疑問文を入れればよいかを考える。余る選択肢はウ(彼らはそんな巨大な石の建造物をどのようにして作ったのか)。

④全訳の＿＿部(A)～(C)を参照。ここに書かれているストーンヘンジから見た位置は次のとおり。

(A) 北に30キロほど離れた場所

(B) 北西に200キロ以上離れた場所

(C) 北に1,000キロほど離れた島

したがって，Aは[3]，Bは[2]，Cは[1]である。

⑤全訳の＿＿部(5a)(5b)を参照。(5a)に書かれている「一番高いトリリトン」とは，図Bの中央の小さなサークルに立つ高さ約7メートルのトリリトンである(*ll*.19-20(The tallest one standing at its center was about seven meters tall.)を参照)。夏至の日にこのトリリトンの前に立つとヒールストーンの真上から太陽が昇ってくる。ウはそれを表している。一方，冬至の日には太陽は「同じ線上の，サークルの反対側に沈む」とある。また(5b)によれば，当時の人々は一番高いトリリトンの2つの立石の間のすき間から夕日を見たのかもしれない。この2つの説明から考えて，冬至の日の太陽の動きと，それを見る人が立っていた位置を表す図はエである。

⑥(1)「私たちは今ではストーンヘンジについて以前より多くのことを理解しているが，それは…からである」という文を完成する。

ア「古代ブリトン人たちがストーンヘンジに残したたくさんの文書の記録を科学者たちが研究してきた」。*ll*.5-6 (The people ...)によれば，古代ブリトン人たちは文書の記録を残さなかったので誤り。

イ「科学者たちは約50年間ストーンヘンジという建造物を見て調査してきた」。*l*.6(Scientists have ...)によれば，50年間ではなく1世紀(100年間)以上だから誤り。

ウ「科学が発達し，科学者たちは現代科学を使ってそれを研究してきた」。第1段落の最後の文(A lot of ...)の内容から考えて正しい。

エ「科学は私たちに，古代ブリトン人たちがいくつのストーンサークルを作ったかを教えてきた」。そのような内容は本文に書かれておらず，常識的に考えても誤り。

(2)「科学者たちは放射性炭素年代測定法を使って…を解明した」という文を完成する。

ア ストーンヘンジという巨大な石の建造物が実際に作られたのはいつか

イ 古代ブリトン人はストーンヘンジを建造するためにどんな種類の石を使ったか

ウ ブルーストーンが氷の動きによってストーンヘンジへ運ばれたこと

エ イギリスには巨大な石を使った1,000以上のストーンサークルがあること

ll.9-10(Around 1970 ...)によれば，科学者たちは放射性炭素年代測定法を使って，ストーンヘンジが4,600年前ごろに作られたことを発見した。したがってアが正解。radio-carbon datingの訳語は「放射性炭素年代測定法」だから，時代を特定する方法であることがわかる。

(3)「一部の科学者たちは，古代ブリトン人がおそらく…使っていたと考えている」という文を完成する。

ア 太陽が空でどのように円を描いて動くかを予測するためにステーションストーンとサーセンストーンサークルを

イ 食べ物を育てるのに十分な雨がいつ降るかを予測するためにヒールストーンとトリリトンを

ウ どのようにして食べ物を手に入れ寒い天候を生き延びるかを予測するためにオーブリーホールとブルーストーンを

エ 太陽の動きを予測するためにオーブリーホールとトリリトンを

*ll.*72-74(And the circle ...)に，エの内容が書かれている。ストーンヘンジの利用方法はこの段落で説明されている点を見抜くのがポイント。

(4)「科学者たちによれば，古代ブリトン人はおそらく…を知っていた」という文を完成する。

ア 氷の動きによって運ばれた多くのブルーストーンがストーンヘンジの近くで発見されたこと

イ ブルーストーンを彫って長期間立ったままにしておく方法

ウ 頑丈で印象的に見えるストーンヘンジという建造物の作り方

エ 夏至の後は日が長くなるということ

*ll.*48-50(The stones for ... knew this.)の内容から考えて，ウが正解。ア・エは常識的に考えても不自然。イは*ll.*46-48(Sarsen stones ... without falling down.)に関連しており，「ブルーストーン」が「サーセンストーン」なら正しい。

⑦[1]「ストーンヘンジの中央にある2種類の巨大な建造物は，サーセンストーンを使って作られた」。第2段落によれば，一方はサーセンストーンサークルであり，もう一方はトリリトンで作られた。そして*l.*18に，They were also made with very large sarsen stones.(それら[＝トリリトン]もまた巨大なサーセンストーンを使って作られた)とある。したがって正しい。

[2]「ストーンヘンジの中央には，5つのトリリトンが今でも立っている」。第2段落の最後の文によれば，現存するトリリトンは3つだけだから誤り。

[3]「科学者たちは大きなブルーストーンがどこから来たかを容易に発見した」。*ll.*34-36(Long ago, ...)に「(より小さな)ブルーストーンがどこから来たのかがわかるまで長い時間がかかった」とあるので誤り。

[4]「ブルーストーンはサーセンストーンよりも大きくて柔らかい」。*l.*46(Sarsen stones are ...)の内容に反するので誤り。

[5]「古代ブリトン人は，大きな石を運んで巨大な石の建造物を作る方法を知っていた」。*l.*41([A]に入る文)に「どのようにして(石を)そんなに遠くまで運んだのか」とある。つまりストーンヘンジを作るための石は遠くから運んできたのであり，彼らが石の運び方(と作り方)を知らなければストーンヘンジは作れなかっただろう。したがって正しい。

[6]「研究によれば，さまざまな村から来てストーンヘンジから2，3キロ離れた村に住んでいた古代ブリトン人が，巨大な建造物を作り始めたのかもしれない」。第6段落([B]で始まる段落)の内容に一致するので正しい。

[7]「ストーンサークルは，おそらく太陽，月，星の動きを示すために作られた」。*ll.*63-64(They probably knew ...)の内容に一致するので正しい。

[8]「科学者たちはストーンヘンジに関するすべての謎を解き，今ではそれ以上の謎はない」。第1段落の最後の文(A lot of mysteries ...)や最後の段落の内容に反するので誤り。

以上から正しいのは[1][5][6][7]であり，サが正解となる。

精読

◆This circle, about 100 meters in diameter, was carved into the ground about 5,100 years ago.(*ll.*21-22)(直径約100メートルのこのサークルは，約5,100年前に地面に彫られた)：下線部は前のThis circleに説明を加えている。This circle, **(which was)** about .... と補って考えるとわかりやすい。

◆A smaller circle was then made inside it with bluestones or timber in holes.(*ll.*22-23)(それからその内側に，穴を掘ってブルーストーンや木材が入ったより小さな円が作られた)：下線部は「穴に入ったブルーストーンや木材を持って」の意味。つまり，穴を掘って，そこにブルーストーンや木材を差し込んだということ。

全訳

ロンドンから西へ200キロほど車で走ると，突然巨大な石の建造物が見える。それはストーンヘンジと呼ばれる。(図Aを参照。)ストーンヘンジは世界で最も有名な建造物の1つであり，毎年100万人以上の人が訪れる。ストーンヘンジには多くの謎がある。それを作った人々は，それに関する文書の記録を残さなかった。科学者たちは100年以上それを研究してきた。まだ多くの謎が残っているが，現代の科学は私たちにかなり多くのことを教えてきた。

その巨大な石の建造物は2,000～3,000年ほど前に作られたと多くの人が考えていたが，そうではなかった。1970年ごろ，科学者たちは放射性炭素年代測定法を用いて，それらが実際には[3]4,600年前ごろに作られたことを発見した。図Bを見てみよう。この図は，ストーンヘンジが4,600年前ごろにおそらくどのような姿をしていたかを示している。[3]中央に2種類の巨大な石の建造物が見える。1つはサーセンストーンサークルと呼ばれる。30個の大きなサーセンストーンが円形に立てられ，その上にさらに輪の形になるよう30個のサーセンストーンが載せられた。高さは約5メートル，直径は約30メートルだった。[3]もう1つはトリリトンで作られた。それぞれのトリリトンは2つの立てた石とその上に載せた1つの石でできていた。サークルの内側には非常に高いトリリトンが5つ作られた。これらも巨大なサーセンストーンでできていた。5つのトリリトンは「U」の形に立っていた。中央に立つ一番高いものは約7メートルの高さがあった。それらのうちの3つは現在も立っている。

(図A，図B，図C)

図Bの最も大きなサークルを見てみよう。[5]直径約100メートルのこのサークルは，約5,100年前に地面に彫られた。[4]それからその内側に，穴を掘ってブルーストーンや木材が入ったより小さな円が作られた。現在では56個の穴だけが残っている。このサークルはオーブリーホールと呼ばれる。[1]約4,800年前に，サークルの近くにステーションストーンと呼ばれる4つの石が加えられ，ヒールストーンと呼ばれる高さ5メートルほどの大きなサーセンストーンが，最も大きなサークルから約25メートル外側の地面に立てられた。ヒールストーンがある地域からエイボン川まで，約3キロの道が作られた。[2]ストーンヘンジの中央の2種類の巨大な建造物が作られた後，他のサークルや形がブルーストーンを使って加えられた。以上のように，ストーンヘンジにはさまざまな変更が加えられた。1995年に現代科学は，約3,500年前にストーンヘンジの建造が最終段階を迎えていたことを発見した。ストーンヘンジは非常に長い年月をかけて建造されたのである。

(A)大きなサーセンストーンは北に30キロほど離れたところから運ばれたことを科学者たちはずっと前に突き止めていたが，より小さなブルーストーンがどこから来たのかがわかるまで長い時間がかかった。氷河期には，氷床がストーンヘンジの周辺地域をおおっていた。「ブルーストーンは氷の移動によって運ばれたのかもしれない」と考える科学者もいた。しかし他のブルーストーンがその付近で発見されなかったので，確信が持てなかった。その後，(B)ストーンヘンジから北西に200キロ以上離れた場所で，ストーンヘンジに使われた種類のブルーストーンが発見された。ここがストーンヘンジのブルーストーンの産地だと彼らは信じている。[A]しかし，どのようにしてそんなに遠くまで運んだのか？ 船に載せて海や川で運んだと考える科学者もいる。

ブルーストーンはとても硬く，一部の科学者によれば，人々はその石に健康を保ち幸運をもたらす力があると信じていた。サーセンストーンはブルーストーンよりも大きくて柔らかい。サーセンストーンは図Cのように彫られた。それらは組み合わせて長い間倒れずに立っていられるように作られた。立てるための石は，真ん中がふくらむようカットされている。そのため，ストーンヘンジは遠くから見ると頑丈で印象的に見える。おそらく，ストーンヘンジを作った人々はそのことを知っていたのだろう。サーセンストーンの内部は真っ白である。カットされたばかりの石はとても美しく見える。ストーンヘンジという巨大な建造物は，それらのサーセンストーンを使って最初に作られたときは，美しい白色に見えただろうと科学者は考えている。

[B]誰がストーンヘンジを作ったのか？ 約5,100年前，現在のイギリスに当たる地域には，古代ブリトン人と呼ばれる人々が住んでいた。彼らがストーンヘンジを作ったと多くの科学者が考えている。研究によると，約4,600年前には，ストーンヘンジから3キロ離れた村に，さまざまな村から集まった約4,000人の古代ブリトン人がともに暮らしていた。この人々がストーンヘンジという巨大な建造物を作り始めた人々なのかもしれない。

イギリスには1,000以上のストーンサークルがあり，(C)最も古いものはストーンヘンジから北に1,000キロほど離れた島にある。ストーンサークルは，おそらくそこからイギリス全土に広がっていったのだろう。科学者たちは，ストーンサークルがおそらく人々にとって特別な意味を持っていたと考えている。人々はたぶん，太陽，月，星が円を描いて動くことを知っていて，それを地上に表そうとしたのだろう。

約5,100年前には，ストーンサークルはより小さな石で作られた簡素なものだった。しかし4,600年前ごろ，何らかの理由でそれらに使う石が大きくなり始めた。[C]その間に何があったのか？ そのころに地球は寒冷化し，人々は食物を育てるのに苦労していた。彼らはおそらく太陽の力を取り戻そうとして，巨大な石の建造物を作ったと言う科学者もいる。

[D]ストーンヘンジはどのように使われていたのか？ 一部の科学者によると，それはおそらく太陽と月の位置を予測することのできる一種の暦として使われていた。ステーションストーンと呼ばれる4つの石は，月の動きを予測するために使われた。そし

て，オーブリーホールと呼ばれるサークルと大きなトリリトンの建造物は，太陽の動きを予測するために使われた。(5a)夏至の日に，一番高いトリリトンの前に立って道の上のヒールストーンを見ると，ヒールストーンの真上から太陽が昇ってくる。夏至の日には太陽が昇り，冬至の日には太陽が同じ線上に沈む，ただしサークルの反対側に。古代ブリトン人にとって，冬至はおそらく特別な意味を持っていた。その日以降は日がだんだん長くなることを彼らは知っていた。その日，彼らはストーンヘンジで特別な行事を行ったのだろう。みんなで集まって，ストーンヘンジまでの道を歩き，(5b)一番高いトリリトンの2つの立石の間のすき間から夕日を見たのかもしれない。彼らは太陽の力がより強くなるよう願ったのかもしれない。

この100年ほどの間に，ストーンヘンジについて多くのことがわかった。将来，科学技術の発展とともに，科学者たちはさらに多くのことを知るかもしれない。彼らのおかげで，いつかストーンヘンジに関する多くの謎が解き明かされるかもしれない。

語句

record「記録」　remain「残っている」
close to ～「～の近くに」
ice sheet「氷床(地表をおおう氷)」
movement「動き，移動」
fit together「組み合わさる，整合する」
fall down「倒れる」　spread「広がる」
directly「ちょうど，まさに」

第5回　実力テスト

① ウ	② **America**	③ イ
④ イ	⑤ ウ	

解説 グラフの説明に「日米韓の3か国」とあるので，会話の内容からA・B・Cがそれぞれどの国かを最初に確定させれば，効率的に問いを解くことができる。

①ア「それぞれの国で，『エンターテイメント』と答えた生徒の割合が最も高い」。グラフ2によれば，B国ではentertainmentよりもpoliticsに興味があると答えた生徒の方が多い。したがって誤り。

イ「それぞれの国で，生徒はスポーツよりも金融に興味を持っている」。グラフ2によれば，3か国すべてでfinanceに興味を持つと答えた生徒の割合の方が低い。したがって誤り。

ウ「ただ1つの国で，50%を超える生徒が文化に興味を持っている」。グラフ2によれば，cultureに興味を持つ生徒の割合が50%を超えているのはB国だけだから正しい。

エ「ただ1つの国で，50%を超える生徒が時々新聞を読んだりニュースを見たりする」。グラフ1によれば，sometimesという回答が50%を超えている国は1つもないから誤り。

②光太の4番目の発言(Look! ...)に「政治に関するニュースに興味を持つアメリカ人の生徒の割合は，70%を超えている」とある。グラフ2でpoliticsと答えた生徒の割合から考えて，Bはアメリカである。

③「光太によれば，新聞を読む方がニュースを見るよりもよい，なぜなら…からだ」という文を完成する。

ア 彼は新聞を毎日読むことができる
イ 新聞は彼により多くの種類の情報を与えてくれる
ウ 新聞は彼にボランティア活動への興味を持たせてくれる
エ 生徒たちは国際ニュースをより容易に理解することができる

光太の最初の発言(I think reading ...)の最後の文の内容から考えて，イが正解。

④「アレックスは政治に興味を持つ日本人の高校生の数が増えるだろうと考えている，なぜなら…からだ」という文を完成する。

ア 彼らは約50年前に選挙で投票し始めた
イ 彼らは投票がどれほど大切かを教える授業を受けている
ウ 彼らは世界の文化に関する多くの授業を受けるだろう
エ 彼らは18歳になった後に投票するための時間が増えるだろう

アレックスの最後の発言(When people ...)中に，「今では日本人の生徒は社会科の授業で投票の大切さを学ぶことができる。日本でも政治に関心を持つ若者がますます増えると思う」とあるので，イが正解。

⑤「ベーカー先生の生徒たちへのメッセージは何か」という問い。

ア 授業中に，生徒たちは大きな声で自分の意見を先生に伝えるべきだ。

イ　20代の人々は投票に行かなければならない，なぜならそれが彼らの責任だからだ。

ウ　生徒たちは投票することによって自分の国をよりよい方向に変えるための力を持っている。

エ　政府は若者から多くの意見を聞くべきだ。

ベーカー先生の発言の最後から2文目(Each person's voice ...)および最後の言葉がYou can change your countries for the better!(皆さんは自分の国をよりよい方向に変えることができます！)であることから考えて，ウが正解。なお，この文でcountriesが複数形になっているのは，美保や光太にとって自分の国は日本だが，アレックスの母国は別の国だからだと考えられる。

全訳

(グラフのタイトル)

グラフ1「あなたはどのくらいの頻度で新聞を読んだりニュースを見たりしますか」

グラフ2「あなたはどんなニュースに興味がありますか」

(グラフは省略)

ベーカー先生：今日は新聞とニュースについて話し合います。皆さんは新聞を読んだりニュースを見たりしますか。

美保：はい，私は毎朝新聞を読みます。以前はよくテレビでニュースを見ていましたが，近ごろは新聞を読むことに興味があります。社会科の先生が授業で新聞を使います。私たちは面白い記事を1つ選んで，各グループで話し合います。他の生徒からいろいろな意見を聞くことができます。そういう授業は私にとって面白いです。

アレックス：ぼくはめったに新聞を読んだりニュースを見たりしませんが，世界で何が起きているかを知ることは大切だと思います。

光太：多くの情報を得るためには，ニュースを見るより新聞を読む方がいい方法だと思います。新聞の方が，政治，文化，スポーツなどより幅広い記事が入っています。

美保：そうです！ 私たちは自分の知らないことに興味を持つようになって，それについての多くの情報を得ることができます。それに新聞は，イベントやボランティア活動など，自分の地域の中の多くのことを知るのにも役立ちます。たとえば，自分の市の役に立つことをしている人たちがいるのを知ることができます。

ベーカー先生：新聞のよい点を話してくれてありがとう。グラフ1を見てください。このグラフは，高校生がどのくらいの頻度で新聞を読んだりニュースを見たりするかを表しています。このグラフから何がわかりますか。

光太：「ほぼ毎日」と答えた日本の高校生の割合は，3か国のうちで最高です。

アレックス：ほぼ40%！ すごい。めったに新聞を読んだりニュースを見たりしない生徒は日本では約17%なのに，アメリカと韓国では約40%の生徒がめったにそれをしません。

光太：それを知って驚きました。高校生はどんなニュースに興味がありますか。

ベーカー先生：グラフ2を見てください。このグラフから何がわかりますか。

アレックス：すべての国で，高校生の50%以上が，映画や歌などのエンターテイメントに関するニュースに興味を持っています。

美保：高校生は金融に興味がないことがわかります。韓国の割合が一番高いけれど，約30%しかありません。生徒には金融を理解するのが難しいからだと思います。

光太：見てください！ 政治に関するニュースに興味を持つアメリカ人の生徒の割合は，日本と韓国の割合よりも高いです。それは70%を超えています！ 日本人の高校生はよく新聞を読んだりニュースを見たりしますが，政治にはアメリカ人の生徒ほど興味を持っていません。

美保：ベーカー先生，あなたは高校生のとき政治に興味がありましたか。

ベーカー先生：ええ，私の高校では政治についての授業がありました。その授業で私たちはあるテーマについて自分の意見を他の生徒に伝えなければならなかったので，よく考える必要がありました。その授業を通して私は多くのことを学び，政治に興味を持つようになりました。

美保：わかりました。

アレックス：18歳になると投票ができます。アメリカでは50年ほど前に始まりましたが，日本でそれが始まったのはわずか6年前です。今では日本人の生徒は社会科の授業で投票の大切さを学ぶことができます。日本でも政治に関心を持つ若者がますます増えると思います。

光太：そうなればいいですね。今，私たちの国には多くの問題があるので，私たちはそれらの問題にもっと関心を持つようになることが大切です。新聞を読んだりニュースを見たりして，それらの問題について考え，自分自身の意見を持つべきです。

ベーカー先生：そのとおりです。皆さん，ありがとう。皆さんは国民の一人です。18歳になれば，投票によって自分の意見を政府に伝えることができます。一人一人の声は小さいかもしれませんが，まとまればとても大きな声になることができます。皆さんは自分の国をよりよい方向へ変えることができるのです！